WEIGHT WATCHERS®

FOOD PLAN DIET
COOKBOOK

WEIGHT WATCHERS®
FOOD PLAN DIET COOKBOOK

BY

JEAN NIDETCH

NAL BOOKS

NEW AMERICAN LIBRARY

TIMES MIRROR

NEW YORK AND SCARBOROUGH, ONTARIO

NAL BOOKS TRADEMARK REG. U.S. PAT. OFF. AND FOREIGN COUNTRIES
REGISTERED TRADEMARK—MARCA REGISTRADA
HECHO EN HARRISONBURG, VA., U.S.A.

SIGNET, SIGNET CLASSICS, MENTOR, PLUME, MERIDIAN and NAL
BOOKS are published *in the United States* by The New American Library, Inc.,
1633 Broadway, New York, New York 10019, *in Canada* by The New American
Library of Canada Limited, 81 Mack Avenue, Scarborough, Ontario MIL 1M8

Designed by Julian Hamer   Drawings by Janet Nelson
Cover photograph by Gus Francisco

Library of Congress Cataloging in Publication Data

Nidetch, Jean.
  Weight Watchers food plan diet cookbook.

  Includes index.
  1. Reducing diets—Recipes. I. Weight Watchers
International. II. Title.
  RM222.2.N515 1982   641.5'63   82–12417
  ISBN 0–453–01007–5

First Printing, September, 1982

1 2 3 4 5 6 7 8 9

PRINTED IN THE UNITED STATES OF AMERICA

Contents

Acknowledgments

The creation of a cookbook is never the work of one individual. This book is no exception and many people have helped in its preparation. Numerous hours were spent in the test kitchens of Weight Watchers International creating and testing recipes, for which we thank Bianca Brown, Nina Procaccini, and Judi Rettmer. The challenging task of researching, writing, and editing the material for this manuscript was accomplished by Patricia Barnett, Anne Hosansky, Lynette McEvoy, Harriet Pollock, Eileen Pregosin, and Isabel Sobol. A large measure of thanks is due to Lucille Corsello, Isabel Fleisher, and Lola Sher for typing and secretarial services.

We also wish to acknowledge the contribution of Felice Lippert, Advisor and Consultant to the Food Research & Development Department, for her inspiration in the conception of this series of Weight Watchers cookbooks.

DR. LELIO G. PARDUCCI
Vice President
Food Research & Development Department

Dear Friend,

Many of us dreamed that in some idyllic life we'd be able to enjoy such delights as peanut butter and popcorn—and still lose weight.

With the 1981 revision of our Program, this fantasy became a reality. On the famous Weight Watchers Food Plan you can now eat food never believed possible on a weight-loss regimen. You can even toast your pound-shedding efforts with wine! And you can use such popular cooking methods as sautéing with oil and stir-frying.

Why was a program that was already so successful changed? Partly because the Weight Watchers organization has never been content to stand still. Partly because we wanted our Food Plan to have increased flexibility and offer even greater freedom.

The medical consultants and nutritionists who staff our Food Research & Development Department evaluated the most up-to-date nutritional findings and produced this new Food Plan, which opened kitchen doors to a vast range of culinary possibilities.

The changes made headlines. Our switchboard lit up like a neon sign and desks were hidden under a deluge of mail. One question kept popping up: "When are you going to update the Weight Watchers Program Cookbook?"

For months, our expert home economists and chefs worked in the test kitchens of Weight Watchers International testing recipes individually and evaluating them to meet our exacting standards. This book is the result of their work—and the answer to your requests.

It offers almost 600 easy ways to serve delectable dishes that blend with equally pleasing weight losses. To ease your way, the recipes are grouped according to Food Plan categories. Whether you're serving a routine family meal, a lavish spread, or a simple snack, you'll find invaluable suggestions on every page of this book.

We are frequently asked how it is possible to include such an incredible array of foods. The answer takes us into another area of Weight Watchers, for we offer more than a Food Plan. We include invaluable eating-management techniques that help Weight Watchers members learn various strategies, including portion control. That is why we felt confident about expanding the choices on our Food Plan.

And "choices" is the word, for we personalized the Plan into three levels—and they are all included in this book. You'll find The Full Choice Plan, for those who wish to enjoy the greatest variety possible; The Limited Choice Plan, for those who prefer fewer options; and The No Choice Plan, for those who feel most comfortable within the strict guidelines of a specific menu plan.

I have watched the Weight Watchers organization grow from a handful of members in one American town to hundreds of thousands around the world. If our new foods seem like a dream-come-true, the more meaningful dreams-come-true are the incredible transformations of the overweight men, women, and teenagers all over the world who have come through our doors to find not just a new eating style but new lives. In almost every language, the Weight Watchers name has come to stand for quality help.

You'll find that kind of quality between the covers of this book, just as you did in our Party and Holiday Cookbook, *our* International Cookbook, *and our* 365-Day Menu Cookbook.

JEAN NIDETCH,
Founder, Weight Watchers
International, Inc.

Weight Watchers Food Plans, Menu Suggestions, and Goal Weights

The purpose of this chapter is to acquaint you with the Food Plans and to help you build a menu based on some of the recipes in this book. It includes the Full, Limited, and No Choice Plans, one week of menu suggestions each for the Full and Limited Choice Plans, a list of Food Plan requirements necessary to complete each of these weeks, an outline for a daily food record, and goal weight charts.

The *Full Choice Plan* is the basic Food Plan with which you should begin. It has been scientifically designed to provide a wide variety of nutritious foods. Choices have been built into this flexible Plan, allowing options to meet your individual needs. You also have choice in regard to quantity, since some servings are listed in ranges.

The *Limited Choice Plan* is more restricted than the Full Choice Plan. There are fewer food choices and no ranges. The choices within each category have been limited to the lowest possible caloric selections. If you do not wish to avail yourself of a wide range of choices and prefer a more specific Food Plan, after following the Full Choice Plan you may elect to follow this Plan.

The *No Choice Plan* is a structured menu planner and may be selected after following the Full Choice Plan. Specific guidelines for this plan are included on pages 11–13.

Our *Goal Weights* are based on sex, height without shoes, and age. If you are shorter or taller than the height given in the table, check with your physician to obtain a goal weight. There is a weight range for each goal, which allows you to decide what weight will best meet your personal needs. The high end of your range is the tentative goal for which you should aim. When you reach it, you may decide to remain at this weight, or you may prefer to go lower within your range.

Guidelines for Using Menu Plans

1. Eat only the foods listed on your Menu Plan, in the quantities and weights specified.

2. The weights indicated on the Menu Plans for Poultry, Meat, and Fish are net cooked (or drained canned) weights (without skin and bones).

3. Refer to guidelines in the following chapters for explanations of food items and cooking procedures.

4. Consume three meals a day and never skip a meal. As you will learn, there is a wide range of possible mealtime splits and combinations, but at least ½ serving of Protein should be consumed at any given meal; the remaining portion should be added to one of the other meals that day.

5. Consume all items that are required, in the amounts specified. All three Plans require that you consume Fruits, Vegetables, Milk, Grains, Protein, and Fats daily; the amounts of some of these items will differ according to the different Plans and for Women, Men, and Youth (females 11 through 14 and males 11 through 17). Be sure to select the amounts appropriate for you.

6. The word *serving* appears throughout the Food Plans. A serving may be defined as a portion of food that equates to the amount of food allowed on the Food Plan.

7. It is suggested that you keep a food record, as outlined on page 14; this will help you to keep track of the food that you consume daily and to plan ahead.

Guidelines for Using Menu Suggestions and Additional Requirements

1. Bold type indicates that recipes are included in this book. Suggestions are based on 1 serving of each recipe.

2. Additional Food Plan Requirements may be added to any meal or taken as Planned Snacks.

3. Additional vegetables may be consumed daily, provided the guidelines in the Vegetables chapter are followed for each respective Plan.

4. On the Full Choice Plan, additional servings of Bonus and Occasional Substitutes may be used throughout the week, provided the total does not exceed the amount permitted on the Plan.

WEIGHT WATCHERS STRONGLY ADVISES YOU TO CONSULT YOUR PHYSICIAN WHILE PARTICIPATNG IN THE FOOD PLAN.

FULL CHOICE PLAN MENU

Food	Quantity

Morning Meal

		Women, Men, and Youth	
	Fruit or Fruit Juice		1 serving
Choice of	Egg		1
or	Cheese, soft		⅓ cup
or	Cheese, semisoft or hard		1 ounce
or	Cereal		1 serving with Milk
or	Peanut Butter		1 tablespoon (omit 1 serving Fats)
or	Poultry, Meat, or Fish		1 ounce*
or	Legumes:		
	Beans, lentils, and peas	Women and Youth	3 ounces*
		Men	4 ounces*
	Tofu	Women and Youth	4 ounces
		Men	5 ounces
	Tempeh	Women and Youth	1½ ounces
		Men	2 ounces
	Beverage, if desired		

Midday and Evening Meal

		Women, Men, and Youth	
Choice of	Eggs		2
or	Cheese, soft		⅔ cup
or	Cheese, semisoft or hard		2 ounces
or	Peanut Butter		3 tablespoons (omit 2 servings Fats)
or	Poultry, Meat, or Fish	Women and Youth	3 to 4 ounces*
		Men	4 to 5 ounces*
or	Legumes:		
	Beans, lentils, and peas	Women and Youth	6 ounces*
		Men	8 ounces*

* Cooked weight.

Tofu	Women and Youth	8 ounces
	Men	10 ounces
Tempeh	Women and Youth	3 ounces
	Men	4 ounces
Beverage, if desired		

Daily, at any time

Fruits	Women	3 servings†
	Men and Youth	4 to 6 servings†
Vegetables	Women, Men, and Youth	2 servings (minimum)
Milk	Women and Men	2 servings
	Youth	3 to 4 servings
Bread	Women	2 to 3 servings
	Men and Youth	4 to 5 servings
Fats	Women, Men, and Youth	3 servings

† Includes fruit at Morning Meal.

Full Choice Plan Menu Suggestions

Fruits that are high in Vitamin C have been asterisked (*). Serving sizes for each food item can be found at the beginning of the chapter dealing with that item.

Day 1

Morning Meal   **Breakfast Raisin Turnover** (see page 121); Skim Milk; 1 serving

Midday Meal   **Cream of Cheddar Soup** (full-meal serving, see page 170); Tomato Wedges, 1 serving; Cucumber Slices, 1 serving; Bread, 1 serving; *Strawberries, 1 serving; Beverage

Evening Meal   **Salmon in Red Wine Sauce** (see page 324); Steamed Spinach, 1 serving; **Frozen Honeydew Soufflé** (see page 39); Beverage

Day 2

Morning Meal   *Orange Juice, 1 serving; **Buttermilk Pancakes** (see page 153) with ¾ serving Margarine; Skim Milk, ½ serving; Beverage

Midday Meal   **Tuna-Stuffed Tomato** (see page 347); **Pear and Yogurt Parfait** (see page 99); Beverage

Evening Meal   **Gazpacho** (see page 88); **Pepper Steak with Mushrooms** (see page 268); Beverage

Day 3

Morning Meal   *Tomato Juice, 1 serving; Hard Cheese, 1 ounce; Bread, 1 serving; Skim Milk, ½ serving; Beverage

Midday Meal	**Veal-Salad Mold** (see page 244); Bread, 1 serving, with ½ serving Margarine; Coffee or Tea with 3 tablespoons Skim Milk
Evening Meal	**Potted Turkey Burgers** (see page 240); **Broccoli-Cauliflower Mold** (see page 62); **Dried Fruit Compote** (see page 45); Beverage

Day 4

Morning Meal	*Orange Sections, 1 serving; **Cornmeal Mush** (see page 118); Skim Milk, 1 serving
Midday Meal	**Pocket Full of Surprises** (see page 198); **Citrus-Cucumber Salad** (see page 69); Beverage
Evening Meal	**Liver-Stuffed Shells** (see page 302); Light Beer, ½ serving; *Cantaloupe, 1 serving

Day 5

Morning Meal	*Tomato Juice, 1 serving; Egg, 1; Bread, 1 serving; Skim Milk, ½ serving; Beverage
Midday Meal	**Calamari (Squid) Salad** (see page 336); Beverage
Evening Meal	**Veal Rouladen** (see page 245); **"Banana Daiquiri"** (see page 36)

Day 6

Morning Meal	Peach, 1 serving; Cottage Cheese, ⅓ cup; Bread, 1 serving; Skim Milk, 1 serving
Midday Meal	*Cantaloupe, 1 serving; **Curried Eggs** (see page 157); **White Wine Spritzer** (see page 406)
Evening Meal	**Stuffed Mushrooms** (see page 78); **Whitefish Piquante** (see page 329); Beverage

Day 7

Morning Meal	Pear, 1 serving: **Grits and Bacon Bits** (see page 119); Skim Milk, ½ serving; Beverage
Midday Meal	**Chilled Tongue with Horseradish Sauce** (see page 286); **Quick Tomato Relish** (see page 87); Beverage
Evening Meal	**Lentil Soup** (see page 356); Bread, 1 serving, with ¾ serving Margarine; *Grapefruit Sections, 1 serving; Beverage

Additional Food Plan Requirements to Complete
Full Choice Plan Menu Suggestions*

Day 1

Women: add ¼ serving Fruits, ¼ serving Milk, and ¾ serving Bread

Men: add 1¼ servings Fruits, ¼ serving Milk, and 2¾ servings Bread

Youth: add 1¼ servings Fruits, 1¼ servings Milk, and 2¾ servings Bread

Day 2

Women: add 1½ servings Fruits and ¾ serving Milk

Men: add 2½ servings Fruits, ¾ serving Milk, and 1½ servings Bread

Youth: add 2½ servings Fruits, 1¾ servings Milk, and 1½ servings Bread

Day 3

Women: add 1 serving Fruits and ¼ serving Milk

Men: add 2 servings Fruits, ¼ serving Milk, and 1 serving Bread

Youth: add 2 servings Fruits, 1¼ servings Milk, and 1 serving Bread

Day 4

Women: add 1 serving Milk and 1½ servings Fats

Men: add 1 serving Fruits, 1 serving Milk, 2 servings Bread, and 1½ servings Fats

Youth: add 1 serving Fruits, 2 servings Milk, 2 servings Bread, and 1½ servings Fats

Day 5

Women: add 1¼ servings Fruits, 1½ servings Milk, ¾ serving Bread, and ½ serving Fats

Men: add 2¼ servings Fruits, 1½ servings Milk, 2¾ servings Bread, and ½ serving Fats

Youth: add 2¼ servings Fruits, 2½ servings Milk, 2¾ servings Bread, and ½ serving Fats

Day 6

Women: add 1 serving Milk

Men: add 1 serving Fruits, 1 serving Milk, and 2 servings Bread

Youth: add 1 serving Fruits, 2 servings Milk, and 2 servings Bread

* Note: These additions fulfill the *minimum* daily requirements of the Full Choice Plan. The Plan includes a serving range for Bread for Women, Fruit and Bread for Men, and Fruit, Milk, and Bread for Youth. Therefore, additional servings of these items may be selected. Refer to your Food Plan for amounts.

Day 7

Women:	add 1 serving Fruits, 1 serving Milk, and 1 serving Bread
Men:	add 2 servings Fruits, 1 serving Milk, and 3 servings Bread
Youth:	add 2 servings Fruits, 2 servings Milk, and 3 servings Bread

LIMITED CHOICE PLAN MENU

Food	*Quantity*

Morning Meal

		Women, Men, and Youth	
	Fruit or Fruit Juice		1 serving
Choice of	Egg		1
or	Cheese, soft		⅓ cup
or	Cheese, semisoft or hard		1 ounce
or	Cereal		1 serving with Milk
or	Poultry, Meat, or Fish		1 ounce*
or	Legumes:		
	Beans, lentils, and peas	Women and Youth	3 ounces*
		Men	4 ounces*
	Tofu	Women and Youth	4 ounces
		Men	5 ounces
	Tempeh	Women and Youth	1½ ounces
		Men	2 ounces
	Beverage, if desired		

Midday and Evening Meal

		Women, Men, and Youth	
Choice of	Eggs		2
or	Cheese, soft		⅔ cup
or	Cheese, semisoft or hard		2 ounces
or	Poultry, Meat, or Fish	Women and Youth	3 ounces*
		Men	4 ounces*
or	Legumes:		
	Beans, lentils, and peas	Women and Youth	6 ounces*
		Men	8 ounces*
	Tofu	Women and Youth	8 ounces
		Men	10 ounces
	Tempeh	Women and Youth	3 ounces
		Men	4 ounces

* Cooked weight.

Daily, at any time

Fruits	Women	3 servings†
	Men and Youth	4 servings†
Vegetables	Women, Men, and Youth	2 servings (minimum)
Milk	Women and Men	2 servings
	Youth	3 servings
Bread	Women	2 servings
	Men and Youth	4 servings
Fats	Women, Men, and Youth	3 servings

† Includes fruit at Morning Meal.

Limited Choice Plan Menu Suggestions

Day 1

Morning Meal *Orange Juice, 1 serving; **Cereal with Peach Sauce** (see page 120); Beverage

Midday Meal **Crab Meat Salad** (see page 331); Beverage

Evening Meal Tomato Juice, ¾ serving; **Chicken Livers "Stroganoff"** (see page 298); **Sautéed Cucumber** (see page 71); **Frozen Cantaloupe "Ice Cream"** (see page 37); Beverage

Day 2

Morning Meal *Cantaloupe or Honeydew, 1 serving; **Not-So-Danish Pastry** (see page 187); Skim Milk, ½ serving; Beverage

Midday Meal **Curried Turkey** (see page 238); **Cucumber in Chived Yogurt** (see page 70); Coffee or Tea with ⅛ serving Skim Milk

Evening Meal **Sautéed Veal Chops** (see page 245); **Piquant Carrots** (see page 66); Tossed Salad with **Creamy Salad Dressing** (see page 385); **Buttermilk Pops** (see page 100); Beverage

Day 3

Morning Meal *Grapefruit, 1 serving; **Soft-Cooked Egg** (see page 150); **Cinnamon Toast** (see page 114); Skim Milk, 1 serving

Midday Meal **Chicken Sukiyaki** (see page 218); Green Salad with Lemon Juice and Herbs; Beverage

Evening Meal **Clam Casserole** (see page 330); **Endive Salad** (see page 73); Beverage

Day 4

Morning Meal *Orange Juice, 1 serving; **Strawberry-Topped Bran Crisps** (see page 122); Skim Milk, ½ serving; Beverage

Midday Meal	**Bean 'n' Cheese Salad** (see page 358); Bread, 1 serving, with 1 serving Margarine; Beverage
Evening Meal	**Japanese Beef Teriyaki** (see page 266); **Broccoli-Carrot Stir-Fry** (see page 62); **Apple Yogurt** (see page 98); Beverage

Day 5

Morning Meal	*Grapefruit, 1 serving; Soft Cheese, ⅓ cup; Bread, 1 serving; **Hot Carob Milk** (see page 102)
Midday Meal	**Eggplant–Tuna Salad** (see page 342); **Buttermilk Coleslaw** (see page 63); Skim Milk, ½ serving; Beverage
·Evening Meal	**Fruited Chicken** (see page 226); **Romaine and Watercress Salad** (see page 76); **Spiced Orange Tea** (see page 404)

Day 6

Morning Meal	*Orange, 1 serving; **Sunny-Side Up Egg** (see page 150); Bread, 1 serving, with ½ serving Margarine; Skim Milk, ½ serving; Beverage
Midday Meal	**Zucchini–Cheese Salad** (see page 177); Beverage
Evening Meal	**Shrimp "Cutlets" with Dipping Sauce** (see page 334); **Green and Wax Bean Salad** (see page 60); **Brandy-Coffee Float** (see page 100)

Day 7

Morning Meal	**Honey-Glazed Grapefruit** (see page 38); Cereal, 1 serving; Skim Milk, ½ serving; Beverage
Midday Meal	*Tomato Juice, 1 serving; **Mushroom–Asparagus Frittata** (see page 158); **Pickled Radishes** (see page 82); Bread, 1 serving; Beverage
Evening Meal	**Turkey Hash** (see page 241); Bread, 1 serving, with 1 serving Margarine; **Mixed Fruit Ambrosia** (see page 45); Beverage

Additional Food Plan Requirements to Complete Limited Choice Plan Menu Suggestions

Day 1

Women:	add 1⅛ servings Milk, 1 serving Bread, and 1 serving Fats
Men:	add 1 serving Fruits, 1⅛ servings Milk, 3 servings Bread, and 1 serving Fats

Youth: add 1 serving Fruits, 2⅛ servings Milk, 3 servings Bread, and 1 serving Fats

Day 2

Women: add 1½ servings Fruits, 1 serving Bread, and ½ serving Fats

Men: add 2½ servings Fruits, 3 servings Bread, and ½ serving Fats

Youth: add 2½ servings Fruits, 1 serving Milk, 3 servings Bread, and ½ serving Fats

Day 3

Women: add 1 serving Fruits and 1 serving Milk

Men: add 2 servings Fruits, 1 serving Milk, and 2 servings Bread

Youth: add 2 servings Fruits, 2 servings Milk, and 2 servings Bread

Day 4

Women: add ½ serving Fruits, ¾ serving Milk, 1 serving Bread, and 1 serving Fats

Men: add 1½ servings Fruits, ¾ serving Milk, 3 servings Bread, and 1 serving Fats

Youth: add 1½ servings Fruits, 1¾ servings Milk, 3 servings Bread, and 1 serving Fats

Day 5

Women: add ½ serving Fruits, ⅓ serving Milk, 1 serving Bread, and 1½ servings Fats

Men: add 1½ servings Fruits, ⅓ serving Milk, 3 servings Bread, and 1½ servings Fats

Youth: add 1½ servings Fruits, 1⅓ servings Milk, 3 servings Bread, and 1½ servings Fats

Day 6

Women: add ½ serving Fruits and ¾ serving Milk

Men: add 1½ servings Fruits, ¾ serving Milk, and 2 servings Bread

Youth: add 1½ servings Fruits, 1¾ servings Milk, and 2 servings Bread

Day 7

Women: add 1½ servings Milk

Men: add 1 serving Fruits, 1½ servings Milk, and 2 servings Bread

Youth: add 1 serving Fruits, 2½ servings Milk, and 2 servings Bread

NO CHOICE PLAN

Guidelines for Using the No Choice Plan

The No Choice Plan is a structured menu plan that has been designed for individuals who find that making food choices causes difficulty and prefer a preselected menu. It will also help those who have reached a temporary plateau in weight loss or who need this type of structure to control the urge to eat indiscriminately.

1. You may follow the No Choice Plan for one or two days or, at most, for *up to* two weeks, at which time you should return to one of the preceding Plans. You may return to the No Choice Plan after following the Full or Limited Choice Plan for one week, but be sure to complete a week on one of these preceding Plans before doing so.

2. The No Choice Plan may be started on any day desired, but follow the sequence thereafter. For example, if you start Day 3 on a Saturday, Day 4 is your menu for Sunday, Day 5 for Monday, etc.

3. Refer to the guidelines specified for the Limited Choice Plan in each food category for explanations of food items, cooking procedures, and food substitutions, but follow the basic format as outlined (e.g., if red snapper is not available or to your taste, substitute one of the *fish* listed as a Limited Choice Plan selection; do *not* substitute poultry or meat).

4. Selections from the Beverage and Condiment sections of the Optional category may be used.

5. On this Plan, *up to* 10 calories per day of diet soda may be consumed.

6. Bold type on the Plan indicates that a recipe has been included. The equivalents for each recipe have been calculated into each day's menu. If the recipe is not used, adjust the menu for the day in accordance with these recipe equivalents.

No Choice Plan

	DAY 1	DAY 2	DAY 3	DAY 4	DAY 5	DAY 6	DAY 7
Morning Meal	**Broiled Spiced Orange,** 1 serving Cereal, 1 serving Skim Milk, ½ serving Beverage	* Grapefruit, 1 serving Cottage Cheese, ⅓ cup Melba Toast, 1 serving Skim Milk, 1 serving	* Tomato Juice, 1 serving **Scrambled Egg,** 1 serving Bread, 1 serving Skim Milk, ½ serving Beverage	* Orange, 1 serving Cereal, 1 serving Bread, 1 serving Skim Milk, ½ serving Beverage	* Melon, 1 serving Cottage Cheese, ⅓ cup **Raisin Bread,** 1 ounce Skim Milk, ½ serving Beverage	* Grapefruit, 1 serving Egg, 1 Bread, 1 serving Margarine, 1 serving Skim Milk, ½ serving Beverage	* Melon, 1 serving Cereal, 1 serving Skim Milk, ½ serving Beverage
Midday Meal	* Tomato Juice, 1 serving **Tuna Salad,** 1 serving Melba Toast, 1 serving Skim Milk, ½ serving Beverage	Cooked Chicken, 3 ounces Carrot Sticks with Green Bell Pepper Strips Mayonnaise, 1 serving Bread, 1 serving Beverage	**Vegetable Cottage Cheese,** 1 serving Melba Toast, 1 serving Margarine, 1 serving Fruit Cocktail, 1 serving Yogurt, 1 serving Beverage	Tuna, 3 ounces Lettuce with Celery Sticks and Cucumber Slices Mayonnaise, 1 serving Bread, 1 serving Skim Milk, ½ serving Beverage	Cooked Turkey, 3 ounces Lettuce with Green Bell Pepper Strips Mayonnaise, 1 serving Bread, 1 serving **Applesauce,** ½ cup Skim Milk, ½ serving Beverage	**Open-Face Grilled Cheese Sandwich,** 1 serving Skim Milk, ½ serving Beverage	Eggs, 2 Lettuce with Celery and Carrot Sticks **Homemade Mayonnaise,** 1 teaspoon Bread, 2 servings * Orange, 1 serving Beverage

Evening Meal	Roast Turkey, 3 ounces Spinach, 1 serving Tossed Salad with **Herb Vinaigrette Dressing** Bread, 1 serving Beverage	**Stir-Fried Liver and Vegetables,** 1 serving Green Salad with Vegetable Oil plus Vinegar and Herbs * Orange, 1 serving Beverage	Broiled Sole, 3 ounces Green Beans, 1 serving Tossed Salad with Vegetable Oil plus Vinegar and Herbs Beverage	**Broiled Chicken,** 1 serving Carrots, 1 serving Green Salad with 1 serving **Herb Vinaigrette Dressing** * Grapefruit, 1 serving Beverage	Cooked Beef, 3 ounces Green Beans, 1 serving Margarine, 1 serving Tossed Salad with Vegetable Oil plus Vinegar and Herbs Beverage	Broiled Red Snapper, 3 ounces Spinach, 1 serving Green Salad with 1 serving Vegetable Oil plus Vinegar and Herbs Tangerine, 1 serving Beverage	**Chicken Rolls with Cauliflower Puree,** 1 serving Tossed Salad with 1 serving Vegetable Oil plus Vinegar and Herbs Skim Milk, ½ serving Beverage
Planned Snacks	Fruit Cocktail, 1 serving Yogurt, 1 serving	Banana, 1 serving Skim Milk, 1 serving	Applesauce, ½ cup Skim Milk, ½ serving	Banana, 1 serving Yogurt, 1 serving	* Orange, 1 serving Skim Milk, 1 serving	Fruit Cocktail, 1 serving Yogurt, 1 serving	Banana, 1 serving Skim Milk, 1 serving

Serving Information	Basic Allowances are for Women. Adjustments for Men and Youth are indicated at right.	Men (add daily): Poultry, Meat, or Fish—Recipes indicate additions for Men's portions. For Midday and Evening Meals at which recipes are not included, add 1 ounce of indicated Protein.
		Bread, 2 servings Fruit, 1 serving
		Youth (add daily): Bread, 2 servings Fruit, 1 serving Milk, 1 serving

To help you keep track of your daily and weekly use of foods, keep a record like the one below.

Sample Daily Food Record

Food	Day 1	Day 2	Day 3	Day 4	Day 5	Day 6	Day 7
Fruit*							
Fruit							
Cereal							
Eggs							
Cheese, soft							
Cheese, semisoft or hard							
Peanut Butter							
Poultry, Veal, or Game							
Meat Group							
Liver							
Fish							
Legumes							
Vegetables							
Limited Vegetables							
Bread							
Bread Substitutes							
Fats							
Milk							
Milk Substitutes							
Extras							
Bonus							
Specialty Foods							
Occasional Substitutes							

GOAL WEIGHTS
WOMEN

Height Range Without Shoes	Age in Years				
	18	19-20	21-22	23-24	25 & Over
Ft. Inches	Weight in Pounds				
4 6 (54)	83- 99	84-101	85-103	86-104	88-106
4 7 (55)	84-100	85-102	86-104	88-105	90-107
4 8 (56)	86-101	87-103	88-105	90-106	92-108
4 9 (57)	89-102	90-104	91-106	92-108	94-110
4 10 (58)	91-105	92-106	93-109	94-111	96-113
4 11 (59)	93-109	94-111	95-113	96-114	99-116
5 0 (60)	96-112	97-113	98-115	100-117	102-119
5 1 (61)	100-116	101-117	102-119	103-121	105-122
5 2 (62)	104-119	105-121	106-123	107-125	108-126
5 3 (63)	106-125	107-126	108-127	109-129	111-130
5 4 (64)	109-130	110-131	111-132	112-134	114-135
5 5 (65)	112-133	113-134	114-136	116-138	118-139
5 6 (66)	116-137	117-138	118-140	120-142	122-143
5 7 (67)	121-140	122-142	123-144	124-146	126-147
5 8 (68)	123-144	124-146	126-148	128-150	130-151
5 9 (69)	130-148	131-150	132-152	133-154	134-155
5 10 (70)	134-151	135-154	136-156	137-158	138-159
5 11 (71)	138-155	139-158	140-160	141-162	142-163
6 0 (72)	142-160	143-162	144-164	145-166	146-167
6 1 (73)	146-164	147-166	148-168	149-170	150-171
6 2 (74)	150-168	151-170	152-172	153-174	154-175

GOAL WEIGHTS
MEN

Height Range Without Shoes	Age in Years				
	18	19-20	21-22	23-24	25 & Over
Ft. Inches	Weight in Pounds				
5 0 (60)	109-122	110-133	112-135	114-137	115-138
5 1 (61)	112-126	113-136	115-138	117-140	118-141
5 2 (62)	115-130	116-139	118-140	120-142	121-144
5 3 (63)	118-135	119-143	121-145	123-147	124-148
5 4 (64)	120-145	122-147	124-149	126-151	127-152
5 5 (65)	124-149	125-151	127-153	129-155	130-156
5 6 (66)	128-154	129-156	131-158	133-160	134-161
5 7 (67)	132-159	133-161	134-163	136-165	138-166
5 8 (68)	135-163	136-165	138-167	140-169	142-170
5 9 (69)	140-165	141-169	142-171	144-173	146-174
5 10 (70)	143-170	144-173	146-175	148-178	150-179
5 11 (71)	147-177	148-179	150-181	152-183	154-184
6 0 (72)	151-180	152-184	154-186	156-188	158-189
6 1 (73)	155-187	156-189	158-190	160-193	162-194
6 2 (74)	160-192	161-194	163-196	165-198	167-199
6 3 (75)	165-198	166-199	168-201	170-203	172-204
6 4 (76)	170-202	171-204	173-206	175-208	177-209

GOAL WEIGHTS
GIRLS

Height Range Without Shoes	Age in Years							
	10	11	12	13	14	15	16	17
Ft. Inches	Weight in Pounds							
3 11 (47)	48- 55							
4 0 (48)	49- 58	51- 61						
4 1 (49)	50- 61	52- 65	53- 69					
4 2 (50)	51- 64	53- 67	55- 71	60- 73				
4 3 (51)	54- 67	55- 70	57- 73	62- 76	63- 84			
4 4 (52)	58- 70	59- 73	60- 76	64- 79	67- 88	77- 91		
4 5 (53)	59- 73	62- 76	63- 79	66- 82	71- 90	78- 93	79- 94	80- 96
4 6 (54)	62- 75	65- 77	66- 81	68- 85	74- 91	79- 94	80- 95	82- 98
4 7 (55)	64- 77	68- 78	69- 84	70- 88	76- 92	80- 95	81- 96	83- 99
4 8 (56)	66- 79	71- 80	72- 87	73- 91	78- 94	81- 96	82- 97	85-100
4 9 (57)	68- 83	74- 84	75- 90	76- 94	81- 97	84- 99	85-100	88-101
4 10 (58)	70- 86	76- 87	77- 93	79- 97	84-100	87-102	88-103	90-104
4 11 (59)	75- 89	78- 90	80- 96	82-100	87-103	90-105	91-106	92-108
5 0 (60)	80- 92	81- 93	82- 98	86-103	90-106	93-108	94-110	95-111
5 1 (61)	82- 95	84- 97	86-101	88-106	94-109	97-111	98-112	99-113
5 2 (62)	84- 98	86-102	89-104	92-109	98-112	101-115	102-117	103-118
5 3 (63)	87-101	89-104	92-106	96-112	101-115	103-122	104-123	105-124
5 4 (64)	90-103	93-106	97-109	100-115	104-118	106-124	107-126	108-128
5 5 (65)	94-105	98-108	102-111	104-118	107-121	109-126	110-129	111-131
5 6 (66)		103-111	106-116	108-121	111-124	113-131	114-132	115-134
5 7 (67)		107-114	110-120	112-124	116-127	118-134	119-135	120-137
5 8 (68)			114-124	117-127	119-130	120-135	121-138	122-140
5 9 (69)			118-127	122-130	124-133	126-141	128-142	129-144
5 10 (70)				127-134	128-137	130-143	132-146	133-148
5 11 (71)				132-138	133-141	135-146	136-150	137-152
6 0 (72)					136-145	138-148	140-151	141-156
6 1 (73)					140-150	142-155	144-158	145-160

GOAL WEIGHTS
BOYS

Height Range Without Shoes	Age in Years							
	10	11	12	13	14	15	16	17
Ft. Inches	Weight in Pounds							
3 11 (47)	48- 52							
4 0 (48)	50- 55	51- 57						
4 1 (49)	52- 57	53- 58						
4 2 (50)	54- 59	55- 60	56- 62					
4 3 (51)	58- 62	59- 63	60- 64					
4 4 (52)	60- 65	61- 66	62- 67					
4 5 (53)	63- 68	64- 69	65- 70	66- 71				
4 6 (54)	65- 71	66- 72	67- 73	68- 75				
4 7 (55)	70- 75	71- 76	72- 77	73- 79	74- 80			
4 8 (56)	75- 80	76- 81	77- 83	78- 85	79- 87			
4 9 (57)	79- 82	80- 84	81- 86	83- 89	84- 90	86- 95		
4 10 (58)	82- 86	83- 87	84- 88	88- 93	89- 94	92-100	95-108	
4 11 (59)	86- 90	87- 91	88- 92	93- 97	94- 98	96-104	98-110	101-114
5 0 (60)	90- 94	91- 95	92- 96	96-101	98-103	100-108	102-113	105-117
5 1 (61)	93- 97	95- 99	96-100	100-105	101-108	103-112	106-116	108-120
5 2 (62)	97-101	99-103	100-104	104-109	106-113	108-116	110-120	112-123
5 3 (63)	100-104	102-106	104-108	107-113	111-118	113-120	114-123	117-126
5 4 (64)	102-107	104-109	108-112	111-117	114-121	116-123	118-127	119-130
5 5 (65)	105-110	107-112	112-116	115-121	117-125	119-127	122-130	123-133
5 6 (66)		111-116	116-120	118-125	121-129	123-131	126-133	127-137
5 7 (67)		115-120	119-124	121-130	125-133	128-134	130-136	131-141
5 8 (68)			122-128	124-133	129-137	132-138	133-140	134-145
5 9 (69)			125-132	127-136	133-141	136-142	138-144	139-149
5 10 (70)				130-140	137-145	140-149	141-155	142-160
5 11 (71)				135-144	141-149	144-155	145-160	146-168
6 0 (72)					146-153	148-156	149-163	150-170
6 1 (73)					150-157	152-163	153-166	154-175
6 2 (74)						157-165	158-170	159-182
6 3 (75)						162-175	163-180	164-190
6 4 (76)						167-185	168-191	169-195

Recipe Information

Tips for Using Recipes
with the Food Plans

1. Each of our Food Plans is actually made up of six food groups: Fruits; Vegetables; Milk; Grains; Protein; and Fats. For ease of recipe selection, we have divided the Grains and Protein groups into separate categories. The food selections in the Bread and Cereal and Bread Substitutes chapters make up the Grains food group; the food selections in the Eggs, Cheese, Peanut Butter, Poultry, Veal, and Game, Meat Group, Liver, Fish, and Legumes chapters make up the Protein food group.

2. Each recipe was developed to fit into a specific Food Plan and is so noted. Full Choice Plan recipes should be used only in conjunction with the Full Choice Plan; however, all Limited and No Choice Plan recipes may be used with the Full Choice Plan also. No Choice Plan recipes may be used with the Limited Choice Plan as well.

3. Occasionally, when Limited or No Choice Plan recipes are used with the Full Choice Plan, due to differences in the Plans some of the equivalents must be adjusted. The recipes to which this applies have been noted accordingly and an appendix incorporating the required changes has been included.

4. When necessary, adjustments for Men's portions have been added to recipes. For poultry, meat, and fish recipes, if no such adjustment has been made, the recipe will provide Men with a low end of the range serving.

5. Always take time to measure and weigh ingredients carefully; this is vital to both recipe results and weight control. Don't try to judge portions by eye.

- To weigh foods, use a scale.
- To measure liquids, use a standard glass or clear plastic measuring cup. Place it on a level surface and read markings at eye level. Fill the cup just to the appropriate marking. To measure less than ¼ cup, use standard measuring spoons.

19

- To measure dry ingredients, use metal or plastic measuring cups that come in sets of four: ¼ cup; ⅓ cup; ½ cup; and 1 cup. Spoon the ingredients into the cup, then level with the straight edge of a knife or metal spatula. To measure less than ¼ cup, use standard measuring spoons and, unless otherwise directed, level as for measuring cup.
- To measure a dash, as a guide consider a dash to be about ⅟₁₆ of a teaspoon (½ of a ⅛-teaspoon measure or ¼ of a ¼-teaspoon measure).

6. In any recipe for more than one serving it is important to mix ingredients well and to *divide evenly*, so that each portion will be the same size.

Tips About Our Ingredients

1. The herbs used in these recipes are dried unless otherwise indicated. If you are substituting fresh herbs, use approximately four times the amount of dried (e.g., 1 teaspoon chopped fresh basil instead of ¼ teaspoon dried basil leaves). If you are substituting ground (powdered) herbs for dried leaves, use approximately half the amount of dried (e.g., ¼ teaspoon ground thyme instead of ½ teaspoon dried thyme leaves).

2. If you are substituting fresh spices for ground, generally use approximately eight times the amount of ground (e.g., 1 teaspoon minced ginger root instead of ⅛ teaspoon ground ginger).

3. Generally, dried herbs and spices should not be kept for more than a year. Date the container at the time of purchase and check periodically for potency. Usually, if the herb (or spice) is aromatic, it is still potent; if the aroma has diminished, the recipe may require a larger amount of the seasoning.

4. Unless otherwise specified, the raisins used in our recipes are dark seedless raisins.

5. We've used fresh vegetables unless otherwise indicated. If you substitute frozen or canned vegetables, it may be necessary to adjust cooking times accordingly.

6. When vegetable oil is called for, oils such as safflower, sunflower, soybean, corn, cottonseed, peanut, or any of these combined may be used. Since olive oil and sesame oil have distinctive flavors, they

have been specifically indicated. There are two types of sesame oil: light and dark. The light oil is relatively flavorless and may be used as a substitute for any other vegetable oil. When sesame oil is specified, use the dark variety. This product, made from *toasted* sesame seeds, has a rich amber color and a characteristic sesame flavor.

7. We have included recipes for Chicken Broth, Beef Broth, and Vegetable Broth. These broths were developed without the addition of salt and have been used in various other recipes throughout the book. If desired, bouillon (made from cubes or instant broth and seasoning mix) may be substituted for homemade broth. Use 1 cube or packet dissolved in ¾ cup hot water for each ¾ cup broth. Since these products do contain salt, the amount of salt called for in the recipe may have to be adjusted. If this substitution is made, the amount of sodium per serving will be increased.

8. Some of our recipes use prepared instant broth and seasoning mix. The amount of sodium in these recipes can be decreased by substituting homemade broth.

Tips for Successful Results

1. Read through a recipe completely before you begin. Make sure you understand the method and have all ingredients and utensils on hand. Gather all ingredients and any special utensils needed in one place and make sure that all items are at proper temperature (e.g., if you're beating evaporated skimmed milk, you'll want to chill the milk, bowl, and beaters; if you're beating egg whites, you'll want them at room temperature).

2. Measure and/or weigh all ingredients carefully.

3. When it is suggested that an ingredient be at room temperature, we are referring to a temperature of 68° to 72°F.

4. It is recommended that foods *not* be marinated in aluminum containers. Certain foods react with aluminum and this can have an adverse effect. Using a plastic bag is an effective way of marinating foods. Place marinade and items to be marinated in a leakproof plastic bag; close bag securely and let marinate according to recipe directions. Using this method makes turning of foods easy, since all you have to do is turn the entire bag. After food has been marinated, the bag can be discarded and there's one pan less to clean.

5. When pounding meat, if a meat mallet is unavailable a saucepan can be substituted. Pound with bottom of the saucepan and, unless otherwise specified, pound until meat is about ¼ inch thick.

6. When using eggs, it's a good idea to break each one into a cup or bowl before combining with other ingredients or additional eggs. This will avoid wasting other items should one egg happen to be spoiled.

7. When dissolving arrowroot, flour, or cornstarch in liquid, to avoid lumping add the dry ingredient to the liquid, not vice versa.

8. When dissolving unflavored gelatin over direct heat, be sure to use a low heat and stir constantly. This is important since gelatin burns very easily.

9. Some of our recipes call for the use of a steamer; if you don't have one available, you can easily improvise. Use a Dutch oven or any large pot that has a tight-fitting cover; add 2 to 3 inches water. Place one or two empty cans, from which the tops and bottoms have been removed, into the Dutch oven (or pot); be sure that they are tall enough to support a dish above the water level. Bring water to a boil. Place food that is to be steamed in a heatproof dish and carefully set dish onto cans, making sure that water does not touch dish; cover tightly and steam as directed in recipe.

As an alternative steaming apparatus, you can use a wire rack set onto two heatproof measuring cups. Whichever form of apparatus you use, remember that the pot containing it should always be tightly covered. And be sure to use a cooking/serving dish, since steam heat is hot enough to damage even good china.

10. When a recipe calls for the use of custard cups, use items made of heatproof glass or heavy ceramic.

11. The cooking times on most recipes are approximate and should be used as guides. There are many variables that can affect timing such as: temperature of food before it is cooked; type of heat being used; shape of food; type of cookware being used; etc. In addition, the flow of both gas and electricity to your appliances may be affected by the total amount being used within your area at the time you are cooking. If you are cooking at "peak-load" times, chances are a recipe may take a little longer than the suggested time; conversely, if a minimum amount of power is being utilized, the recipe may be done in a shorter period of time. Therefore, to ensure optimum results, be sure to always check for doneness as directed.

12. Some recipes include instructions to preheat the oven. When preparing these recipes, if you do not preheat, generally allow an additional 5 to 10 minutes cooking time.

13. When baking, be sure that pans are placed on oven rack so that air can circulate freely. It's best to use one oven rack at a time. If you're using two racks, place them so that the oven is divided into thirds, then stagger the pans so that one is not directly above the other.

14. When baking in a muffin pan and using only some of the cups, it's a good idea to partially fill the empty cups with water. This will prevent the pan from warping or burning. When ready to remove items from pan, drain off the water very carefully; remember, it will be boiling hot.

15. When broiling, 4 inches is the standard distance from the heat source and should be used with any recipes that do not specify otherwise. If it is necessary to broil closer to or farther away from the heat, the appropriate distance will be indicated.

16. If a dish is to be chilled or frozen after cooking, always allow it to cool slightly before refrigerating or freezing. Placing a very hot item into the refrigerator or freezer can adversely affect the functioning of the appliance. Additionally, cover all items that are to be refrigerated; cover or properly wrap all items that are to be placed in the freezer. If a dish is not covered: odors from other foods may permeate it, or vice versa; drying may occur, particularly in frost-free refrigerators; the flavor may be spoiled by the accidental dripping of other foods; freezer burn may occur.

17. It is recommended that chilled foods be served on chilled plates and hot foods on warmed plates. Plates and glassware should be chilled in the refrigerator for approximately 5 minutes before serving. Plates and platters can be heated by placing them in a warm oven (no more than 200°F.) for 5 to 10 minutes before serving, in a warmer, or on a warming tray.

Pan Substitutions

It's best to use the pan size that's recommended in a recipe; however, if your kitchen isn't equipped with that particular pan, chances are a substitution will work just as well. The pan size is determined by the volume of food. When substituting, use a pan as close to the recommended size as possible; food cooked in too small a pan may boil over, in too large a pan may dry out or burn. To determine the dimensions of a baking pan, measure across the top, between the inside edges. To determine the volume, measure the amount of water the pan holds when completely filled.

When you use a pan that is a different size from the one recommended, it may be necessary to adjust the suggested cooking time. Depending on the size of the pan and the depth of the food in it, you may need to add or subtract 5 to 10 minutes. If you substitute glass or glass-ceramic for metal, it is recommended that the oven temperature be reduced by 25°F.

The following chart provides some common pan substitutions:

Recommended Size	Approximate Volume	Possible Substitutions
8 x 1½-inch round baking pan	1½ quarts	10 x 6 x 2-inch baking dish 9 x 1½-inch round baking pan 8 x 4 x 2-inch loaf pan 9-inch pie plate
8 x 8 x 2-inch baking pan	2 quarts	11 x 7 x 1½-inch baking pan 12 x 7½ x 2-inch baking pan 9 x 5 x 3-inch loaf pan two 8 x 1½-inch round baking pans
13 x 9 x 2-inch baking pan	3 quarts	14 x 11 x 2-inch baking dish two 9 x 1½-inch round baking pans three 8 x 1½-inch round baking pans

Oven Temperatures

Oven thermostats should be checked at least once a year. If your oven does not have a thermostat or regulator, the following chart will give you an idea of the equivalent amount of heat required for each temperature range:

250° to 275°F.	Very slow oven
300° to 325°F.	Slow oven
350° to 375°F.	Moderate oven
400° to 425°F.	Hot oven
450° to 475°F.	Very hot oven
500° to 525°F.	Extremely hot oven

An oven thermometer can be purchased and placed in the oven to help determine the degree of heat.

Microwave Ovens

Many of our recipes can be cooked in a microwave oven. Since there is no one standard that applies to all ovens, you will have to experiment with your unit and follow the manufacturer's advice for timing. Generally, you should allow about ¼ of the suggested cooking time. This means that if our recipe suggests 20 minutes, allow 5 minutes in your microwave oven (or slightly less, since it's wiser to undercook than overcook). Please note that our roasting procedures for beef, ham, lamb, and pork require the use of a rack so that fat can drain off into the pan. Racks designed for use in microwave ovens are available.

Slow Cookers

If you enjoy cooking with a slow cooker, there's no reason why you can't adapt many of our recipes to its use. For a headstart on Chicken Broth (see page 401), combine all ingredients; cook covered on low for 12 hours. Strain and proceed as in the basic recipe.

Artificial Sweeteners

The use of artificial sweeteners on the Weight Watchers Food Plan has always been optional. Natural sweetness is available in the form of fruits and honey. You may also use white and brown sugar, fructose, molasses, and syrup. The use of artificial sweeteners is completely optional, and we believe that the decision about using them should be made by you and your physician.

Nutrition Notes

Nutrition is defined as the process by which we utilize foods in order to maintain healthy bodily functions. Foods provide the nutrients necessary for energy, growth, and repair of body tissues, as well as for regulation and control of body processes. You need about forty different nutrients to stay healthy. These include proteins, fats, carbohydrates, vitamins, minerals, and water. It is the amount of proteins, carbohydrates, and fats in foods that determines their energy value or caloric content. The objective of daily menu planning is to provide yourself with basic nutrients while staying within your caloric limit.

Proteins are necessary for building and maintaining body tissues. Poultry, meat, fish, eggs, milk, and cheese are the best sources of protein. Fats and carbohydrates provide energy in addition to assisting other body functions. Fruits, vegetables, cereals, and grains are rich in carbohydrates. Margarine, vegetable oils, poultry, meat, and fish supply the fats we need.

Vitamins and minerals are also essential for the body's proper functioning. Sodium is especially important for maintaining body water balance and therefore has a significant effect on weight control. Sodium occurs naturally in some foods, and additional amounts are often added in processing prepared foods.

Variety is the key to success. No single food supplies all the essential nutrients in the amounts needed. The greater the variety of food the less likely you are to develop either a deficiency or an excess of any single nutrient, and the more interesting and attractive your diet will be.

Fruits

"Apple polishing" may reap favors, but you can gain more substantial results by polishing not just apples but a whole array of fruits into delectable stand-ins for more dangerous desserts. Or try our figure-saving versions of cakes, tarts, and soufflés. Fruits spruce up thirst-quenchers like our lemonade blended with blueberries, or form the base of a calorie-wise, liquorless "daiquiri."

Guidelines for Using Fruits

1. Amounts:

	Full Choice Plan	Limited Choice Plan
Women	3 servings daily	3 servings daily
Men	4 to 6 servings daily	4 servings daily
Youth	4 to 6 servings daily	4 servings daily

2. Individual fruits vary widely in the amount of nutrients they supply; therefore it is important to vary your selections.

3. One serving should be selected at the Morning Meal; remaining servings may be selected at any time. However, on the Full Choice Plan, 1 cup tomato or mixed vegetable juice may be selected in place of a fruit serving at the Morning Meal; this may be counted as a Bonus (see Optional, page 389) and all fruit servings may be used later in the day.

4. Daily, choose *at least* one fruit marked with an asterisk (*). However, on the Full Choice Plan, if 1 cup tomato juice is selected as a Bonus, it is not necessary to select an asterisked fruit that day. These fruits supply almost all of the vitamin C required daily. Since heating destroys vitamin C, if an asterisked fruit is cooked, one of your remaining fruit selections should be another asterisked fruit.

5. Use only those fruits and fruit juices listed on the Food Plan; they may be fresh, canned, or frozen. Canned and frozen products should have *no sugar added*.

6. The serving size for canned fruits, except pineapple slices and spears, is ½ cup with the juice that adheres to fruit while measuring or the fresh equivalent with 2 tablespoons juice. Two slices or 4 spears of canned pineapple with 2 tablespoons juice is 1 serving Fruits.

7. Frozen fruit should be measured in its frozen state, never totally or partially thawed.

8. Equate frozen concentrated fruit juice (no sugar added) as follows:

> 2 tablespoons concentrated orange or grapefruit juice equals 1 serving Fruits

29

>1 tablespoon plus 1 teaspoon concentrated apple,
>grape, pineapple, or pineapple-orange juice equals
>1 serving Fruits

9. Use only those dried fruits listed on the Food Plan; they should have *no sugar added*.

10. Freeze-dried and home-dried fruits may be used; equate to the amount of fresh fruit used before drying.

11. One serving of the approved commercially prepared dietary frozen dessert used in our recipes equates to 1 serving Fruits and ½ serving Milk.

Fruit Servings

The fruits in italics are for the Full Choice Plan only and should *not* be used with the Limited Choice Plan. The other fruits may be used on both plans.

Selections	One Serving
JUICES	
apple juice or cider (may be carbonated but not fermented)	⅓ cup
grape juice	*⅓ cup*
*grapefruit juice	½ cup
*orange juice	½ cup
*orange–grapefruit juice	½ cup
pineapple juice	*⅓ cup*
pineapple–orange juice	*⅓ cup*
prune juice	*⅓ cup*
tangerine juice	*½ cup*
*tomato juice (may be homemade—no sugar added)	1 cup
mixed vegetable juice (may be homemade— no sugar added)	1 cup
FRUITS (fresh unless otherwise specified)	
apple, whole	*1 small*
slices	*¾ cup*
applesauce	½ cup
apricots	2 medium
dried	4 medium halves
banana	½ medium
berries:	
blackberries	½ cup
blueberries	½ cup
boysenberries	½ cup
cranberries	1 cup
elderberries	*½ cup*

Selections	One Serving
*gooseberries	¾ cup
huckleberries	½ cup
loganberries	½ cup
mulberries	½ cup
raspberries	½ cup
*strawberries, whole	1 cup
sliced	¾ cup
*cantaloupe	½ small or 1 cup chunks or balls (Limited Choice— use only 1 cup chunks or balls, not ½ small)
*carambola	1 medium
cherries	10 large
crab apples	2
*currants	¾ cup
currants, dried	2 tablespoons
dates	2
fig	1 large
dried	1
fruit cocktail or salad	½ cup
gineps	2
*grapefruit, whole	½ medium
sections	½ cup
grapes	20 small or 12 large
*honeydew or similar melon	2-inch wedge or 1 cup chunks or balls
*kiwi fruit	1 medium
kumquats	3 medium
litchis	8
loquats	10 pitted
mandarin, whole	1 large
sections	½ cup
*mango	½ small
murcot (similar to tangerine)	1 medium
nectarine	1 small
*orange, whole	1 small
sections	½ cup
*papaya	½ medium
peach	1 medium
pear	1 small
persimmon	1 medium
pineapple	¼ small
plums	2 medium
prickly pear (cactus pear)	1 medium
prunes	3 medium or 2 large
quince	1 medium
raisins	2 tablespoons

Selections	One Serving
rhubarb (raw or cooked)	1 cup
soursop	⅓ *cup*
sweetsop (sugar apple)	⅓ *cup*
tangelo	1 large
tangerine	1 large
ugli fruit	1 *medium*
watermelon	3 x 1½-inch triangle or 1 cup chunks or balls

APPLESAUCE
No Choice Plan
Makes about 2 cups

1½ pounds cooking apples, pared, cored, and quartered
½ cup water
1½-inch piece cinnamon stick

Artificial sweetener to equal 2 teaspoons sugar, or to taste (optional)

In 2-quart saucepan combine apples, water, and cinnamon stick. Bring to a boil. Reduce heat, cover, and simmer, stirring occasionally, until apples are tender, 15 to 20 minutes. (If necessary, add more water to prevent scorching.) Cool.

Remove and discard cinnamon stick. Transfer mixture to blender container or work bowl of food processor and process until desired consistency. Stir in sweetener if desired. Serve at room temperature or transfer to container, cover, and chill.

½ cup applesauce is equivalent to: 1 serving Fruits.

Per ½-cup serving: 79 calories, 0.3 g protein, 0.4 g fat, 21 g carbohydrate, 1 mg sodium
With sweetener: 80 calories, 0.3 g protein, 0.4 g fat, 21 g carbohydrate, 1 mg sodium

Variation: Add 2 teaspoons lemon juice and dash ground nutmeg to apples and water.

Per ½-cup serving: 80 calories, 0.3 g protein, 0.5 g fat, 21 g carbohydrate, 2 mg sodium

NO-COOK APPLESAUCE
Full Choice Plan
Makes 1 serving

1 small apple, pared and cored
1 tablespoon lemon juice

1 teaspoon granulated sugar
Dash ground cinnamon (optional)

Chop apple into small pieces. In blender container combine apple and lemon juice and process until smooth (when necessary, stop machine and, using a rubber scraper, scrape apple from sides into bottom of container). Stir in sugar and, if desired, cinnamon. Serve immediately.

Each serving is equivalent to: 1 serving Fruits; 2 servings Extras.

Per serving: 78 calories, 0.3 g protein, 0.3 g fat, 21 g carbohydrate, 1 mg sodium

APPLESAUCE CRISP
Limited Choice Plan
Makes 1 serving

1 teaspoon margarine
2 graham crackers (2½-inch
  squares), made into crumbs

½ teaspoon firmly packed light
  brown sugar
½ cup applesauce (no sugar added)
⅛ teaspoon ground allspice

Preheat oven to 375°F. In small saucepan melt margarine. Add graham cracker crumbs and sugar; stir to combine and set aside.

In small bowl combine applesauce and allspice. Spoon half of applesauce mixture into a 6-ounce custard cup; top with half of crumb mixture. Repeat layers. Bake 15 minutes. Serve warm or chilled.

Each serving is equivalent to: 1 serving Fats; 1 serving Bread; 1 serving Extras; 1 serving Fruits.

Per serving: 148 calories, 1 g protein, 5 g fat, 26 g carbohydrate, 142 mg sodium

POACHED APPLE SECTIONS
Full Choice Plan
Makes 2 servings

2 small apples
2 teaspoons lemon juice, divided
¾ cup water

2-inch strip lemon peel
2 teaspoons honey
1 teaspoon vanilla extract

Pare and core apples; cut into thin wedges and place in bowl with water to cover. Add 1 teaspoon lemon juice and set aside.

In small saucepan combine ¾ cup water and lemon peel; bring to a boil and cook 5 minutes. Drain apples; add to saucepan along with honey, vanilla, and remaining 1 teaspoon lemon juice. Cook until apples are tender, 8 to 10 minutes. Remove and discard lemon peel. Serve apple wedges in poaching liquid. May be served warm or chilled.

Each serving is equivalent to: 1 serving Fruits; 2 servings Extras.

Per serving: 89 calories, 0.3 g protein, 0.3 g fat, 21 g carbohydrate, 1 mg sodium

MAPLE–APPLE BAKE
Full Choice Plan
Makes 2 servings

2 small apples
2 teaspoons reduced-calorie
  pancake syrup (60 calories per 1
  fluid ounce), divided

½ teaspoon poppy seed
⅓ cup apple juice (no sugar added)
2 tablespoons evaporated skimmed
  milk

Remove core from each apple to ½ inch from bottom. Remove a thin strip of skin from around center of each apple (this helps keep skin from bursting). Spoon ½ teaspoon pancake syrup and ¼ teaspoon poppy seed into each apple cavity and place apples upright in small baking dish. Pour apple juice over fruit and drizzle with remaining pancake syrup. Bake at 350°F. until tender, about 40 minutes.

Transfer each apple to a plate and set aside. To prepare sauce, pour juice remaining in baking dish into a small saucepan; add milk and cook over high heat, stirring constantly, until sauce thickens. Pour half of sauce over each apple.

Each serving is equivalent to: 1½ servings Fruits; 10 calories Specialty Foods; ½ serving Extras; ⅛ serving Milk.

Per serving: 106 calories, 2 g protein, 1 g fat, 24 g carbohydrate, 20 mg sodium

Variation: Substitute 2 small pears for the apples.

Per serving: 125 calories, 2 g protein, 1 g fat, 29 g carbohydrate, 22 mg sodium

APPLE TART (TARTE AUX POMMES)
Full Choice Plan
Makes 1 serving

2 tablespoons plus 1½ teaspoons enriched all-purpose flour
Dash salt
2 teaspoons margarine
1 tablespoon plain unflavored yogurt

1 small apple, pared, cored, and thinly sliced
Dash each ground nutmeg and cinnamon
2 teaspoons reduced-calorie apricot spread (16 calories per 2 teaspoons)

1. In small bowl combine flour and salt.
2. With pastry blender, or 2 knives used scissor-fashion, cut in margarine until mixture resembles coarse meal. Add yogurt and mix thoroughly.
3. Form dough into a ball; wrap in plastic wrap or wax paper and chill at least 1 hour.
4. Roll dough between 2 sheets of wax paper, forming a 4½-inch circle, about ⅛ inch thick. Carefully remove wax paper and place dough on foil or small cookie sheet. Preheat oven to 375°F.
5. Arrange apple slices decoratively over dough; sprinkle with nutmeg and cinnamon.
6. Bake until crust is golden, 20 to 30 minutes.
7. While tart is baking, in small metal measuring cup or other small flameproof container heat apricot spread. As soon as tart is done, brush with warm spread.

Each serving is equivalent to: 1 serving Bread; 2 servings Fats; ⅛ serving Milk; 1 serving Fruits; 16 calories Specialty Foods.

Per serving: 225 calories, 3 g protein, 9 g fat, 35 g carbohydrate, 226 mg sodium

CIDER COOLER
Limited Choice Plan
Makes 2 servings

1¼ cups chilled lemon- or
  lemon-lime-flavored diet soda
  (4 calories per 12 fluid ounces)

⅔ cup chilled apple juice or
  unfermented cider (no sugar
  added)

Garnish
2 cinnamon sticks (2 inches each)

Chill two 8-ounce glasses. Combine soda and juice or cider in a 4-cup measure or pitcher. Pour an equal amount into each chilled glass. Garnish each with a cinnamon stick.

Each serving is equivalent to: ⅕ serving Extras; 1 serving Fruits. (See page 407 for Full Choice Plan adjustments.)

Per serving: 41 calories, 0.1 g protein, trace fat, 10 g carbohydrate, 43 mg sodium

BANANA–CHOCOLATE CAKE
Limited Choice Plan
Makes 8 Midday or Evening Meal servings, ¼ meal each; supplement as required

4 eggs, separated
2 tablespoons granulated sugar
Artificial sweetener to equal 2
  teaspoons sugar
¼ cup cold water
2 tablespoons unsweetened cocoa
¼ teaspoon vanilla extract

Dash salt
4 slices raisin bread, made into fine
  crumbs
Dash salt
Whipped Topping (see page 103)
2 medium bananas
1 tablespoon lemon juice

1. Preheat oven to 350°F. Line bottom of an 8-inch springform pan with wax paper. Spray sides of pan with nonstick cooking spray and set aside.

2. In large mixing bowl combine egg yolks, sugar, and sweetener; using an electric mixer, beat for 2 minutes. Gradually add water and cocoa and beat at medium-high speed until thick, about 5 minutes; beat in vanilla.

3. In separate bowl, using clean beaters, beat egg whites with salt until stiff peaks form.

4. Fold bread crumbs into yolk mixture and lightly stir in about ¼ of the egg whites. Carefully fold in remaining egg whites.

5. Pour mixture into prepared baking pan and bake for 20 to 25 minutes (until a cake tester, inserted in center, comes out clean). Let cool in pan for 5 minutes; remove from pan and place on wire rack to cool.

6. Using a sharp knife, cut cake in half horizontally. Spread half of Whipped Topping on bottom layer. Peel bananas and slice into bowl; gently toss with lemon juice. Arrange half of banana slices over Whipped Topping; cover with remaining cake layer. Spread remaining Whipped Topping over top and sides of cake and arrange remaining banana slices over top.

Each serving is equivalent to: ½ Egg; 2¼ servings Extras; ½ serving Bread; Whipped Topping (see page 103); ½ serving Fruits.

Per serving: 122 calories, 5 g protein, 3 g fat, 19 g carbohydrate, 122 mg sodium

Variation: *Full Choice Plan*—Substitute 2 cups strawberries for the bananas and omit lemon juice. Reserve 8 strawberries for garnish; slice remaining strawberries and use between layers. Garnish top of cake with reserved berries. Change equivalent listing to ¼ serving Fruits.

Per serving: 110 calories, 5 g protein, 4 g fat, 15 g carbohydrate, 122 mg sodium

"BANANA DAIQUIRI"
Full Choice Plan
Makes 1 serving

½ medium banana, peeled and chopped
1 tablespoon thawed frozen concentrated pineapple juice (no sugar added)
1 teaspoon lime juice (no sugar added)
½ cup crushed ice

Chill an 8-ounce glass. In blender container combine all ingredients except ice; process at medium speed until smooth. Increase speed to high and add ice, a little at a time, until all ice has been processed. Mixture should be thick, smooth, and cold. Serve immediately in chilled glass.

Each serving is equivalent to: 1¾ servings Fruits.

Per serving: 84 calories, 1 g protein, 0.1 g fat, 22 g carbohydrate, 1 mg sodium

"BANANAS FOSTER"
Full Choice Plan
Makes 2 servings

1 medium banana
1 tablespoon lemon juice
2 teaspoons margarine
1 teaspoon granulated brown sugar
Dash each ground cinnamon, banana extract, and rum extract
2 scoops (3 ounces each) vanilla dietary frozen dessert

1. Peel banana and cut in half lengthwise, then cut each piece in half crosswise. Sprinkle banana quarters with lemon juice and set aside.

2. In small skillet heat margarine; add brown sugar, cinnamon, and extracts and cook over low heat, stirring constantly, until sugar melts.

3. Using a wooden spoon, roll banana pieces in sugar mixture.

4. In each of 2 champagne glasses or dessert dishes place 1 scoop frozen dessert; top each scoop with 2 banana quarters and half of any remaining sugar mixture.

Each serving is equivalent to: 2 servings Fruits; 1 serving Fats; 1 serving Extras; ½ serving Milk.

Per serving: 197 calories, 5 g protein, 5 g fat, 36 g carbohydrate, 116 mg sodium

STRAWBERRY–GRAHAM BANANAS
Limited Choice Plan
Makes 2 servings

4 graham crackers (2½-inch
  squares), made into crumbs
2 teaspoons shredded coconut

1 tablespoon plus 1 teaspoon
  reduced-calorie strawberry spread
  (16 calories per 2 teaspoons)
1 medium banana, peeled and cut
  in half lengthwise

In small skillet combine graham cracker crumbs and coconut. Toast lightly over low heat, *being careful not to burn*. Transfer to sheet of wax paper or paper towel. In same skillet heat strawberry spread until melted; remove from heat. Roll each banana half in spread, then quickly roll in crumb mixture, pressing crumbs so they adhere to banana; chill.

Each serving is equivalent to: 1 serving Bread; 2⅗ servings Extras; 1 serving Fruits. (See page 407 for Full Choice Plan adjustments.)

Per serving: 128 calories, 2 g protein, 2 g fat, 28 g carbohydrate, 95 mg sodium

Variation: Add ¼ teaspoon ground cinnamon to graham cracker crumbs and substitute reduced-calorie apricot spread (16 calories per 2 teaspoons) for the strawberry spread.

Per serving: 129 calories, 2 g protein, 2 g fat, 28 g carbohydrate, 95 mg sodium

BLUEBERRY LEMONADE
Limited Choice Plan
Makes 2 servings

2 small lemons
1 cup frozen blueberries (no sugar
  added), thawed

1 cup water
1 tablespoon granulated sugar
4 ice cubes

Cut a ¼-inch-thick slice from center of each lemon and reserve. Squeeze juice from remaining lemon halves into blender container. Add blueberries, water, and sugar and process at high speed until berries are pureed. Place 2 ice cubes in each of two 10-ounce glasses; pour half of the blueberry mixture into each glass. Garnish each with a reserved lemon slice.

Each serving is equivalent to: 1 serving Fruits; 3 servings Extras.

Per serving: 80 calories, 1 g protein, 0.4 g fat, 21 g carbohydrate, 1 mg sodium

FROZEN CANTALOUPE "ICE CREAM"
Limited Choice Plan
Makes 4 servings, about ½ cup each

Soften 6 ounces vanilla dietary frozen dessert. In work bowl of food processor puree 1 cup very ripe cantaloupe chunks or balls. Add softened frozen dessert and process until smooth. Transfer mixture to bowl, cover, and freeze until solid.

Break mixture into pieces and place in work bowl of food processor; process until smooth. Spoon into 4 dessert dishes, cover with plastic wrap, and refreeze until firm. Remove from freezer 5 minutes before serving.

Each serving is equivalent to: ¾ serving Fruits; ¼ serving Milk.

Per serving: 62 calories, 2 g protein, 1 g fat, 13 g carbohydrate, 40 mg sodium

CARAMBOLA

The carambola has a bright, golden-yellow, thick, waxy skin and may vary in size from as small as a hen's egg to as large as a large orange. This fruit is often referred to as the Golden Star Fruit and is ovoid in shape (egg-shaped) with 4 to 6 prominent longitudinal ribs. The flesh is juicy and crisp in texture. Fully ripened fruits have an agreeable flavor ranging from mildly sub-acidic to sweet. Carambolas are delicious eaten fresh and are frequently used in beverages, jams, and jellies.

CHOCOLATE–FIG DESSERT

Full Choice Plan
Makes 2 servings

2 ripe large figs, stems removed
2 tablespoons water
2 strips orange peel
1 teaspoon unsweetened cocoa

1 teaspoon confectioners' sugar
6 ounces vanilla dietary frozen
   dessert

Place figs in a small (about 1 cup) shallow baking dish just large enough to hold them. Add water and orange peel and bake at 375°F. until figs are soft to the touch but still hold their shape, about 15 minutes.

Sift cocoa and sugar into a small, shallow bowl. Roll warm figs in cocoa mixture. Cut each fig in half. For each portion serve 2 halves with 3 ounces frozen dessert; pour half each of the remaining cocoa mixture and any liquid remaining from cooked figs over each serving.

Each serving is equivalent to: 2 servings Fruits; 1½ servings Extras; ½ serving Milk.

Per serving: 160 calories, 5 g protein, 1 g fat, 34 g carbohydrate, 71 mg sodium

HONEY-GLAZED GRAPEFRUIT

Limited Choice Plan
Makes 1 serving

Using the point of a sharp knife, remove seeds from ½ **medium grapefruit;** then, using a grapefruit knife, cut around each section to loosen flesh from membrane and skin. Place grapefruit half in small, shallow baking dish and spoon ½ **teaspoon honey** onto center of fruit; sprinkle with **dash ground cinnamon.** Broil 3 inches from heat source until fruit is lightly browned and honey has melted, 8 to 10 minutes.*

Each serving is equivalent to: 1 serving Fruits; 1 serving Extras.

Per serving: 51 calories, 1 g protein, 0.1 g fat, 13 g carbohydrate, 1 mg sodium

Variation: Substitute 2 teaspoons reduced-calorie orange marmalade or apricot spread (16 calories per 2 teaspoons) for the honey and cinnamon. Change equivalent listing to 1⅗ servings Extras. (See page 407 for Full Choice Plan adjustments.)

Per serving: 56 calories, 0.5 g protein, 0.1 g fat, 14 g carbohydrate, 1 mg sodium

* This can be broiled in a conventional broiler or toaster-oven.

FROZEN HONEYDEW SOUFFLÉ
Full Choice Plan
Makes 4 servings, about ½ cup each

1 cup very ripe honeydew chunks or balls	2 egg whites (at room temperature)
6 ounces vanilla dietary frozen dessert, softened	*Garnish*
	4 mint sprigs

In work bowl of food processor puree honeydew. Add softened frozen dessert; process until smooth and well blended. Transfer to bowl, cover, and freeze until solid.

Remove from freezer, break into pieces, and place in work bowl of food processor; process until smooth. Spoon into a large bowl.

In medium bowl beat egg whites until stiff but not dry. Beat ⅓ of egg whites into melon mixture; gently fold in remaining egg whites. Spoon into 4 dessert dishes, cover with plastic wrap, and freeze until firm. Remove from freezer 5 minutes before serving. Garnish with mint sprigs.

Each serving is equivalent to: ¾ serving Fruits; ¼ serving Milk; 1 serving Extras.

Per serving: 72 calories, 4 g protein, 1 g fat, 13 g carbohydrate, 65 mg sodium

Variation: Substitute 1 cup watermelon chunks or balls for the honeydew.

Per serving: 69 calories, 4 g protein, 1 g fat, 12 g carbohydrate, 60 mg sodium

HUCKLEBERRIES
The true huckleberry is very rare and probably not one person in a thousand has ever tasted it. That fondly remembered old-fashioned huckleberry pie was probably made from lowbush blueberries. The huckleberry has several large, bony seeds that do not disappear when the berries are eaten fresh or baked. Blueberries, on the other hand, have many tiny seeds that are so soft as to be unnoticeable. There is a huckleberry plant in western Pennsylvania that is probably the oldest living thing on earth. It covers several hundred square acres and botanists estimate it to be over 13,000 years old. It is the last surviving example of the Box Huckleberry.

LITCHI

The litchi is the product of the handsome, ornamental, tropical litchi tree, a native of southeastern Asia. This round, bright red, rough-surfaced fruit is considered a delicacy in China and is usually consumed fresh in the United States. The shimmery, firm, white flesh surrounds a single seed and has a pleasant mild aroma and slightly acidic flavor. This fruit is in peak season June through July.

LOQUAT

The loquat is a small, yellow-orange, round, downy fruit that grows on a small, tropical, ornamental evergreen tree that has broad leaves and fragrant white flowers. This native of China is not as rich and sweet-tasting as most tropical fruits; it has a slightly acid flavor. The juicy flesh is pale yellow to orange and surrounds up to ten large black seeds. Loquats are best eaten fresh, but are also used stewed and in preserves or jellies.

BROILED SPICED ORANGE

No Choice Plan
Makes 1 serving

Cut **1 small orange** in half and place in broiler pan, cut-side up. Sprinkle each half with a **dash each ground cinnamon and artificial sweetener.** Broil 4 to 6 inches from heat source until lightly browned, about 5 minutes.*

Each serving is equivalent to: 1 serving Fruits.

Per serving: 60 calories, 1 g protein, 0.3 g fat, 15 g carbohydrate, 1 mg sodium

Variation: Substitute ½ medium grapefruit for the orange.

Per serving: 41 calories, 1 g protein, 0.1 g fat, 11 g carbohydrate, 1 mg sodium

* This can also be broiled in a toaster-oven; adjust timing accordingly.

ORANGE–APRICOT SOUFFLÉ

Full Choice Plan
Makes 4 servings

1 cup orange juice (no sugar added)	1 tablespoon lemon juice
1 cup water	2 egg whites (at room temperature)
1 envelope (four ½-cup servings) apricot-flavored gelatin	2 teaspoons confectioners' sugar

Cut 4 pieces of foil, each long enough to go around a ½-cup soufflé dish or 6-ounce custard cup and about 4 inches wide. Wrap a piece of foil around each dish or cup so that it extends 2 inches above rim; secure with cellophane tape and set aside.

In small saucepan combine orange juice and water and bring to a boil. Reduce heat, add gelatin, and stir until dissolved. Remove from heat; add lemon juice, cover, and chill until slightly thickened.

In medium bowl combine egg whites with sugar and beat until stiff peaks form. Fold egg whites into chilled gelatin mixture. Divide evenly into prepared dishes. Cover lightly and chill until set, about 2 hours. Carefully remove foil collars before serving.

Each serving is equivalent to: ½ serving Fruits; 1 serving Occasional Substitutes; 2 servings Extras.

Per serving: 123 calories, 4 g protein, 0.1 g fat, 28 g carbohydrate, 93 mg sodium

Variation: Substitute 1 cup grapefruit juice (no sugar added) for the orange juice and 1 envelope (four ½-cup servings) lime-flavored gelatin for the apricot-flavored gelatin.

Per serving: 116 calories, 4 g protein, 0.1 g fat, 26 g carbohydrate, 93 mg sodium

ORANGE–BANANA CHIFFON PIE
Full Choice Plan
Makes 8 servings

Crust

½ cup plus 2 tablespoons enriched all-purpose flour
⅛ teaspoon salt

2 tablespoons plus 2 teaspoons margarine
¼ cup plain unflavored yogurt

Filling

1 envelope (four ½-cup servings) orange-flavored gelatin
1 cup boiling water
½ cup orange juice (no sugar added)
2 egg whites (at room temperature)

1 tablespoon plus 1 teaspoon granulated sugar
2 medium bananas, peeled and sliced
20 small seedless green grapes, cut into halves

Glaze

¼ cup reduced-calorie apple spread (16 calories per 2 teaspoons)

To Prepare Crust: Preheat oven to 400°F. In mixing bowl combine flour and salt; with pastry blender, or 2 knives used scissor-fashion, cut in margarine until mixture resembles coarse meal. Add yogurt and mix thoroughly. Form dough into a ball; wrap in plastic wrap or wax paper and chill 1 hour.

Roll dough between 2 sheets of wax paper, forming an 11-inch circle, about ⅛ inch thick. Carefully remove paper and fit dough into 9-inch pie pan; fold under any dough that extends beyond edge of pan and flute or crimp edge. Using a fork, prick bottom and sides of pie shell. Bake until lightly browned, 15 to 20 minutes; cool.

To *Prepare Filling:* In large bowl sprinkle gelatin over boiling water; stir until dissolved. Add orange juice; cover and chill until slightly thickened but not firm.

In medium bowl beat egg whites until stiff; gradually beat in sugar. Fold into gelatin mixture; pour into cooled pie shell. Arrange banana slices and grape halves attractively over gelatin mixture.

To *Glaze:* In metal measuring cup or other small flameproof container heat apple spread until melted; spread over fruit to glaze. Cover carefully and chill until ready to serve.

Each serving is equivalent to: ½ serving Bread; 1 serving Fats; 1½ teaspoons Yogurt (1⁄16 serving Milk); ½ serving Occasional Substitutes; ¾ serving Fruits; 1½ servings Extras; 12 calories Specialty Foods.

Per serving: 180 calories, 4 g protein, 4 g fat, 33 g carbohydrate, 130 mg sodium

Variation: Substitute 1 envelope (four ½-cup servings) lime-flavored gelatin for the orange-flavored gelatin.

SPICED PEACH PUDDING
Limited Choice Plan
Makes 4 servings, about ½ cup each

1 cup plain unflavored yogurt
1 tablespoon plus 1 teaspoon
  reduced-calorie orange
  marmalade (16 calories per 2
  teaspoons)
1 teaspoon unflavored gelatin
¼ cup water
Artificial sweetener to equal 2
  teaspoons sugar

Dash each ground nutmeg and
  mace
2 teaspoons margarine
1 teaspoon granulated brown sugar
1 small orange
½ cup canned sliced peaches (no
  sugar added)

1. In small bowl combine yogurt and marmalade and set aside.

2. In small saucepan sprinkle gelatin over water; let stand a few minutes to soften. Cook over low heat, stirring constantly, until gelatin is completely dissolved.

3. Stir dissolved gelatin into yogurt mixture; add sweetener, nutmeg, and mace and stir to combine. Cover and chill until almost firm, about 2 hours.

4. While yogurt mixture is chilling, in small skillet melt margarine over low heat; add brown sugar and stir until dissolved. Remove from heat.

5. Holding orange over skillet to catch juices, cut away and discard peel and membrane; cut orange into sections and add to skillet. Add peaches and cook, stirring, until fruits are well coated and heated through.

6. Transfer fruit mixture to blender container and process until smooth; chill covered.

7. In each of 4 custard cups or dessert dishes make alternate layers of yogurt mixture and peach-orange puree; cover and chill until firm.

Each serving is equivalent to: ½ serving Milk; 1½ servings Extras; ½ serving Fats; ½ serving Fruits. (See page 407 for Full Choice Plan adjustments.)

Per serving: 91 calories, 3 g protein, 4 g fat, 12 g carbohydrate, 50 mg sodium

PEARS WITH CHOCOLATE SAUCE

Full Choice Plan
Makes 4 servings

1 tablespoon plus 1 teaspoon
   unsweetened cocoa
2 teaspoons cornstarch
2 teaspoons granulated sugar
1 cup evaporated skimmed milk,
   divided

¼ teaspoon vanilla extract
Artificial sweetener to equal 2
   teaspoons sugar
8 canned pear halves with ½ cup
   juice (no sugar added)

In small saucepan mix cocoa with cornstarch and sugar. Gradually add ¼ cup milk, stirring until sugar is completely dissolved. Add remaining milk and vanilla and cook over medium heat, stirring constantly, until mixture comes to a boil. Continue to stir and cook until thickened, about 2 minutes longer. Remove from heat and stir in sweetener. Cover with plastic wrap and chill.

To Serve: Place 2 pear halves and 2 tablespoons juice in each of 4 dessert dishes; top each with an equal amount of sauce.

Each serving is equivalent to: 2½ servings Extras; ½ serving Milk; 1 serving Fruits.

Per serving: 119 calories, 5 g protein, 1 g fat, 25 g carbohydrate, 75 mg sodium

Variation: *Limited Choice Plan*—Substitute 8 canned peach halves with ½ cup juice (no sugar added) for the pears.

Per serving: 117 calories, 6 g protein, 1 g fat, 24 g carbohydrate, 77 mg sodium

CARROT–PINEAPPLE–LIME MOLD

Full Choice Plan
Makes 4 servings

1 envelope (four ½-cup servings)
   lime-flavored gelatin
½ cup shredded carrot

½ cup canned crushed pineapple
   (no sugar added)

Prepare gelatin according to package directions but do not chill. Rinse four 1-cup molds with cold water; press ¼ of the shredded carrot in bottom and up the sides of each mold. Spoon ¼ of the crushed pineapple into center of each mold; carefully pour ½ cup prepared gelatin over each portion. Cover and chill until firm. Unmold and serve.

Each serving is equivalent to: 1 serving Occasional Substitutes; ¼ serving Vegetables; ¼ serving Fruits.

Per serving: 103 calories, 2 g protein, 0.1 g fat, 25 g carbohydrate, 75 mg sodium

Variation: Substitute 1 envelope (four ½-cup servings) orange-flavored gelatin for the lime-flavored gelatin.

PRICKLY PEAR (CACTUS PEAR)

This fruit, which comes from the cactus plant, is very juicy, red in color, and has a sweet-tart taste. It contains a large number of edible seeds. The prickly pear is delicious eaten out of hand and in salads, breads, muffins, and drinks.

STRAWBERRY TARTS

Full Choice Plan
Makes 4 servings, 1 tart each

Tart Shells

½ cup plus 2 tablespoons enriched all-purpose flour
⅛ teaspoon salt

2 tablespoons plus 2 teaspoons margarine
¼ cup plain unflavored yogurt

Strawberry Filling

1 cup boiling water
1 envelope (four ½-cup servings) strawberry-flavored gelatin

2 cups strawberries, sliced
1 teaspoon grated orange peel
½ teaspoon grated lemon peel

To Prepart Tart Shells: In mixing bowl combine flour and salt; with pastry blender, or 2 knives used scissor-fashion, cut in margarine until mixture resembles coarse meal. Add yogurt and mix thoroughly to form dough. Wrap dough in plastic wrap or wax paper and chill for at least 1 hour.

Preheat oven to 400°F. Divide dough into 4 pieces and roll each, between 2 sheets of wax paper, to a thickness of about ⅛ inch. Carefully remove paper and fit each piece into a 5¼ x 1½-inch foil tart pan. Using a fork, prick bottom and sides of each; flute or crimp edges. Bake until golden brown, 15 to 20 minutes; cool.

To Prepare Filling: In heatproof 1-quart bowl combine water and gelatin and stir until gelatin is completely dissolved; stir in remaining ingredients. Let cool to syrupy consistency.

To Prepare Tarts: Pour cooled gelatin mixture into prepared tart shells, cover, and chill until firm.

Each serving is equivalent to: 1 serving Bread; 2 servings Fats; ⅛ serving Milk; 1 serving Occasional Substitutes; ½ serving Fruits.

Per serving: 258 calories, 5 g protein, 9 g fat, 41 g carbohydrate, 234 mg sodium

UGLI FRUIT

This badly-disfigured-looking, light green fruit is a native of Jamaica. It is about the size of a grapefruit and has an extremely rough peel with blemishes that turn orange as the fruit matures. In spite of its sad appearance, however, the ugli fruit has a delightful orange flavor and is very juicy. Use and store this fruit as you would any other citrus fruit.

MIXED FRUIT AMBROSIA

Limited Choice Plan
Makes 4 servings, about ½ cup each

1 small orange	1 tablespoon lemon juice
1 cup honeydew balls	½ teaspoon almond extract
1 medium banana, peeled and	1 tablespoon plus 1 teaspoon
sliced	shredded coconut, toasted

Over medium bowl to catch juice, remove skin and membrane from orange and section orange into bowl. Add melon balls, banana slices, lemon juice, and extract; toss gently to combine. Divide into 4 dessert dishes; sprinkle each portion with 1 teaspoon toasted coconut.

Each serving is equivalent to: 1 serving Fruits; 1 serving Extras.

Per serving: 64 calories, 1 g protein, 1 g fat, 15 g carbohydrate, 6 mg sodium

DRIED FRUIT COMPOTE

Full Choice Plan
Makes 2 servings

Pastry Topping

2 tablespoons plus 1½ teaspoons	2 teaspoons margarine
enriched all-purpose flour	1 tablespoon plain unflavored
Dash salt	yogurt

Dried Fruit Mixture

4 medium dried apricot halves,	1 teaspoon lemon juice
chopped	¼ teaspoon apple pie spice
2 tablespoons raisins	1 small apple, pared, cored, and
1 dried fig, chopped	diced
1 teaspoon granulated brown sugar	

To Prepare Pastry Topping: In mixing bowl combine flour and salt; with a pastry blender, or 2 knives used scissor-fashion, cut in margarine until mixture resembles coarse meal. Add yogurt and mix until thoroughly combined. Form dough into a ball; wrap in plastic wrap or wax paper and chill about 1 hour.

To Prepare Dried Fruit Mixture: In a small saucepan combine remaining ingredients except apple. Cook over low heat, stirring constantly, until sugar begins to melt and glaze fruit mixture slightly. If necessary, add about 1 tablespoon water to keep fruit from burning. Simmer until fruit softens and raisins are plump, about 5 minutes. Add apple and stir to combine.

To Prepare Compote: Preheat oven to 400°F. Divide fruit mixture into two 1-cup ovenproof dishes. Roll dough between 2 sheets of wax paper to about ⅛-inch thickness; carefully remove paper and cut dough in half. Place one half on top of each fruit mixture, molding dough to inside edges of dish. Bake until topping is golden brown, about 20 minutes. Serve warm or at room temperature.

Each serving is equivalent to: ½ serving Bread; 1 serving Fats; 1½ teaspoons Yogurt (⅟₁₆ serving Milk); 2 servings Fruits; 1 serving Extras.

Per serving: 166 calories, 2 g protein, 4 g fat, 32 g carbohydrate, 118 mg sodium

Variation: Substitute 2 large prunes, pitted and chopped, for the fig.

Per serving: 193 calories, 2 g protein, 4 g fat, 39 g carbohydrate, 119 mg sodium

FRUIT BARS
Full Choice Plan
Makes 4 Midday or Evening Meal servings, ⅛ meal each; supplement as required

1 small apple, pared, cored, and grated
1 egg
2 tablespoons plus 2 teaspoons margarine
2 tablespoons granulated brown sugar
Artificial sweetener to equal 6 teaspoons sugar

½ cup plus 2 tablespoons enriched all-purpose flour
½ teaspoon double-acting baking powder
¼ teaspoon each salt, ground cinnamon, and apple pie spice
½ cup plus 2 tablespoons raisins

In small bowl combine apple, egg, margarine, sugar, and sweetener; stir in remaining ingredients except raisins. Beat until smooth; fold in raisins. Spray an 8 x 8-inch nonstick baking pan with nonstick cooking spray and spoon mixture into pan. Bake at 350°F. until golden brown, about 25 minutes. Cool; cut into 4 bars.

Each serving is equivalent to: 1½ servings Fruits; ¼ Egg;* 2 servings Fats; 3 servings Extras; 1 serving Bread.

Per serving: 271 calories, 4 g protein, 9 g fat, 45 g carbohydrate, 301 mg sodium

* Serve at same meal as Egg-Stuffed Peppers (page 158), which contains ¾ egg per serving.

FRUIT 'N' HONEY BALLS
Full Choice Plan
Makes 2 servings

¼ cup raisins, finely chopped
2 dried figs, finely chopped
½ teaspoon apple pie spice
1 teaspoon honey

½ teaspoon lemon juice
2 teaspoons sunflower seed, finely crushed

In small bowl combine raisins, figs, and apple pie spice; roll into 10 small balls, each about 1 inch in diameter. In a metal measuring cup or other small flameproof container combine honey and lemon juice; place over low heat and stir constantly until honey melts. Remove from heat and immediately roll each fruit ball in honey-lemon mixture, then in crushed sunflower seed to coat. Arrange on small plate, cover, and chill.

Each serving is equivalent to: 2 servings Fruits; 3 servings Extras.

Per serving: 136 calories, 2 g protein, 2 g fat, 32 g carbohydrate, 13 mg sodium

Variation: Substitute 2 medium dried apricot halves, finely chopped, for the figs. Change equivalent listing to 1¼ servings Fruits.

Per serving: 91 calories, 1 g protein, 2 g fat, 20 g carbohydrate, 7 mg sodium

Vegetables

Versatile vegetables take many roles: in soups and slaws, stir-fries and sautés, dips and mousses, as well as raw, their most nutritious version. From our fiery Sicilian caponata to our version of guacamole made with asparagus, these recipes expand menu choices without stretching budgets or waistlines. Although cooking times vary, it's safer to undercook than overcook vegetables.

Guidelines for Using Vegetables

1. Amounts:
    A. *Full Choice Plan*
        a. Women, Men, and Youth—2 servings daily (minimum).
        b. One serving vegetables (raw or cooked) is ½ cup or ½ medium (e.g., tomato; cucumber; etc.).
        c. Limited Vegetables—the following may be selected daily, up to a combined total of ½ cup. One-half cup Limited Vegetables fulfills half of the minimum daily vegetable requirement.

artichoke, whole, medium	lotus root	water chestnuts ❦
artichoke hearts	okra	winter squash:
		acorn (table queen)
beets	onions	banana
		buttercup
brussels sprouts	parsnips	butternut
		calabaza
burdock	peas	cushaw
		Des Moines
celeriac (celery root)	pumpkin	gold nugget
		hubbard
Chinese pea pods (snow peas)	rutabagas	peppercorn
		warren turban
Jerusalem artichokes (sunchokes)	salsify (oyster plant)	yellow turnips
jicama	scallions (green onions)	
leeks	shallots	

        d. If a canned or frozen mixed vegetable product contains a Limited Vegetable, consider this product to be a Limited Vegetable and do not use more than ½ cup daily (e.g., peas and carrots).
    B. *Limited Choice Plan*
        a. Women, Men, and Youth—2 to 4 servings daily.
        b. To fulfill the daily requirement, use 2 to 4 servings daily of the following vegetables. One serving (raw or cooked) is ½ cup or ½ medium (e.g., tomato; cucumber; etc.).

51

asparagus	cucumbers	summer squash:
		caserta
beans (green and	eggplant	chayote
yellow wax)		cocozelle
bean sprouts	mushrooms	mirleton
		scallop (pattypan,
broccoli	peppers	cymling)
		spaghetti
cabbage	pickles	straightneck and
		crookneck
carrots	pimientos	vegetable marrow
		zucchini
cauliflower	spinach	
		tomatoes

  c. The following vegetables may be used as desired but do
not fulfill the daily requirement.

celery	endive	radishes
	(Belgian or French)	
chicory		
	escarole	watercress
Chinese cabbage		
(celery cabbage)	lettuce	

2. Vegetables may be selected at any time; since they differ in their
nutritional content, *variety* is the key to vegetable selections.

3. Fresh, canned, frozen, dried, and freeze-dried vegetables may
be used. Canned, frozen, dried, and freeze-dried products should not
contain butter, sugar, cornstarch, etc., except for canned peas and
stewed tomatoes; these two items may contain sugar.

4. Equate asparagus spears and cherry tomatoes as follows:

> 6 medium asparagus spears equal 1 serving Vege-
> tables
> 6 small, medium, or large cherry tomatoes equal 1
> serving Vegetables

5. Equate dried and freeze-dried vegetables to the amount of fresh
vegetables used before drying.

6. It is recommended that the liquid used for cooking vegetables
be consumed.

Average Approximate Size/Dimensions and Weight for Vegetables
(fresh, including seeds and skin, unless otherwise specified)

Vegetables	Number	Approx. Size/Dimensions	Approx. Weight	Number of Servings/Cups
Artichokes, Globe	1	medium	11 ounces	½ cup
hearts:				
fresh	2		4 ounces	½ cup
frozen	6		6 ounces	1 cup
drained canned	6		8 ounces	1 cup
Asparagus Spears	4	large (¾ to ⅞-inch diameter at base)	3½ ounces	1 serving
	6	medium (½-inch diameter at base)	3 ounces	1 serving
	12	small (⅜-inch diameter at base)	4 ounces	1 serving
Broccoli, bunch	1	medium (2 large, 3 medium, or 4 small stalks)	1 pound	8 servings
frozen spears	4			1 serving
Cabbage, head:				
Chinese (celery)	1		12 ounces	8 servings
green	1	medium	1 pound	12 servings
red	1	medium	1½ pounds	18 servings
leaves:				
green	2	medium/large	3¾ ounces	1 serving
	3	small	3 ounces	1 serving
red	1	medium/large	2½ ounces	1 serving
	2	small	3 ounces	1 serving

(Continued)

Vegetables	Number	Approx. Size/Dimensions	Approx. Weight	Number of Servings/Cups
Carrots, whole	1	medium (1⅛-inch diameter at top x 7½ inches long) or large	3 to 4 ounces	2 servings
sticks	6	3½ inches x ½ inch each		1 serving
Cauliflower, head	1	medium (6- to 7-inch diameter)	1½ pounds	12 servings
Celery, ribs	1	large (8 x 1½ inches)		1 serving
	2	medium (6 inches x 1 inch)		1 serving
	3	small (5 inches x ¾ inch)		1 serving
sticks	6	3½ inches x ½ inch each		½ serving
Cucumbers, whole	1	large (6½-inch circumference at widest part x 8¼ inches long)	9½ ounces	2¼ servings
	1	medium (6-inch circumference at widest part x 7 inches long)	8 ounces	2 servings
	1	small (5¼-inch diameter at widest part x 6¼ inches long)	6 ounces	1 serving
sticks	6	4 inches x ½ inch each		½ serving
Eggplants, whole	1	large	1½ pounds	8 servings
	1	medium	1 to 1¼ pounds	6 servings
	1	small	12 ounces	4 servings
	1	tiny	8 ounces	3 servings
slices, round	6	thin (¼ inch thick each)		1½ servings
Endives (Belgian or French)	1		2¾ ounces	1 serving
Grape Leaves	12			1 serving
Kohlrabi	1	medium		1 serving
Leeks (white portion only)	2	medium		½ cup

Lettuce, head:				
Boston and Bibb	1	16-inch circumference at widest part	8 ounces	2½ servings
iceberg	1	medium to large	2½ pounds	8 servings
	1	small	1¼ pounds	4 servings
romaine (cos) and loose-leaf	1	medium	1¼ pounds	12 servings
leaves:	1	small	10 ounces	8 servings
Boston and Bibb	8			1 serving
iceberg	4	small, medium, and large		1 serving
romaine (cos) and loose-leaf	4	small, medium, and large		1 serving
Peppers, Bell, green/red, whole	1	large (3-inch diameter x 3¾ inches high)	7 ounces	4 servings
	1	medium (2½-inch diameter x 2¾ inches high)	3¼ ounces	2 servings
sticks	7	2¾ inches x ½ inch each		½ serving
rings	4			1 serving
Chilies, canned	2			1 serving
Pickles, whole	1	large (5½-inch circumference at widest part x 4 inches long)	4¾ ounces	4 servings
	1	medium (4-inch circumference at widest part x 3¾ inches long)	2¼ ounces	2 servings
slices	3	large	1½ ounces	1 serving
	5	medium	1⅛ ounces	1 serving
Pimientos, whole	1			⅓ serving
Radishes	12	medium to large (2- to 4-inch circumference each at widest part)	2 to 3½ ounces	1 serving

(Continued)

Vegetables	Number	Approx. Size/Dimensions	Approx. Weight	Number of Servings/Cups
Scallions (green onions)	8	medium	4 ounces	½ cup
Squash:				
Acorn	1		1 pound	1 cup
Scallop	1	4-inch diameter	5 ounces	2 servings
Spaghetti	1		2½ to 3 pounds	8 servings
Zucchini	1	medium	5 ounces	2 servings
Tomatoes, whole	1	large (3-inch diameter x 2⅛ inches high)	7 ounces	3 servings
	1	medium (2½-inch diameter x 2 inches high)	4¾ ounces	2 servings
	1	small (2¼-inch diameter)	3½ ounces	1½ servings
slices:				
regular	4 to 6	⅛ inch thick each		1 serving
thin	10			1 serving
wedges	6	large		1½ servings
	6	medium		1 serving
	6	small		¾ serving
Cherry	6	small, medium, and large		1 serving
Turnips	1	medium	2 ounces	1 serving

CRUDITÉS

For party-goers or party-givers who want taste without waist, these crisp raw vegetables, called crudités in France, are a favorite hors d'oeuvre. Prepare them ahead and refrigerate until party time.

Beans (Green or Yellow Wax)—Snap off ends, blanch, and use whole or cut on diagonal.

Broccoli—Rinse tiny florets in ice water containing 1 teaspoon lemon juice or vinegar. Drain and dry.

Carrots—Using a paring knife, cut off slivers or strips. To make curls, roll up strips, secure with toothpicks, and place in ice water to set the curl.

Cauliflower—Dip tiny florets in ice water containing 1 teaspoon lemon juice or vinegar. Drain and dry.

Celeriac (Celery Root)—Pare and cut into long strips; blanch for 1 or 2 minutes in water containing lemon juice. Drain and serve. (Limited Vegetable)

Celery—Cut tender ribs into long, slim fingers. If ribs are stringy, pare before cutting. Celery sticks look pretty served with the green leaves left on.

Chinese Cabbage—Use halved stalks or rolled-up leaf sections.

Chinese Pea Pods (Snow Peas)—Remove stem ends and strings. Serve whole and crisp. (Limited Vegetable)

Cucumbers—Pare or, if young, rinse and use. With tines of a fork, make parallel gashes from top to bottom around the whole cucumber, then slice into rounds or cut into long, thin strips. If desired, sprinkle with chopped fresh dill or chives.

Fennel—Cut into slices and serve.

Kale—Cut off and discard root ends. Rinse leaves and dry.

Kohlrabi—Pare, slice, and serve.

Mushrooms—Dip whole mushroom caps in lemon juice or cut mushroom through cap and stem into slices and drip in lemon juice.

Parsley—Use crisp sprigs, rinsed and dried.

Peppers (Bell)—Use both red and green for color contrast. Seed peppers and cut into strips or rings.

Pimientos—Use for color; chop and use as stuffing in celery ribs.

Radishes—Prepare radish roses or accordions (see page 82).

Salad Greens—Rinse and drain crisp, firm leaves of chicory and an assortment of other available greens.

Scallions (Green Onions)—Trim off roots and any wilted portion of leaves. Cut thick scallions in half lengthwise. (Limited Vegetable)

Spinach—Rinse several times to remove sand; drain well. Using scissors, cut out any tough ribs.

Squash—Use young zucchini. Cut into fingers or slices.

Tomatoes—Use whole cherry tomatoes or serve medium tomatoes cut into quarters and sprinkled with chopped fresh basil or dill or minced fresh garlic.

Watercress—Use fresh sprigs, rinsed and dried.

Suggested Dips for Crudités:
Pimiento Dressing (see page 386)
Yogurt–Mint Dressing or Dip (see page 387)
Yogurt–Onion Dip (see page 388)

ARTICHOKES (Limited Vegetable)
Full Choice Plan

To Prepare Whole Artichokes for Cooking: Use artichokes that weigh about 11 ounces each; wash thoroughly in cold water to remove all grit. Using a large stainless-steel knife, cut off stem flush with base so that artichoke will stand upright; snap off any small or discolored leaves at base. Cut off and discard about 1 inch of the top; rub cut edges of artichoke with lemon juice. To remove barbed tips of leaves, using stainless-steel scissors, cut about ½ inch off tip of each leaf; rub cut edges of leaves with lemon juice.

To Cook Whole Artichokes: Pour about 3 inches water into saucepan (not aluminum or cast-iron) that is just large enough to hold artichokes snugly; add ¼ teaspoon salt per artichoke and 1 tablespoon lemon juice. Stand artichokes in pan. Cover pan and simmer until bases of artichokes can be pierced easily with a fork, about 35 minutes. Remove artichokes from liquid and stand upside down to drain.

Each 11-ounce artichoke is equivalent to: ½ cup Limited Vegetables.

Per 11-ounce artichoke: 38 calories, 4 g protein, 0.3 g fat, 14 g carbohydrate, 188 mg sodium

Artichoke Hearts: The artichoke heart is the tender, innermost portion of the artichoke, directly below the choke. Artichoke hearts can be purchased canned or frozen.

STUFFED ARTICHOKES
Full Choice Plan
Makes 2 servings

2 medium artichokes, about 11 ounces each
1½ teaspoons lemon juice
½ teaspoon salt
Freshly ground pepper
3 tablespoons plain dried bread crumbs
1 tablespoon chopped fresh parsley
2 teaspoons olive oil
2 teaspoons grated Parmesan cheese
1 small garlic clove, minced

Prepare artichokes for cooking according to directions on page 58; sprinkle each artichoke with ¾ teaspoon lemon juice, ¼ teaspoon salt, and dash pepper. In small bowl combine bread crumbs, parsley, oil, cheese, and garlic. Spread open leaves of artichokes and stuff half of mixture into each artichoke.

Stand artichokes upright in deep baking pan (not aluminum) that is just large enough to hold them snugly. Pour about 1 inch water into pan and cover with foil. Bake at 375°F. until base of each artichoke is tender when pierced with a fork, about 45 minutes. Serve warm.

Each serving is equivalent to: ½ cup Limited Vegetables; ½ serving Bread; 1 serving Fats; 1 serving Extras.

Per serving: 126 calories, 6 g protein, 6 g fat, 21 g carbohydrate, 695 mg sodium

ASPARAGUS GUACAMOLE
Full Choice Plan
Makes 2 servings, about ½ cup each

This is delicious served as a dip with fresh vegetables or on tortillas. May also be frozen.

12 medium asparagus spears, cooked and chopped
2 tablespoons drained canned green chili peppers
1 tablespoon chopped red onion
2 teaspoons olive oil
2 teaspoons lemon juice
½ teaspoon salt
½ garlic clove, crushed
Dash each ground nutmeg and pepper

In blender container or work bowl of food processor combine all ingredients and process until smooth. Chill covered.

Each serving is equivalent to: 1⅛ servings Vegetables; 1½ teaspoons Limited Vegetables; 1 serving Fats.

Per serving: 67 calories, 2 g protein, 5 g fat, 5 g carbohydrate, 541 mg sodium

Variation: Add ½ cup plain unflavored yogurt to ingredients and process as directed. Add ½ serving Milk to equivalent listing.

Per serving: 101 calories, 4 g protein, 7 g fat, 8 g carbohydrate, 567 mg sodium

BAMBOO SHOOTS
Bamboo shoots are the edible, ivory-colored, tender young stalks of a species of bamboo plant and are used extensively in Oriental cooking. After they have pushed above the soil, these stalks can grow up to one foot in height in a 24-hour period. Bamboo shoots are imported canned

from the Orient and are not inexpensive, but a little goes a long way. Once the can has been opened, place any unused shoots in a container with water to cover. Cover container and refrigerate. To prevent bamboo shoots from losing their unique crisp texture and nutlike flavor, change the water daily and use the shoots as soon as possible.

GREEN AND WAX BEAN SALAD
Limited Choice Plan
Makes 2 servings

1 cup cooked cut green beans	2 teaspoons Dijon-style mustard
1 cup cooked cut wax beans	1 garlic clove
½ cup water	½ teaspoon salt
1 teaspoon arrowroot	¼ teaspoon pepper
2 tablespoons fresh parsley leaves	4 iceberg or romaine lettuce leaves

In bowl combine beans and set aside.

In small saucepan combine water and arrowroot and stir to dissolve. Cook over high heat until mixture is slightly thickened; cool a few minutes. Transfer to blender container; add parsley, mustard, garlic, salt, and pepper and process until smooth.

Pour parsley mixture over beans and toss to coat. Cover and refrigerate for at least 2 hours. Serve on lettuce leaves.

Each serving is equivalent to: 2 servings Vegetables; ½ serving Extras. (See page 407 for Full Choice Plan adjustments.)

Per serving: 49 calories, 2 g protein, 1 g fat, 10 g carbohydrate, 693 mg sodium

BORSCHT (BEET SOUP)
Full Choice Plan
Makes 4 servings

Borscht is delicious served hot or chilled.

3 cups Beef Broth (see page 401)	½ cup sliced carrot
1½ cups pared and coarsely shredded beets	½ cup tomato puree
	1 tablespoon plus 1½ teaspoons red wine vinegar*
½ cup chopped onion	
1 bay leaf	Dash each salt and pepper
2 cups shredded green cabbage	½ cup plain unflavored yogurt

In 3-quart saucepan combine broth, beets, onion, and bay leaf; bring to a boil, cover, and cook for 10 minutes. Add cabbage, carrot, tomato puree, vinegar, salt, and pepper. Simmer until vegetables are tender, about 25 minutes. Remove bay leaf. Pour borscht into 4 soup bowls and top each portion with 2 tablespoons yogurt.

Each serving is equivalent to: 1 serving Extras; ½ cup Limited Vegetables; 1¼ servings Vegetables; ¼ serving Bonus; ¼ serving Milk.

Per serving: 89 calories, 4 g protein, 1 g fat, 17 g carbohydrate, 229 mg sodium

* For a slightly more tart flavor, add an additional 1½ teaspoons red wine vinegar.

QUICK BORSCHT
Full Choice Plan
Makes 4 servings, about 1 cup each

For a refreshing summer soup, serve borscht chilled.

1½ cups drained canned sliced beets, divided (reserve 1 cup liquid)
1 cup water
¼ cup chopped onion
1 packet instant beef broth and seasoning mix
1 tablespoon lemon juice
Dash each salt and pepper
¼ cup plain unflavored yogurt

In 2-quart saucepan combine ¾ cup beets, the reserved beet liquid, water, onion, and broth mix; bring to a boil. Reduce heat, cover, and simmer for 10 minutes.

Pour half of mixture into blender container and process until smooth; transfer to a 1-quart bowl. Puree remaining beet mixture and return all of pureed mixture to saucepan.

Cut remaining beets into long, thin strips. Add julienne beets and lemon juice to saucepan and bring to a boil. Reduce heat, cover, and simmer for 10 minutes. Stir in salt and pepper. Serve immediately or cool slightly, cover, and refrigerate until chilled. Top each portion with 1 tablespoon yogurt.

Each serving is equivalent to: ¼ cup plus 3 tablespoons Limited Vegetables; ¼ serving Extras; ⅛ serving Milk.

Per serving: 48 calories, 2 g protein, 1 g fat, 10 g carbohydrate, 446 mg sodium

SAUTÉED BEETS
Full Choice Plan
Makes 2 servings

2 teaspoons margarine
1 cup pared and shredded beets
1½ teaspoons water
½ teaspoon granulated brown sugar
¼ teaspoon salt

In small skillet heat margarine until bubbly; add beets and sauté over medium heat, stirring occasionally, until tender. Add water, sugar, and salt. Reduce heat to low, cover, and cook 5 minutes longer. Serve hot.

Each serving is equivalent to: 1 serving Fats; ½ cup Limited Vegetables; ½ serving Extras.

Per serving: 65 calories, 1 g protein, 4 g fat, 7 g carbohydrate, 349 mg sodium

BROCCOLI–CARROT STIR-FRY
Limited Choice Plan
Makes 2 servings

1½ teaspoons peanut or vegetable oil
½ teaspoon Chinese sesame oil
½ cup diagonally sliced carrot (¼-inch-thick slices)

¼ teaspoon minced fresh garlic or ⅛ teaspoon garlic powder
1 cup broccoli florets

In small nonstick skillet combine oils and heat until just hot. Add carrot and garlic or garlic powder and, over medium-high heat, stir-fry briefly. Reduce heat, cover, and cook about 3 minutes (carrot slices should still be crisp). Add broccoli and sauté until tender-crisp, about 5 minutes.

Each serving is equivalent to: 1 serving Fats; 1½ servings Vegetables.

Per serving: 76 calories, 3 g protein, 5 g fat, 7 g carbohydrate, 27 mg sodium

BROCCOLI–CAULIFLOWER MOLD
Full Choice Plan
Makes 4 servings

5 cups broccoli florets
Salt
6 cups cauliflower florets

¼ cup pimiento squares (1-inch squares)

1. Place broccoli in steamer insert; add dash salt and set insert into saucepan containing boiling water. Cover pan and steam broccoli until tender-crisp, 5 to 6 minutes. Transfer broccoli to bowl, being careful not to break florets, and set aside.
2. Repeat procedure with cauliflower, steaming 4 to 5 minutes.
3. Preheat oven to 300°F. Spray a 1½-quart ovenproof bowl with non-stick cooking spray. Place a circle of broccoli florets, stem-side up, in center of bowl and push tightly together; arrange a few pieces of pimiento between the florets. Arrange some of the cauliflower florets around the broccoli, covering the bottom of the bowl; place a few pimiento pieces between cauliflower florets. Cover vegetables in bowl with remaining broccoli florets, pressing down slightly; place pimiento pieces between the florets at the outer edge. Repeat with remaining cauliflower.
4. Cut a piece of wax paper into a circle the same size as top of bowl; spray with nonstick cooking spray.
5. Set bowl into baking pan, cover with paper circle, sprayed-side down, and weight paper with an ovenproof plate that fits snugly into the bowl. Pour enough boiling water into the pan to reach halfway up the sides of bowl. Carefully transfer pan to oven and bake for 15 to 20 minutes.
6. Remove bowl from water; remove plate and paper and unmold onto a round serving platter.

Each serving is equivalent to: 5⅔ servings Vegetables.

Per serving: 102 calories, 11 g protein, 1 g fat, 19 g carbohydrate, 121 mg sodium

BURDOCK (Limited Vegetable)

Burdock is a root vegetable that is also referred to as great burdock and is well known in Japan as gobo. This burr-producing, thistle-like plant grows wild in the United States. Its long, tapering, tender root has an excellent flavor, a crisp and crunchy texture, and can be eaten raw in salads or cooked.

To prepare, split the root and remove the outer layer. Use the smooth, white inner core.

BACON-FLAVORED COLESLAW

Full Choice Plan
Makes 2 servings

2 cups finely shredded green
   cabbage
2 tablespoons thinly sliced scallion
   (green onion)
¼ teaspoon caraway seed

3 tablespoons white wine vinegar
2 tablespoons water
1 teaspoon olive oil
2 teaspoons imitation bacon bits,
   divided

In medium bowl toss cabbage with scallion and caraway seed; set aside.

In small saucepan combine vinegar, water, oil, and 1 teaspoon bacon bits; bring mixture to a boil. Pour over cabbage mixture and toss to combine. Cover and refrigerate at least 3 hours.

Just before serving, sprinkle cabbage with remaining bacon bits and toss to combine.

Each serving is equivalent to: 2 servings Vegetables; 1 tablespoon Limited Vegetables; 1¼ servings Extras; ½ serving Fats.

Per serving: 58 calories, 2 g protein, 3 g fat, 7 g carbohydrate, 116 mg sodium

BUTTERMILK COLESLAW

Limited Choice Plan
Makes 4 servings

2 cups shredded green cabbage
½ cup buttermilk
1 tablespoon lemon juice
Artificial sweetener to equal 1
   teaspoon sugar

1 teaspoon salt
¼ teaspoon celery seed
¼ teaspoon pepper
Dash garlic powder

In bowl combine all ingredients; cover and refrigerate until chilled, at least 1 hour. Toss before serving.

Each serving is equivalent to: 1 serving Vegetables; ⅙ serving Milk.

Per serving: 25 calories, 2 g protein, 0.4 g fat, 4 g carbohydrate, 579 mg sodium

CREAMY COLESLAW
Full Choice Plan
Makes 4 servings

4 cups shredded green cabbage
2 cups shredded carrots
2 tablespoons each diced green bell pepper and celery
1 tablespoon minced onion
2 tablespoons plain unflavored yogurt

2 teaspoons mayonnaise
1 teaspoon granulated sugar
¼ teaspoon salt
Dash white pepper
Dash celery seed (optional)

In medium bowl combine cabbage, carrots, green pepper, celery, and onion.

In small bowl mix yogurt with mayonnaise, sugar, salt, pepper, and celery seed if desired; pour over vegetables and toss until well coated. Cover and chill.

Each serving is equivalent to: 3⅛ servings Vegetables; ¾ teaspoon Limited Vegetables; 1½ teaspoons Yogurt (¹⁄₁₆ serving Milk); ½ serving Fats; ½ serving Extras.

Per serving: 73 calories, 2 g protein, 2 g fat, 12 g carbohydrate, 200 mg sodium

FRENCH CABBAGE SOUP
Full Choice Plan
Makes 4 servings

This soup can be prepared in advance and frozen for later use.

2 teaspoons vegetable oil
3 cups shredded green cabbage
1 cup sliced onions
⅛ teaspoon minced fresh garlic
1½ cups Beef Broth (see page 401)
1 cup water
½ cup sliced carrot

½ cup tomato puree
1 teaspoon granulated brown sugar
1 whole clove
1 bay leaf
8 ounces peeled cooked potato, diced

In medium saucepan heat oil. Add cabbage, onions, and garlic. Cook, stirring often, until cabbage is soft, about 10 minutes. Add remaining ingredients except potato; cook over low heat 20 minutes longer. Add potato and cook until heated. Remove and discard clove and bay leaf before serving.

Each serving is equivalent to: ½ serving Fats; 1¾ servings Vegetables; ¼ cup Limited Vegetables; 1 serving Extras; ¼ serving Bonus; ½ serving Bread Substitutes.

Per serving: 118 calories, 4 g protein, 3 g fat, 22 g carbohydrate, 154 mg sodium

CAPERS
Capers are the unopened flower buds of the caper bush; they are used in the cuisines of many lands as a seasoning and condiment. The variety

imported from France is usually preferred because of its small size, firmness, and perfect round shape. The lively, puckery flavor of capers complements seafood, poultry, and lamb as well as some vegetables. They are available bottled in brine or vinegar.

FRUITED CARROT SALAD
Limited Choice Plan
Makes 2 servings

2 cups shredded carrots
24 large seedless green grapes,
   cut into halves
2 teaspoons mayonnaise

½ teaspoon poppy seed
¼ teaspoon salt
4 lettuce leaves

In bowl combine all ingredients except lettuce leaves. Cover and chill at least 2 hours. Serve on lettuce leaves.

Each serving is equivalent to: 2 servings Vegetables; 1 serving Fruits; 1 serving Fats; ½ serving Extras. (See page 407 for Full Choice Plan adjustments.)

Per serving: 138 calories, 2 g protein, 5 g fat, 23 g carbohydrate, 352 mg sodium

Variation: *Full Choice Plan*—Substitute ¼ cup raisins for the grapes.

Per serving: 139 calories, 2 g protein, 4 g fat, 26 g carbohydrate, 354 mg sodium

MANDARIN–CARROT LOAF WITH CHIVE–YOGURT DRESSING
Limited Choice Plan
Makes 4 servings

Mold
1 envelope (four ½-cup servings)
   low-calorie orange-flavored
   gelatin (8 calories per ½ cup)
1¼ cups boiling water

2 cups shredded carrots
1 teaspoon salt
1 cup canned mandarin orange
   sections (no sugar added)

Dressing
¼ cup plain unflavored yogurt
2 tablespoons chopped chives

Dash each salt and pepper

To Prepare Mold: In medium bowl stir gelatin into boiling water until dissolved. In another bowl toss carrots with salt. Add carrots and orange sections to gelatin and stir to combine. Pour into a 7⅜ x 3⅝ x 2¼-inch loaf pan; cover and chill until firm.

To Prepare Dressing: In small bowl combine yogurt, chives, salt, and pepper; cover and chill.

To Serve: Unmold loaf onto serving platter and serve with dressing.

Each serving is equivalent to: ⅘ serving Extras; 1 serving Vegetables; ½ serving Fruits; ⅛ serving Milk. (See page 407 for Full Choice Plan adjustments.)

Per serving: 77 calories, 3 g protein, 1 g fat, 16 g carbohydrate, 609 mg sodium

PIQUANT CARROTS

Limited Choice Plan
Makes 2 servings

1 teaspoon margarine
1 cup slivered carrots, blanched
1 teaspoon granulated brown sugar

⅛ teaspoon powdered mustard
Dash each salt and hot sauce

In small skillet heat margarine until bubbly. Add remaining ingredients and cook, stirring occasionally, until carrots are tender-crisp, about 5 minutes.

Each serving is equivalent to: ½ serving Fats; 1 serving Vegetables; 1 serving Extras.

Per serving: 50 calories, 1 g protein, 2 g fat, 8 g carbohydrate, 115 mg sodium

SLOW-COOKED CARROT MEDLEY

Limited Choice Plan
Makes 2 servings

2 cups sliced carrots (¼-inch-thick slices)
1½ cups sliced celery (½-inch slices)

2 teaspoons margarine, softened
1 teaspoon onion flakes
Dash each salt and pepper

Garnish
1 tablespoon chopped fresh dill

Preheat oven to 325°F. Combine all ingredients except garnish in 1-quart casserole; cover and bake, stirring occasionally, until vegetables are tender, about 30 minutes. Remove cover; bake 15 minutes longer. Garnish with dill and serve hot.

Each serving is equivalent to: 2 servings Vegetables; 1 serving Fats. (See page 407 for Full Choice Plan adjustments.)

Per serving: 98 calories, 2 g protein, 4 g fat, 15 g carbohydrate, 275 mg sodium

Variation: *Full Choice Plan*—Substitute 1 tablespoon minced onion for the onion flakes. Add 1½ teaspoons Limited Vegetables to Full Choice Plan equivalents.

Per serving: 98 calories, 2 g protein, 4 g fat, 15 g carbohydrate, 275 mg sodium

CAULIFLOWER–BROCCOLI SOUP
Full Choice Plan
Makes 2 servings

1 cup cauliflower florets
1 cup broccoli florets
3 cups boiling water
½ teaspoon salt
2 teaspoons olive oil
¼ cup diced onion
¼ teaspoon minced fresh garlic

2 teaspoons enriched all-purpose
  flour
¾ cup Chicken Broth (see
  page 401)
Dash each ground nutmeg and
  white pepper
⅔ cup cooked enriched small
  macaroni shells*

In medium saucepan combine cauliflower and broccoli florets with boiling water and salt. Cook until vegetables are fork-tender, about 5 minutes. Drain vegetables and reserve 1 cup liquid. Cool slightly; separate cauliflower and broccoli and set each aside.

In small skillet heat oil; add onion and garlic and sauté until onion is translucent, about 3 minutes. Transfer to blender container. Add cauliflower, reserved cup of vegetable liquid, and flour; process until smooth.

Return pureed vegetables to saucepan. Bring to a simmer; add broth, nutmeg, and pepper. Simmer until slightly thickened, about 5 minutes longer. Add broccoli and macaroni; cook until heated.

Each serving is equivalent to: 2 servings Vegetables; 1 serving Fats; ⅛ cup Limited Vegetables; 1½ servings Extras; ½ serving Bread Substitutes.

Per serving: 186 calories, 18 g protein, 6 g fat, 31 g carbohydrate, 632 mg sodium

Variation: Substitute 1 cup chopped asparagus for the broccoli.

Per serving: 182 calories, 18 g protein, 6 g fat, 30 g carbohydrate, 619 mg sodium

* Any other small macaroni may be substituted for the shells (e.g., elbow macaroni).

CAULIFLOWER SALAD
Limited Choice Plan
Makes 2 servings

1 cup cauliflower florets, blanched
¼ cup chopped pimientos
1 tablespoon lemon juice
2 teaspoons olive oil

⅛ teaspoon minced fresh garlic or
  dash garlic powder
⅛ teaspoon Dijon-style mustard
Dash each salt and white pepper

Garnish
1 teaspoon chopped fresh parsley

In small bowl combine all ingredients except parsley. Toss well; cover and chill. Sprinkle with parsley just before serving.

Each serving is equivalent to: 1¼ servings Vegetables; 1 serving Fats.

Per serving: 63 calories, 2 g protein, 5 g fat, 5 g carbohydrate, 86 mg sodium

Variation: Substitute 1 cup chopped broccoli, blanched, for the cauliflower.

Per serving: 74 calories, 3 g protein, 5 g fat, 6 g carbohydrate, 94 mg sodium

CAULIFLOWER WITH YOGURT–CHEESE SAUCE
Limited Choice Plan
Makes 2 servings

2 teaspoons reduced-calorie margarine
1 teaspoon enriched all-purpose flour
2 tablespoons plain unflavored yogurt (at room temperature)

2 teaspoons grated Parmesan cheese
Dash each salt, pepper, and ground nutmeg
1 cup cauliflower florets, blanched

Garnish
1 teaspoon chopped fresh parsley

In small saucepan heat margarine until bubbly; stir in flour. Remove from heat and, using a wire whisk, blend in yogurt, cheese, salt, pepper, and nutmeg. Return to low heat and cook, stirring constantly, until smooth (*do not boil*). Add cauliflower and cook, stirring occasionally, until hot.

Transfer mixture to flameproof 1½-cup casserole; broil 6 inches from heat source until browned, about 1 minute. Sprinkle with parsley and serve.

Each serving is equivalent to: ½ serving Fats; 1½ servings Extras; ⅛ serving Milk; 1 serving Vegetables.

Per serving: 51 calories, 3 g protein, 3 g fat, 4 g carbohydrate, 155 mg sodium

BRAISED CELERY
Limited Choice Plan
Makes 2 servings

¾ cup Chicken Broth (see page 401)
Dash each salt and pepper

4 medium celery ribs (each about 6 inches long), cut into halves, then into thin strips

Garnish
Chopped fresh parsley

In small saucepan combine broth, salt, and pepper and bring to a boil. Add celery. Reduce heat and simmer until tender-crisp, about 5 minutes. Using a slotted spoon, remove celery from pan and place on serving platter. Sprinkle with parsley and serve.

Each serving is equivalent to: ½ serving Extras. (See page 407 for Full Choice Plan adjustments.)

Per serving: 45 calories, 12 g protein, 0.4 g fat, 11 g carbohydrate, 199 mg sodium

CHINESE WINTER MELON

This large, pumpkinlike melon weighs anywhere from 20 to 30 pounds and has a frosty green skin and delicate flavor. Even though it is called winter melon, it is available year round.

To prepare, pare melon, cut into thin slices, and stir-fry; serve as a side dish.

BRAISED CUCUMBERS

Limited Choice Plan
Makes 2 servings

¾ cup sliced cucumbers
  (¼-inch-thick slices)
¼ cup diced pimientos
1 packet instant chicken broth and
  seasoning mix

1 tablespoon water
1 teaspoon lemon juice
⅛ teaspoon garlic powder

In small saucepan combine cucumbers and pimientos; sprinkle with broth mix and stir in remaining ingredients. Bring to a boil. Reduce heat, cover, and simmer until cucumbers are tender-crisp, about 3 minutes.

Each serving is equivalent to: 1 serving Vegetables; ½ serving Extras.

Per serving: 18 calories, 1 g protein, 0.2 g fat, 4 g carbohydrate, 425 mg sodium

CITRUS–CUCUMBER SALAD

Full Choice Plan
Makes 2 servings

1 medium cucumber, scored and
  thinly sliced
½ cup each orange sections and
  grapefruit sections (no sugar
  added)
2 tablespoons thinly sliced scallion
  (green onion)

1 teaspoon each olive oil, red wine
  vinegar, and lemon juice
½ teaspoon salt
¼ teaspoon oregano leaves
Dash pepper
2 iceberg or romaine lettuce leaves

In a bowl combine all ingredients except lettuce; toss well. Cover and refrigerate until chilled. Serve on lettuce leaves.

Each serving is equivalent to: 1¼ servings Vegetables; 1 serving Fruits; 1 tablespoon Limited Vegetables; ½ serving Fats.

Per serving: 80 calories, 2 g protein, 3 g fat, 15 g carbohydrate, 545 mg sodium

CUCUMBER IN CHIVED YOGURT
Limited Choice Plan
Makes 2 servings

1 medium cucumber, scored and thinly sliced
½ cup plain unflavored yogurt
1 tablespoon chopped chives

1 tablespoon onion flakes, reconstituted in 2 tablespoons water
½ teaspoon salt
Dash pepper

In small bowl combine all ingredients; mix well. Cover and chill for at least 1 hour before serving.

Each serving is equivalent to: 1 serving Vegetables; ½ serving Milk.

Per serving: 53 calories, 3 g protein, 2 g fat, 7 g carbohydrate, 571 mg sodium

Variation: *Full Choice Plan*—Substitute 1 tablespoon thinly sliced scallion (green onion) for the chives. Add 1½ teaspoons Limited Vegetables to equivalent listing.

Per serving: 53 calories, 3 g protein, 2 g fat, 7 g carbohydrate, 569 mg sodium

CUCUMBER MOUSSE
Full Choice Plan
Makes 4 servings

1½ teaspoons unflavored gelatin
¼ cup water
2 large cucumbers (about 8 inches each), pared and seeded
½ cup plain unflavored yogurt
¼ cup reduced-calorie mayonnaise

2 teaspoons finely chopped scallion (green onion)
1½ teaspoons Worcestershire sauce
1 teaspoon lemon juice
Dash each salt, white pepper, and ground red pepper

In small saucepan sprinkle gelatin over water; let stand 1 minute. Cook over low heat, stirring constantly, until gelatin is completely dissolved; set aside.

Coarsely grate cucumbers into a bowl; set aside. In separate bowl combine yogurt, mayonnaise, scallion, Worcestershire sauce, and lemon juice; stir in dissolved gelatin. Squeeze moisture from cucumbers; add cucumbers and seasonings to yogurt mixture and stir to combine. Pour mixture into a 1¾- or 2-cup mold that has been rinsed with cold water. Cover and chill until firm, at least 3 hours. Unmold onto serving platter.

Each serving is equivalent to: ¼ serving Extras; 1⅛ servings Vegetables; ¼ serving Milk; 1½ servings Fats; ½ teaspoon Limited Vegetables.

Per serving: 129 calories, 2 g protein, 12 g fat, 3 g carbohydrate, 128 mg sodium

CUCUMBER RELISH
Full Choice Plan
Makes 2 servings

1 large cucumber (about 8 inches
  long), pared and seeded
1 tablespoon diced pimiento
1 tablespoon coarsely grated carrot
2 teaspoons finely chopped scallion
  (green onion)

1 tablespoon plus 1 teaspoon white
  wine vinegar
1 teaspoon olive oil
½ teaspoon granulated sugar
¼ teaspoon salt
⅛ teaspoon powdered mustard
⅛ teaspoon pepper

Coarsely grate cucumber into a small bowl; pour off any liquid. Add pimiento, carrot, and scallion. In another small bowl combine remaining ingredients except pepper. Pour over cucumber mixture and toss well. Sprinkle with pepper.

Each serving is equivalent to: 1¼ servings Vegetables; 1 teaspoon Limited Vegetables; ½ serving Fats; ½ serving Extras.

Per serving: 43 calories, 1 g protein, 3 g fat, 5 g carbohydrate, 279 mg sodium

SAUTÉED CUCUMBER
Limited Choice Plan
Makes 1 serving

1 teaspoon margarine
½ cup pared, seeded, and sliced
  cucumber

1 teaspoon chopped fresh parsley
Dash each salt and pepper

In small skillet heat margarine until bubbly; add cucumber and sauté until tender-crisp. Toss with parsley, salt, and pepper.

Each serving is equivalent to: 1 serving Fats; 1 serving Vegetables.

Per serving: 45 calories, 1 g protein, 4 g fat, 3 g carbohydrate, 178 mg sodium

DAIKONS
The daikon is a spongy, mildly pungent Oriental radish that has large-growing white roots; it has a light tan outer covering and, when pared, is white. Daikons can be shredded and used raw in salads, cooked and used as a side dish (usually served with soy sauce), or pickled. Leaves of the young plant can be served as a piquant green vegetable. The Japanese carve daikons into flowers and use them as a garnish. Purchase daikons with the roots removed; they can be found in fruit and vegetable markets, some supermarkets, and Oriental specialty food shops.

To prepare, pare daikons and cook in boiling water to cover until tender.

EGGPLANT AND PIMIENTO PARMESAN
Limited Choice Plan
Makes 2 servings

1 tablespoon teriyaki sauce	2 teaspoons onion flakes,
1 garlic clove, minced	reconstituted in 1 tablespoon
6 thin eggplant slices (about	water
¼ inch thick each)	1½ teaspoons grated Parmesan
¼ cup chopped pimientos	cheese

In shallow 1-quart casserole combine teriyaki sauce with garlic. Place eggplant slices in teriyaki mixture, turning to coat both sides. Let marinate for at least 20 minutes, turning occasionally.

Transfer eggplant to a 12 x 15-inch nonstick baking sheet and broil 5 inches from heat source until crisp and browned, about 3 minutes; turn slices and brown other side.

In small bowl combine pimientos and reconstituted onion flakes; spread ⅙ of mixture onto each eggplant slice and sprinkle each with ¼ teaspoon Parmesan cheese. Broil until topping is thoroughly heated and crisp, about 3 minutes.

Each serving is equivalent to: 1 serving Vegetables; ¾ serving Extras.

Per serving: 35 calories, 2 g protein, 1 g fat, 6 g carbohydrate, 333 mg sodium

Variation: *Full Choice Plan*—Substitute 2 tablespoons minced onion for the onion flakes. Add 1 tablespoon Limited Vegetables to equivalent listing.

Per serving: 36 calories, 2 g protein, 1 g fat, 7 g carbohydrate, 333 mg sodium

EGGPLANT CAPONATA
Full Choice Plan
Makes 4 servings

Store in a tightly covered glass or stainless steel container for up to one week.

3 cups cubed eggplant	1 cup diced celery
1 teaspoon salt	1 cup chopped tomatoes
1 tablespoon plus 1 teaspoon olive	2 teaspoons wine vinegar
oil	1 teaspoon granulated sugar
1 cup thinly sliced onions	8 black olives, pitted and chopped
1 teaspoon minced fresh garlic	1 tablespoon capers

On paper towels place eggplant in a single layer. Sprinkle with salt and allow to stand for at least 1 hour. Pat dry and set aside.

In a 9- or 10-inch skillet heat oil; add onions and garlic and sauté over medium heat until onions are translucent, 3 to 5 minutes. Add eggplant; cook, stirring occasionally, until eggplant begins to soften, about 5 minutes. Add celery and tomatoes; cover and simmer until celery is tender, about 15 minutes. Add vinegar and sugar; cook 5 minutes longer.

Remove from heat; add olives and capers and toss to combine. Cover and chill before serving.

Each serving is equivalent to: 2½ servings Vegetables; 1 serving Fats; ¼ cup Limited Vegetables; 1½ servings Extras.

Per serving: 112 calories, 2 g protein, 7 g fat, 13 g carbohydrate, 698 mg sodium

BRAISED ENDIVE
Limited Choice Plan
Makes 2 servings

5 heads Belgian endive (about 14 ounces)
2 teaspoons margarine
1 tablespoon lemon juice

1 packet instant chicken broth and seasoning mix
Dash pepper

Garnish
1 teaspoon chopped fresh parsley

Preheat oven to 300°F. Cut off and discard hard core from bottom of each endive; slice endives into 1-inch pieces and set aside.

In 1-quart flameproof casserole melt margarine; add lemon juice, broth mix, and pepper and stir to combine. Add endives and toss until thoroughly coated.

Bake endives until tender, 20 to 30 minutes. Sprinkle with parsley and serve.

Each serving is equivalent to: 1 serving Fats; ½ serving Extras. (See page 407 for Full Choice Plan adjustments.)

Per serving: 71 calories, 3 g protein, 4 g fat, 8 g carbohydrate, 475 mg sodium

ENDIVE SALAD
Limited Choice Plan
Makes 2 servings

Salad
5 small heads Belgian endive (about 14 ounces)

½ cup chopped watercress leaves
6 cherry tomatoes, cut into quarters

Dressing
1 teaspoon sesame seed, toasted
1 teaspoon each lemon juice, rice vinegar, and water

½ garlic clove, mashed
Dash salt

To Prepare Salad: Separate each endive into individual leaves. Line a clear 1-quart salad bowl with endive leaves with tips facing rim of bowl like flower petals. Fill center of bowl with chopped watercress; top watercress with cherry tomato quarters, arranged in a circular pattern. Chill for at least 30 minutes.

To Prepare Dressing: Using a mortar and pestle, mash sesame seed. In small bowl or cup combine mashed seed with lemon juice, vinegar, water, garlic, and salt; mix well. Chill for at least 30 minutes.

To Serve: Stir dressing and pour over salad.

Each serving is equivalent to: ½ serving Vegetables; 1 serving Extras. (See page 407 for Full Choice Plan adjustments.)

Per serving: 49 calories, 3 g protein, 1 g fat, 9 g carbohydrate, 84 mg sodium

GRAPE LEAVES

These edible leaves of the grapevine are often stuffed with fish, fowl, rice, or various other combinations. Cooked as a vegetable, grape leaves offer a special texture and unique flavor.

To prepare fresh leaves for stuffing, blanch for 1 minute, then drain and pat dry with paper towels. Grape leaves are also available packed in brine; remove the tough stem ends and rinse and dry leaves before stuffing.

HEART OF PALM

This vegetable is also referred to as "swamp cabbage," "palmetto cabbage," and "cabbage palm." It is the heart of a tropical palm tree from Brazil or Florida, weighs 3 to 4 pounds, and has a fairly bland, delicate flavor. Rarely seen fresh, heart of palm is widely available canned; it may be used in salads or heated and eaten as a side dish.

JERUSALEM ARTICHOKES ITALIANO

Full Choice Plan
Makes 4 servings

2 teaspoons olive oil
1½ cups pared and thinly sliced Jerusalem artichokes
½ cup thinly sliced scallions (green onions)

2 teaspoons grated Parmesan cheese
Dash each salt, pepper, and oregano leaves

In 8- or 9-inch nonstick skillet heat oil; add artichokes and scallions and sauté over high heat, stirring frequently, until tender. Remove from heat and toss with remaining ingredients. Serve immediately.

Each serving is equivalent to: ½ serving Fats; ½ cup Limited Vegetables; ½ serving Extras.

Per serving: 50 calories, 2 g protein, 3 g fat, 9 g carbohydrate, 49 mg sodium

LETTUCE AND OTHER GREENS

Lettuce, which has been cultivated for more than 2,500 years, was once known as the "water plant" because it refreshed travelers. It is deliciously refreshing for us too. The most popular kinds are crisphead (iceberg), butterhead (Bibb, limestone), cos (romaine), and loose-leafed (red-edged ruby, green-leaf, oakleaf). Curly endive (chicory), escarole, Belgian endive, raw spinach, watercress, and arugula are also frequently used in salads. You might want to try some lesser known greens, too; they will add variety to your salads.

All greens should be rinsed thoroughly to restore lost moisture and to remove soil. Dry quickly and tear into bite-size pieces. If greens are prepared in advance, wrap them in paper or cloth towels and refrigerate until ready to use. Whenever possible, use more than one type of green in a salad.

Arugula—This salad green, which is similar to watercress, is frequently found in Italian markets.

Beet Greens—These are the tops or leaves of the beet plant. They may be eaten raw or cooked.

Comfrey Leaves—This green grows wild and can be used raw in salads or cooked in soups, stews, and as a side dish.

Dandelion Greens—This familiar weed belongs to the chicory family. The tender inner leaves have a slightly bitter flavor. These greens are delectable raw in salads or cooked as a green vegetable. Discard the mature outer leaves; they are tough and bitter.

Fiddlefern (Fiddlehead)—The young shoots of fern fronds get their name from their coiled shape, which is reminiscent of the scrolled head of a violin. This springtime delicacy has a very short season, usually around the first two weeks in May. The ferns are best when picked in the morning and used the same day; however, they can be kept in the refrigerator for several days. The flavor of fiddlefern is a cross between that of asparagus and mushrooms. These greens are excellent raw in salads, steamed and eaten as a side dish, or in soups.

To prepare, rub off the fuzz from the fronds, wash ferns thoroughly, and steam for 3 to 5 minutes.

Lambs-Quarters—This plant is one of the most common weeds in the United States. It is often called pigweed, goosefoot, or wild spinach. The irregular-shaped edible leaves are white on the underside and green on top; they taste much like spinach, although considerably milder. Use lambs-quarters raw in salads.

Mustard Greens—Mustard greens include several species of the mustard plant, grown for their young leaves. The leaves vary in shape but are similar in flavor. They are used raw in salads or cooked as a side dish.

Nasturtium Leaves—This plant, nicknamed "Indian cress," is a member of the watercress family. Its pale green leaves have the flavor of watercress but are more delicate and less peppery. Nasturtium leaves make a delightful salad, either alone or combined with other greens. The leaves may also be blanched and used as a substitute in recipes calling for grape leaves.

Peppergrass—This plant is one of the many members of the mustard family. It grows wild throughout much of the United States and Canada. The young leaves are delicious in salads or cooked and mixed with other cooked greens.

Turnip Greens—These are the tops from the young turnip plant. The greens may be served raw in salads, or cooked and eaten as a side dish.

LETTUCE STIR-FRY
Limited Choice Plan
Makes 2 servings

2 teaspoons peanut or vegetable oil
⅛ teaspoon minced fresh garlic
4 cups coarsely chopped romaine or
  green-leaf lettuce

2 teaspoons soy sauce
½ packet instant chicken broth
  and seasoning mix

In medium skillet heat oil; add garlic and stir-fry until golden. Add remaining ingredients and stir-fry until lettuce is tender-crisp, about 3 minutes.

Each serving is equivalent to: 1 serving Fats; ¼ serving Extras. (See page 407 for Full Choice Plan adjustments.)

Per serving: 67 calories, 2 g protein, 5 g fat, 5 g carbohydrate, 661 mg sodium

Variation: *Full Choice Plan*—Add ½ cup chopped onion with the garlic and stir-fry until onion is translucent. Proceed as directed. Add ¼ cup Limited Vegetables to Full Choice Plan equivalents.

Per serving: 83 calories, 3 g protein, 5 g fat, 9 g carbohydrate, 666 mg sodium

ROMAINE AND WATERCRESS SALAD
Limited Choice Plan
Makes 4 servings

4 cups torn romaine lettuce (1-inch
  pieces)
2 cups watercress leaves (stems
  removed)
1 tablespoon plus 1½ teaspoons
  garlic-flavored wine vinegar

2 teaspoons olive oil
1 teaspoon each chopped chives
  and chopped fresh parsley
⅛ teaspoon each salt and
  powdered mustard
Dash pepper

In salad bowl combine romaine lettuce with watercress. In small bowl mix wine vinegar with remaining ingredients. Pour over greens, toss, and serve.

Each serving is equivalent to: ½ serving Fats. (See page 407 for Full Choice Plan adjustments.)

Per serving: 36 calories, 1 g protein, 3 g fat, 3 g carbohydrate, 85 mg sodium

LOTUS ROOT (Water-Lily Root) (Limited Vegetable)
The lotus root is the reddish brown, tuberous stem of the water lily. It measures about 2 inches in diameter and about 8 inches in length per section and looks like several sweet potatoes linked together. Similar in texture to the potato but less woody, the lotus root is quite popular in

the Orient. It can be purchased fresh, from July through February, in Oriental specialty food shops and is also available canned and dried. Store fresh lotus root in a cool, dry place or refrigerate; it will keep for up to 3 weeks.

To prepare, pare and soak for about 20 minutes in acidulated hot water; drain, rinse, and stir-fry or use in slow-simmering soups and stews.

MARINATED MUSHROOMS
Limited Choice Plan
Makes 4 servings

6 cups small mushroom caps*
2 tablespoons each lemon juice
  and cider vinegar
1 teaspoon each salt and olive oil

½ teaspoon each tarragon leaves
  and pepper
¼ teaspoon ground thyme

In small saucepan (not aluminum or cast-iron) combine all ingredients; bring to a boil. Reduce heat and simmer for 5 minutes, stirring occasionally. Cover and refrigerate at least 8 hours.

Each serving is equivalent to: 3 servings Vegetables; ¼ serving Fats.

Per serving: 45 calories, 3 g protein, 2 g fat, 6 g carbohydrate, 554 mg sodium

* Save and freeze the mushroom stems. Use in soup or sauce.

MUSHROOM PÂTÉ
Full Choice Plan
Makes 2 Midday or Evening Meal servings, ½ meal each; supplement as required

This pâté may be prepared ahead, unmolded, garnished, wrapped in plastic wrap, and refrigerated until ready to serve.

4 cups sliced mushrooms
2 tablespoons sliced scallion (green
  onion)
2 teaspoons dry red wine
1 packet instant onion broth and
  seasoning mix

⅔ cup cottage cheese
3 tablespoons plain dried bread
  crumbs
2 large lettuce leaves

Garnish
Watercress sprigs and 4 sliced
  radishes

In 8- or 9-inch nonstick skillet combine mushrooms, scallion, wine, and broth mix; cook over medium heat, stirring occasionally, until no liquid remains in pan.

Transfer mixture to blender container or work bowl of food processor and process until smooth. Turn motor off and add cheese and bread crumbs; process until combined. Spoon into two 6-ounce custard cups that have been sprayed with nonstick cooking spray, or two ¾-cup nonstick molds. Tap cups or molds on a hard surface to release air bubbles. Cover with plastic wrap and refrigerate for at least 2 hours.

To Unmold and Serve: Run the point of a small knife around the edge of each cup or mold. Place 1 lettuce leaf on each of 2 plates and invert pâtés onto lettuce. Garnish each portion with watercress sprigs and 2 sliced radishes.

Each serving is equivalent to: 4¼ servings Vegetables; 1 tablespoon Limited Vegetables; 1 serving Extras; ⅓ cup Soft Cheese; ½ serving Bread.

Per serving: 168 calories, 15 g protein, 4 g fat, 17 g carbohydrate, 777 mg sodium

STUFFED MUSHROOMS
Full Choice Plan
Makes 4 servings

16 mushrooms, each about 2 inches in diameter (about 4 cups)
Acidulated water*
⅔ cup water
⅓ cup rice vinegar or white wine vinegar
1 small onion
2 pieces celery (3 inches each)

2 parsley sprigs
½ teaspoon pickling spice
½ teaspoon salt
3 tablespoons finely diced carrot
2 tablespoons finely diced green bell pepper
2 teaspoons minced scallion (green onion)

Garnish
16 pimiento squares (¼ inch each)

Clean mushrooms and remove stems. Place mushroom caps and stems into a bowl of acidulated water* to keep the mushrooms from turning dark, and set aside.

In a stainless steel or glass-ceramic saucepan combine ⅔ cup water with the vinegar. Tie onion, celery, parsley, and pickling spice in a piece of cheesecloth and add, along with salt, to vinegar mixture; bring to a boil. Drain mushrooms and add caps to saucepan, reserving stems; return to a boil and cook for 2 minutes. Set aside to cool.

Chop mushroom stems. In small bowl combine stems with carrot, green pepper, and scallion; pour about half of the vinegar mixture from mushroom caps over vegetables. Let cool. Cover and refrigerate mushroom caps and bowl of chopped vegetables; let chill for at least 4 hours, stirring each occasionally.

To Serve: Using a slotted spoon, remove mushroom caps to a serving platter. Drain vegetables and stuff each mushroom cap with an equal amount of vegetable mixture. Garnish each with a pimiento square.

Each serving is equivalent to: 2⅛ servings Vegetables; ½ teaspoon Limited Vegetables.

Per serving: 24 calories, 2 g protein, 0.2 g fat, 4 g carbohydrate, 283 mg sodium

* 1 quart water and 1 tablespoon lemon juice.

QUICK BLENDER PEA SOUP
Full Choice Plan
Makes 4 servings, about ½ cup each

2 cups skim milk
1 cup frozen peas, thawed
2 teaspoons enriched all-purpose
   flour
2 teaspoons reduced-calorie
   margarine

1 teaspoon salt
½ teaspoon onion powder
Dash each ground nutmeg and
   pepper

In blender container combine skim milk and peas and process until smooth. Add remaining ingredients and process to combine.

Pour mixture into 1-quart saucepan and bring to a boil; reduce heat and simmer until mixture thickens slightly. Pour into 4 soup bowls and serve immediately.

Each serving is equivalent to: ½ serving Milk; ¼ cup Limited Vegetables; ½ serving Extras; ¼ serving Fats.

Per serving: 87 calories, 7 g protein, 1 g fat, 12 g carbohydrate, 677 mg sodium

OLIVE AND PEPPER SALAD
Full Choice Plan
Makes 2 servings

2 teaspoons olive oil
½ cup thinly sliced onion
1 garlic clove, minced
1½ cups each thinly sliced green
   and red bell peppers
2 teaspoons red wine vinegar

1½ teaspoons capers
½ teaspoon each salt and
   granulated sugar
Dash each oregano leaves and
   pepper
4 pitted black olives, sliced

In 9-inch nonstick skillet heat oil; add onion and garlic and sauté briefly (just until onion is tender-crisp). Add sliced peppers; toss lightly, cover, and cook until peppers are tender-crisp, 3 to 5 minutes.

Transfer vegetable mixture to medium bowl; add remaining ingredients except olives and toss. Garnish with olives. Chill salad for at least 2 hours before serving.

Each serving is equivalent to: 1 serving Fats; ¼ cup Limited Vegetables; 3 servings Vegetables; 1½ servings Extras.

Per serving: 140 calories, 4 g protein, 7 g fat, 19 g carbohydrate, 687 mg sodium

PUMPKIN LOG
Full Choice Plan
Makes 4 servings

1 envelope unflavored gelatin
2 tablespoons thawed frozen
  concentrated orange juice
  (no sugar added)
1 cup canned pumpkin
Artificial sweetener to equal
  4 teaspoons sugar
2 teaspoons granulated sugar

½ teaspoon ground cinnamon
¼ teaspoon vanilla extract
Dash each ground nutmeg and
  ginger
1 cup low-calorie whipped topping
  (6 calories per 2 tablespoons)
8 graham crackers (2½-inch
  squares)

1. In a small heatproof bowl sprinkle gelatin over juice and let stand about 5 minutes to soften. Place bowl in pan of hot water and stir until gelatin is completely dissolved; set aside.

2. To prepare frosting, in bowl combine pumpkin, sweetener, sugar, cinnamon, vanilla, nutmeg, and ginger; stir in gelatin mixture. Carefully fold in whipped topping. Cover and chill for 10 minutes.

3. Break each graham cracker in half. Spread a ¼-inch-thick layer of pumpkin frosting over 1 side of each of 3 cracker halves; stack halves and top with a fourth half. Set on a plate. Repeat with remaining cracker halves and some of the frosting (reserve about 1 cup frosting to cover complete log); cover lightly and chill for 10 minutes.

4. To form log, on a long, narrow, serving platter stand frosted cracker stacks on edge, long-side down, with long edge of crackers parallel to long edge of platter, making 1 continuous row. Place 3-inch-wide strips of wax paper on platter around log to keep platter clean. Frost top and sides of log with remaining frosting. Using the tines of a fork, score top and sides of log lengthwise. Cover lightly and chill for at least 4 hours. Carefully remove wax paper strips before serving.

Each serving is equivalent to: 1½ servings Extras; ¼ serving Fruits; ¼ cup Limited Vegetables; 12 calories Specialty Foods; 1 serving Bread.

Per serving: 119 calories, 3 g protein, 2 g fat, 25 g carbohydrate, 242 mg sodium

PUMPKIN PUDDING PIE
Full Choice Plan
Makes 8 servings

Crust
16 graham crackers (2½-inch
  squares), made into crumbs

⅓ cup reduced-calorie margarine

Filling
1 envelope (four ½-cup servings)
  reduced-calorie vanilla pudding
  mix
2 cups skim milk
1 tablespoon plus 1 teaspoon
  granulated sugar

⅛ teaspoon ground cloves
Dash each ground nutmeg and
  ginger
2 cups canned pumpkin

To Prepare Crust: Preheat oven to 325°F. In bowl combine graham cracker crumbs and margarine, mixing thoroughly. Using the back of a spoon, press crumb mixture over bottom and up sides of a 9-inch pie pan. Bake until crisp and brown, about 15 minutes. Remove from oven and place pan on rack to cool.

To Prepare Filling: In 1½-quart saucepan prepare pudding with skim milk according to package directions, but do not chill. When cool, stir in sugar, cloves, nutmeg, and ginger. Add pumpkin and mix until thoroughly combined.

To Prepare Pie: Pour filling into prepared crust; cover and refrigerate until firm.

Each serving is equivalent to: 1 serving Bread; 1 serving Fats; ½ serving Milk Substitutes; 1 serving Extras; ¼ cup Limited Vegetables.

Per serving: 157 calories, 4 g protein, 5 g fat, 25 g carbohydrate, 367 mg sodium

SPICED PUMPKIN MOUSSE
Full Choice Plan
Makes 4 servings

Vanilla "Cream"

½ teaspoon unflavored gelatin
1½ teaspoons water
¼ cup evaporated skimmed milk, chilled

1 teaspoon granulated sugar
¼ teaspoon vanilla extract

Spiced Pumpkin

1 envelope unflavored gelatin
2 tablespoons thawed frozen concentrated orange juice (no sugar added)
1 cup canned pumpkin

2 teaspoons granulated sugar
½ teaspoon ground cinnamon
¼ teaspoon vanilla extract
Dash each ground nutmeg and ginger

To Prepare Vanilla "Cream": Chill small mixing bowl and beaters of electric mixer.

In small heatproof cup sprinkle ½ teaspoon gelatin over water and let stand to soften. Place cup in pan containing heated water and stir until gelatin is completely dissolved. Pour milk into chilled bowl; stir in dissolved gelatin, 1 teaspoon sugar, and ¼ teaspoon vanilla. Beat at high speed until mixture stands in peaks, 8 to 10 minutes. Cover and refrigerate until ready to use.

To Prepare Spiced Pumpkin: In small heatproof cup sprinkle gelatin over juice and let stand to soften. Place cup in pan containing heated water and stir until gelatin is dissolved. In 1-quart bowl combine pumpkin, sugar, cinnamon, vanilla, nutmeg, and ginger; stir in gelatin mixture.

To Prepare Mousse: Carefully fold vanilla "cream" into spiced pumpkin, reserving some for garnish. Spoon mousse into serving bowl and garnish center with reserved "cream."

Each serving is equivalent to: 2½₂ servings Extras; ⅛ serving Milk; ¼ serving Fruits; ¼ cup Limited Vegetables.

Per serving: 70 calories, 4 g protein, 0.3 g fat, 14 g carbohydrate, 167 mg sodium

RADISHES

The red radish most frequently seen in the market is one of several varieties available. There are also white radishes, black radishes, and the large Japanese radish called daikon.

To Make Radish Roses: Using a red radish, slice off top. Make 4 or 5 cuts, each about ¼ inch deep, all around radish to create petals. Place in bowl of ice water, cover, and refrigerate until "rose" opens, 1 to 2 hours. Drain and use as garnish.

To Make Radish Accordions: Using a red radish, trim away a thin slice from each end. Cut parallel slashes, about ⅛ inch apart, along 1 side of radish, being careful not to cut through to other side. Refrigerate as for radish roses.

PICKLED RADISHES

Limited Choice Plan
Makes 2 servings

2 cups thinly sliced red radishes
½ teaspoon salt
2 tablespoons rice vinegar

1 teaspoon granulated sugar
1 tablespoon chopped fresh parsley

1. In small bowl sprinkle sliced radishes with salt; toss well and set aside for ½ hour.
2. Drain liquid from radishes and pat dry with paper towels to remove moisture. Return radishes to bowl.
3. In small saucepan combine vinegar and sugar and bring to a boil. Remove from heat and pour over radishes. Add parsley and toss to combine.
4. Cover and refrigerate for at least 1 hour before serving.

Each serving is equivalent to: 1 serving Extras. (See page 407 for Full Choice Plan adjustments.)

Per serving: 30 calories, 1 g protein, 0.1 g fat, 7 g carbohydrate, 290 mg sodium

FRUITED RUTABAGA

Full Choice Plan
Makes 4 servings

2 cups pared and diced rutabaga
½ teaspoon salt
½ cup applesauce (no sugar added)

1 tablespoon plus 1 teaspoon
  margarine
2 teaspoons honey
2 tablespoons raisins

In 1-quart saucepan combine rutabaga and salt with enough water to cover; bring to a boil and cook until tender, 20 to 25 minutes.

Drain and transfer rutabaga to blender container or work bowl of food processor; process until smooth. Turn motor off and push rutabaga down from sides of container with rubber scraper. Add applesauce, margarine, and honey and process until smooth.

Transfer mixture to 1-quart baking dish; stir in raisins and bake at 350°F. for 20 to 25 minutes. Serve hot.

Each serving is equivalent to: ½ cup Limited Vegetables; ½ serving Fruits; 1 serving Fats; 1 serving Extras.

Per serving: 103 calories, 1 g protein, 4 g fat, 18 g carbohydrate, 319 mg sodium

SALSIFY (Limited Vegetable)

This fleshy root is also known as oyster plant and vegetable oyster. It is shaped like a carrot and has leaves that resemble those of a leek, but are smaller. Salsify is available in black and white varieties; the black is large and reputed to have a better flavor. Serve salsify hot as a side dish.

QUICK SPINACH SAUTÉ

Limited Choice Plan
Makes 1 serving

1 teaspoon vegetable oil
⅛ teaspoon minced fresh garlic

6 ounces spinach leaves, washed
   well and drained*
Dash each salt and pepper

In 10-inch skillet heat oil; add garlic and sauté just until garlic begins to turn golden. Add spinach, salt, and pepper and cook, stirring frequently, until spinach is cooked, about 5 minutes.

Each serving is equivalent to: 1 serving Fats; 1 serving Vegetables.*

Per serving: 62 calories, 3 g protein, 5 g fat, 3 g carbohydrate, 179 mg sodium

Variation: Substitute 1 teaspoon olive oil for the vegetable oil. Sprinkle cooked spinach with 2 teaspoons grated Parmesan cheese. Add 2 servings Extras to cquivalent listing.

Per serving: 77 calories, 5 g protein, 6 g fat, 3 g carbohydrate, 241 mg sodium

* 6 ounces fresh spinach leaves will yield about ½ cup cooked vegetable.

SQUASH

Summer Squash

Caserta—Cylindrical in shape with alternating stripes of dark and light green. Usually 6 to 7 inches long and 1 to 1½ inches thick.

Cocozelle—Cylindrical in shape with smooth, slightly ribbed skin with alternating stripes of yellow and dark green. Usually 6 to 8 inches long and 2 inches thick.

Chayote—Pear-shaped with either smooth or corrugated surface, varying in color from ivory to dark green. A one-seeded vegetable, usually 3 to 4 inches long with a weight range of from 3 ounces to 2 pounds. Flesh should be fibrous and delicately flavored.

Scallop (also known as Pattypan and Cymling)—Dish- or bowl-shaped with smooth or slightly bumpy skin and prominent ribbing on edges giving the squash a scalloped appearance. Usually 3 to 4 inches in diameter and pale green when young but white when mature. Flesh is green-tinged.

Spaghetti—Nearly cylindrical in shape with dark yellow shell and orange flesh that, when cooked, can be pulled apart with a fork into strands resembling spaghetti. (The spaghetti squash has the characteristics of a winter squash but is considered a summer squash on the Food Plan.)

Vegetable Marrow—Green and cucumber-shaped with thin yellow stripes; should be eaten young. Much prized in Europe, but less popular in the United States.

Yellow Crookneck—Curved at the neck with moderately bumpy skin which is light yellow when young and deeper yellow when mature. Usually 8 to 10 inches long and 3 inches thick. Flesh is creamy yellow.

Yellow Straightneck—Similar to crookneck squash but neck is relatively straight. Usually grows to 20 inches long and 4 inches thick.

Zucchini—Cylindrical in shape but larger at the base. Skin is dark green with hints of yellow throughout, giving a striped appearance. Usually 2 to 3 inches thick and may grow as long as 10 to 12 inches. Flesh is greenish white.

Winter Squash (Limited Vegetable)

Acorn (also known as Table Queen)—Acorn-shaped, with smooth, thin, hard, widely ribbed shell, which is dark green when young but turns orange-green when mature. Usually 5 to 8 inches long and 4 to 5 inches thick. Flesh is pale orange.

Banana—Nearly cylindrical in shape with moderately tapering base and apex. Usually from 18 to 24 inches long and 5 to 6½ inches thick. Skin is moderately smooth to wrinkled and pitted and pale olive-gray, but changes to creamy pink in storage. Flesh is thick, moderately dry, and orange-buff in color.

Buttercup—Shaped somewhat like a drum with a turbanlike formation at blossom end. Usually 4 to 5 inches long and 6 to 8 inches in diameter. Skin is dark green with faint gray spots and stripes. Flesh is sweet, dry, and orange in color.

Butternut—Nearly cylindrical but with slightly bulbous base. Skin is smooth, hard, and creamy brown or dark yellow. Usually 9 to 12 inches long and the bulbous end is often 5 inches in diameter. The fine-grained flesh is yellow or orange.

Calabaza—Generally round, but may be elongated and almost pear-shaped, with heavy rind that is either white or light yellow with dark green spots or blotches. Flesh is slightly fibrous and a vivid orange-yellow in color. Flavor is a delicate variation of the North American pumpkin.

Hubbard—Globe-shaped with thick, tapered neck at stem end and somewhat smaller taper at blossom end. Can be dark bronze-green, blue-gray, or red-orange with a very hard rind and warted, ridged skin. Usually from 10 to 16 inches long and 9 to 12 inches thick at largest diameter. Flesh is thick, yellow-orange, and sweet.

Warren Turban—Drum-shaped with turbanlike formation at blossom end. Usually from 8 to 10 inches long and 12 to 15 inches in diameter. Skin is bright red-orange with scattered striping at blossom end; the turban is blue. The hard, thick shell is heavily warted and the flesh is bright orange, thick, sweet, fairly dry, and often rather stringy.

ACORN–CARROT BAKE

Full Choice Plan
Makes 2 servings

This can be prepared ahead of time and reheated when ready to use.

1 acorn squash, 1 to 1¼ pounds   Dash each ground nutmeg and
1 cup cooked sliced carrots   cinnamon
2 teaspoons margarine

Place acorn squash on baking sheet; bake at 350°F. until tender, 45 to 50 minutes.

Cut squash in half; remove and discard seeds and membranes. Scoop out pulp, being careful not to tear shells; reserve shells. Measure 1 cup pulp; in work bowl of food processor or blender container combine pulp with carrots and margarine and process until pureed.

Divide mixture into the 2 reserved shells. Sprinkle each with nutmeg and cinnamon. Return to oven for 10 to 15 minutes or wrap in foil, refrigerate, and reheat when ready to use.

Each serving is equivalent to: ½ cup Limited Vegetables; 1 serving Vegetables; 1 serving Fats.

Per serving: 104 calories, 2 g protein, 4 g fat, 17 g carbohydrate, 69 mg sodium

ZUCCHINI–MUSHROOM SALAD

Limited Choice Plan
Makes 2 servings

3 tablespoons lemon juice   1 cup thinly sliced zucchini
2 teaspoons olive or vegetable oil   1 cup thinly sliced mushrooms
½ teaspoon granulated sugar   1 tablespoon chopped fresh parsley
¼ teaspoon Dijon-style mustard   ½ teaspoon basil leaves or
⅛ teaspoon minced fresh garlic   1 tablespoon chopped fresh basil
Dash each salt and pepper

In salad bowl combine lemon juice, olive or vegetable oil, sugar, mustard, garlic, salt, and pepper. Add remaining ingredients and toss to combine. Cover and chill for several hours, tossing occasionally.

Each serving is equivalent to: 1 serving Fats; ½ serving Extras; 2 servings Vegetables.

Per serving: 75 calories, 2 g protein, 5 g fat, 7 g carbohydrate, 91 mg sodium

ZUCCHINI–TOMATO SAUTÉ
Full Choice Plan
Makes 2 servings

2 teaspoons olive oil
¼ teaspoon minced fresh garlic
1½ cups sliced zucchini
3 medium tomatoes, blanched, peeled, seeded, and chopped

1 tablespoon chopped fresh basil or ½ teaspoon dried basil leaves
Dash each salt and pepper

In 9- or 10-inch skillet heat oil; add garlic and sauté just until golden. Add zucchini and cook, stirring occasionally, for 10 minutes. Add remaining ingredients and cook until zucchini is fork-tender, about 10 minutes longer. If mixture becomes dry, add water to adjust consistency.

Each serving is equivalent to: 1 serving Fats; 4½ servings Vegetables.

Per serving: 104 calories, 3 g protein, 5 g fat, 13 g carbohydrate, 72 mg sodium

Variation: Add ½ cup fresh or frozen peas along with "remaining ingredients." Proceed as directed. Add ¼ cup Limited Vegetables to equivalent listing.

Per serving: 131 calories, 6 g protein, 5 g fat, 18 g carbohydrate, 118 mg sodium

CREAM OF TOMATO SOUP
Full Choice Plan
Makes 4 servings, about ¾ cup each

2 cups canned crushed tomatoes
½ cup diced onion
½ teaspoon salt
½ bay leaf
2 tablespoons reduced-calorie margarine

1 tablespoon enriched all-purpose flour
1 cup evaporated skimmed milk, heated
Dash pepper

In 1-quart saucepan combine tomatoes, onion, salt, and bay leaf; bring to a boil. Remove from heat and discard bay leaf. Transfer mixture to blender container; set aside and allow to cool slightly.

In same saucepan heat margarine, over low heat, until bubbly. Using a wire whisk, add flour and cook, stirring constantly, until smooth. Gradually stir in milk; continue stirring and cook until thickened. Remove from heat and set aside.

Process tomato mixture in blender container until smooth. Slowly add tomato mixture to milk mixture; add pepper and stir to combine. Reheat soup over low heat before serving, stirring occasionally (*do not boil*).

Each serving is equivalent to: 1 serving Vegetables; ⅛ cup Limited Vegetables; ¾ serving Fats; ¾ serving Extras; ½ serving Milk.

Per serving: 116 calories, 7 g protein, 3 g fat, 16 g carbohydrate, 571 mg sodium

QUICK TOMATO RELISH
Full Choice Plan
Makes 4 servings

This is also delicious served over cottage cheese.

36 cherry tomatoes, cut into quarters
½ cup each finely diced green bell pepper and celery
¼ cup finely diced onion
½ garlic clove, minced

1 teaspoon each salt, red wine vinegar, olive oil, and honey
½ teaspoon lemon juice
¼ teaspoon oregano leaves
Dash each powdered mustard and pepper
4 iceberg or romaine lettuce leaves

In medium bowl combine tomatoes with remaining ingredients except lettuce; toss thoroughly. Cover and refrigerate until well chilled, about 2 hours. Serve on lettuce leaves.

Each serving is equivalent to: 2¼ servings Vegetables; 1 tablespoon Limited Vegetables; ¼ serving Fats; ½ serving Extras.

Per serving: 49 calories, 2 g protein, 1 g fat, 9 g carbohydrate, 563 mg sodium

TOMATO BAKE
Limited Choice Plan
Makes 1 serving

1 teaspoon margarine
½ garlic clove, minced
1 slice enriched white bread, made into crumbs

1 teaspoon each grated Parmesan cheese and chopped chives
1 medium tomato, sliced
Dash each salt and pepper

In small skillet heat margarine, over medium heat, until bubbly; add garlic and sauté until golden. In small bowl combine crumbs, cheese, and chives and add to skillet, stirring until margarine is completely absorbed.

Place tomato slices in shallow individual casserole. Season with salt and pepper and spoon crumb mixture evenly over slices. Bake at 350°F. until thoroughly heated, about 10 minutes.

Each serving is equivalent to: 1 serving Fats; 1 serving Bread; 1 serving Extras; 2 servings Vegetables.

Per serving: 137 calories, 4 g protein, 5 g fat, 19 g carbohydrate, 327 mg sodium

TOMATO–CLAM BISQUE
Full Choice Plan
Makes 2 servings

1 teaspoon margarine
¼ cup diced onion
2 teaspoons enriched all-purpose flour
1 cup bottled clam juice

1 cup canned crushed tomatoes
¼ cup diced celery
⅛ teaspoon thyme leaves
Dash pepper

In 1-quart saucepan heat margarine until bubbly; add onion and sauté until softened. Add flour and cook over medium heat, stirring constantly, for 2 minutes. Remove from heat and gradually stir in clam juice; return to heat. Add tomatoes, celery, thyme, and pepper and bring to a boil. Reduce heat, partially cover, and simmer for 20 minutes.

Each serving is equivalent to: ½ serving Fats; ⅛ cup Limited Vegetables; 1 serving Extras; ½ serving Bonus; 1¼ servings Vegetables.

Per serving: 86 calories, 5 g protein, 2 g fat, 12 g carbohydrate, 679 mg sodium

TRUFFLES

Truffles are tuberlike, warty, fleshy, edible fungi found underground in the woodlands of England, France, and other European countries. This prized delicacy is solid and roughly spherical in shape; it ranges in size from small as a pea to large as a potato and in color from white to shades of pink and brown to black. The most preferred truffles are the black ones. The pleasant aroma produced by truffles is detectable by trained dogs and pigs, which are used to harvest them. Truffles are not easily cultivated artificially and are rarely grown in America.

WATER CHESTNUTS (Limited Vegetable)

Also referred to as Chinese water chestnut and waternut, this vegetable has long been cultivated for its crunchy tubers. It has a chestnut-brown skin, firm white flesh, and a chestnutty flavor and texture and is valued as a nutritious delicacy in Chinese cookery. Water chestnuts can be eaten raw or used in a wide array of Oriental dishes. They are difficult to find fresh, but are worth searching for. They are available canned in most supermarkets.

GAZPACHO (CHILLED SALAD–SOUP)

Full Choice Plan
Makes 4 servings

1 cup tomato juice
1 packet instant beef broth and
  seasoning mix
2 medium tomatoes, coarsely
  chopped
1 medium cucumber, pared and
  coarsely chopped
½ cup coarsely chopped celery
½ cup coarsely chopped green bell
  pepper

¼ cup coarsely chopped onion
1 tablespoon olive oil
2 teaspoons red wine vinegar
1 teaspoon lemon juice
1 garlic clove
¼ teaspoon salt
2 drops hot sauce
Dash pepper

In small saucepan combine tomato juice and broth mix and bring to a boil. Remove from heat and allow to cool.

In blender container combine remaining ingredients and process until vegetables are finely chopped. Turn motor off and add cooled tomato juice mixture; process just until combined (*do not puree*). Refrigerate at least 2 hours before serving.

Each serving is equivalent to: ¼ serving Bonus; ¼ serving Extras; 2 servings Vegetables; 1 tablespoon Limited Vegetables; ¾ serving Fats.

Per serving: 78 calories, 2 g protein, 4 g fat, 10 g carbohydrate, 469 mg sodium

MIXED VEGETABLE KABOBS
Limited Choice Plan
Makes 2 servings

1 cup cut-up celery (1-inch pieces)
1 medium zucchini (about 5 ounces), cut in half lengthwise and then into 1-inch pieces
½ cup small mushrooms
6 cherry tomatoes

2 tablespoons reduced-calorie pancake syrup (12 calories per tablespoon)
1½ teaspoons onion flakes
1 teaspoon each lemon juice and teriyaki sauce

On each of two 6-inch wooden skewers, alternating ingredients, thread ½ cup celery pieces, half of the zucchini pieces, ¼ cup mushrooms, and 3 cherry tomatoes. Place skewers in an oblong dish large enough to hold them so they lie flat.

In small saucepan combine remaining ingredients and heat to just under a boil. Pour mixture over kabobs; let marinate in refrigerator for 2 hours, turning and basting with marinade once.

Transfer skewers to broiler pan, reserving marinade. Broil 6 inches from heat source until vegetables are browned; turn skewers and broil until other side is browned. Serve kabobs with reserved marinade.

Each serving is equivalent to: 2 servings Vegetables; 1⅕ servings Extras. (See page 407 for Full Choice Plan adjustments.)

Per serving: 52 calories, 2 g protein, 0.3 g fat, 11 g carbohydrate, 181 mg sodium

RATATOUILLE
Full Choice Plan
Makes 4 servings

2 teaspoons olive oil
3 medium tomatoes, blanched, peeled, quartered, and seeded
½ cup chopped onion
1 garlic clove, sliced
2 cups cubed eggplant
2 cups chopped zucchini

½ cup chopped green bell pepper
¼ teaspoon salt
Dash pepper
Bouquet garni (2 celery tops, 3 parsley sprigs, and 1 bay leaf, tied in cheesecloth)

In a 4-quart saucepan heat oil over medium heat; add tomatoes, onion, and garlic and cook, stirring occasionally, until onion is translucent. Add remaining ingredients. Reduce heat to low and cook until vegetables are tender, 20 to 30 minutes.

Strain and reserve liquid from vegetables; remove and discard bouquet garni. Transfer vegetables to a bowl and keep warm. Return liquid to pan and bring to a boil; cook until liquid is reduced by half. Return vegetables to liquid and stir to combine. Serve hot or chilled.

Each serving is equivalent to: ½ serving Fats; 3¾ servings Vegetables; ⅛ cup Limited Vegetables.

Per serving: 79 calories, 3 g protein, 3 g fat, 13 g carbohydrate, 144 mg sodium

Variations: *To use as a Midday or Evening Meal entrée—1 serving each*
1. Place 1 serving Ratatouille in individual casserole; top with 2 ounces sliced hard cheese and bake at 350°F. until cheese is melted. Add 2 ounces Hard Cheese to equivalent listing.

Per serving: 308 calories, 17 g protein, 22 g fat, 13 g carbohydrate, 495 mg sodium

2. Place 4 ounces boned cooked beef or fish or skinned and boned cooked poultry in individual casserole; top with 1 serving Ratatouille and bake at 350°F. until heated through, about 20 minutes. Add 4 ounces Meat Group, Fish, or Poultry to equivalent listing.

Per serving with beef: 298 calories, 39 g protein, 10 g fat, 13 g carbohydrate, 231 mg sodium
With fish: 261 calories, 24 g protein, 13 g fat, 13 g carbohydrate, 386 mg sodium
With poultry: 295 calories, 36 g protein, 11 g fat, 13 g carbohydrate, 241 mg sodium

3. Place 2 ounces boned cooked beef or fish or skinned and boned cooked poultry in individual casserole. Top with 1 serving Ratatouille, then 1 ounce sliced hard cheese. Bake at 350°F. until heated through and cheese is melted. Add 2 ounces Meat Group, Fish, or Poultry and 1 ounce Hard Cheese to equivalent listing.

Per serving with beef: 308 calories, 28 g protein, 16 g fat, 13 g carbohydrate, 363 mg sodium
With fish: 214 calories, 31 g protein, 4 g fat, 13 g carbohydrate, 276 mg sodium
With poultry: 301 calories, 27 g protein, 16 g fat, 13 g carbohydrate, 368 mg sodium

VEGETABLES À LA GRECQUE
Limited Choice Plan
Makes 4 servings

1 medium cucumber, scored and thinly sliced
1 cup thinly sliced mushrooms
1 cup diagonally sliced carrots (¼-inch-thick slices), blanched
1 cup diagonally cut green beans (1-inch pieces), blanched

1 cup each cauliflower and broccoli florets, blanched
1½ teaspoons each salt, granulated sugar, and lemon juice
1 teaspoon each dill weed, tarragon vinegar, and olive oil

In medium bowl combine all ingredients and toss well to thoroughly coat vegetables. Cover and refrigerate for at least 8 hours.

Each serving is equivalent to: 3 servings Vegetables; ¾ serving Extras; ¼ serving Fats.

Per serving: 68 calories, 4 g protein, 2 g fat, 12 g carbohydrate, 837 mg sodium

VEGETABLE SOUP
Full Choice Plan
Makes 2 servings

¾ cup quartered small mushrooms
¼ cup each diced celery, carrot, zucchini, and onion
1 packet instant chicken broth and seasoning mix
2 cups water
½ cup tomato juice

2 teaspoons margarine
1 tablespoon enriched all-purpose flour
⅛ teaspoon thyme leaves
Dash pepper
2 teaspoons chopped fresh parsley

In 1½-quart saucepan combine mushrooms, celery, carrot, zucchini, onion, and broth mix; add water and tomato juice and bring to a boil. Reduce heat and simmer 15 minutes.

In small skillet heat margarine until bubbly; add flour and cook over low heat, stirring constantly, for 3 minutes. Remove from heat. Measure ½ cup liquid from cooked vegetables and add gradually to flour mixture, stirring constantly until mixture is smooth.

Add flour mixture to soup remaining in saucepan; stir in thyme and pepper. Simmer 15 minutes longer. Just before serving sprinkle with parsley.

Each serving is equivalent to: 1½ servings Vegetables; ⅛ cup Limited Vegetables; 2 servings Extras; ¼ serving Bonus; 1 serving Fats.

Per serving: 93 calories, 3 g protein, 4 g fat, 12 g carbohydrate, 613 mg sodium

VEGETABLE STIR-FRY
Limited Choice Plan
Makes 2 servings

2 teaspoons Chinese sesame oil
1 cup diagonally sliced celery
¾ cup bean sprouts

¼ cup chopped pimientos
1 tablespoon soy sauce
1 teaspoon sesame seed, toasted

In small skillet heat oil; add celery and stir-fry until tender. Add sprouts, pimientos, and soy sauce and stir-fry 1 minute. Transfer to serving dish and sprinkle with sesame seed.

Each serving is equivalent to: 1 serving Fats; 1 serving Vegetables; 1 serving Extras. (See page 407 for Full Choice Plan adjustments.)

Per serving: 84 calories, 3 g protein, 6 g fat, 7 g carbohydrate, 748 mg sodium

Variation: *Full Choice Plan*—Add 1 tablespoon thinly sliced scallion (green onion) to skillet with sprouts, pimientos, and soy sauce. Proceed as directed. Add 1½ teaspoons Limited Vegetables to Full Choice Plan equivalents.

Per serving: 86 calories, 3 g protein, 6 g fat, 8 g carbohydrate, 749 mg sodium

Milk

*Remember childhood days when "Drink your milk" was
a dull command? There's nothing dull about the ways
we've blended milk products into a rainbow array of con-
fections for children of all ages! You'll find your sweet
tooth's dream dish here: floats, milk shakes, parfaits, and
molds—take your pick with a clear conscience, for we've
deleted the fattening and left in the flavorful.*

Milk and milk products supply Calcium, Phosphorus, Riboflavin, Protein, Vitamin A, and Vitamin D.

Guidelines for Using Milk

1. Amounts:

	Full Choice Plan	Limited Choice Plan
Women	2 servings daily	2 servings daily
Men	2 servings daily	2 servings daily
Youth	3 to 4 servings daily	3 servings daily

2. Milk servings may be consumed at any time and may be mixed-and-matched (e.g., 1 cup skim milk, ¼ cup plain unflavored yogurt, and ¼ cup evaporated skimmed milk equal a total of 2 servings Milk—see chart below).

3. A milk serving may contain up to 90 calories.

4. Commercially prepared whole-milk, low-fat, or low-calorie plain unflavored yogurts or homemade yogurt may be used. Homemade yogurt may be made from whole or skim milk. Mix yogurt thoroughly before consuming; the clear liquid component contains valuable nutrients that should not be discarded.

5. One serving of the approved commercially prepared dietary frozen dessert used in our recipes equates to ½ serving Milk and 1 serving Fruits.

Milk Servings

Selections	One Serving
milk powder, instant nonfat dry	⅓ cup
milk, skim	1 cup
buttermilk	¾ cup
milk, evaporated skimmed	½ cup
yogurt:	
plain unflavored (commercially prepared)	½ cup
homemade (made from skim milk)	1 cup
homemade (made from whole milk)	½ cup
yogurt drinks, instant plain unflavored	1 packet
Milk Substitutes	
flavored milk beverages, low-calorie	1 packet or serving
flavored milk puddings, low-calorie	½ cup

CREAM OF CELERY SOUP
Full Choice Plan
Makes 2 servings, about 1 cup each

2 teaspoons margarine
¼ cup diced onion
2 teaspoons enriched all-purpose
  flour
1 packet instant chicken broth and
  seasoning mix, dissolved in
  1½ cups hot water

1 cup chopped celery
½ cup evaporated skimmed milk
Dash each ground nutmeg, salt,
  and white pepper

In a 1-quart saucepan heat margarine until bubbly; add onion and sauté until softened. Add flour and cook, stirring constantly, for 2 minutes. Add dissolved broth mix and celery and bring mixture to a boil. Reduce heat and simmer until celery is soft, 20 to 25 minutes.

Pour mixture into blender container or work bowl of food processor and process until smooth. Return soup to saucepan; stir in milk and nutmeg and simmer 5 minutes. Season with salt and pepper.

Each serving is equivalent to: 1 serving Fats; ⅛ cup Limited Vegetables; 1½ servings Extras; 1 serving Vegetables; ½ serving Milk.

Per serving: 117 calories, 7 g protein, 4 g fat, 14 g carbohydrate, 677 mg sodium

CREAM OF MUSHROOM SOUP
Full Choice Plan
Makes 2 servings, about 1 cup each

2 teaspoons margarine
2 tablespoons minced onion
2 cups sliced mushrooms
1 tablespoon enriched all-purpose
  flour
1½ cups water
1 packet instant chicken broth and
  seasoning mix

Dash ground thyme
½ cup evaporated skimmed milk
2 teaspoons dry sherry
Dash each salt and white pepper
1 teaspoon chopped fresh parsley

In a 1-quart saucepan heat margarine until bubbly; add onion and sauté, stirring occasionally, until softened. Add mushrooms; sauté 5 minutes longer. Remove and reserve 2 tablespoons of mushrooms. Sprinkle flour over vegetables in saucepan; cook, stirring constantly, for 2 minutes. Gradually stir in water, broth mix, and thyme. Bring mixture to a boil; reduce heat, cover, and simmer for 15 minutes.

Pour 2 cups soup into blender container and process until smooth. Transfer mixture to a 1-quart bowl and repeat procedure with remaining soup.

Pour soup back into saucepan. Stir in evaporated milk, sherry, and reserved mushrooms and simmer 5 minutes longer; season with salt and pepper. Serve garnished with parsley.

Each serving is equivalent to: 1 serving Fats; 1 tablespoon Limited Vegetables; 2 servings Vegetables; 2½ servings Extras; ½ serving Milk.

Per serving: 135 calories, 8 g protein, 4 g fat, 16 g carbohydrate, 611 mg sodium

RASPBERRY "CREAM"
Limited Choice Plan
Makes 2 servings

½ envelope (two ½-cup servings) low-calorie raspberry-flavored gelatin (8 calories per ½ cup)
¼ cup boiling water

6 ounces vanilla dietary frozen dessert
½ cup raspberries

In small heatproof bowl sprinkle gelatin over water and stir until completely dissolved; blend in frozen dessert. Spray two 1-cup molds with nonstick cooking spray; pour half of mixture into each. Cover and refrigerate until set, at least 2 hours.

To Serve: Unmold each portion onto a plate; garnish each with ¼ cup raspberries and serve immediately.

Each serving is equivalent to: ⅘ serving Extras; ½ serving Milk; 1½ servings Fruits. (See page 407 for Full Choice Plan adjustments.)

Per serving: 147 calories, 11 g protein, 1 g fat, 24 g carbohydrate, 89 mg sodium

Variation: *Orange "Cream"*—Substitute low-calorie orange-flavored gelatin for the raspberry-flavored gelatin and omit raspberries. In equivalent listing reduce Fruits to 1 serving.

Per serving: 101 calories, 4 g protein, 1 g fat, 19 g carbohydrate, 70 mg sodium

ORANGE–YOGURT MOLD
Limited Choice Plan
Makes 2 servings

1 envelope unflavored gelatin
2 tablespoons thawed frozen concentrated orange juice (no sugar added)
½ cup boiling water
1 cup plain unflavored yogurt
½ cup canned mandarin orange sections (no sugar added)

2 thin strips orange peel (each about 1 inch long)
1 teaspoon lemon juice
Artificial sweetener to equal 2 teaspoons sugar

In small heatproof bowl sprinkle gelatin over orange juice and let stand to soften; add boiling water and stir until gelatin is dissolved.

In another bowl combine yogurt and orange sections; gently fold in dissolved gelatin. Rinse a 2-cup mold with cold water; pour mixture into mold. Cover and refrigerate overnight or until mold has set.

In small saucepan combine orange peel, lemon juice, and sweetener; cook over low heat, stirring constantly, until lemon juice has evaporated.

Turn out each mold onto a plate and garnish each with orange peel. Serve immediately.

Each serving is equivalent to: 1 serving Extras; 1 serving Fruits; 1 serving Milk.

Per serving: 149 calories, 7 g protein, 4 g fat, 22 g carbohydrate, 55 mg sodium

RIBBON MOLD
Limited Choice Plan
Makes 4 servings

1 envelope unflavored gelatin
¼ cup water
1 cup lemon-lime-flavored diet soda (4 calories per 12 fluid ounces), divided
2 tablespoons lemon juice
Artificial sweetener to equal 4 teaspoons sugar

2 teaspoons granulated sugar
1 to 2 drops green food color
¼ cup evaporated skimmed milk
Dash coconut extract
1 cup canned fruit cocktail (no sugar added)

1. In small saucepan sprinkle gelatin over water and let stand 1 minute to soften; cook over low heat, stirring constantly, until gelatin is completely dissolved. Remove from heat and add ⅓ cup soda, the lemon juice, sweetener, sugar, and food color and stir to combine.

2. Pour ⅓ cup soda mixture into a bowl; stir in milk and extract (mixture may look curdled). Cover and chill until the consistency of heavy cream, about 20 minutes.

3. Using an electric mixer or hand beater, beat milk mixture until fluffy. Pour mixture into a 4-cup ring mold that has been rinsed with cold water; cover and chill until set, about 30 minutes.

4. While milk mixture is chilling, combine remaining soda mixture with remaining ⅔ cup soda; cover and chill until syrupy, 20 to 30 minutes.

5. Stir fruit cocktail into syrupy soda mixture and spoon over set milk mixture; cover and chill overnight.

6. To unmold, dip point of small knife in warm water; with point, loosen gelatin mixture around edge of mold. Quickly dip mold, just to rim, in warm (*not hot*) water; remove from water and shake gently. Invert platter on mold, then invert platter and mold together and gently lift off mold.

Each serving is equivalent to: 1⅗ servings Extras; ⅛ serving Milk; ½ serving Fruits. (See page 407 for Full Choice Plan adjustments.)

Per serving: 54 calories, 3 g protein, 0.1 g fat, 11 g carbohydrate, 40 mg sodium

APPLE YOGURT
Limited Choice Plan
Makes 1 or 2 servings, 1 cup or ½ cup each

½ cup plain unflavored yogurt
½ cup applesauce (no sugar added)

Artificial sweetener to equal 2 teaspoons sugar
Dash apple pie spice

In bowl combine all ingredients; cover and chill.
Each 1-cup serving is equivalent to: 1 serving Milk; 1 serving Fruits.
Per serving: 123 calories, 4 g protein, 4 g fat, 20 g carbohydrate, 54 mg sodium

Each ½-cup serving is equivalent to: ½ serving Milk; ½ serving Fruits.
Per serving: 62 calories, 2 g protein, 2 g fat, 10 g carbohydrate, 27 mg sodium

CHOCOLATE YOGURT
Limited Choice Plan
Makes 1 serving, about ½ cup

½ cup plain unflavored yogurt
1½ teaspoons chocolate syrup
¼ teaspoon vanilla extract

Artificial sweetener to equal 2
teaspoons sugar

In small bowl combine all ingredients. Cover and chill.

Each serving is equivalent to: 1 serving Milk; 3 servings Extras.
Per serving: 100 calories, 4 g protein, 4 g fat, 12 g carbohydrate, 57 mg sodium

MOCHA YOGURT
Limited Choice Plan
Makes 1 serving, about ½ cup

1 teaspoon chocolate syrup
½ teaspoon vanilla extract
⅛ teaspoon instant coffee powder

Artificial sweetener to equal 2
teaspoons sugar
½ cup plain unflavored yogurt

In small bowl combine syrup, extract, coffee, and sweetener, stirring until
coffee is dissolved. Stir in yogurt; cover and chill.
Each serving is equivalent to: 2 servings Extras; 1 serving Milk.
Per serving: 96 calories, 4 g protein, 4 g fat, 10 g carbohydrate, 55 mg sodium

PEAR AND YOGURT PARFAIT
Full Choice Plan
Makes 4 servings

1 cup plain unflavored yogurt
2 very ripe small pears, pared,
  cored, and diced
2 teaspoons honey

⅛ teaspoon ground cinnamon
8 graham crackers (2½-inch
  squares), crushed

In bowl thoroughly combine yogurt, pears, honey, and cinnamon; cover
and chill.
Just before serving, in each of 4 parfait glasses spoon alternate layers
of yogurt mixture and graham cracker crumbs, starting with yogurt and
ending with crumbs.
Each serving is equivalent to: ½ serving Milk; ½ serving Fruits; 1 serving Extras; 1 serving Bread.
Per serving: 142 calories, 4 g protein, 3 g fat, 27 g carbohydrate, 121 mg sodium

BUTTERMILK POPS
Limited Choice Plan
Makes 2 servings

Thaw 2 tablespoons frozen concentrated orange juice (no sugar added). In small bowl thoroughly combine ¾ cup buttermilk, thawed orange juice, and liquid artificial sweetener to equal 1 teaspoon sugar. Divide mixture into two 4- or 5-ounce plastic-coated paper cups; cover and freeze until partially frozen. Insert a wooden ice cream bar stick in each cup and freeze until completely frozen.

To remove frozen pop from cup, hold cup, bottom-side up, under running warm water until loose.

Each serving is equivalent to: ½ serving Fruits; ½ serving Milk.

Per serving: 68 calories, 4 g protein, 1 g fat, 12 g carbohydrate, 98 mg sodium

FROZEN STRAWBERRY YOGURT
Full Choice Plan
Makes 4 servings, about 1 cup each

½ envelope unflavored gelatin	1 tablespoon plus 1 teaspoon honey
2 tablespoons cold water	Artificial sweetener to equal 4
3 cups strawberries, divided	teaspoons sugar
2 cups plain unflavored yogurt	¼ teaspoon vanilla extract

In small saucepan or metal measuring cup sprinkle gelatin over water and let stand to soften; cook over low heat, stirring constantly, until gelatin is completely dissolved.

In blender container combine 2 cups strawberries with dissolved gelatin and process until smooth. Add yogurt, honey, sweetener, and extract; process until combined. Add remaining 1 cup strawberries and process until coarsely chopped. Pour mixture into a shallow metal 1½-quart pan; cover and freeze, stirring every 30 minutes, until consistency of ice cream.

Just before serving, remove from freezer and stir until mixture is creamy.

Each serving is equivalent to: 2¼ servings Extras; ¾ serving Fruits; 1 serving Milk.

Per serving: 138 calories, 5 g protein, 4 g fat, 21 g carbohydrate, 54 mg sodium

BRANDY-COFFEE FLOAT
Limited Choice Plan
Makes 1 serving, about 1 cup

In an 8-ounce coffee mug combine ½ cup hot black coffee and ¼ teaspoon brandy extract. Add 3 ounces chocolate dietary frozen dessert and serve immediately.

Each serving is equivalent to: ½ serving Milk; 1 serving Fruits.

Per serving: 105 calories, 4 g protein, 1 g fat, 19 g carbohydrate, 71 mg sodium

APPLE-YOGURT FROST
Limited Choice Plan
Makes 2 servings

1 cup plain unflavored yogurt
2 tablespoons plus 2 teaspoons
  thawed frozen concentrated
  apple juice (no sugar added)

2 teaspoons granulated sugar
2 ice cubes
Dash artificial sweetener
  (optional)

In blender container combine yogurt, apple juice, sugar, and ice cubes; process until mixture is thick and foamy. Add sweetener if desired and process to combine.
Each serving is equivalent to: 1 serving Milk; 1 serving Fruits; 2 servings Extras.

Per serving: 124 calories, 4 g protein, 4 g fat, 19 g carbohydrate, 53 mg sodium
Without artificial sweetener: 124 calories, 4 g protein, 4 g fat, 19 g carbohydrate, 52 mg sodium

BANANA-YOGURT SHAKE
Limited Choice Plan
Makes 2 servings, about ¾ cup each

1 cup plain unflavored yogurt
1 medium banana, peeled and cut
  into chunks
¼ cup skim milk

Artificial sweetener to equal 2
  teaspoons sugar
1 teaspoon granulated sugar
½ teaspoon vanilla extract

In blender container combine all ingredients; process until smooth.
Each serving is equivalent to: 1⅛ servings Milk; 1 serving Fruits; 1 serving Extras.

Per serving: 144 calories, 6 g protein, 4 g fat, 23 g carbohydrate, 68 mg sodium

HONEY-VANILLA MILK SHAKE
Limited Choice Plan
Makes 1 serving, about 1 cup

½ cup skim milk
3 ounces vanilla dietary frozen
  dessert

½ teaspoon honey
¼ teaspoon vanilla extract

In blender container combine all ingredients and process until smooth, about 1 minute. Serve immediately.
Each serving is equivalent to: 1 serving Milk; 1 serving Fruits; 1 serving Extras.

Per serving: 159 calories, 8 g protein, 1 g fat, 28 g carbohydrate, 134 mg sodium

Variation: Substitute ⅛ teaspoon coconut extract or pineapple extract for the vanilla extract.

Per serving: 156 calories, 8 g protein, 1 g fat, 28 g carbohydrate, 134 mg sodium

RICH CHOCOLATE MILK SHAKE
Limited Choice Plan
Makes 1 serving, about 1 cup

½ cup skim milk
3 ounces chocolate dietary frozen
  dessert

1 teaspoon chocolate syrup
¼ teaspoon vanilla extract

In blender container combine all ingredients and process until smooth, about 1 minute. Serve immediately or cover and chill in freezer for 1 to 2 minutes, then reprocess.

Each serving is equivalent to: 1 serving Milk; 1 serving Fruits; 2 servings Extras.

Per serving: 164 calories, 8 g protein, 1 g fat, 29 g carbohydrate, 138 mg sodium

HOT CAROB MILK
Limited Choice Plan
Makes 1 serving

1½ teaspoons unsweetened carob
  powder
½ teaspoon granulated sugar

¾ cup skim milk
⅛ teaspoon vanilla extract

In small saucepan combine carob powder and sugar; using a wire whisk, gradually stir in milk. Add vanilla and, over medium heat, bring mixture to a boil, beating with whisk until frothy. Pour into a mug and serve immediately.

Each serving is equivalent to: 2½ servings Extras; ¾ serving Milk.

Per serving: 83 calories, 7 g protein, 1 g fat, 13 g carbohydrate, 97 mg sodium

HOT MOCHA
Limited Choice Plan
Makes 2 servings

1 tablespoon chocolate syrup
1 teaspoon instant coffee powder
2 cups skim milk

Artificial sweetener to equal 2
  teaspoons sugar
½ teaspoon vanilla extract

In a small saucepan combine chocolate syrup and instant coffee. Add milk and cook over medium heat, stirring constantly, to just below the boiling point. Remove from heat; stir in sweetener and vanilla.

Each serving is equivalent to: 3 servings Extras; 1 serving Milk.

Per serving: 117 calories, 9 g protein, 1 g fat, 19 g carbohydrate, 134 mg sodium

WHIPPED TOPPING
Limited Choice Plan
Makes 8 servings, about 3 tablespoons each

½ teaspoon unflavored gelatin
1½ teaspoons water
¼ cup evaporated skimmed milk, chilled

Artificial sweetener to equal 1 teaspoon sugar
⅛ teaspoon vanilla extract

Chill small bowl and beaters of an electric mixer. In a small saucepan or metal measuring cup sprinkle gelatin over water and let stand for 1 minute to soften; cook over low heat, stirring constantly, until gelatin is completely dissolved. Remove from heat.

In chilled bowl combine milk, sweetener, and extract. Beat milk mixture at high speed, gradually adding dissolved gelatin; continue beating until mixture stands in peaks, about 5 minutes.

Each serving is equivalent to: ¼₄ serving Extras; 1½ teaspoons Evaporated Skimmed Milk (¹⁄₁₆ serving Milk).

Per serving: 7 calories, 1 g protein, trace fat, 1 g carbohydrate, 9 mg sodium

Variation: Substitute 2 teaspoons granulated sugar for the artificial sweetener. Add ½ serving Extras to equivalent listing.

Per serving: 11 calories, 1 g protein, trace fat, 2 g carbohydrate, 9 mg sodium

Bread and Cereal

Bread is often the first thing dieters give up, without realizing it's a nutritious filler that helps ward off hunger pangs. Wheat forms the basis for both bread and some cereals. We've transformed these commonplace items into Spoon-Dropped Biscuits, Fruit 'n' Spice Cake, and Fruited Cereal Bars. Or top your morning cereal with our Peach Sauce; it makes getting up early worthwhile.

Bread and Cereal products supply Carbohydrates,
B Vitamins, Iron, and Fiber.

Guidelines for Using Bread

1. Amounts:

	Full Choice Plan	*Limited Choice Plan*
Women	2 to 3 servings daily	2 servings daily
Men	4 to 5 servings daily	4 servings daily
Youth	4 to 5 servings daily	4 servings daily

2. Bread servings may be consumed at any time and may be mixed-and-matched (e.g., 3 melba toast rounds, ½ English muffin, and 1 graham cracker equal a total of 2 servings Bread).

3. Although Bread is not required at the Morning Meal, it is recommended that it be consumed when Cereal is not selected in order to provide an even distribution of calories and carbohydrates (see Guidelines for Using Cereal, page 117).

4. Items in the Bread category, except cereal, should contain up to 80 calories per serving. Cereal may contain up to 85 calories per serving.

5. All breads, rolls, buns, and biscuits *must* be made with enriched or whole grain flour. Enriched flour contains added vitamins and minerals to restore the nutrients lost during milling and processing. Whole grain flour contains those parts of the seed and kernel that provide good sources of vitamins and minerals. Examples of bread and flour selections are:

  A. Bread—cracked wheat; enriched white; gluten; pumpernickel; raisin; rye; whole wheat
  B. Flour—enriched white all-purpose, bread, and self-rising; gluten; oatmeal; rye; soybean; whole wheat

6. When cereal is used as a Bread selection (Full Choice Plan only), it does not have to be consumed with milk.

7. For increased fiber intake, select whole grain breads and bran cereals.

Bread Servings

The bread selections in italics are for Full Choice Plan only and should *not* be used with the Limited Choice Plan. The other selections may be used on both plans.

Selections	One Serving
bagel, enriched or whole grain, small	½ (1 ounce)
biscuits	1 ounce
bread or rolls, enriched or whole grain	1 ounce
bread crumbs, dried, seasoned or plain	3 tablespoons
cereal (not presweetened), ready-to-eat or	¾ ounce
uncooked	
cornflake crumbs	¾ ounce
crispbread	¾ ounce
English muffin	½
flour, enriched or whole grain, sifted or	2 tablespoons plus
unsifted	1½ teaspoons
frankfurter roll	½ (1 ounce)
graham crackers	2 (2½-inch squares)
hamburger roll	½ (1 ounce)
matzo	½ board
matzo meal	3 tablespoons
matzo cake meal	2 tablespoons plus
	1½ teaspoons
melba toast	6 rounds or 4 slices
oyster crackers	20
pita	1 ounce
refrigerated roll or biscuit	1 ounce
rice cakes	2
saltines	6
taco shell	1
tortilla, corn	1 (6-inch diameter)
	or 1 ounce

HEARTY WHEAT BREAD
Limited Choice Plan
Makes 2 loaves, about 1¼ pounds each

Whole or sliced loaves can be frozen for use at a later date.

2 packets (¼ ounce each) active
   dry yeast or 2 cakes (0.6 ounce
   each) compressed yeast
¼ cup firmly packed light brown
   sugar, divided
1½ cups lukewarm skim milk

2 tablespoons vegetable oil
2 teaspoons salt
2 cups whole wheat flour
3½ to 4 cups enriched all-purpose
   or bread flour

1. Pour ¼ cup warm or lukewarm water* into 4-quart mixing bowl; add yeast and 2 tablespoons sugar and stir to dissolve. Set aside in a warm

(80° to 85°F.), draft-free place until bubbles form and the liquid foams, about 5 minutes.

2. Stir milk, oil, salt, and remaining 2 tablespoons sugar into yeast mixture. Add whole wheat flour, all at once, and beat with a spoon until batter is smooth. Add 3 cups all-purpose or bread flour, 1 cup at a time, mixing with a spoon and, as mixture becomes stiffer, by hand.

3. When dough becomes a rough mass and pulls away from sides of bowl, scrape sides of bowl and turn dough onto a lightly floured surface. Keep coating of flour on dough as you begin to knead.

4. With floured hands, knead dough by pushing the heels of your hands, with a rolling motion, down into dough and away from you, then folding dough over and giving it a quarter turn. Repeat kneading, adding remaining flour as needed, until dough becomes smooth and elastic (springs back when pressed lightly), 5 to 10 minutes.

5. Shape dough into a ball and place in greased 4-quart bowl; turn dough to coat lightly. Cover bowl with clean towel and let stand in warm place (80° to 85°F.) until dough has doubled in volume, about 1 hour. When 2 fingers, pressed lightly into dough, leave a dent, the dough is ready to shape.

6. Punch dough down, shape into a ball, and divide into 2 portions of equal weight; shape each into an oval. Place each loaf, seam-side down, in greased 9 x 5 x 2½-inch loaf pan. Cover pans with clean towels and let stand in warm place until dough is doubled in volume, about 45 minutes.

7. Place loaves in cold oven; set oven temperature at 375°F. Bake about 45 minutes (until loaves are nicely browned and just starting to pull away from sides of pans). Remove pans from oven; turn loaves out onto wire racks to cool. To serve, cut into 1-ounce slices.

1 ounce Hearty Wheat Bread is equivalent to: 1 serving Bread.

Per 1 ounce: 79 calories, 3 g protein, 1 g fat, 15 g carbohydrate, 113 mg sodium

* For active dry yeast use warm water (105° to 115°F.); for compressed yeast use lukewarm water (80° to 90°F.).

RAISIN BREAD
No Choice Plan
Makes 2 loaves

Bread can be frozen, whole or sliced, for use at a later date.

1 tablespoon plus 1 teaspoon active dry yeast	4 cups whole wheat flour
2½ cups warm water (105° to 115°F.), divided	½ cup wheat germ
	½ cup unprocessed bran
2 tablespoons dark molasses	2 teaspoons salt
1 tablespoon honey	1 cup raisins

1. In 3- or 4-quart mixing bowl, sprinkle yeast over 1 cup water; add molasses and honey and stir to combine. Set aside for about 5 minutes (bubbles will form and liquid will foam).

2. In another bowl combine flour, wheat germ, bran, and salt; gradually stir into yeast mixture. Add raisins and remaining 1½ cups water and stir until thoroughly combined (mixture will be sticky).

3. Spray two 7⅞ x 3⅞ x 2½-inch foil loaf pans with nonstick cooking spray. Weigh dough and divide in half, making sure that each half weighs the same. Place one half into each prepared pan and let pans stand in a warm, draft-free place (80° to 85°F.) until dough has doubled in volume, about 1 hour.

4. Preheat oven to 375°F. Place loaf pans in middle of center oven rack and bake 50 to 55 minutes (until loaves begin to pull away from sides of pans).

5. Remove pans from oven and turn each loaf out, on its side, onto wire rack to cool. To serve, cut into 1-ounce slices.

1 ounce Raisin Bread is equivalent to: 1 serving Bread.

Per 1 ounce: 68 calories, 3 g protein, 0.5 g fat, 15 g carbohydrate, 122 mg sodium

BRAN MUFFINS

Full Choice Plan
Makes 4 Midday or Evening Meal servings; ¼ meal each; supplement as required

Muffins can be baked, then frozen for use at a later date.

½ cup plus 2 tablespoons whole wheat flour
2 teaspoons double-acting baking powder
½ teaspoon salt
2 large eggs
1 cup skim milk

2 tablespoons plus 2 teaspoons vegetable oil
2 tablespoons honey
3 ounces unprocessed bran
2 tablespoons plus 2 teaspoons any flavor reduced-calorie spread (16 calories per 2 teaspoons), optional

1. Preheat oven to 400°F. In bowl, using a fork, combine flour, baking powder, and salt and set aside.

2. In medium bowl, using a fork, beat eggs; stir in milk, oil, and honey. Stir bran into egg mixture and allow to soak for 1 to 2 minutes.

3. Add flour mixture to egg mixture, stirring until just mixed (do not overmix).

4. Spray eight 2½-inch-diameter muffin pan cups with nonstick cooking spray. Spoon ⅛ of batter into each prepared cup. (If a 12-cup muffin pan is used, fill empty cups with water.)

5. Bake 25 to 30 minutes (until muffins are lightly browned).

6. Remove muffins to wire rack to cool. Serve 2 muffins per portion. If desired, top each muffin with 1 teaspoon reduced-calorie spread.

Each serving is equivalent to: 2 servings Bread; ½ Egg; ¼ serving Milk; 2 servings Fats; 3 servings Extras; 16 calories Specialty Foods (optional).

Per serving: 302 calories, 11 g protein, 14 g fat, 43 g carbohydrate, 543 mg sodium
Without reduced-calorie spread: 286 calories, 11 g protein, 14 g fat, 39 g carbohydrate, 543 mg sodium

Variation: Add ¼ cup raisins, chopped, to batter; bake as directed. Add ½ serving Fruits to equivalent listing.

Per serving: 328 calories, 11 g protein, 14 g fat, 50 g carbohydrate, 546 mg sodium
Without reduced-calorie spread: 312 calories, 11 g protein, 14 g fat, 46 g carbohydrate, 546 mg sodium

ROLLED BISCUITS
Full Choice Plan
Makes 6 servings, 2 biscuits each

Biscuits can be baked, then frozen for use at a later date.

1 cup less 1 tablespoon enriched all-purpose flour	¼ teaspoon salt
1 teaspoon double-acting baking powder	¼ cup reduced-calorie margarine
	¼ cup skim milk

1. Preheat oven to 400°F. In bowl combine flour, baking powder, and salt; sift into mixing bowl. With a pastry blender, or 2 knives used scissor-fashion, cut in margarine until mixture resembles coarse meal.
2. Add milk and, using a fork, mix until a soft dough forms and leaves sides of bowl.
3. Between 2 sheets of wax paper roll dough to about ½-inch thickness. Using a 2-inch-diameter biscuit cutter or rim of glass, cut out biscuits. Roll scraps of dough and continue cutting until all dough has been used (should make 12 biscuits).
4. Transfer biscuits to nonstick baking sheet and bake 12 to 15 minutes (until golden brown). Serve hot or allow to cool on wire rack.
Each serving is equivalent to: 1 serving Bread; 1 serving Fats; 2 teaspoons Skim Milk (¹⁄₂₄ serving Milk).

Per serving: 111 calories, 3 g protein, 4 g fat, 16 g carbohydrate, 256 mg sodium

Variation: Crush 2 tablespoons imitation bacon bits. Before baking, sprinkle each biscuit with an equal amount of crushed bacon bits; bake as directed. Add 1 serving Extras to equivalent listing.

Per serving: 120 calories, 3 g protein, 4 g fat, 17 g carbohydrate, 351 mg sodium

SPOON-DROPPED BISCUITS
Full Choice Plan
Makes 4 servings, 1 biscuit each

This recipe can be doubled and unused baked biscuits can be frozen for use at another time.

½ cup plus 2 tablespoons enriched all-purpose flour	1 tablespoon plus 1 teaspoon margarine
¼ teaspoon baking soda	½ cup buttermilk
Dash salt	

1. Preheat oven to 450°F. In bowl combine flour, baking soda, and salt; sift into a medium bowl. With a pastry blender, or 2 knives used scissor-fashion, cut in margarine until mixture resembles coarse meal.

2. Make a well in the center of the flour mixture and pour buttermilk into the well. Stir batter until thoroughly blended but *do not overmix*.

3. Drop batter by tablespoonsful onto nonstick baking sheet, forming 4 biscuits.

4. Bake about 20 minutes (until biscuits are golden brown and crisp). Serve warm or transfer to wire rack to cool.

Each serving is equivalent to: 1 serving Bread; 1 serving Fats; ⅙ serving Milk.

Per serving: 119 calories, 3 g protein, 4 g fat, 17 g carbohydrate, 131 mg sodium

Variation: Before baking, sprinkle each biscuit with ½ teaspoon imitation bacon bits or grated Parmesan cheese, or ¼ teaspoon caraway, poppy, or sesame seed. Add ½ serving Extras to equivalent listing.

Per serving with bacon bits: 120 calories, 3 g protein, 4 g fat, 17 g carbohydrate, 143 mg sodium
With Parmesan cheese: 120 calories, 3 g protein, 4 g fat, 17 g carbohydrate, 135 sodium
With seeds: 120 calories, 3 g protein, 4 g fat, 17 g carbohydrate, 131 mg sodium

BREAD STUFFING
Full Choice Plan
Makes 2 servings

2 teaspoons margarine
½ cup diced celery (with some leaves)
¼ cup diced onion
2 slices day-old enriched white bread, diced

½ cup Chicken Broth (see page 401)
¼ teaspoon salt
⅛ to ¼ teaspoon each thyme leaves and ground savory
⅛ teaspoon pepper
Dash rosemary leaves

In small skillet heat margarine until bubbly; add celery and onion and sauté until onion is translucent. Transfer mixture to 1¾-cup casserole; add remaining ingredients and stir to combine. Bake at 350°F. until slightly browned, about 20 minutes.

Each serving is equivalent to: 1 serving Fats; ½ serving Vegetables; ⅛ cup Limited Vegetables; 1 serving Bread; ⅓ serving Extras.

Per serving: 114 calories, 4 g protein, 5 g fat, 16 g carbohydrate, 478 mg sodium

VEGETABLE–BREAD STUFFING
Full Choice Plan
Makes 4 servings

1 tablespoon plus 1 teaspoon reduced-calorie margarine
¼ cup minced onion
1 cup diced zucchini
1 cup sliced mushrooms
½ cup diced celery
1 tablespoon chopped fresh parsley

¼ teaspoon thyme leaves
4 slices enriched white bread, toasted and cut into ¼-inch cubes
¼ cup Chicken Broth (see page 401)
Dash each salt and pepper

Preheat oven to 350°F. In 9-inch skillet heat margarine until bubbly; add onion and sauté until softened. Add zucchini, mushrooms, celery, parsley, and thyme and sauté until vegetables are tender-crisp, about 5 minutes. Remove from heat and stir in bread cubes, broth, salt, and pepper.

Spray a 3-cup casserole with nonstick cooking spray; spoon vegetable mixture into casserole, cover, and bake for 15 minutes. Remove cover and bake 5 minutes longer.

Each serving is equivalent to: ½ serving Fats; 1 tablespoon Limited Vegetables; 1¼ servings Vegetables; 1 serving Bread; ½₂ serving Extras.

Per serving: 98 calories, 4 g protein, 3 g fat, 16 g carbohydrate, 222 mg sodium

PIZZA APPETIZERS
Full Choice Plan
Makes 6 servings, 2 pizza rounds each

1 cup less 1 tablespoon enriched all-purpose flour
½ teaspoon baking soda
¼ teaspoon salt
2 tablespoons margarine

1 tablespoon onion flakes
¾ cup buttermilk
½ cup tomato sauce
2 tablespoons grated Parmesan cheese, divided

1. In bowl combine flour, baking soda, and salt; sift into medium bowl. With a pastry blender, or 2 knives used scissor-fashion, cut in margarine until mixture resembles coarse meal. Stir in onion flakes; add buttermilk and stir until all ingredients are blended.

2. Preheat oven to 350°F. Drop batter by teaspoonsful onto nonstick baking sheet, forming 12 mounds and leaving a space of about 3 inches between each. Using back of spoon, flatten each mound into a 2- to 2½-inch round.

3. Bake until browned, about 15 minutes.

4. Remove baking sheet from oven and spread 2 teaspoons tomato sauce over each round; sprinkle each with ½ teaspoon Parmesan cheese. Return to oven and bake until cheese melts, 5 to 10 minutes.

Each serving is equivalent to: 1 serving Bread; 1 serving Fats; ⅙ serving Milk; ⅙ serving Bonus; 1 serving Extras.

Per serving: 135 calories, 4 g protein, 5 g fat, 19 g carbohydrate, 326 mg sodium

PIZZAIOLA SPECIAL
Full Choice Plan
Makes 1 Midday or Evening Meal serving, ½ meal; supplement as required

½ English muffin, well toasted
1 tablespoon low-calorie Italian dressing (4 calories per tablespoon)
2 tablespoons tomato sauce

1 teaspoon each thinly sliced scallion (green onion) and mushroom
Dash oregano leaves
1 ounce mozzarella cheese, shredded

Place muffin half on baking sheet or sheet of foil; spread dressing evenly over muffin and top with tomato sauce. Arrange scallion and mushroom slices over sauce and sprinkle with oregano, then cheese. Broil 6 inches from heat source until cheese is melted, 4 to 6 minutes.*

Each serving is equivalent to: 1 serving Bread; 4 calories Specialty Foods; ¼ serving Bonus; 1 teaspoon Limited Vegetables; 1 teaspoon Vegetables; 1 ounce Hard Cheese.

Per serving: 160 calories, 8 g protein, 7 g fat, 17 g carbohydrate, 623 mg sodium

* This can also be broiled in a toaster-oven; adjust timing accordingly.

CINNAMON TOAST
Limited Choice Plan
Makes 1 serving

1 slice enriched white bread, lightly toasted
1 teaspoon margarine

½ teaspoon granulated sugar
⅛ teaspoon ground cinnamon

Spread 1 side of toast with margarine, covering entire surface. Place toast, margarine-side up, on sheet of foil or tray of toaster-oven. In small cup combine sugar and cinnamon; sprinkle evenly over toast. Broil 3 inches from heat source until golden brown, about 1 minute.

Each serving is equivalent to: 1 serving Bread; 1 serving Fats; 1 serving Extras.

Per serving: 105 calories, 2 g protein, 5 g fat, 14 g carbohydrate, 162 mg sodium

COCONUT TOAST
Limited Choice Plan
Makes 2 servings

2 teaspoons reduced-calorie margarine
2 tablespoons evaporated skimmed milk
2 teaspoons shredded coconut

1 teaspoon granulated brown sugar
⅛ teaspoon each vanilla and coconut extracts
2 slices raisin bread, toasted

In small saucepan melt margarine over medium heat. Remove from heat; add milk, coconut, sugar, and extracts and stir to combine. Spread half of mixture over 1 side of each slice of toast, covering entire surface. Transfer toast to nonstick baking sheet and broil 3 inches from heat source until heated, about 1 minute.* Cut each slice diagonally into 4 triangles and serve immediately.

Each serving is equivalent to: ½ serving Fats; ⅛ serving Milk; 2 servings Extras; 1 serving Bread.

Per serving: 113 calories, 3 g protein, 3 g fat, 18 g carbohydrate, 159 mg sodium

* This can be broiled in a conventional broiler or toaster-oven.

GRAHAM WAFERS
Full Choice Plan
Makes 4 servings, about 7 wafers each

½ cup plus 2 tablespoons whole wheat flour
1½ ounces wheat germ
Artificial sweetener to equal 3 teaspoons sugar
2 teaspoons firmly packed light brown sugar

2 teaspoons double-acting baking powder
¼ teaspoon ground cinnamon
2 tablespoons margarine
¼ cup skim milk

1. Preheat oven to 350°F. In medium bowl combine flour, wheat germ, sweetener, brown sugar, baking powder, and cinnamon; with a pastry blender, or 2 knives used scissor-fashion, cut in margarine until mixture resembles coarse meal. Gradually stir in milk, forming dough into a ball.
2. On a board lightly knead dough; cut in half. Between 2 sheets of wax paper roll out one half of the dough to ⅛-inch thickness; repeat with other half.
3. Using a sharp knife, cut dough into 2½ x 1¼-inch rectangles, forming about 28 wafers.
4. Transfer wafers to nonstick cookie sheet and bake until lightly browned, 10 to 12 minutes. Remove wafers to wire rack and let cool.
Each serving is equivalent to: 1½ servings Bread; 1 serving Extras; 1½ servings Fats; 1 tablespoon Skim Milk (¹⁄₁₆ serving Milk).

Per serving: 172 calories, 6 g protein, 7 g fat, 23 g carbohydrate, 281 mg sodium

VANILLA-CRISP COOKIES
Full Choice Plan
Makes 2 Midday or Evening Meal servings, ¼ meal each; supplement as required

1 tablespoon granulated sugar
2 teaspoons margarine, softened
½ teaspoon vanilla extract
1 large egg

2 tablespoons plus 1½ teaspoons enriched self-rising flour, sifted
¾ ounce ready-to-eat oven-toasted rice cereal

1. Preheat oven to 350°F. In bowl combine sugar, margarine, and extract and mix until creamy; add egg and beat well.
2. Blend in sifted flour, then fold in cereal until just combined.
3. Spray baking sheet with nonstick cooking spray; drop batter by heaping teaspoonful onto baking sheet, forming 12 cookies and leaving a space of about 2 inches between each. Using moistened tines of a fork, flatten each cookie slightly.
4. Bake until golden brown, 8 to 10 minutes. Remove cookies to wire rack to cool.
Each serving is equivalent to: 3 servings Extras; 1 serving Fats; ½ Egg; 1 serving Bread.

Per serving: 179 calories, 5 g protein, 7 g fat, 23 g carbohydrate, 315 mg sodium

Variations:

1. *Lemon-Crisp Cookies*—Add 2 teaspoons each grated lemon peel and lemon juice to batter before adding cereal.

Per serving: 182 calories, 5 g protein, 7 g fat, 24 g carbohydrate, 316 mg sodium

2. *Raisin-Crisp Cookies*—Add ¼ cup raisins to batter before adding cereal. Add 1 serving Fruits to equivalent listing.

Per serving: 231 calories, 5 g protein, 7 g fat, 37 g carbohydrate, 320 mg sodium

3. *Spiced Raisin-Crisp Cookies*—Add ½ teaspoon ground cinnamon and dash ground ginger to sifted flour. Add ¼ cup raisins to batter before adding cereal. Add 1 serving Fruits to equivalent listing.

Per serving: 233 calories, 5 g protein, 7 g fat, 38 g carbohydrate, 320 mg sodium

4. *Chocolate-Crisp Cookies*—Decrease sugar to 2 teaspoons. Add 1 teaspoon chocolate syrup to batter before adding cereal.

Per serving: 179 calories, 5 g protein, 7 g fat, 23 g carbohydrate, 317 mg sodium

CINNAMON COFFEE CAKE

Full Choice Plan

Makes 8 Midday or Evening Meal servings, ⅛ meal each; supplement as required

2 cups less 2 tablespoons enriched all-purpose flour	2 eggs
2 tablespoons plus 2 teaspoons granulated sugar	⅔ cup skim milk
2 teaspoons double-acting baking powder	1 teaspoon vanilla extract
¼ teaspoon salt	1 tablespoon granulated brown sugar
¼ cup margarine	½ teaspoon ground cinnamon
	1 teaspoon confectioners' sugar

1. Preheat oven to 400°F. In bowl combine flour, granulated sugar, baking powder, and salt; sift into mixing bowl. With a pastry blender, or 2 knives used scissor-fashion, cut in margarine until mixture resembles coarse meal.

2. Add eggs, milk, and extract; using electric mixer, beat just until smooth.

3. Spray an 8-inch square nonstick baking pan with nonstick cooking spray; pour batter into pan.

4. In small cup or bowl combine brown sugar and cinnamon; sprinkle over batter.

5. Bake 25 to 30 minutes (cake should pull away slightly from sides of pan and be springy to the touch).

6. Transfer pan to wire rack and allow cake to cool in pan. To serve, remove cooled cake from pan and sprinkle with confectioners' sugar.

Each serving is equivalent to: 1½ servings Bread; 3 servings Extras; 1½ servings Fats; ¼ Egg;* 1 tablespoon plus 1 teaspoon Skim Milk (¹⁄₁₂ serving Milk).

Per serving: 214 calories, 5 g protein, 7 g fat, 31 g carbohydrate, 265 mg sodium

* At least an additional ¼ egg must be consumed at same meal as this cake.

FRUIT 'N' SPICE CAKE
Full Choice Plan
Makes 12 servings

2 cups less 2 tablespoons enriched
  self-rising flour
2 teaspoons ground cinnamon
½ teaspoon ground cloves
½ cup reduced-calorie margarine
¼ cup granulated sugar

1 teaspoon baking soda
1½ cups applesauce (no sugar
  added)
⅓ cup plus 2 teaspoons golden
  raisins

1. Into medium bowl sift together flour, cinnamon, and cloves and set aside.
2. Preheat oven to 350°F. In medium bowl cream margarine; add sugar and stir to combine. Stir baking soda into applesauce; add to margarine mixture and stir to combine.
3. Add sifted ingredients to applesauce mixture and, using an electric mixer, beat at medium speed until thoroughly combined, about 30 seconds; fold in raisins.
4. Spray an 8 x 8 x 2-inch baking pan with nonstick cooking spray; pour batter into pan and bake 40 to 45 minutes (until cake is browned and a cake tester or toothpick, inserted in center, comes out dry).
5. Remove cake from pan; transfer to wire rack to cool.

Each serving is equivalent to: 1 serving Bread; 1 serving Fats; 2 servings Extras; ½ serving Fruits.

Per serving: 147 calories, 2 g protein, 4 g fat, 26 g carbohydrate, 340 mg sodium

Guidelines for Using Cereal (Full and Limited Choice Plans)

1. Amounts (ready-to-eat or uncooked):

	Morning Meal
Women, Men, and Youth	¾ ounce with at least ½ serving Milk

2. Cereal may be selected as a Protein entrée at the Morning Meal *only* and then *must* be consumed with at least ½ Milk serving.
3. Different varieties of cereal may be combined provided the total amount per portion does not exceed the serving size indicated above.

4. Cereals may contain up to 110 calories per ounce (85 calories per ¾ ounce).

5. Select ready-to-eat or hot cereals (always weigh hot cereal *before* cooking). Do not use cereals that are presweetened or that have descriptive names or titles indicating that they are sweetened. Examples of cereal selections are:

A. *Ready-to-Eat*—cornflakes; puffed rice; wheat bran flakes with raisins; unprocessed bran; wheat germ

B. *Hot*—enriched cornmeal; cracked wheat (bulgur); farina; enriched whole hominy or hominy grits; millet; old-fashioned or quick oats

6. For increased fiber intake, select bran cereals.

CORNMEAL MUSH
Limited Choice Plan
Makes 1 Morning Meal serving; supplement as required

In small heavy saucepan add ¼ **teaspoon salt** to **1 cup water** and bring to a boil; slowly stir in **¾ ounce uncooked enriched yellow cornmeal.** Continue stirring until mixture returns to a boil and is smooth. Cover and cook until mixture thickens, 12 to 15 minutes; serve immediately.

Each serving is equivalent to: 1 serving Cereal.

Per serving: 77 calories, 2 g protein, 0.3 g fat, 17 g carbohydrate, 537 mg sodium

Variation: Top with ½ teaspoon honey or maple syrup before serving. Add 1 serving Extras to equivalent listing.

Per serving with maple syrup: 86 calories, 2 g protein, 0.3 g fat, 19 g carbohydrate, 538 mg sodium
With honey: 88 calories, 2 g protein, 0.3 g fat, 20 g carbohydrate, 538 mg sodium

"FRIED" CORNMEAL MUSH
Limited Choice Plan
Makes 1 Morning Meal serving; supplement as required

Spray a 7⅜ x 3⅝ x 2¼-inch loaf pan with nonstick cooking spray; pour **Cornmeal Mush** (see above) into pan, cover, and refrigerate until firm.

Invert chilled mush onto flat surface and cut into 2-inch strips. In small nonstick skillet melt **1 teaspoon margarine** over medium heat. Increase heat to high, add Cornmeal Mush strips, and cook until browned on bottom; turn strips over and brown other side. Serve immediately with ½ **teaspoon honey.**

Each serving is equivalent to: 1 serving Cereal; 1 serving Fats; 1 serving Extras.

Per serving: 122 calories, 2 g protein, 4 g fat, 20 g carbohydrate, 582 mg sodium

Variations:
1. Substitute ½ teaspoon maple syrup for the honey.

Per serving: 119 calories, 2 g protein, 4 g fat, 19 g carbohydrate, 582 mg sodium

2. Substitute ½ cup applesauce (no sugar added) for the honey. Add 1 serving Fruits to equivalent listing and omit Extras.

Per serving: 162 calories, 2 g protein, 4 g fat, 30 g carbohydrate, 584 mg sodium

FARINA WITH RAISINS
Full Choice Plan
Makes 1 Morning Meal serving

¾ cup skim milk, divided
⅓ cup water
⅛ teaspoon salt
¾ ounce quick enriched farina
1 tablespoon raisins

1 teaspoon granulated sugar
1 teaspoon margarine
Artificial sweetener to equal 1
    teaspoon sugar (optional)
⅛ teaspoon vanilla extract

In small saucepan combine ½ cup milk with water and salt and bring to a boil. Gradually stir in farina; add raisins and cook, stirring constantly, 2 to 3 minutes. Stir in sugar, margarine, sweetener if desired, and vanilla. Spoon into a bowl and serve with remaining ¼ cup milk.

Each serving is equivalent to: ¾ serving Milk; 1 serving Cereal; ½ serving Fruits; 2 servings Extras; 1 serving Fats.

Per serving: 224 calories, 9 g protein, 4 g fat, 37 g carbohydrate, 423 mg sodium
Without artificial sweetener: 222 calories, 9 g protein, 4 g fat, 37 g carbohydrate, 423 mg sodium

GRITS AND BACON BITS
Full Choice Plan
Makes 1 Morning Meal serving; supplement as required

½ teaspoon salt
1 cup water
¾ ounce uncooked enriched
    hominy grits

1 teaspoon imitation bacon bits
1 teaspoon margarine

In small saucepan add salt to water and bring to a boil; slowly stir in hominy grits. Allow mixture to return to a boil. Reduce heat, cover, and simmer until grits are cooked, about 20 minutes. Remove from heat and stir in bacon bits; cover and let stand 1 minute. Transfer grits to cereal bowl and top with 1 teaspoon margarine.

Each serving is equivalent to: 1 serving Cereal; 1 serving Extras; 1 serving Fats.

Per serving: 120 calories, 3 g protein, 4 g fat, 17 g carbohydrate, 1,214 mg sodium

MILLET WITH APRICOTS

Limited Choice Plan
Makes 2 Morning Meal servings

1 cup skim milk, divided
½ cup water
1½ ounces uncooked hulled millet
⅛ teaspoon salt
4 canned apricot halves with 2 tablespoons juice (no sugar added)

Artificial sweetener to equal 2 teaspoons sugar
1 teaspoon granulated sugar
1 teaspoon margarine
⅛ teaspoon vanilla extract

In top half of double boiler combine ½ cup milk and water; bring to a boil over direct heat. Gradually stir in millet and salt and cook, stirring constantly, about 5 minutes. Place over hot water, cover tightly, and cook until all liquid is absorbed, 35 to 40 minutes.

Cut apricots into ½-inch pieces. In bowl combine apricots, 2 tablespoons juice, sweetener, sugar, margarine, vanilla, and remaining ½ cup milk. Fold into millet mixture and cook until almost all liquid is absorbed, about 5 minutes.

Each serving is equivalent to: ½ serving Milk; 1 serving Cereal; ½ serving Fruits; 1 serving Extras; ½ serving Fats.

Per serving: 162 calories, 7 g protein, 3 g fat, 30 g carbohydrate, 227 mg sodium

CEREAL WITH PEACH SAUCE

Limited Choice Plan
Makes 2 Morning Meal servings

½ cup skim milk
½ cup canned sliced peaches (no sugar added)
¼ cup plain unflavored yogurt
1 teaspoon honey

1 teaspoon lemon juice
¼ teaspoon grated lemon peel
Dash artificial sweetener
1½ ounces ready-to-eat cereal (not presweetened)

In blender container combine milk, peaches, yogurt, and honey and process until smooth. Add lemon juice, lemon peel, and sweetener and process until combined. Pour ¾ ounce cereal into each of 2 bowls and top each portion with half of the sauce.

Each serving is equivalent to: ½ serving Milk; ½ serving Fruits; 1 serving Extras; 1 serving Cereal.

Per serving: 153 calories, 5 g protein, 1 g fat, 31 g carbohydrate, 309 mg sodium

BREAKFAST RAISIN TURNOVER
Full Choice Plan
Makes 1 Morning Meal serving; supplement as required

Fruit Filling
½ teaspoon arrowroot   2 tablespoons raisins, chopped
1 tablespoon lemon juice

Dough for Turnover
¾ ounce puffed rice   2 tablespoons water
2 teaspoons reduced-calorie
  margarine

To *Prepare Filling:* In small saucepan dissolve arrowroot in lemon juice; add raisins and cook over low heat, stirring constantly, until hot and mixture thickens, about 1 minute. Remove from heat and set aside.

To *Prepare Dough:* Preheat oven to 375°F. In work bowl of food processor or blender container process cereal until consistency of flour; transfer to small bowl. With a pastry blender, or 2 knives used scissor-fashion, cut in margarine until mixture resembles coarse meal. Add water and, using a fork, stir until mixture leaves sides of bowl.

To *Prepare Turnover:* Form dough into a ball. Between 2 sheets of wax paper roll dough into a circle, 5 inches in diameter. Remove top sheet of wax paper and spread fruit filling over half of dough. Carefully fold remaining half of dough over fruit and press to seal edges. Spray a nonstick baking sheet with nonstick cooking spray; peel wax paper from bottom of turnover and transfer turnover to prepared sheet. Bake until crisp on bottom, about 20 minutes; turn and bake 10 minutes longer.

Each serving is equivalent to: ½ serving Extras; 1 serving Fruits; 1 serving Cereal; 1 serving Fats.

Per serving: 179 calories, 2 g protein, 4 g fat, 35 g carbohydrate, 99 mg sodium

FRUITED CEREAL BARS
Full Choice Plan
Makes 4 Morning Meal servings, 1 bar each; supplement as required

3 ounces crunchy nutlike cereal   ⅓ cup thawed frozen concentrated
  nuggets   apple juice (no sugar added)
¼ cup raisins, chopped   1 teaspoon honey
1 teaspoon shredded coconut   1 envelope unflavored gelatin

1. In small bowl combine cereal, raisins, and coconut; set aside.
2. In small saucepan combine apple juice and honey; sprinkle gelatin over mixture and let stand to soften.
3. Cook over low heat, stirring constantly, until gelatin is completely dissolved; pour over cereal mixture and stir until thoroughly combined.
4. Spray a 7⅜ x 3⅝ x 2¼-inch loaf pan with nonstick cooking spray;

pack cereal mixture firmly into pan, cover, and refrigerate overnight or until firm.

5. Loosen edges of fruited cereal with the point of a knife and invert onto plate. Cut into 4 equal bars. Wrap each bar in foil or plastic wrap and store in refrigerator until ready to use.

Each serving is equivalent to: 1 serving Cereal; 1½ servings Fruits; 1¼ servings Extras.

Per serving: 154 calories, 4 g protein, 0.2 g fat, 36 g carbohydrate, 187 mg sodium

STRAWBERRY-TOPPED BRAN CRISPS

Limited Choice Plan
Makes 1 Morning Meal serving, 4 bran crisps; supplement as required

¾ ounce unprocessed bran
1 teaspoon whole wheat flour
1 tablespoon plus 1 teaspoon
  thawed frozen concentrated
  apple juice (no sugar added)

1 teaspoon water
2 teaspoons reduced-calorie
  strawberry spread (16 calories
  per 2 teaspoons)

1. Preheat oven to 250°F. In small bowl, using a fork, combine bran and flour. Add apple juice and water and stir until all bran mixture is moistened.

2. Spray a 15 x 9-inch nonstick cookie sheet with nonstick cooking spray. Spoon bran mixture onto prepared sheet, forming 4 mounds and leaving a space of about 6 inches between each.

3. Cover entire surface with a sheet of wax paper and, using a rolling pin, roll each mound into a circle, about 3 inches in diameter.

4. Bake until crisps are dry, about 30 minutes.

5. Using a metal spatula, remove bran crisps to a rack; let cool.

6. Spread each crisp with ½ teaspoon strawberry spread and serve.

Each serving is equivalent to: 1 serving Cereal; 2⅗ servings Extras; 1 serving Fruits. (See page 407 for Full Choice Plan adjustments.)

Per serving: 109 calories, 4 g protein, 1 g fat, 29 g carbohydrate, 3 mg sodium

Variation: Spoon ¼ cup plain unflavored yogurt into cereal bowl; break cooled bran crisps into bowl and top with strawberry spread. Add ½ serving Milk to equivalent listing.

Per serving: 143 calories, 6 g protein, 3 g fat, 31 g carbohydrate, 29 mg sodium

Bread Substitutes

This section includes a world of ethnic dishes based on potatoes, pasta, and other grains, foods once deemed out of bounds if you were trying to trim down. Select from American yams, German potato salad, Russian kasha varnishkes, Italian lasagna or ditalini, French vichyssoise, and pilaf, the national dish of Turkey, and discover how to be a round-the-world diner without excess "baggage."

Guidelines for Using Bread Substitutes (Full Choice Plan Only)

1. Amounts:
Women, Men, and Youth—1 serving in place of 1 Bread serving.
2. Bread Substitutes may be selected *up to* 3 times weekly. On any given day, *only* one such substitution may be made.
3. Bread Substitute items may be split and combined provided the total serving, per portion, does not exceed 1 serving.
4. Do *not* use homemade cream-style corn.
5. Canned Bread Substitute items should *not* contain sugar, except for canned corn.
6. If 1 ounce of unpopped popping corn, when popped in a hot air popper, yields more than 2 cups, the additional popcorn may be consumed. However, popcorn may be prepared with fat according to manufacturer's directions; if so prepared, 2 cups is the appropriate serving size, regardless of yield. Do not equate the fat used for popping to the daily allotted servings of Fats.
7. Cornmeal, cracked wheat (bulgur), hominy, and millet may be selected as Cereal servings and, therefore, Bread servings, provided the Cereal serving size is used.
8. Uncooked and cooked serving sizes are listed for Bread Substitute items. Depending upon the cooking method used and the length of cooking time, as well as other variables, the uncooked serving size may not yield the indicated cooked amount. For most items, nutritionally the difference is negligible. Therefore, except for very small macaroni products (pastena, orzo, tubettini, etc.), choose whichever serving size is more appropriate to your needs. Use *only* the uncooked weight for very small macaroni products, then cook according to package directions or use as indicated in recipes.

Bread Substitutes Servings

| Selections | One Serving | |
	Uncooked	Cooked
barley	1 ounce	½ cup
buckwheat groats (kasha)	1 ounce	½ cup
corn, fresh, frozen, or canned:		
ear (approximately 5 inches long)	1 medium	1 medium
whole-kernel or cream-style	½ cup	½ cup
cornmeal, enriched	1 ounce	¾ cup
couscous	1 ounce	½ cup
cracked wheat (bulgur)	1 ounce	½ cup
hominy, enriched:		
grits or whole	1 ounce	¾ cup
legumes:		
fresh, frozen, or canned	3 ounces	3 ounces
dry	1 ounce	3 ounces
millet	1 ounce	½ cup
pasta, enriched (commercial or homemade):		
macaroni or spaghetti	1 ounce	⅔ cup
noodles	1 ounce	½ cup
popcorn, plain	1 ounce	2 cups
potato, white	4 ounces	4 ounces
rice, enriched white, or brown, or wild	1 ounce	½ cup
sweet potato or yam	3 ounces	3 ounces
tempeh (fermented soybean cake)	1½ ounces	1½ ounces
tofu (soybean curd)	4 ounces	4 ounces

VICHYSSOISE
Full Choice Plan
Makes 2 servings, about 1⅛ cups each

1 tablespoon plus 1 teaspoon
   reduced-calorie margarine
4 ounces pared potato, diced
½ cup sliced leeks (white portion
   only)

Dash each salt and white pepper
1½ cups Chicken Broth (see
   page 401)
1 cup skim milk

Garnish
1 tablespoon chopped chives

In 1-quart saucepan heat margarine until bubbly; add potato, leeks, salt, and pepper and sauté, over medium heat, until leeks are soft. Add broth and bring mixture to a boil, stirring occasionally. Reduce heat to low, cover, and simmer until potatoes are tender.

Allow potato mixture to cool slightly, then transfer to blender container or work bowl of food processor; process until smooth. Return mixture to saucepan and stir in milk; cook over low heat until soup is hot (*do not boil*). Cool slightly, then cover and refrigerate until thoroughly chilled.

To Serve: Pour into 2 soup bowls and garnish each serving with 1½ teaspoons chopped chives.

Each serving is equivalent to: 1 serving Fats; ½ serving Bread Substitutes; ¼ cup Limited Vegetables; 1 serving Extras; ½ serving Milk.

Per serving: 154 calories, 10 g protein, 4 g fat, 24 g carbohydrate, 250 mg sodium

CREAM OF POTATO SOUP
Full Choice Plan
Makes 2 servings, about 1½ cups each

1 tablespoon plus 1 teaspoon
reduced-calorie margarine
8 ounces pared potatoes, diced
½ cup sliced leeks (white portion
only)

½ teaspoon salt
⅛ teaspoon white pepper
1½ cups Chicken Broth (see
page 401)
1 cup evaporated skimmed milk

Garnish
2 tablespoons chopped chives and
dash ground nutmeg

In 1-quart saucepan heat margarine until bubbly; add potatoes, leeks, salt, and pepper and sauté over medium heat until leeks are soft. Add broth; cover and simmer until potatoes are tender.

Using a slotted spoon, remove half of cooked potatoes and reserve. Pour remaining soup mixture into blender container and process until smooth; return to saucepan. Stir in milk and reserved potatoes and heat (*do not boil*). Divide soup into 2 soup bowls and garnish each portion with chives and nutmeg.

Each serving is equivalent to: 1 serving Fats; 1 serving Bread Substitutes; ¼ cup Limited Vegetables; 1 serving Extras; 1 serving Milk.

Per serving: 254 calories, 17 g protein, 4 g fat, 42 g carbohydrate, 807 mg sodium

WATERCRESS–POTATO SOUP
Full Choice Plan
Makes 2 servings, about ¾ cup each

1 tablespoon plus 1 teaspoon
reduced-calorie margarine
4 ounces pared potato, chopped
1 cup watercress leaves, chopped
½ cup chopped leeks (white
portion only)

2 packets instant chicken broth and
seasoning mix
1½ cups water
Dash each salt and white pepper

1. In 1-quart saucepan heat margarine until bubbly; add potato, watercress, and leeks and sauté, over low heat, until leeks are soft.

2. Sprinkle broth mix over vegetables, then add water, salt, and pepper. Increase heat and bring to a boil, stirring occasionally. Reduce heat, cover, and simmer until potato is tender, 10 to 15 minutes; cool slightly.

3. Transfer soup to blender container and process until smooth.

4. Return soup to saucepan and heat.

Each serving is equivalent to: 1 serving Fats; ½ serving Bread Substitutes; 1 serving Vegetables; ¼ cup Limited Vegetables; 1 serving Extras.

Per serving: 112 calories, 4 g protein, 4 g fat, 16 g carbohydrate, 1,003 mg sodium

OVEN-CRISPED POTATO SLICES

Full Choice Plan
Makes 2 servings

Using a vegetable brush, thoroughly scrub an 8-ounce potato. Preheat oven to 450°F. Using a sharp knife, cut potato into ¼-inch-thick round slices, or slice in work bowl of food processor fitted with slicing disk. On nonstick baking sheet arrange potato slices in 1 layer and sprinkle with dash each salt and white pepper. Bake 10 minutes; using a pancake turner, turn slices over, sprinkle with dash each salt and white pepper, and bake 10 minutes longer.

Each serving is equivalent to: 1 serving Bread Substitutes.

Per serving: 87 calories, 2 g protein, 0.1 g fat, 19 g carbohydrate, 132 mg sodium

OVEN "FRIED" POTATOES

Full Choice Plan
Makes 2 servings

Preheat oven to 350°F. Pare 8 ounces baking potatoes and cut potatoes into thin strips. In medium bowl combine potato strips, 2 teaspoons vegetable oil, and dash each salt and pepper; toss thoroughly so that all oil is used to coat potatoes.

On nonstick baking sheet arrange potatoes, leaving space between strips; bake for 20 minutes. Using a spatula, turn potatoes over; bake until browned and crisp, about 20 minutes longer.

Each serving is equivalent to: 1 serving Bread Substitutes; 1 serving Fats.

Per serving: 128 calories, 2 g protein, 5 g fat, 19 g carbohydrate, 68 mg sodium

CREAMY BAKED POTATOES

Full Choice Plan
Makes 4 servings

4 potatoes (4 ounces each), well
   scrubbed and baked
½ cup plain unflavored yogurt

1 tablespoon plus 1 teaspoon
   margarine, melted
2 teaspoons chopped chives
Dash each salt and white pepper

Preheat oven to 350°F. Cut each baked potato in half lengthwise. Scoop pulp from 4 halves into bowl, leaving firm shells; reserve shells. Scoop pulp from remaining 4 halves, discarding skins; add pulp to bowl and mash until smooth. Add remaining ingredients and stir to combine. Spoon ¼ of potato mixture into each reserved shell; transfer to baking sheet and bake until thoroughly heated, about 20 minutes.

Each serving is equivalent to: 1 serving Bread Substitutes; ¼ serving Milk; 1 serving Fats.

Per serving: 138 calories, 3 g protein, 5 g fat, 21 g carbohydrate, 93 mg sodium

CREAMY SCALLOPED POTATOES

Full Choice Plan
Makes 2 servings

1 tablespoon plus 1 teaspoon
  reduced-calorie margarine
1 tablespoon plus ¾ teaspoon
  enriched all-purpose flour
Dash each salt and white pepper

1 cup skim milk, heated
8 ounces pared potatoes, thinly
  sliced
¼ cup diced onion

In small saucepan heat margarine, over low heat, until bubbly; add flour, salt, and pepper and cook, stirring constantly, for 2 minutes. Add milk and cook, stirring constantly, until mixture is smooth and thickened. Remove from heat.

Preheat oven to 350°F. Spray shallow 1-quart casserole with nonstick cooking spray; layer half of the potatoes in casserole, then half of the diced onion. Stir sauce and spoon half over onion layer. Repeat layers with remaining potatoes, onion, and sauce. Cover and bake until potatoes are tender, about 20 minutes. Remove cover and bake until golden, about 10 minutes longer.

Each serving is equivalent to: 1 serving Fats; ¼ serving Bread; ½ serving Milk; 1 serving Bread Substitutes; ⅛ cup Limited Vegetables.

Per serving: 190 calories, 8 g protein, 4 g fat, 31 g carbohydrate, 228 mg sodium

CONFETTI POTATOES

Full Choice Plan
Makes 2 servings

2 teaspoons vegetable oil
8 ounces peeled boiled potatoes,
  cut into cubes*
1 medium red bell pepper, seeded
  and cut into 1 x ¼-inch strips

1 medium green bell pepper,
  seeded and cut into 1 x ¼-inch
  strips
1 tablespoon chopped chives
Dash each salt and pepper

In small skillet heat oil; add potatoes and pepper strips and sauté, turning occasionally, until potatoes are lightly browned and peppers are tender-crisp. Gently stir in chives, salt, and pepper and cook 2 to 4 minutes longer.

Each serving is equivalent to: 1 serving Fats; 1 serving Bread Substitutes; 2 servings Vegetables.

Per serving: 143 calories, 4 g protein, 5 g fat, 23 g carbohydrate, 82 mg sodium

* For Parisian potatoes, use potato balls.

OVEN-BAKED POTATO PANCAKES

Full Choice Plan
Makes 2 servings, 3 pancakes each

Delicious served with applesauce or "Sour Cream" (see page 374).

4 ounces peeled cooked potato,
    mashed and cooled
⅓ cup plus 2 teaspoons skim milk
2 tablespoons plus 1½ teaspoons
    enriched self-rising flour

2 teaspoons margarine, softened
1 tablespoon chopped chives
⅛ teaspoon salt

Preheat oven to 400°F. In small bowl combine mashed potato, milk, flour, and margarine; using an electric mixer, beat at low speed until blended. Increase speed to high and beat about 1 minute longer; stir in chives.

Drop batter by tablespoonsful onto nonstick baking sheet, forming 6 pancakes; sprinkle each with salt. Bake until pancakes are golden brown, about 10 minutes; turn pancakes over and bake until crisp, 3 to 5 minutes longer.

Each serving is equivalent to: ½ serving Bread Substitutes; 3 tablespoons Skim Milk (³⁄₁₆ serving Milk); ½ serving Bread; 1 serving Fats.

Per serving: 124 calories, 4 g protein, 4 g fat, 18 g carbohydrate, 320 mg sodium

POTATO–ONION BISCUITS

Full Choice Plan
Makes 2 servings, 3 biscuits each

4 ounces peeled cooked potato,
    mashed and cooled
2 tablespoons plus 1½ teaspoons
    enriched self-rising flour

2 tablespoons skim milk
2 tablespoons minced onion
2 teaspoons margarine, softened
⅛ teaspoon salt

Preheat oven to 350°F. In small mixing bowl combine all ingredients except salt; using an electric mixer, beat at low speed until blended. Increase speed to high and beat for about 1 minute longer.

Drop batter by heaping tablespoonsful onto nonstick baking sheet, forming 6 biscuits; sprinkle each with salt. Bake until biscuits are golden brown, 12 to 15 minutes. Serve immediately.

Each serving is equivalent to: ½ serving Bread Substitutes; ½ serving Bread; 1 tablespoon Skim Milk (¹⁄₁₆ serving Milk); 1 tablespoon Limited Vegetables; 1 serving Fats.

Per serving: 116 calories, 3 g protein, 4 g fat, 17 g carbohydrate, 303 mg sodium

HOT GERMAN POTATO SALAD
Full Choice Plan
Makes 2 servings

2 teaspoons vegetable oil
¼ cup thinly sliced onion
2 teaspoons imitation bacon bits
2 tablespoons cider vinegar

1 teaspoon granulated sugar
Dash each salt and pepper
8 ounces peeled cooked potatoes, thinly sliced

In small skillet heat oil over medium heat; add onion slices and bacon bits and sauté until slices are translucent. Add vinegar, sugar, salt, and pepper and cook, stirring occasionally, until mixture starts to boil. Add potatoes and cook, stirring gently, until thoroughly heated. Serve hot.

Each serving is equivalent to: 1 serving Fats; ⅛ cup Limited Vegetables; 2 servings Extras; 1 serving Bread Substitutes.

Per serving: 142 calories, 3 g protein, 5 g fat, 22 g carbohydrate, 164 mg sodium

STUFFED SWEET POTATOES
Full Choice Plan
Makes 4 servings, ½ potato each

Using a vegetable brush, scrub **two 6-ounce sweet potatoes** well. Wrap each potato in foil and place on baking sheet; bake at 425°F. until tender, 40 to 45 minutes. Remove foil and let potatoes stand until cool enough to handle.

Cut each potato in half lengthwise; scoop pulp out into medium bowl and reserve shells. Add **2 teaspoons honey** and ⅛ **teaspoon each ground cinnamon and nutmeg** to bowl and, using an electric mixer, beat until potato mixture is smooth and fluffy. Spoon ¼ of mixture into each reserved shell. Bake on baking sheet at 350°F. until heated through, 15 to 20 minutes.

Each serving is equivalent to: 1 serving Bread Substitutes; 1 serving Extras.

Per serving: 108 calories, 1 g protein, 0.4 g fat, 25 g carbohydrate, 9 mg sodium

"FRENCH-FRIED" YAMS
Full Choice Plan
Makes 4 servings

2 medium yams
2 teaspoons margarine

1 teaspoon vegetable oil
½ teaspoon salt

Garnish
Parsley sprigs

On baking sheet bake yams at 350°F. until just tender, about 25 minutes (*do not overbake*). Cool yams; peel and discard skins. Cut yams into 2 x ¼-inch sticks; weigh 12 ounces potato sticks (remaining yam can be frozen for use at a later date).

In 9-inch skillet combine margarine and oil; heat. Add yams and cook over medium heat, stirring constantly, until crispy outside and tender inside. Sprinkle with salt and serve garnished with parsley.

Each serving is equivalent to: 1 serving Bread Substitutes; ¾ serving Fats.

Per serving: 119 calories, 2 g protein, 3 g fat, 21 g carbohydrate, 332 mg sodium

Variation: Omit salt and sprinkle cooked yams with 1 teaspoon granulated brown sugar. Add ½ serving Extras to equivalent listing.

Per serving: 124 calories, 2 g protein, 3 g fat, 22 g carbohydrate, 63 mg sodium

PINEAPPLE-STUFFED YAMS

Full Choice Plan
Makes 4 servings, ½ stuffed yam each

2 yams (6 ounces each), well
  scrubbed and baked
1 tablespoon plus 1 teaspoon
  margarine

½ cup canned crushed pineapple
  (no sugar added)
¼ teaspoon apple pie spice, or to
  taste
Dash salt

Preheat oven to 400°F. Cut each yam in half lengthwise. Scoop out pulp into mixing bowl, leaving firm shells; reserve shells. Mash pulp until smooth. Stir in margarine; add crushed pineapple, apple pie spice, and salt and stir to combine. Spoon ¼ of yam mixture into each reserved shell, mounding mixture. Set stuffed shells in shallow baking pan and bake until thoroughly heated, about 15 minutes. Turn oven control to broil and broil yams until slightly browned, about 3 minutes.

Each serving is equivalent to: 1 serving Bread Substitutes; 1 serving Fats; ¼ serving Fruits.

Per serving: 145 calories, 2 g protein, 4 g fat, 26 g carbohydrate, 118 mg sodium

LASAGNA

Full Choice Plan
Makes 4 Midday or Evening Meal servings

1 tablespoon plus 1 teaspoon olive
  or vegetable oil
¾ cup chopped onions
1 teaspoon minced fresh garlic
8 ounces cooked ground beef,
  crumbled
1 cup sliced mushrooms
3 cups canned plum tomatoes,
  crushed
2 teaspoons basil leaves
1 teaspoon granulated sugar

1 teaspoon salt
¼ teaspoon pepper, divided
⅔ cup part-skim ricotta cheese
2 ounces mozzarella cheese
2 tablespoons chopped fresh
  parsley
4 ounces uncooked enriched
  lasagna macaroni, cooked
  according to package directions
1 tablespoon plus 1 teaspoon grated
  Parmesan cheese

1. In 2-quart saucepan heat oil; add onions and garlic and sauté until onions are translucent, about 3 minutes.
2. Add beef and mushrooms and cook until mushrooms begin to soften, about 3 minutes.
3. Add tomatoes, basil, sugar, salt, and ⅛ teaspoon pepper; bring to a boil. Reduce heat and simmer for 20 minutes.
4. While sauce is simmering, in bowl combine ricotta and mozzarella cheeses with parsley and remaining ⅛ teaspoon pepper; set aside.
5. In bottom of an 8 x 8-inch baking pan spread a thin layer of meat sauce; top with alternate layers of cooked lasagna macaroni, cheese mixture, and meat sauce, ending with a layer of meat sauce. Sprinkle with Parmesan cheese.
6. Bake at 375°F. for 40 minutes. Remove from oven and allow to stand 15 minutes before serving.

Each serving is equivalent to: 1 serving Fats; 3 tablespoons Limited Vegetables; 2 ounces Meat Group; 2 servings Vegetables; 1½ servings Extras; ⅙ cup Soft Cheese; ½ ounce Hard Cheese; 1 serving Bread Substitutes.

Per serving: 438 calories, 30 g protein, 19 g fat, 37 g carbohydrate, 953 mg sodium

PASTA ALFREDO STYLE
Full Choice Plan
Makes 4 Midday or Evening Meal servings*

1 tablespoon plus 1 teaspoon margarine
1 garlic clove, minced
6 ounces diced boiled ham
4 ounces uncooked enriched linguine or spaghetti, cooked according to package directions

⅔ cup cottage cheese, creamed in blender
2 ounces grated Parmesan cheese
Dash white pepper, or to taste

In 10-inch skillet heat margarine until bubbly; add garlic and sauté until golden. Add ham and sauté until lightly browned. Add remaining ingredients and cook, tossing occasionally, until heated through. Serve immediately.

Each serving is equivalent to: 1 serving Fats; 1½ ounces Meat Group (cured); 1 serving Bread Substitutes; ⅙ cup Soft Cheese; ½ ounce Hard Cheese.

Per serving: 322 calories, 25 g protein, 14 g fat, 23 g carbohydrate, 846 mg sodium

Variation: For a creamier pasta, add ¼ cup plain unflavored yogurt with "remaining ingredients." Add ⅛ serving Milk to equivalent listing.

Per serving: 331 calories, 25 g protein, 14 g fat, 24 g carbohydrate, 853 mg sodium

* Men—One serving provides ⅞ of a meal. Supplement with an additional ⅛ serving of Protein at the Midday or Evening Meal.

DITALINI SALAD
Full Choice Plan
Makes 4 servings

4 ounces uncooked enriched ditalini,* cooked according to package directions and chilled
1 medium tomato, blanched, peeled, and diced
1 medium green bell pepper, seeded and diced
1 medium dill pickle, diced, with 2 teaspoons brine

½ cup diced pimientos
¼ cup diced red onion
¼ cup mayonnaise
8 green olives, pitted and diced
2 tablespoons chopped fresh parsley
2 tablespoons lemon juice
¼ teaspoon each salt and pepper

In medium bowl combine all ingredients and toss. Cover and chill for at least 1 hour before serving.

Each serving is equivalent to: 1 serving Bread Substitutes; 1¾ servings Vegetables; 1 tablespoon Limited Vegetables; 3 servings Fats; 1 serving Extras.

Per serving: 242 calories, 5 g protein, 13 g fat, 28 g carbohydrate, 646 mg sodium

* Other small tube macaroni (e.g., tubetti, elbow macaroni, etc.) can be substituted for the ditalini.

NOODLE SALAD
Full Choice Plan
Makes 2 servings

Dressing

1 teaspoon each salt and chopped fresh dill
1 teaspoon each vegetable oil and cider vinegar

½ teaspoon minced fresh garlic
¼ teaspoon lemon juice
Dash pepper

Salad

2 ounces uncooked enriched egg bows, cooked according to package directions and chilled

1 medium tomato, diced
¼ cup thinly sliced onion, separated into rings

To Prepare Dressing: In jar with tight-fitting cover or bowl combine all ingredients for dressing and mix thoroughly; chill, covered.

To Prepare Salad: In salad bowl combine all ingredients for salad and toss; shake or stir chilled dressing, pour over salad, and toss to coat. Serve immediately.

Each serving is equivalent to: ½ serving Fats; 1 serving Bread Substitutes; 1 serving Vegetables; ⅛ cup Limited Vegetables.

Per serving: 151 calories, 5 g protein, 3 g fat, 27 g carbohydrate, 1,080 mg sodium

DILLED CARROT–NOODLE MIX
Full Choice Plan
Makes 2 servings

1 tablespoon margarine	½ teaspoon salt
1 cup grated carrots	Dash pepper
2 tablespoons diced onion	2 ounces uncooked enriched egg
1 tablespoon chopped fresh dill	bows, cooked according to
1 teaspoon minced fresh garlic	package directions

In 9-inch nonstick skillet heat margarine, over medium heat, until bubbly; add remaining ingredients except egg bows and sauté until vegetables are tender. Reduce heat to low, stir in egg bows, and cook until noodles are heated and flavors are blended, 2 to 3 minutes. Serve immediately.

Each serving is equivalent to: 1½ servings Fats; 1 serving Vegetables; 1 tablespoon Limited Vegetables; 1 serving Bread Substitutes.

Per serving: 195 calories, 5 g protein, 7 g fat, 28 g carbohydrate, 636 mg sodium

NOODLE PUDDING
Full Choice Plan
Makes 4 Mealtime servings, 1 Morning or ½ Midday or Evening Meal each; supplement as required

1 cup skim milk	1 teaspoon grated lemon or orange
1-inch piece vanilla bean, cut in	peel
half lengthwise	½ teaspoon ground cinnamon
½ cup raisins	⅛ teaspoon each salt and ground
1 tablespoon plus 1 teaspoon	nutmeg
margarine	4 ounces uncooked enriched wide
4 eggs, separated	noodles, cooked according to
2 teaspoons granulated sugar	package directions
Artificial sweetener to equal 2	
teaspoons sugar	

1. In small saucepan heat milk with vanilla bean until tiny bubbles form around edge.
2. Remove pan from heat and add raisins and margarine; let stand for 10 minutes.
3. Preheat oven to 350°F. In large bowl beat together egg yolks, sugar, sweetener, lemon or orange peel, cinnamon, salt, and nutmeg; gently stir in noodles. Remove vanilla bean from milk and add milk to noodle mixture.
4. In small mixing bowl beat egg whites until soft peaks form; fold whites, ⅓ at a time, into noodle mixture.
5. Spray 1½-quart casserole with nonstick cooking spray. Transfer noodle mixture to casserole and bake until firm, about 25 minutes.

Each serving is equivalent to: ¼ serving Milk; 1 serving Fruits; 1 serving Fats; 1 Egg; 1 serving Extras; 1 serving Bread Substitutes.

Per serving: 309 calories, 12 g protein, 11 g fat, 41 g carbohydrate, 222 mg sodium

RICE

Rice is a grain that has been consumed since ancient times. Available brown and white, its versatility makes it appropriate for almost any cuisine. Add new interest to your menus by trying different varieties.

Brown rice, sometimes called natural brown rice, hulled rice, or whole unpolished rice, has had the outer husk and a small amount of the bran removed. Due to the presence of the bran, brown rice requires a longer cooking time than white rice; the bran also supplies it with a delicate, nutlike flavor.

White rice is available in short-, medium-, and long-grain varieties. Short- and medium-grain rice become tender, moist, and glutinous when cooked, making them ideal for molding, as well as for dishes in which a creamy consistency is desired.

Long-grain rice, the type most preferred in the United States, is four to five times longer than it is wide. When cooked, the grains are fluffy and separate. Long-grain rice requires a longer growing season than the short and medium varieties and is, therefore, more expensive.

Three types of long-grain rice are available. Since they each require a different cooking method, when using uncooked rice be sure to use the type specified in the recipe. Once cooked, however, they are virtually interchangeable. The three types of long-grain rice are:

Regular rice, sometimes called white or polished, is the most widely used rice on the market today. It has had the outer husk removed, then several outer layers ground away in the milling process.

Converted rice, sometimes called parboiled, has undergone a special steam-pressure process in order to retain much of the nutrient value lost in the milling. When cooked, this type of rice holds up well; its grains are firmer, plumper, and more separate than those of regular rice.

Quick-cooking rice, sometimes called instant or precooked, has been milled, cooked, and dehydrated. Therefore, when this type is used, it is actually reconstituted rather than cooked. Generally, quick-cooking rice is slightly more expensive than regular and converted rice.

CHINESE RICE AND VERMICELLI

Full Choice Plan
Makes 4 servings

2 teaspoons margarine
½ cup chopped scallions (green onions) or onion
½ teaspoon minced fresh garlic
2 ounces uncooked enriched vermicelli, broken into ½-inch pieces
2 ounces uncooked regular long-grain enriched rice

½ cup sliced mushrooms
2 packets instant beef broth and seasoning mix, dissolved in 1½ cups hot water
2 teaspoons soy sauce
½ cup frozen peas
Dash each salt and pepper

Garnish
1 tablespoon chopped fresh parsley

1. In 9-inch skillet heat margarine, over medium heat, until bubbly; add scallions or onion and garlic and sauté briefly (about 1 minute).
2. Add vermicelli and rice and cook, stirring constantly, until browned (*be careful not to burn*).
3. Add mushrooms and stir to combine. Stir in dissolved broth mix and soy sauce; cover and simmer for 15 minutes.
4. Add peas, salt, and pepper; cover and continue simmering until rice is tender, 5 to 10 minutes longer (all liquid should be absorbed and mixture should be dry). Serve garnished with chopped parsley.

Each serving is equivalent to: ½ serving Fats; ¼ cup Limited Vegetables; 1 serving Bread Substitutes; ¼ serving Vegetables; ½ serving Extras.

Per serving: 151 calories, 5 g protein, 2 g fat, 28 g carbohydrate, 678 mg sodium

SESAME RICE
Full Choice Plan
Makes 2 servings

Delicious as a side dish with chicken or pork.

2 teaspoons Chinese sesame oil
¼ cup each finely diced celery, carrot, and green bell pepper
2 tablespoons thinly sliced scallion (green onion)
1 teaspoon minced fresh garlic

2 ounces uncooked brown rice
1 packet instant onion broth and seasoning mix, dissolved in 1½ cups hot water
2 teaspoons sesame seed, toasted

Garnish
Parsley sprigs

In 1-quart saucepan heat oil over medium heat; add celery, carrot, green pepper, scallion, and garlic and sauté until vegetables are tender-crisp. Add rice and dissolved broth mix; bring to a boil. Reduce heat, cover, and simmer, stirring occasionally, until all moisture is absorbed.

Remove pan from heat and stir in sesame seed. Transfer to serving plate and garnish with parsley sprigs.

Each serving is equivalent to: 1 serving Fats; ¾ serving Vegetables; 1 tablespoon Limited Vegetables; 1 serving Bread Substitutes; 2½ servings Extras.

Per serving: 181 calories, 4 g protein, 7 g fat, 27 g carbohydrate, 415 mg sodium

RISI E BISI
Full Choice Plan
*Makes 2 Midday or Evening Meal servings**

Serve with mixed green salad. In Italy, this popular Venetian dish is usually made with prosciutto and is therefore more salty than our version. If desired, prosciutto can be substituted for the boiled ham.

1 tablespoon plus 1 teaspoon
    margarine, divided
½ cup diced onion
4½ ounces diced boiled ham
2 ounces uncooked converted
    enriched rice

½ cup peas
1½ cups Chicken Broth (see
    page 401)
1 ounce grated Parmesan cheese

Garnish
Parsley sprigs

In 1½- or 2-quart saucepan heat 2 teaspoons margarine, over medium heat, until bubbly; add onion and sauté until translucent. Stir in ham, rice, and peas and cook until rice is "buttery" and opaque, about 2 minutes. Add broth; bring to a boil. Reduce heat and simmer, stirring occasionally, until all liquid is absorbed.

Remove pan from heat; stir in cheese and remaining 2 teaspoons margarine. Transfer to serving dish, garnish with parsley, and serve immediately.

Each serving is equivalent to: 2 servings Fats; ½ cup Limited Vegetables; 2¼ ounces Meat Group (cured); 1 serving Bread Substitutes; 1 serving Extras; ½ ounce Hard Cheese.

Per serving: 413 calories, 31 g protein, 18 g fat, 35 g carbohydrate, 1,013 mg sodium

* Men—Add ¾ ounce diced boiled ham to each portion of Risi e Bisi. Change equivalent listing to 3 ounces Meat Group (cured).

CURRIED RAISIN-RICE
Full Choice Plan
Makes 2 servings

1 cup cooked enriched rice
¾ cup Chicken Broth (see page
    401)
½ cup diced celery
¼ cup diced onion

¼ cup raisins
½ teaspoon each curry powder and
    salt
Dash pepper

Preheat oven to 375°F. In shallow 1-quart casserole combine all ingredients; bake, stirring occasionally, until broth is absorbed, about 30 minutes.

Each serving is equivalent to: 1 serving Bread Substitutes; ½ serving Extras; ½ serving Vegetables; ⅛ cup Limited Vegetables; 1 serving Fruits.

Per serving: 186 calories, 5 g protein, 0.3 g fat, 44 g carbohydrate, 594 mg sodium

CUSTARD–RICE PUDDING
Full Choice Plan
Makes 4 servings, about ¾ cup each

2 cups skim milk
2 envelopes (two 4-ounce servings
    each) reduced-calorie custard
    mix

1 cup cooked enriched rice
½ cup raisins
1 teaspoon vanilla extract

Garnish
Ground cinnamon or nutmeg

In small saucepan heat milk to a simmer; stirring constantly, add custard mix and cook until dissolved, at least 1 minute. Allow to cool for 3 to 5 minutes. In bowl combine rice, raisins, and extract; stir into cooled custard. Spoon ¼ of mixture into each of four 6-ounce custard cups or dessert dishes; garnish each portion with dash cinnamon or nutmeg. Cover and refrigerate until set.

Each serving is equivalent to: 1 serving Milk Substitutes; ½ serving Bread Substitutes; 1 serving Fruits.

Per serving: 193 calories, 7 g protein, 0.1 g fat, 42 g carbohydrate, 110 mg sodium

CONFETTI CORN SAUTÉ
Full Choice Plan
Makes 2 servings

1 teaspoon margarine
2 tablespoons each diced red and
   green bell pepper
1 tablespoon minced onion

1 cup drained canned whole-kernel
   corn
Dash ground red pepper

In small nonstick skillet heat margarine, over medium heat, until bubbly; add bell peppers and onion and sauté until tender. Stir in corn and ground red pepper. Increase heat and cook, stirring constantly, until corn is lightly browned, about 1 minute.

Each serving is equivalent to: ½ serving Fats; ¼ serving Vegetables; 1½ teaspoons Limited Vegetables; 1 serving Bread Substitutes.

Per serving: 110 calories, 3 g protein, 2 g fat, 23 g carbohydrate, 271 mg sodium

POPCORN–RAISIN TREAT
Full Choice Plan
Makes 2 servings

1 teaspoon margarine
1 cup prepared plain popcorn
¾ ounce bite-size shredded wheat
   biscuits
2 tablespoons raisins

1 teaspoon dry-roasted sunflower
   seed
½ teaspoon granulated brown
   sugar
¼ teaspoon ground cinnamon

In 9-inch skillet melt margarine over medium heat; add remaining ingredients except cinnamon and, using a spoon, toss lightly to coat. Sprinkle with cinnamon.

Each serving is equivalent to: ½ serving Fats; ¼ serving Bread Substitutes; ½ serving Bread; ½ serving Fruits; 1½ servings Extras.

Per serving: 126 calories, 3 g protein, 3 g fat, 23 g carbohydrate, 28 mg sodium

BULGUR PILAF
Full Choice Plan
Makes 2 servings

¾ cup Chicken Broth* (see page 401)
2 ounces uncooked cracked wheat (bulgur)
¼ cup shredded carrot

2 tablespoons sliced scallion (green onion)
1 tablespoon each finely diced celery and green bell pepper
Dash each salt and pepper

Preheat oven to 325°F. Spray a 1-quart casserole with nonstick cooking spray; combine all ingredients in prepared casserole. Bake until bulgur has absorbed all of the broth, 25 to 30 minutes.

Each serving is equivalent to: ½ serving Extras; 1 serving Bread Substitutes; ⅓ serving Vegetables; 1 tablespoon Limited Vegetables.

Per serving: 118 calories, 5 g protein, 1 g fat, 27 g carbohydrate, 90 mg sodium

* When pilaf is used as an accompaniment to a beef dish, substitute Beef Broth (see page 401) for the Chicken Broth.

GRITS AND BACON
Full Choice Plan
Makes 1 Midday or Evening Meal serving*

1 ounce uncooked enriched hominy grits
3 ounces Canadian-style bacon, cut into ⅛-inch-thick slices

1 teaspoon margarine
½ medium tomato, sliced

Garnish
1 teaspoon chopped fresh parsley

1. In small saucepan bring 1¼ cups water to a boil; slowly stir in hominy grits and allow mixture to return to a boil.
2. Reduce heat to low, cover, and simmer until grits are cooked, about 20 minutes.
3. In small nonstick skillet cook bacon, turning once, until browned on both sides.
4. Spoon cooked grits onto plate and top with margarine; serve with bacon and tomato slices and garnish with parsley. Serve immediately.

Each serving is equivalent to: 1 serving Bread Substitutes; 3 ounces Meat Group (cured); 1 serving Fats; 1 serving Vegetables.

Per serving: 384 calories, 26 g protein, 19 g fat, 26 g carbohydrate, 2,223 mg sodium

* Men—Use 4 ounces Canadian-style bacon for each portion of Grits and Bacon. Change equivalent listing to 4 ounces Meat Group (cured).

KASHA VARNISHKES
Full Choice Plan
Makes 4 servings

1½ cups Beef Broth (see page
    401)
2 ounces uncooked fine buckwheat
    groats (kasha)
1 tablespoon plus 1 teaspoon
    vegetable oil

½ cup diced onion
1 cup sliced mushrooms
2 ounces uncooked enriched
    bowtie macaroni, cooked
    according to package directions
Dash pepper, or to taste

In 1-quart saucepan bring broth to a boil; add kasha. Reduce heat, cover, and simmer until all liquid is absorbed, 15 to 20 minutes.

While kasha is cooking, in 9-inch skillet heat oil; add onion and sauté until softened. Add mushrooms and sauté until mushrooms are cooked.

Add mushroom mixture and macaroni to cooked kasha and, using a fork, toss to combine. Season with pepper and serve immediately.

Each serving is equivalent to: ½ serving Extras; 1 serving Bread Substitutes; 1 serving Fats; ⅛ cup Limited Vegetables; ½ serving Vegetables.

Per serving: 160 calories, 5 g protein, 5 g fat, 24 g carbohydrate, 10 mg sodium

MUSHROOM–BARLEY SOUP
Full Choice Plan
Makes 4 servings

1 quart plus ½ cup Beef Broth
    (see page 401)
2 cups water
1 cup each diced celery and carrots
2 ounces uncooked barley
2 teaspoons margarine, divided

½ cup diced onion
4 cups sliced mushrooms
1 tablespoon chopped fresh parsley
1 teaspoon salt
¼ teaspoon pepper

1. In 3-quart saucepan combine broth and water and bring to a boil; add celery, carrots, and barley. Reduce heat, cover, and simmer for 20 minutes.

2. In 12-inch nonstick skillet heat 1 teaspoon margarine until bubbly; add onion and sauté until translucent.

3. Add sautéed onion to broth mixture and continue simmering, partially covered, for 25 minutes longer, adding additional water if mixture becomes too thick.

4. In same skillet heat remaining teaspoon margarine until bubbly; add mushrooms and sauté for 5 minutes.

5. Add sautéed mushrooms to soup and continue simmering, partially covered, for 15 minutes longer. Just before serving stir in parsley, salt, and pepper.

Each serving is equivalent to: 1½ servings Extras; 3 servings Vegetables; ½ serving Bread Substitutes; ½ serving Fats; ⅛ cup Limited Vegetables.

Per serving: 128 calories, 5 g protein, 3 g fat, 23 g carbohydrate, 638 mg sodium

Variation: *Beef–Barley Soup* (makes 4 Midday or Evening Meal Servings)—Add 1 pound diced cooked beef to broth with carrots, celery, and barley. Add 4 ounces Meat Group to equivalent listing.

Per serving: 275 calories, 35 g protein, 11 g fat, 6 g carbohydrate, 219 mg sodium

BLACK BEAN SOUP
Full Choice Plan
Makes 4 Midday or Evening Meal servings, ¼ meal each; supplement as required

This recipe yields about 1 cup soup per serving.

4 ounces uncooked black beans
1 quart water
1 tablespoon plus 1 teaspoon margarine
¼ cup diced onion
1 teaspoon chopped fresh garlic
2¼ cups Chicken Broth (see page 401)
½ cup each chopped carrot and celery

1½ teaspoons white vinegar
1 bay leaf
2 tablespoons plus 2 teaspoons dry red wine
¼ teaspoon salt
⅛ teaspoon pepper
1 teaspoon lemon juice*
2 eggs, hard-cooked and chopped

1. Sort and rinse beans. In 2-quart saucepan add beans to water and bring to a boil. Boil for 2 minutes, then remove from heat and let stand for 1 hour.
2. Return saucepan to heat, bring mixture to a boil, and cook for 30 minutes. Drain beans, reserving 1 cup cooking liquid; set beans and liquid aside.
3. In same saucepan heat margarine until bubbly; add onion and garlic and sauté until softened. Add broth, carrot, celery, beans, reserved cooking liquid, vinegar, and bay leaf to saucepan and bring to a boil. Reduce heat, cover, and cook until beans are very soft, about 1½ hours. Cool slightly and remove bay leaf.
4. Pour 1½ cups soup into blender container or work bowl of food processor and process until smooth. Transfer mixture to a 2-quart bowl and repeat procedure with remaining soup, 1½ cups at a time, until all soup is processed.
5. Pour soup back into saucepan; add wine, salt, and pepper and bring to a boil. Reduce heat and simmer 5 minutes.
6. Stir in lemon juice and pour soup into 4 bowls; garnish each portion with ¼ of the chopped eggs.

Each serving is equivalent to: 1 serving Bread Substitutes; 1 serving Fats; 1 tablespoon Limited Vegetables; 1¾ servings Extras; ½ serving Vegetables; ½ Egg.

Per serving: 202 calories, 13 g protein, 7 g fat, 24 g carbohydrate, 266 mg sodium

* For a slightly more tart flavor increase lemon juice to 2 teaspoons.

HOT TOFU SOUP
Full Choice Plan
Makes 1 serving

Cut 4 ounces tofu (soybean curd) into small cubes. In small saucepan heat 1 cup tomato or mixed vegetable juice; add tofu and simmer until tofu is thoroughly heated, 1 to 2 minutes. Pour into soup bowl and garnish with a **parsley sprig.**
Each serving is equivalent to: 1 serving Bread Substitutes; 1 serving Bonus.

Per serving: 128 calories, 11 g protein, 5 g fat, 13 g carbohydrate, 488 mg sodium

Variation: *Chilled Tofu Soup*—In blender container combine tofu and tomato or mixed vegetable juice and process until smooth. Chill, covered, and serve garnished with parsley sprig.

ROASTED SOYBEAN SNACK
Full Choice Plan
Makes 3 servings, about ⅓ cup each

Enjoy as a snack or on a tossed salad.

9 ounces drained canned soybeans	**1 teaspoon imitation butter-**
1½ teaspoons grated Parmesan	**flavored salt**
cheese	**⅛ teaspoon each garlic powder and**
	onion powder

Preheat oven to 250°F. On nonstick baking sheet spread soybeans in a single layer; bake in middle of center oven rack until dry, about 1 hour.
Turn oven control to broil and broil soybeans 6 inches from heat source until extra crispy, about 1 minute. Remove from broiler and allow to cool.
Transfer beans to small bowl; add remaining ingredients and toss thoroughly. Serve immediately or transfer to an air-tight container, cover, and refrigerate.
Each serving is equivalent to: 1 serving Bread Substitutes; ½ serving Extras.

Per serving: 119 calories, 10 g protein, 5 g fat, 10 g carbohydrate, 733 mg sodium (estimated)

GARBANZO DIP
Full Choice Plan
Makes 2 servings

6 ounces drained canned chick-peas	**⅛ teaspoon each salt and minced**
(garbanzo beans)	**fresh garlic**
¼ cup reduced-calorie mayonnaise	**Dash white pepper**
2 teaspoons finely chopped scallion	
(green onion)	

In blender container combine chick-peas and mayonnaise; process until smooth. Add remaining ingredients and process until just combined.

Each serving is equivalent to: 1 serving Bread Substitutes; 3 servings Fats; 1 teaspoon Limited Vegetables.

Per serving: 173 calories, 6 g protein, 7 g fat, 22 g carbohydrate, 296 mg sodium (estimated)

CANNELLINI BEAN SALAD
Full Choice Plan
Makes 2 servings

2 teaspoons olive oil
½ cup each finely diced celery and carrot
2 garlic cloves, minced
6 ounces drained canned white kidney beans (cannellini beans)

1 tablespoon minced fresh parsley
1 teaspoon red wine vinegar
½ teaspoon each salt and lemon juice
Dash each dill weed and pepper

In small skillet heat oil; add celery, carrot, and garlic and sauté until tender. Transfer to a bowl and add remaining ingredients; toss to combine. Cover and chill at least 1 hour before serving.

Each serving is equivalent to: 1 serving Fats; 1 serving Vegetables; 1 serving Bread Substitutes.

Per serving: 161 calories, 7 g protein, 5 g fat, 23 g carbohydrate, 596 mg sodium (estimated)

SPICY PEACHES 'N' BEANS
Full Choice Plan
Makes 2 servings

6 ounces drained canned white kidney beans (cannellini beans)
1 cup canned sliced peaches (no sugar added)

1 medium tomato, blanched, peeled, and diced
2 teaspoons granulated brown sugar
2 teaspoons Dijon-style mustard
¼ teaspoon ground ginger

Preheat oven to 350°F. In shallow 1-quart casserole combine all ingredients, reserving some peach slices for garnish. Arrange reserved peach slices over bean mixture and bake until peaches are lightly browned, 25 to 30 minutes.

Each serving is equivalent to: 1 serving Bread Substitutes; 1 serving Fruits; 1 serving Vegetables; 2 servings Extras.

Per serving: 174 calories, 8 g protein, 1 g fat, 36 g carbohydrate, 161 mg sodium (estimated)

CITRUS BEAN BAKE
Full Choice Plan
Makes 2 servings

6 ounces drained canned small
    white beans
1 medium tomato, blanched,
    peeled, and diced
2 tablespoons thawed frozen
    concentrated orange juice
    (no sugar added)

1 teaspoon granulated brown sugar
1 teaspoon chili sauce
½ teaspoon Worcestershire sauce
Dash each salt and pepper

Preheat oven to 350°F. In 1¾-cup casserole combine all ingredients. Bake for 45 minutes, stirring twice during baking.

Each serving is equivalent to: 1 serving Bread Substitutes; 1 serving Vegetables; ½ serving Fruits; 1¼ servings Extras.

Per serving: 154 calories, 8 g protein, 1 g fat, 31 g carbohydrate, 111 mg sodium (estimated)

VEGETARIAN BAKED BEANS IN TOMATO SAUCE
Full Choice Plan
Makes 2 servings

6 ounces drained canned small pink
    beans
½ medium tomato, diced
1 garlic clove, minced
1 cinnamon stick (2 inches)

1 teaspoon each onion flakes,
    granulated brown sugar, and
    cider vinegar
½ teaspoon dark molasses
¼ teaspoon each salt and
    Worcestershire sauce

Preheat oven to 350°F. In bowl thoroughly combine all ingredients; transfer to 1¾-cup casserole. Cover and bake for 20 minutes; uncover and bake 10 minutes longer. Remove cinnamon stick before serving.

Each serving is equivalent to: 1 serving Bread Substitutes; ½ serving Vegetables; 1½ servings Extras.

Per serving: 122 calories, 7 g protein, 1 g fat, 24 g carbohydrate, 278 mg sodium (estimated)

HOPPIN' JOHN
Full Choice Plan
Makes 2 servings

Serve with ham or pork.

2 teaspoons vegetable oil
½ cup diced onion
1 bay leaf
½ teaspoon minced fresh garlic
½ teaspoon each salt and crushed
    marjoram leaves
⅛ teaspoon pepper

4 drops hot sauce
Dash ground red pepper
3 ounces drained canned
    black-eyed peas
½ cup cooked enriched rice
1 tablespoon imitation bacon bits

In 9-inch nonstick skillet heat oil; add onion and seasonings and cook, stirring occasionally, until onion is translucent. Stir in peas, rice, and bacon bits and cook until thoroughly heated; remove bay leaf and serve immediately.

Each serving is equivalent to: 1 serving Fats; ¼ cup Limited Vegetables; 1 serving Bread Substitutes; 1½ servings Extras.

Per serving: 163 calories, 5 g protein, 6 g fat, 24 g carbohydrate, 689 mg sodium (estimated)

Eggs

Eggs may be everyday items but they needn't be ordinary. We serve them up in a variety of unusual ways for a slimming menu: in soufflés and pancakes, even in quiche. Eggs can be a thrifty meal, especially when combined with vegetables like zucchini, mushrooms, asparagus, or peppers. Our easy egg recipes will make your life lighter in more ways than one.

Eggs supply Protein, Iron, Vitamin A, and B Vitamins.

Guidelines for Using Eggs
(Full and Limited Choice Plans)

1. Amounts:

Women, Men, and Youth	Serving
Morning Meal	1 egg
Midday and Evening Meals	2 eggs

2. Eggs should be consumed at mealtime *only* and may be split with items from the Cheese, Peanut Butter (Full Choice Plan only), Poultry, Veal, and Game, Meat Group, Fish, and Legumes categories.
3. Select 4 eggs a week, small, medium, large, or extra-large. If an egg or portion thereof is used in combination with any of the above categories, it *must* be counted toward the weekly total of 4 eggs.
4. Egg whites and yolks may be prepared in separate recipes provided both whites and yolks are consumed as part of the same meal.
5. Chicken eggs (white or brown), egg substitutes, and quail eggs may be selected.
6. Four quail eggs equal 1 chicken egg.
7. Raw eggs may be used but should be carefully inspected for cracks. Cracked raw eggs may contain salmonella, a bacteria that causes intestinal upset.
8. Cooking Procedures—Eggs may be cooked over or under direct heat, cooked in the shell, poached, or baked. A measured amount of Fats may be used for cooking over or under direct heat and for baking; equate Fats to the Food Plan.

SCRAMBLED EGG
No Choice Plan
Makes 1 Morning Meal serving

In small bowl, using a fork, beat **1 egg** with up to **1 tablespoon water.** In small nonstick skillet heat **1 teaspoon margarine,** over low heat, until bubbly, tilting pan so bottom is coated. Pour in egg mixture and, as egg begins to set, using a wooden spoon or spatula, stir mixture, scraping bottom and sides and allowing uncooked portions to flow to bottom of pan. Stir frequently but not constantly, allowing egg to form large, soft curds. Remove from heat while egg is still moist, as it will continue to cook from retained heat. Serve immediately on a warm plate.

Each serving is equivalent to: 1 Egg; 1 serving Fats.

Per serving: 113 calories, 6 g protein, 9 g fat, 1 g carbohydrate, 113 mg sodium

Variation: *Limited Choice Plan*—Eliminate margarine. Spray skillet with nonstick cooking spray and heat; proceed as above. Omit Fats from equivalent listing.

Per serving: 79 calories, 6 g protein, 6 g fat, 1 g carbohydrate, 69 mg sodium

Note: On the Full and Limited Choice Plans this recipe may be used as ½ Midday or Evening Meal; supplement as required.

SUNNY-SIDE UP EGG

Limited Choice Plan

Makes 1 Mealtime serving, 1 Morning or ½ Midday or Evening Meal; supplement as required

Break **1 egg** into small dish or cup and set aside. In small nonstick skillet heat **½ teaspoon margarine,** over low heat, until bubbly, tilting pan to coat as much of bottom as possible. Slide egg into skillet and cook until done to taste. (A very fresh egg, which has a great deal of white clinging to the yolk, may need to be covered during cooking so that the top cooks at the same time as the bottom.) Using spatula or pancake turner, loosen cooked egg and slide onto warm plate.

Each serving is equivalent to: 1 Egg; ½ serving Fats.

Per serving: 96 calories, 6 g protein, 7 g fat, 1 g carbohydrate, 91 mg sodium

Variation: Eliminate margarine. Spray skillet with nonstick cooking spray and heat; proceed as above. Omit Fats from equivalent listing.

Per serving: 79 calories, 6 g protein, 6 g fat, 1 g carbohydrate, 69 mg sodium

SOFT- OR HARD-COOKED EGG

Limited Choice Plan

Makes 1 Mealtime serving, 1 Morning or ½ Midday or Evening Meal; supplement as required

If possible, choose an egg that has been stored for several days. This allows the air space inside the shell at large end to expand, thus making the egg easier to shell after cooking.

In small saucepan place **1 egg in enough cold water to cover egg by about 1 inch.** Over high heat bring water just to a boil; cover pan and remove from heat. For soft-cooked egg, let stand 3 to 6 minutes (the longer it stands, the firmer the egg will become); for hard-cooked egg, let stand 17 minutes.*

When done to taste, drain egg immediately and plunge into cold water for several seconds to prevent further cooking and aid in shelling. Soft-cooked egg can be placed in an eggcup, large end up, and eaten directly from the shell, or spooned into a small dish. To shell a hard-cooked egg, crack large end of shell by tapping gently against a flat surface. Place under running water and, starting with large end of egg, gently peel off pieces of shell, being careful not to peel off any egg white along with the shell.
Each serving is equivalent to: 1 Egg.

Per serving: 79 calories, 6 g protein, 6 g fat, 1 g carbohydrate, 69 mg sodium

* If using an egg at room temperature, decrease cooking time by about 2 minutes.

POACHED EGG
Limited Choice Plan
Makes 1 Mealtime serving, 1 Morning or ½ Midday or Evening Meal; supplement as required

In order to achieve the best possible results, choose the freshest egg you can find; during cooking the white will cling to the yolk better, thus producing a neater, more evenly poached egg.
In shallow pan bring about 1½ inches water to a boil. Reduce heat so that water stays at a simmer (there should be bubbles at the bottom of the pan rising almost to the top and then collapsing). Break 1 egg into a small dish or cup and gently slide it into the water. Cook 3 to 5 minutes or until done to taste. Using slotted spoon or skimmer, remove cooked egg from liquid and let drain. Serve immediately or place in container with cold water, cover, and refrigerate for up to 1 day. Drain and serve cold or reheat by immersing in hot water just until heated.*
Eggs may also be poached in nonstick egg poacher insert or one that has been sprayed with nonstick cooking spray.
Each serving is equivalent to: 1 Egg.

Per serving: 79 calories, 6 g protein, 6 g fat, 1 g carbohydrate, 69 mg sodium

* If you are planning to reheat a poached egg, it is best to slightly undercook it initially.

GREEK LEMON SOUP
Full Choice Plan
Makes 2 Midday or Evening Meal servings, ¼ meal each; supplement as required

1½ cups Chicken Broth (see
   page 401)
1 ounce uncooked regular
   long-grain enriched rice
1 egg
1 tablespoon plus 1 teaspoon lemon
   juice
Dash each salt and white pepper

In 1-quart saucepan bring broth to a boil. Reduce heat; add rice, cover, and simmer until rice is tender, about 20 minutes.

In small bowl beat egg with lemon juice; stirring constantly, add ½ cup of the hot soup, a tablespoon at a time. Stir mixture into soup in saucepan and heat (*do not boil*). Season with salt and pepper and serve immediately.

Each serving is equivalent to: 1 serving Extras; ½ serving Bread Substitutes; ½ Egg.

Per serving: 106 calories, 8 g protein, 3 g fat, 16 g carbohydrate, 124 mg sodium

QUICK EGG-DROP SOUP

Full Choice Plan

Makes 1 Mealtime serving (about 1 cup), 1 Morning or ½ Midday or Evening Meal; supplement as required

1 packet instant chicken broth and seasoning mix
¾ cup water

2 teaspoons thinly sliced scallion (green onion), green portion only
1 large egg, beaten
¼ teaspoon soy sauce (optional)

Empty packet of broth mix into a small saucepan; add water and stir to combine. Add scallion and bring to a boil. Remove from heat and gradually stir in egg and, if desired, soy sauce. Serve immediately.

Each serving is equivalent to: 1 serving Extras; 2 teaspoons Limited Vegetables; 1 Egg.

Per serving: 91 calories, 7 g protein, 6 g fat, 3 g carbohydrate, 902 mg sodium
With soy sauce: 92 calories, 7 g protein, 6 g fat, 3 g carbohydrate, 1,013 mg sodium

MUSHROOM APPETIZER PUFFS

Full Choice Plan

Makes 4 Midday or Evening Meal servings, ½ meal each; supplement as required

Puff Shells

¼ cup margarine
½ cup water

½ cup less 1½ teaspoons enriched all-purpose flour
3 medium eggs

Mushroom Filling

2 cups sliced mushrooms
1 tablespoon sliced scallion (green onion)
1 teaspoon dry red wine

½ packet instant onion broth and seasoning mix
⅓ cup cottage cheese
1 tablespoon plus 1½ teaspoons plain dried bread crumbs

To Prepare Puff Shells: Preheat oven to 400°F. In a small saucepan combine margarine with water and, over medium heat, bring to a boil. Add flour all at once and, using a wooden spoon, stir vigorously until mixture leaves sides of pan and forms a ball. Remove from heat. Add eggs

1 at a time, beating well with wooden spoon after each addition until well blended (dough should be smooth and shiny).

Make 24 puff shells by dropping dough, by rounded ½ teaspoonsful, onto a heavy aluminum baking sheet, leaving a space of about 2 inches between each. Bake 12 to 15 minutes; reduce oven temperature to 350°F. and bake until golden, 12 to 15 minutes longer.

Turn oven off and remove baking sheet. Using the point of a sharp knife, pierce side of each shell. Return to turned-off oven and let stand 10 minutes, leaving oven door ajar.

Carefully transfer shells to wire rack away from drafts and let cool.

To Prepare Mushroom Filling: In 8-inch nonstick skillet combine mushrooms, scallion, wine, and broth mix; cook over medium heat, stirring occasionally, until no liquid remains in pan.

Transfer mixture to blender container or work bowl of food processor; process until smooth. Turn motor off and add cheese and bread crumbs; process until combined.

To Prepare Appetizer Puffs: Shortly before serving, using a sharp knife, slice off top of each puff shell. Spoon an equal amount of mushroom filling (about 1½ teaspoons) into each shell. Replace tops and serve 6 puffs per portion.

Each serving is equivalent to: 3 servings Fats; ¾ serving Bread; 1¼ servings Extras; ¾ Egg; 1 serving Vegetables; ¾ teaspoon Limited Vegetables; 1 tablespoon plus 1 teaspoon Soft Cheese.

Per serving: 252 calories, 10 g protein, 16 g fat, 17 g carbohydrate, 376 mg sodium

BUTTERMILK PANCAKES

Full Choice Plan

Makes 1 Mealtime serving, 1 Morning or ½ Midday or Evening Meal; supplement as required

2 tablespoons plus 1½ teaspoons
 enriched all-purpose flour
¼ teaspoon double-acting baking
 powder

⅛ teaspoon baking soda
1 large egg, separated
3 tablespoons buttermilk
½ teaspoon vegetable oil

1. Into small bowl or onto sheet of wax paper sift together flour, baking powder, and baking soda.

2. In separate bowl, using a wire whisk or electric mixer, beat egg white until soft peaks form; set aside.

3. In another bowl combine yolk, buttermilk, and oil. Add sifted ingredients and stir until smooth; fold in white.

4. Spray a 12-inch skillet with nonstick cooking spray and heat. Form 4 pancakes by spooning about 2 tablespoons of batter for each into hot skillet. Cook until bubbles appear on surface and edges are browned. Turn pancakes and brown other side. Serve immediately.

Each serving is equivalent to: 1 serving Bread; 1 Egg; ¼ serving Milk; ½ serving Fats.

Per serving: 193 calories, 10 g protein, 9 g fat, 18 g carbohydrate, 266 mg sodium

FLOURLESS CRÊPES WITH RICOTTA FILLING

Full Choice Plan
Makes 2 Mealtime servings, 1 Morning or ½ Midday or Evening Meal; supplement as required

Filling

⅓ cup part-skim ricotta cheese
¾ teaspoon granulated sugar

2 teaspoons reduced-calorie orange marmalade (16 calories per 2 teaspoons)

Crêpes

1 large egg
1 tablespoon evaporated skimmed milk

1 teaspoon vegetable oil
¼ teaspoon granulated sugar
⅛ teaspoon vanilla extract

To Prepare Filling: In small bowl combine all ingredients for filling; set aside while preparing crêpes.

To Prepare Crêpes: In blender container combine all ingredients for crêpes and process until smooth. Heat 10-inch nonstick skillet over medium heat. When skillet is hot, pour half the batter into pan, making 1 crêpe. Cook until underside is lightly browned. Using a pancake turner, turn crêpe and brown other side. Transfer crêpe to serving platter. Repeat procedure, making 1 more crêpe.

To Serve: Spoon half of filling onto center of each crêpe and roll to enclose filling. Serve 1 crêpe per portion.

Each serving is equivalent to: ⅙ cup Soft Cheese; 1 serving Extras; 8 calories Specialty Foods; ½ Egg; 1½ teaspoons Evaporated Skimmed Milk (1⁄16 serving Milk); ½ serving Fats.

Per serving: 133 calories, 8 g protein, 8 g fat, 6 g carbohydrate, 95 mg sodium

EGG SALAD SANDWICH

Full Choice Plan
Makes 1 Mealtime serving, 1 Morning or ½ Midday or Evening Meal; supplement as required

1 egg, hard-cooked and chopped
2 black olives, pitted and diced
2 teaspoons diced celery
2 teaspoons reduced-calorie mayonnaise

¼ teaspoon Dijon-style mustard
Dash pepper
2 slices enriched white bread
1 iceberg or romaine lettuce leaf

In small bowl combine all ingredients except bread and lettuce; mix well. Spread egg salad on 1 slice of bread; top with lettuce and remaining bread slice to form a sandwich.

Each serving is equivalent to: 1 Egg; 1 serving Extras; ⅓ serving Vegetables; 1 serving Fats; 2 servings Bread.

Per serving: 245 calories, 10 g protein, 11 g fat, 26 g carbohydrate, 457 mg sodium

OPEN-FACE GOLDENROD EGG SALAD SANDWICH
Limited Choice Plan
Makes 1 Midday or Evening Meal serving

2 eggs, hard-cooked and shelled
2 teaspoons reduced-calorie
 mayonnaise
1 teaspoon chopped capers
¼ teaspoon each salt and onion
 powder
Dash pepper

2 iceberg or romaine lettuce
 leaves
2 slices enriched white bread,
 toasted
Paprika
½ medium tomato, sliced

1. Cut each egg in half and remove yolk; in small bowl mash yolks and set aside.
2. Chop egg whites. In another small bowl combine whites with mayonnaise, capers, salt, onion powder, and pepper; stir to combine.
3. Place 1 lettuce leaf on each slice of toast and top with half of the egg white mixture, then half of the mashed yolks; sprinkle each with dash paprika.
4. Transfer sandwich to plate and surround with tomato slices.

Each serving is equivalent to: 2 Eggs; 1 serving Fats; 2 servings Bread; 1 serving Vegetables. (See page 407 for Full Choice Plan adjustments.)

Per serving: 326 calories, 17 g protein, 15 g fat, 30 g carbohydrate, 1,038 mg sodium

CHUNKY EGG SALAD WITH OLIVES
Full Choice Plan
Makes 4 Midday or Evening Meal servings

¼ cup plain unflavored yogurt
¼ cup reduced-calorie mayonnaise
¼ cup chopped scallions (green
 onions)
2 teaspoons Dijon-style mustard
½ teaspoon salt
1 cup diced celery
8 eggs, hard-cooked and coarsely
 chopped

8 pitted black olives, sliced
2 teaspoons chopped drained
 capers
Dash white pepper
8 iceberg or romaine lettuce
 leaves
1 medium tomato, sliced

In large bowl combine yogurt, mayonnaise, scallions, mustard, and salt. Add celery, eggs, olives, capers, and pepper and mix well. Cover and chill.

To Serve: On serving platter arrange bed of lettuce leaves; top with egg salad and garnish with tomato slices.

Each serving is equivalent to: ⅛ serving Milk; 1½ servings Fats; 1 tablespoon Limited Vegetables; 1½ servings Vegetables; 2 Eggs; 1 serving Extras.

Per serving: 237 calories, 14 g protein, 16 g fat, 9 g carbohydrate, 700 mg sodium

CAESAR SALAD
Full Choice Plan
Makes 2 Midday or Evening Meal servings

Dressing
1 tablespoon mashed drained
  canned anchovies
2 teaspoons each olive oil, red wine
  vinegar, and lemon juice

1 garlic clove, mashed
Dash pepper

Salad Mixture
2 large eggs (in the shell)
8 cups torn romaine lettuce
  (bite-size pieces)

2 ounces grated Parmesan cheese
2 slices enriched white bread,
  toasted and cut into small cubes

To *Prepare Dressing:* In small bowl combine all dressing ingredients and mix well; set aside.

To *Prepare Salad:* Place eggs in small heatproof bowl; slowly pour in boiling water to cover. Let stand 3 minutes; drain off water. Crack eggs into bowl and beat lightly.

In large salad bowl arrange torn lettuce leaves; pour eggs over lettuce and toss to coat. Add dressing and cheese and toss again, making sure all greens are thoroughly coated. Add bread cubes and toss to combine. Serve immediately.

Each serving is equivalent to: 1½ servings Extras; 1 serving Fats; 1 Egg; 8 servings Vegetables; 1 ounce Hard Cheese; 1 serving Bread.

Per serving: 373 calories, 25 g protein, 21 g fat, 22 g carbohydrate, 810 mg sodium

GARDEN LUNCHEON SALAD
Full Choice Plan
Makes 4 Midday or Evening Meal servings, ½ meal each; supplement as required

Salad
4 cups torn salad greens (chicory,
  iceberg, romaine, Boston lettuce,
  etc.)
3 eggs, hard-cooked, chilled, and
  sliced
2 medium tomatoes, cut into
  wedges

½ cup alfalfa sprouts
½ cup sliced scallions (green
  onions)
1 ounce Cheddar cheese, cut into
  strips
4 radishes, sliced or cut into roses

Dressing
2 tablespoons olive oil
1 tablespoon wine vinegar
1½ teaspoons lemon juice
1 teaspoon chopped fresh basil

¼ teaspoon Dijon-style mustard
¼ garlic clove, minced
Dash salt

To *Prepare Salad:* In salad bowl combine all salad ingredients; cover and chill.

To Prepare Dressing: In blender container combine all dressing ingredients; process for 1 minute.
To Serve: Pour dressing over salad and toss gently to combine.
Each serving is equivalent to: 3⅓ servings Vegetables; ¾ Egg; ⅛ cup Limited Vegetables; ¼ ounce Hard Cheese; 1½ servings Fats.

Per serving: 186 calories, 8 g protein, 14 g fat, 7 g carbohydrate, 147 mg sodium

CURRIED EGGS
Full Choice Plan
Makes 2 Midday or Evening Meal servings

A quick, colorful dish, delicious served with a mixed green salad.

2 teaspoons margarine	1 cup canned pineapple chunks
½ cup sliced onion	(no sugar added)
¾ cup Chicken Broth (see	4 eggs, hard-cooked and shelled
page 401), at room temperature	1 cup cooked enriched rice, warm
1 tablespoon enriched all-purpose	2 medium tomatoes, cut into
flour	wedges
¼ teaspoon curry powder	

In 8- or 9-inch skillet heat margarine, over medium heat, until bubbly; add onion and sauté until translucent. In measuring cup or small bowl combine broth, flour, and curry powder and stir until flour is completely dissolved and mixture is smooth. Add to skillet and cook, stirring, until mixture thickens. Stir in pineapple and cook until heated. Add eggs to skillet and cook 1 minute longer; remove from heat.

Make a bed of rice on serving platter. Arrange tomato wedges around outside edge of rice. Spoon curried egg mixture over rice and serve immediately.

Each serving is equivalent to: 1 serving Fats; ¼ cup Limited Vegetables; 2 servings Extras; 1 serving Fruits; 2 Eggs; 1 serving Bread Substitutes; 2 servings Vegetables.

Per serving: 447 calories, 19 g protein, 16 g fat, 60 g carbohydrate, 204 mg sodium

EGGS FLORENTINE
Full Choice Plan
Makes 2 Midday or Evening Meal servings

2 teaspoons margarine	¼ teaspoon salt
1 garlic clove, chopped	⅛ teaspoon each ground nutmeg
1 cup well-drained cooked chopped	and pepper
spinach	2 ounces sharp Cheddar cheese,
2 teaspoons enriched all-purpose	shredded
flour	2 eggs
1 cup skim milk	

Preheat oven to 350°F. In 8-inch skillet heat margarine until bubbly; add garlic and sauté for 1 minute. Add spinach and cook over medium heat, stirring constantly, for 3 minutes. Sprinkle flour over spinach; add milk and cook, stirring constantly, until slightly thickened. Remove from heat and stir in salt, nutmeg, and pepper; add cheese and stir to combine.

Spray two 10-ounce custard cups with nonstick cooking spray; fill each with half of the spinach mixture. Using the back of a spoon, make a depression in the center of each portion. Being careful not to break yolk, break 1 egg into a small dish, then slide into depression in 1 portion of spinach mixture; repeat with remaining egg and spinach mixture. Bake until eggs are firm, 12 to 15 minutes.

Each serving is equivalent to: 1 serving Fats; 1 serving Vegetables; 1 serving Extras; ½ serving Milk; 1 ounce Hard Cheese; 1 Egg.

Per serving: 305 calories, 21 g protein, 19 g fat, 13 g carbohydrate, 669 mg sodium

EGG-STUFFED PEPPERS

Full Choice Plan
Makes 4 Midday or Evening Meal servings, ⅜ meal each; supplement as required

4 medium red bell peppers
1 tablespoon plus 1 teaspoon olive
  oil
1 cup sliced onions
½ teaspoon minced fresh garlic
1 cup sliced mushrooms

8 ounces peeled boiled potatoes,
  diced
3 eggs, hard-cooked and chopped
1 tablespoon chopped fresh parsley
½ teaspoon salt
Dash freshly ground pepper

1. Cut top off each pepper; remove and discard seeds and membranes.
2. In 3-quart saucepan bring approximately 2 inches of water to a boil. Add peppers, cover, and boil for 5 minutes; drain and place cut-side down to cool.
3. In small skillet heat oil. Add onions and garlic and sauté until onions are soft. Add mushrooms and cook, stirring occasionally, until mushrooms are tender, about 3 minutes.
4. Transfer mushroom mixture to medium bowl. Add remaining ingredients except peppers and toss to combine.
5. Stuff each pepper with ¼ of mushroom mixture. Place stuffed peppers in a casserole just large enough to hold them in an upright position. Cover and bake at 375°F. for 40 to 45 minutes.

Each serving is equivalent to: 2½ servings Vegetables; 1 serving Fats; ¼ cup Limited Vegetables; ½ serving Bread Substitutes; ¾ Egg.

Per serving: 191 calories, 8 g protein, 9 g fat, 20 g carbohydrate, 342 mg sodium

MUSHROOM–ASPARAGUS FRITTATA

Limited Choice Plan
Makes 1 Midday or Evening Meal serving

2 eggs, beaten
½ cup cooked chopped asparagus
½ cup thinly sliced mushrooms

Dash each salt, pepper, and onion
  powder
1 teaspoon olive oil
⅛ teaspoon minced fresh garlic

Garnish
1 teaspoon chopped fresh parsley

In small bowl combine eggs, asparagus, mushrooms, salt, pepper, and onion powder; set aside. In 8-inch nonstick skillet that has a metal or removable handle, heat oil. Add garlic and sauté briefly (just until garlic is golden). Pour egg mixture into skillet and cook until eggs are set but surface is still moist. Transfer skillet to broiler; with door open and skillet handle away from heat source, broil frittata until surface is dry and puffy, about 3 minutes. Remove skillet from broiler and slide frittata onto warmed plate. Sprinkle with parsley.

Each serving is equivalent to: 2 Eggs; 2 servings Vegetables; 1 serving Fats.

Per serving: 231 calories, 16 g protein, 16 g fat, 6 g carbohydrate, 273 mg sodium

WESTERN ZUCCHINI BAKE
Full Choice Plan
Makes 2 Midday or Evening Meal servings

2 teaspoons vegetable oil	¼ teaspoon pepper
½ cup diced onion	2 medium zucchini
½ garlic clove, minced	(about 5 ounces each), cut into
½ cup each diced red bell pepper	quarters lengthwise and
and mushrooms	blanched
2 eggs, beaten	2 ounces Monterey Jack cheese,
½ teaspoon salt	shredded

Preheat oven to 350°F. In 9-inch nonstick skillet heat oil; add onion and garlic and sauté, stirring occasionally, until onion is translucent. Add diced red pepper and mushrooms; cook until pepper is tender-crisp, about 5 minutes longer. Add eggs and scramble until eggs are cooked but still moist. Remove from heat and sprinkle with salt and pepper.

Line a shallow 1-quart baking dish with zucchini. Spread egg mixture over zucchini and top with cheese. Bake until cheese melts, 10 to 15 minutes.

Each serving is equivalent to: 1 serving Fats; ¼ cup Limited Vegetables; 3 servings Vegetables; 1 Egg; 1 ounce Hard Cheese.

Per serving: 285 calories, 16 g protein, 19 g fat, 13 g carbohydrate, 772 mg sodium

ASPARAGUS "QUICHE"
Limited Choice Plan
Makes 2 Midday or Evening Meal servings

1 cup cooked chopped asparagus	2 ounces low-fat Swiss cheese,
2 eggs, beaten	shredded
½ cup evaporated skimmed milk	2 teaspoons mayonnaise
⅛ teaspoon minced fresh garlic or	2 teaspoons grated Parmesan
dash garlic powder	cheese
Dash each salt, pepper, and onion	
powder	

Garnish
Cooked asparagus spears

Preheat oven to 375°F. In small bowl combine chopped asparagus, eggs, milk, garlic or garlic powder, salt, pepper, and onion powder. Spray a shallow 1-quart casserole with nonstick cooking spray. Pour egg mixture into casserole and sprinkle with Swiss cheese. Bake for about 35 minutes or until a knife, inserted in center, comes out clean.

In small bowl combine mayonnaise with Parmesan cheese. Spread over "quiche" and return to oven; bake until lightly browned, about 5 minutes. Remove from oven and allow to set for 10 minutes. Garnish with asparagus spears.

Each serving is equivalent to: 1 serving Vegetables; 1 Egg; ½ serving Milk; 1 ounce Hard Cheese; 1 serving Fats; 1 serving Extras.

Per serving: 241 calories, 22 g protein, 12 g fat, 12 g carbohydrate, 715 mg sodium

CARROT AND DILL "QUICHE"

Limited Choice Plan
Makes 4 Midday or Evening Meal servings, ¼ meal each; supplement as required

2 teaspoons salt, divided	2 eggs
2 cups shredded carrots	½ teaspoon white pepper
1 cup evaporated skimmed milk	1 tablespoon fresh dill leaves*

1. Preheat oven to 350°F. In 2-quart saucepan bring 1 quart water and 1 teaspoon salt to a boil. Add carrots and boil for 3 minutes. Drain carrots in a colander and refresh under cold water.
2. Spray a 9-inch pie pan with nonstick cooking spray. Spread carrots, in an even layer, in pie pan.
3. In blender container combine milk, eggs, pepper, and remaining 1 teaspoon salt; process for 10 seconds. Add dill and process until dill is chopped. Pour milk mixture over carrots.
4. Set pie pan in a baking pan; pour hot water into baking pan to within 1 inch of rim of pie pan. Bake until "quiche" is firm, about 30 minutes (a knife, inserted in center, should come out clean).

Each serving is equivalent to: 1 serving Vegetables; ½ serving Milk; ½ Egg.

Per serving: 114 calories, 9 g protein, 3 g fat, 13 carbohydrate, 1,209 mg sodium

* If fresh dill is not available, substitute fresh parsley leaves.

PASSOVER PROVENÇALE "QUICHE"

Full Choice Plan
Makes 4 Midday or Evening Meal servings

2 matzo boards	¼ teaspoon each salt and pepper
2 tablespoons margarine	2 medium tomatoes, blanched,
4 medium eggs, beaten	peeled, and sliced
1 cup sliced onions	4 ounces American cheese,
2 garlic cloves, minced	shredded
1 tablespoon chopped fresh parsley	

1. Preheat oven to 375°F. Break 1 matzo board into quarters; in a shallow pan soak in hot water until soft. Using a pancake turner, lift matzo from water; gently press out water and place matzo in an 8 x 8 x 2-inch nonstick baking pan.

2. In small nonstick skillet melt margarine; stir half of the margarine into beaten eggs. Add onions and garlic to margarine remaining in skillet and sauté until onions are translucent.

3. Add parsley, salt, and pepper to egg mixture and stir to combine.

4. Pour ¼ of egg mixture over matzo. Layer half each of the tomato slices, onion mixture, and cheese over matzo, beginning with tomato and ending with cheese.

5. Repeat Step 1 with second matzo board, topping cheese in baking pan with matzo.

6. Repeat Step 4, then pour remaining egg mixture over all. Bake for 30 minutes (a knife, inserted in center, should come out clean).

Each serving is equivalent to: 1 serving Bread; 1½ servings Fats; 1 Egg; ¼ cup Limited Vegetables; 1 serving Vegetables; 1 ounce Hard Cheese.

Per serving: 330 calories, 15 g protein, 20 g fat, 23 g carbohydrate, 674 mg sodium

Variation: *Not* for Passover—Substitute 4 ounces grated sharp Cheddar cheese for the American cheese.

Per serving: 338 calories, 16 g protein, 20 g fat, 23 g carbohydrate, 445 mg sodium

SPINACH QUICHE WITH RICE CRUST
Full Choice Plan
Makes 3 Midday or Evening Meal servings

Crust

1½ cups cooked brown rice
1 egg
1½ ounces Swiss cheese, shredded

1 tablespoon chopped fresh parsley
½ teaspoon salt
⅛ teaspoon pepper

Filling

1 tablespoon vegetable oil
¾ cup diced onions
1 garlic clove, minced
1 cup well-drained and squeezed
   cooked spinach leaves
¾ cup skim milk

2 eggs
1½ ounces Swiss cheese, shredded
½ teaspoon salt
⅛ teaspoon pepper
Dash ground nutmeg

To Prepare Crust: In small bowl combine all crust ingredients. Spray a 9-inch quiche dish or pie plate with nonstick cooking spray; press rice mixture, in an even layer, onto bottom and up sides of prepared dish. Bake at 425°F. for 25 minutes. Remove quiche dish from oven and reduce temperature to 375°F.

To Prepare Filling: While crust is baking, heat oil in 10- or 12-inch nonstick skillet; add onions and garlic and sauté until lightly browned. Add spinach and sauté until liquid has evaporated. In medium bowl combine spinach mixture with remaining filling ingredients.

To Prepare Quiche: Pour filling into baked crust. Bake for 35 minutes. Each serving is equivalent to: 1 serving Bread Substitutes; 1 Egg; 1 ounce Hard Cheese; 1 serving Fats; ¼ cup Limited Vegetables; ⅔ serving Vegetables; ¼ serving Milk.

Per serving: 396 calories, 21 g protein, 19 g fat, 35 g carbohydrate, 927 mg sodium

BROCCOLI–RICE SOUFFLÉ
Full Choice Plan
Makes 4 Midday or Evening Meal servings

4 large eggs, separated	¼ teaspoon salt
1 tablespoon plus 1 teaspoon margarine	Dash each white pepper, ground red pepper, and ground nutmeg
1 tablespoon plus 1 teaspoon minced onion	4 ounces extra-sharp Cheddar cheese, shredded
2 tablespoons enriched all-purpose flour	1 cup cooked enriched rice
1 cup skim milk, heated	1 cup cooked broccoli florets
	Dash cream of tartar

1. In small bowl beat egg yolks and set aside.
2. In small saucepan heat margarine, over medium heat, until bubbly; add onion and sauté until softened. Reduce heat to low; add flour and cook, stirring constantly, for 3 minutes. Remove from heat.
3. Using small wire whisk, gradually stir in hot milk; continue to stir until mixture is smooth. Add salt, white and red peppers, and nutmeg.
4. Return saucepan to medium heat and cook, stirring constantly, until thickened. Reduce heat to low and cook, stirring frequently, for 10 minutes longer. Add cheese and cook, stirring constantly, until cheese is melted. Gradually stir beaten egg yolks into cheese sauce, stirring until well blended. Remove sauce from heat. Preheat oven to 350°F.
5. Gently stir rice into cheese sauce and transfer mixture to a large mixing bowl; gently fold in broccoli.
6. In another large bowl beat egg whites with cream of tartar until stiff but not dry. Lightly stir ¼ of the whites into broccoli mixture, then fold in remaining whites.
7. Spray a 1½-quart soufflé or ovenproof glass dish with nonstick cooking spray; turn mixture into dish. To form a crown, using the back of a spoon, make a shallow indentation about 1 inch from edge of dish, all the way around soufflé. Bake 40 minutes and serve immediately.

Each serving is equivalent to: 1 Egg; 1 serving Fats; 1 teaspoon Limited Vegetables; 1½ servings Extras; ¼ serving Milk; 1 ounce Hard Cheese; ½ serving Bread Substitutes; ½ serving Vegetables.

Per serving: 334 calories, 18 g protein, 19 g fat, 22 g carbohydrate, 463 mg sodium

OMELET SOUFFLÉ
Limited Choice Plan
Makes 2 Midday or Evening Meal servings, ¾ meal each; supplement as required

⅓ cup low-fat cottage cheese
1 ounce low-fat American cheese
1 egg, separated
1 tablespoon chopped fresh parsley
   or dill

¼ teaspoon each powdered
   mustard and Worcestershire
   sauce
⅛ teaspoon pepper

Garnish
Parsley or dill sprig

1. Preheat broiler. In blender container combine cheeses, egg yolk, chopped parsley or dill, and seasonings; process until smooth. Pour into a small bowl.
2. In another small bowl beat egg white until stiff but not dry. Beat ⅓ of the egg white into cheese mixture, then fold in remaining egg white.
3. Spray a 6- or 7-inch omelet pan or skillet that has a metal or removable handle with nonstick cooking spray and place over medium heat. Pour omelet mixture into pan and cook until partially set, about 2 minutes.
4. Transfer pan to broiler; broil until top of omelet is golden brown. Transfer omelet to a warm plate and garnish with parsley or dill sprig. Serve immediately.
Each serving is equivalent to: ⅙ cup Soft Cheese; ½ ounce Hard Cheese; ½ Egg.

Per serving: 79 calories, 9 g protein, 4 g fat, 2 g carbohydrate, 318 mg sodium

LEMON SOUFFLÉ
Limited Choice Plan
Makes 8 Midday or Evening Meal servings, ¼ meal each; supplement as required

2 envelopes unflavored gelatin
½ cup water
4 large eggs
¼ cup less 2 teaspoons granulated
   sugar

Artificial sweetener to equal
   6 teaspoons sugar
1 cup evaporated skimmed milk,
   chilled
¼ cup fresh lemon juice
1 tablespoon grated lemon peel

Garnish
Strips of lemon peel

Chill a medium mixing bowl. Cut a piece of foil long enough to go around a 4-quart soufflé dish and about 6 inches wide. Wrap foil around outside of dish so that it extends 3 inches above rim; secure with cellophane tape and set aside.

In small saucepan sprinkle gelatin over water and let stand about 5 minutes to soften. Cook over low heat, stirring constantly, until gelatin is completely dissolved; remove from heat.

In large bowl, using an electric mixer at high speed, beat eggs with sugar and sweetener until lemon-colored, about 5 minutes. In chilled bowl, using clean beaters, beat chilled milk until peaks form. Add milk to egg mixture and slowly beat in dissolved gelatin, beating until combined. Add lemon juice and grated lemon peel and beat until thoroughly combined. Pour into prepared soufflé dish. Cover lightly with piece of foil or wax paper and refrigerate until set, about 2 hours.

Carefully remove foil collar before serving. Garnish with strips of lemon peel.

Each serving is equivalent to: 3 servings Extras; ½ Egg; ¼ serving Milk.

Per serving: 95 calories, 7 g protein, 3 g fat, 10 g carbohydrate, 73 mg sodium

BAKED EGG CUSTARD

Full Choice Plan
Makes 2 Midday or Evening Meal servings, ¼ meal each; supplement as required

The term "water bath" is used to describe the method of baking indicated below. This method provides excellent heat control and is ideal for baking delicate items such as egg custards.

1 cup skim milk
1 tablespoon granulated sugar
½ teaspoon vanilla extract
Dash salt
1 large egg, lightly beaten

½ cup canned mandarin orange sections (no sugar added) or
½ cup canned crushed pineapple (no sugar added)

Preheat oven to 325°F. In bowl combine milk, sugar, extract, and salt; add egg and stir to combine. Spray two 6-ounce custard cups with non-stick cooking spray and pour half of milk mixture into each cup. Place cups in an 8 x 8 x 2-inch baking pan and pour boiling water into pan to a depth of about 1 inch. Bake 30 to 40 minutes (a knife, inserted in center of custard, should come out clean).

Remove baking pan from oven and cups from water bath. Allow custard to stand at room temperature for about 15 minutes. Serve warm or cover and chill.

To Serve: Unmold custard by inverting custard cups onto plates. When unmolding chilled custard, insert point of knife around edges to loosen before inverting. Garnish each portion with ¼ cup fruit.

Each serving is equivalent to: ½ serving Milk; 3 servings Extras; ½ Egg; ½ serving Fruits.

Per serving with mandarin orange sections: 148 calories, 7 g protein, 3 g fat, 22 g carbohydrate, 164 mg sodium
With pineapple: 149 calories, 8 g protein, 3 g fat, 22 g carbohydrate, 164 mg sodium

SUGAR CAKES
Limited Choice Plan
Makes 4 Midday or Evening Meal servings, ¼ meal each; supplement as required

2 large eggs
½ cup plus 2 tablespoons enriched
  cake flour
1 tablespoon granulated sugar
1½ teaspoons double-acting baking
  powder

Dash salt
2 tablespoons plus 2 teaspoons
  reduced-calorie margarine
¼ cup evaporated skimmed milk
1 teaspoon confectioners' sugar

1. Separate 1 egg and set aside yolk and white.
2. In bowl combine flour, granulated sugar, baking powder, and salt. With a pastry blender, or 2 knives used scissor-fashion, cut in margarine until mixture resembles coarse meal.
3. In another bowl combine 1 whole egg, milk, and reserved yolk; beat slightly. Add to flour mixture and blend thoroughly, forming a thin batter.
4. Preheat oven to 425°F. Spray a cookie sheet with nonstick cooking spray. Spoon batter onto prepared sheet, forming 8 cakes and leaving a space of about 2 inches between each.
5. Bake for 5 minutes; remove cookie sheet from oven and brush top of each cake with egg white, reserving some of the white.
6. Return to oven and repeat Step 5, using all of remaining egg white.
7. Return to oven and bake until golden brown, about 5 minutes longer. Sprinkle each cake with ⅛ teaspoon confectioners' sugar.

Each serving is equivalent to: ½ Egg; 1 serving Bread; 2 servings Extras; 1 serving Fats; ⅛ serving Milk.

Per serving: 156 calories, 5 g protein, 7 g fat, 18 g carbohydrate, 333 mg sodium

Variation: Substitute 1 tablespoon plus 1 teaspoon reduced-calorie strawberry spread (16 calories per 2 teaspoons) for the confectioners' sugar; spread ½ teaspoon over each baked cake. Change equivalent listing to 2⅓ servings Extras. (See page 407 for Full Choice Plan adjustments.)

Per serving: 162 calories, 5 g protein, 7 g fat, 20 g carbohydrate, 333 mg sodium

Cheese

Gone are the days when slim meant a regimen of nothing but cottage cheese. Now cheese, an economical source of protein, can add variety to your menu in many ways, from Gougère, a French cheese ring, to Welsh Rarebit to "danish" pastries and cheesecakes.

Cheese supplies Protein, Calcium, and many of the other nutrients found in Milk.

Guidelines for Using Cheese

1. Amounts (Full and Limited Choice Plans):

Women, Men, and Youth	Serving
Morning Meal	
Soft Cheese	⅓ cup (2½ ounces)
Semisoft and Hard Cheese	1 ounce
Midday and Evening Meals	
Soft Cheese	⅔ cup (5 ounces)
Semisoft and Hard Cheese	2 ounces

2. Cheese may be consumed at mealtime *only* and may be split with items from the Eggs, Peanut Butter (Full Choice Plan only), Poultry, Veal, and Game, Meat Group, Fish, and Legumes categories.

3. Limit semisoft and hard cheese to 4 ounces weekly. If used in combination with any of the above items, the amount used *must* be counted toward the weekly limit of 4 ounces.

4. A. *Full Choice Plan:*

Examples of cheese selections:

Soft—cottage; pot; part-skim ricotta

Semisoft—bleu; Brie; Camembert; pasteurized process cheese products, foods, and spreads

Hard—Cheddar; Muenster; Swiss; Jarlsberg; Parmesan; Romano; Edam

B. *Limited Choice Plan:*

a. Select low-fat varieties only.

b. Hard cheese made from skim milk (e.g., Jarlsberg) is not considered a low-fat cheese.

c. Examples of cheese selections:

Soft—low-fat cottage cheese

Semisoft and Hard Cheeses—lattost, pasteurized process low-fat cheese products

169

CREAM OF CHEDDAR SOUP
Full Choice Plan
Makes 2 or 4 Midday or Evening Meal servings, 1 or ½ meal each; supplement as required

2 teaspoons margarine
¼ cup thinly sliced scallions (green onions)
1 tablespoon plus ¾ teaspoon enriched all-purpose flour
¾ cup Chicken Broth (see page 401), heated

2 tablespoons diced celery
2 tablespoons shredded carrot
1 cup skim milk, heated
4 ounces sharp Cheddar cheese, shredded
Dash white pepper

In small saucepan heat margarine, over low heat, until bubbly; add scallions and sauté until tender. Blend in flour. Add broth and cook, stirring constantly, until mixture is smooth and thickened. Stir in celery and carrot and simmer until celery is tender. Gradually stir in milk and cook until heated (*do not boil*). Add cheese and cook, stirring constantly, until cheese melts. Season with pepper and serve immediately.

Each full-meal serving is equivalent to: 1 serving Fats; ⅛ cup Limited Vegetables; ¼ serving Bread; ½ serving Extras; ¼ serving Vegetables; ½ serving Milk; 2 ounces Hard Cheese.

Per serving: 340 calories, 21 g protein, 23 g fat, 15 g carbohydrate, 486 mg sodium

Each ½-meal serving is equivalent to: ½ serving Fats; 1 tablespoon Limited Vegetables; ⅛ serving Bread; ¼ serving Extras; ⅛ serving Vegetables; ¼ serving Milk; 1 ounce Hard Cheese.

Per serving: 170 calories, 11 g protein, 11 g fat, 7 g carbohydrate, 243 mg sodium

CAPERS 'N' CHEESE DIP
Full Choice Plan
Makes 2 Midday or Evening Meal servings, ½ meal each; supplement as required

⅔ cup cottage cheese
¼ cup buttermilk
1 tablespoon finely chopped scallion (green onion)
1 tablespoon minced capers

½ teaspoon prepared brown mustard
¼ teaspoon mashed fresh garlic
⅛ teaspoon Hungarian paprika
Dash white pepper

In small bowl combine all ingredients; cover and chill for 30 minutes.
Each serving is equivalent to: ⅓ cup Soft Cheese; ⅙ serving Milk; 1½ teaspoons Limited Vegetables.

Per serving: 93 calories, 10 g protein, 4 g fat, 4 g carbohydrate, 455 mg sodium

CHEDDAR CHEESE DIP
Full Choice Plan
Makes 2 or 4 Midday or Evening Meal servings, 1 or ½ meal each; supplement as required

4 ounces sharp Cheddar cheese, shredded
½ cup plain unflavored yogurt
¼ cup diced celery

2 teaspoons minced scallion (green onion)
¾ teaspoon Dijon-style mustard
¼ teaspoon Worcestershire sauce

In small bowl mix cheese with yogurt. Add celery, scallion, mustard, and Worcestershire; stir to combine.

Each full-meal serving is equivalent to: 2 ounces Hard Cheese; ½ serving Milk; ¼ serving Vegetables; 1 teaspoon Limited Vegetables.

Per serving: 269 calories, 16 g protein, 21 g fat, 4 g carbohydrate, 452 mg sodium

Each ½-meal serving is equivalent to: 1 ounce Hard Cheese; ¼ serving Milk; ⅛ serving Vegetables; ½ teaspoon Limited Vegetables.

Per serving: 134 calories, 8 g protein, 10 g fat, 2 g carbohydrate, 226 mg sodium

CHEESE 'N' OLIVE APPETIZER
Full Choice Plan
Makes 4 Midday or Evening Meal servings, ⅛ meal each; supplement as required

½ cup plus 2 tablespoons enriched all-purpose flour
½ teaspoon double-acting baking powder
2 tablespoons plus 2 teaspoons reduced-calorie margarine

1 ounce sharp Cheddar cheese, shredded
4 pimiento-stuffed green olives, minced
1 tablespoon chopped chives
¼ cup skim milk

1. Into small bowl sift together flour and baking powder. With pastry blender, or 2 knives used scissor-fashion, cut in margarine until mixture resembles coarse meal. Stir in cheese, olives, and chives, then milk, stirring until well blended.
2. Place mixture on sheet of plastic wrap or wax paper and form into a 2-inch-thick log. Wrap tightly and freeze for at least 30 minutes.
3. Preheat oven to 375°F. Remove log from freezer and slice into 4 equal portions. Cut each portion into 4 slices.
4. Place slices on a 15½ x 12-inch nonstick baking sheet. Bake until golden brown, 10 to 15 minutes. Remove from oven and serve hot or place on rack to cool.

Each serving is equivalent to: 1 serving Bread; 1 serving Fats; ¼ ounce Hard Cheese; ½ serving Extras; 1 tablespoon Skim Milk (1/16 serving Milk).

Per serving: 147 calories, 5 g protein, 7 g fat, 17 g carbohydrate, 294 mg sodium

CHEESE-STIX APPETIZERS

Full Choice Plan
Makes 2 or 4 Midday or Evening Meal servings, ¼ or ⅛ meal each; supplement as required

⅓ cup less 1 teaspoon enriched
all-purpose flour
1 ounce grated Parmesan cheese
Dash each salt, ground red pepper,
and garlic powder

1 tablespoon plus 1 teaspoon
margarine
2 tablespoons plain unflavored
yogurt

1. In mixing bowl combine flour, cheese, and seasonings. With pastry blender, or 2 knives used scissor-fashion, cut in margarine until mixture resembles coarse meal. Add yogurt and mix thoroughly.
2. Form dough into a ball; wrap in plastic wrap and refrigerate until chilled, about 1 hour.
3. Preheat oven to 400°F. Between 2 sheets of wax paper roll dough to ⅛-inch thickness. Remove wax paper and cut dough into strips, each about 4 inches long and ½ inch wide. Fold each strip in half and twist slightly.
4. Place twists on nonstick baking sheet; bake until golden, about 15 minutes.* Serve warm.

Each ¼-meal serving is equivalent to: 1 serving Bread; ½ ounce Hard Cheese; 2 servings Fats; ⅛ serving Milk.

Per serving: 215 calories, 9 g protein, 13 g fat, 17 g carbohydrate, 424 mg sodium

Each ⅛-meal serving is equivalent to: ½ serving Bread; ¼ ounce Hard Cheese; 1 serving Fats; 1½ teaspoons Yogurt (1⁄16 serving Milk).

Per serving: 107 calories, 4 g protein, 6 g fat, 8 g carbohydrate, 212 mg sodium

Variation: *Sesame-Cheddar Stix*—In small skillet toast 1 teaspoon sesame seed. Transfer to plate and let cool. Substitute 1 ounce shredded Cheddar cheese for the Parmesan. Press folded cheese strips into cooled seeds, then twist and bake. Add 1 serving Extras to equivalent listing for ¼ meal; add ½ serving Extras to equivalent listing for ⅛ meal.

Per ¼-meal serving: 223 calories, 9 g protein, 13 g fat, 17 g carbohydrate, 425 mg sodium
Per ⅛-meal serving: 111 calories, 4 g protein, 7 g fat, 8 g carbohydrate, 212 mg sodium

* These can be baked in a conventional oven or toaster-oven.

GOUGÈRE (GRUYÈRE CHEESE RING)

Full Choice Plan
Makes 4 Midday or Evening Meal servings, ½ meal each; supplement as required

Gougère, a delicious cheese ring, is thought to have originated in the Burgundy district of France. Today, it is a favorite throughout France. Try it as an appetizer or accompanied by a salad and a glass of wine.

2 tablespoons plus 2 teaspoons
   reduced-calorie margarine
1 tablespoon plus 1 teaspoon
   margarine
½ cup water
½ teaspoon salt

Dash pepper
½ cup plus 2 tablespoons enriched
   all-purpose flour, sifted
2 large eggs
2 ounces Gruyère cheese, shredded

Preheat oven to 375°F. In 2-quart saucepan combine margarines with water, salt, and pepper and bring to a boil. Reduce heat to low; add flour all at once and, using a wooden spoon, stir vigorously until mixture leaves sides of pan. Remove from heat and continue stirring until mixture cools slightly. Add eggs 1 at a time, beating after each addition until mixture is smooth. Stir in cheese.

Spray a 15 x 9-inch nonstick baking sheet with nonstick cooking spray; form dough into an 8-inch ring by spooning mixture onto baking sheet in 8 adjoining mounds. Bake until golden brown and mounds are puffed, 35 to 40 minutes. Remove ring to rack to cool slightly; serve warm.

Each serving is equivalent to: 2 servings Fats; 1 serving Bread; ½ Egg; ½ ounce Hard Cheese.

Per serving: 239 calories, 9 g protein, 15 g fat, 16 g carbohydrate, 489 mg sodium

Variation: Substitute Swiss cheese for the Gruyère.

Per serving: 234 calories, 9 g protein, 14 g fat, 16 g carbohydrate, 478 mg sodium

SWISS 'N' BACON PINWHEELS
Full Choice Plan
Makes 2 Midday or Evening Meal servings, ¼ meal each; supplement as required

These can be prepared ahead and refrigerated until ready to bake.

2 slices enriched white bread,
   lightly toasted
2 teaspoons reduced-calorie
   margarine

1 ounce Swiss cheese, shredded
2 teaspoons imitation bacon bits,
   crushed

1. Using a rolling pin, lightly roll each slice of toast as flat as possible without breaking the bread. Spread 1 teaspoon margarine on each slice.
2. In small bowl combine cheese and bacon bits; sprinkle half of mixture on each slice of toast, covering entire surface.
3. Roll each slice and wrap tightly in wax paper or plastic wrap. Freeze for 30 minutes.
4. Preheat oven to 350°F. Unwrap bread rolls and cut each into 5 equal pinwheels, securing each pinwheel with a toothpick.
5. Place pinwheels, cut-side down, on nonstick baking sheet. Bake 10 minutes.* Serve immediately, 5 pinwheels per portion.

Each serving is equivalent to: 1 serving Bread; ½ serving Fats; ½ ounce Hard Cheese; 1 serving Extras.

Per serving: 142 calories, 7 g protein, 7 g fat, 13 g carbohydrate, 296 mg sodium

* For convenience, these can be baked in a toaster-oven.

OPEN-FACE GRILLED CHEESE SANDWICH
No Choice Plan
Makes 1 Midday Meal serving

1 teaspoon margarine
1 slice rye bread, toasted
2 ounces low-fat American cheese, sliced

½ medium tomato, thinly sliced
Dash each garlic powder, onion powder, oregano leaves, and pepper

Spread margarine on toast. Top with cheese, then tomato slices; sprinkle with seasonings. Place on piece of foil or in broiler pan; broil in toaster-oven or broiler until cheese melts.

Each serving is equivalent to: 1 serving Fats; 1 serving Bread; 2 ounces Hard Cheese; 1 serving Vegetables.

Per serving: 211 calories, 17 g protein, 8 g fat, 19 g carbohydrate, 1,087 mg sodium

Variation: *Full Choice Plan*—Substitute Swiss or Jarlsberg cheese for the American cheese.

Per serving: 325 calories, 19 g protein, 20 g fat, 19 g carbohydrate, 336 mg sodium

Note: On the Full and Limited Choice Plans this recipe may be used at the Midday or Evening Meal.

OPEN-FACE GRILLED CHEESE AND BACON SANDWICH
Full Choice Plan
Makes 1 Midday or Evening Meal serving

1 teaspoon margarine
1 slice enriched white bread, toasted
2 ounces Swiss cheese, sliced

1 teaspoon imitation bacon bits
½ medium tomato, thinly sliced
Dash each salt and pepper

Spread margarine on toast; top with cheese and bacon bits. Arrange tomato slices over bacon bits and sprinkle with salt and pepper. Place on piece of foil or in broiler pan; broil in toaster-oven or broiler until cheese melts.

Each serving is equivalent to: 1 serving Fats; 1 serving Bread; 2 ounces Hard Cheese; 1 serving Extras; 1 serving Vegetables.

Per serving: 334 calories, 20 g protein, 21 g fat, 18 g carbohydrate, 536 mg sodium

Variation: Substitute sharp Cheddar cheese for the Swiss cheese.

Per serving: 349 calories, 18 g protein, 24 g fat, 16 g carbohydrate, 740 mg sodium

CHEESE PIZZA
Full Choice Plan
Makes 2 Mealtime servings, 1 Morning or ½ Midday or Evening Meal each; supplement as required

⅓ cup plus 2 teaspoons tomato sauce
Dash each garlic and onion powder

1 English muffin, split and toasted
2 ounces mozzarella cheese, sliced
¼ teaspoon oregano leaves

In measuring cup or small bowl season tomato sauce with garlic and onion powders. Place muffin halves on tray of toaster-oven or piece of foil. Spread 2 tablespoons tomato sauce over each muffin half; top each with 1 ounce cheese and sprinkle with ⅛ teaspoon oregano. Spread half of remaining sauce over each muffin half. Broil in toaster-oven or broiler until cheese melts.

Each serving is equivalent to: ⅜ serving Bonus; 1 serving Bread; 1 ounce Hard Cheese.

Per serving: 161 calories, 8 g protein, 7 g fat, 17 g carbohydrate, 474 mg sodium

TOMATO–CHEESE TOAST
Full Choice Plan
Makes 2 Midday or Evening Meal servings

1 tablespoon plus 1 teaspoon margarine
2 tablespoons minced onion
1 tablespoon plus ¾ teaspoon enriched all-purpose flour
¼ cup skim milk, heated
3 ounces sharp Cheddar cheese, shredded

¼ teaspoon powdered mustard
2 tablespoons dry white wine
Dash ground red pepper
1 egg, lightly beaten
2-ounce piece enriched French bread, cut in half horizontally
1 medium tomato, cut into 4 slices

In small saucepan heat margarine until bubbly; add onion and sauté until softened. Add flour; cook, stirring constantly, for 2 minutes. Remove from heat and, using a wire whisk, stir in hot milk. Return to heat and cook, stirring constantly, until sauce is thickened and smooth. Add cheese and mustard; cook, stirring, until cheese is melted. Add wine and red pepper and stir to combine. Remove from heat and beat in egg.

Spread ⅓ of the cheese sauce on each piece of bread. Top each with 2 tomato slices and half of the remaining sauce. Transfer to broiler pan that has been lined with foil and broil until tops are lightly browned, about 3 minutes.

Each serving is equivalent to: 2 servings Fats; 1 tablespoon Limited Vegetables; 1¼ servings Bread; ⅛ serving Milk; 1½ ounces Hard Cheese; 1½ servings Extras; ½ Egg; 1 serving Vegetables.

P r serving: 424 calories, 19 g protein, 26 g fat, 27 g carbohydrate, 571 mg sodium

"GUACAMOLE" SALAD

Full Choice Plan
Makes 2 Midday or Evening Meal servings, ¾ meal each; supplement as required

2 cups torn lettuce (bite-size pieces)
½ cup chopped tomato
½ cup chopped celery
2 ounces Cheddar cheese, shredded
1 tablespoon plus 2 teaspoons
 lemon juice, divided
1 cup cooked fresh or frozen cut
 asparagus

2 tablespoons plain unflavored
 yogurt
1 teaspoon onion flakes
¼ teaspoon garlic powder
Dash each salt and ground red
 pepper
1 egg, hard-cooked and cut into
 quarters

In medium salad bowl combine lettuce, tomato, celery, cheese, and 2 teaspoons lemon juice; toss well, cover, and chill.

In blender container combine asparagus, yogurt, seasonings, and remaining tablespoon lemon juice; process until smooth. Spoon mixture over chilled salad and garnish with egg quarters.

Each serving is equivalent to: 4 servings Vegetables; 1 ounce Hard Cheese; ⅛ serving Milk; ½ Egg.

Per serving: 212 calories, 15 g protein, 13 g fat, 11 g carbohydrate, 327 mg sodium

VEGETABLE COTTAGE CHEESE

No Choice Plan
Makes 1 Midday Meal serving

⅔ cup low-fat cottage cheese
¼ cup shredded carrot
¼ cup chopped radishes
1 large lettuce leaf

½ medium tomato, cut into wedges
Dash each salt and freshly ground
 pepper

In small bowl combine cheese, shredded carrot, and chopped radishes. Serve on lettuce leaf, surrounded by tomato wedges; sprinkle with salt and pepper before serving.

Each serving is equivalent to: ⅔ cup Soft Cheese; 1½ servings Vegetables. (See page 407 for Full Choice Plan adjustments.)

Per serving: 139 calories, 20 g protein, 2 g fat, 11 g carbohydrate, 750 mg sodium

Note: On the Full and Limited Choice Plans this recipe may be used at the Midday or Evening Meal.

WATERCRESS PINWHEEL PLATTER

Full Choice Plan
Makes 4 Midday or Evening Meal servings

⅔ cup cottage cheese
¼ cup tightly packed watercress
 leaves
2 teaspoons chopped scallion
 (green onion)
½ teaspoon Dijon-style mustard

Dash each salt and white pepper
6 slices enriched white bread
¾ cup shredded lettuce
6 hard-cooked eggs, cut into
 quarters
8 radishes, cut into roses

1. In blender container or work bowl of food processor combine cottage cheese, watercress, chopped scallion, and mustard; process until smooth. Stir in salt and pepper; cover and refrigerate for at least 30 minutes.
2. Using a rolling pin, flatten bread until very thin, being careful not to break bread.
3. Spread ⅙ of the cottage cheese mixture onto each slice of bread; roll each so that it resembles a jelly roll. Wrap each roll tightly in plastic wrap and refrigerate for at least 3 hours.
4. Remove wrap and, using a serrated knife, cut each bread roll into 6 equal pinwheels.
5. To serve, on each of 4 plates arrange a row of 9 overlapping pinwheels. Arrange a row of ¼ of the shredded lettuce next to each row of pinwheels, then a row of 6 egg quarters. Garnish each portion with 2 radish roses.

Each serving is equivalent to: ⅙ cup Soft Cheese; ⅔ serving Vegetables; ½ teaspoon Limited Vegetables; 1½ servings Bread; 1½ Eggs.

Per serving: 255 calories, 17 g protein, 11 g fat, 20 g carbohydrate, 483 mg sodium

ZUCCHINI–CHEESE SALAD

Limited Choice Plan
Makes 1 Midday or Evening Meal serving

2 tablespoons plain unflavored yogurt
½ teaspoon each Dijon-style mustard and prepared horseradish
Dash each salt and pepper

½ cup each coarsely shredded zucchini and celery
¼ cup coarsely shredded carrot
4 radishes, coarsely shredded
2 ounces low-fat American cheese, cut into thin strips
2 iceberg or romaine lettuce leaves

In bowl combine yogurt, mustard, horseradish, salt, and pepper. Add shredded vegetables and cheese and toss to combine. Serve on lettuce leaves.

Each serving is equivalent to: ¼ serving Milk; 1½ servings Vegetables; 2 ounces Hard Cheese. (See page 407 for Full Choice Plan adjustments.)

Per serving: 160 calories, 17 g protein, 5 g fat, 12 g carbohydrate, 1,212 mg sodium

BLEU CHEESE MOLD

Full Choice Plan
Makes 4 Midday or Evening Meal servings, ½ meal each; supplement as required

1½ teaspoons unflavored gelatin
¼ cup water
⅔ cup cottage cheese, put through sieve
2 ounces bleu cheese, put through sieve

¼ cup reduced-calorie mayonnaise
1 tablespoon minced shallots
½ teaspoon Worcestershire sauce
Dash white pepper

In small saucepan sprinkle gelatin over water; let stand 1 minute to soften. Cook over low heat, stirring constantly, until gelatin is completely dissolved.

In small bowl combine cottage cheese, bleu cheese, and mayonnaise. Stir in dissolved gelatin, shallots, Worcestershire sauce, and pepper. Rinse a 2-cup mold with cold water and spoon cheese mixture into mold. Cover and refrigerate until firm, at least 3 hours.

To Unmold: Dip the point of a small knife in warm water; with point, loosen mixture around edge of mold. Invert platter on top of mold; quickly invert mold and platter together. Place a damp hot cloth over inverted mold and shake mold gently to release. Carefully lift off mold.

Each serving is equivalent to: ¼ serving Extras; ⅙ cup Soft Cheese; ½ ounce Hard Cheese; 1½ servings Fats; ¾ teaspoon Limited Vegetables.

Per serving: 128 calories, 9 g protein, 9 g fat, 4 g carbohydrate, 423 mg sodium

STUFFED CUCUMBER BOATS

Full Choice Plan
Makes 2 or 4 Midday or Evening Meal servings, ½ or ¼ meal each; supplement as required

2 medium cucumbers, pared and scored	½ teaspoon granulated sugar
1 teaspoon salt	¼ teaspoon curry powder
⅔ cup cottage cheese	1 garlic clove, minced
2 tablespoons minced Italian parsley	Dash pepper
1 tablespoon chopped chives	1 tablespoon plus 1 teaspoon shredded carrot

Cut each cucumber in half lengthwise and, using a spoon, scoop out and discard seeds. Sprinkle inside of each cucumber half with ¼ teaspoon salt; place cut-side down on paper towels and let drain.

In small bowl combine remaining ingredients except shredded carrot. Dry inside of cucumber boats with paper towels and stuff each with ¼ of the cheese mixture; garnish each with 1 teaspoon shredded carrot. Cover and refrigerate until chilled.

Each ½-meal serving is equivalent to: 2 servings Vegetables; ⅓ cup Soft Cheese; ½ serving Extras.

Per serving: 122 calories, 11 g protein, 4 g fat, 12 g carbohydrate, 1,126 mg sodium

Each ¼-meal serving is equivalent to: 1 serving Vegetables; ⅙ cup Soft Cheese; ¼ serving Extras.

Per serving: 61 calories, 6 g protein, 2 g fat, 6 g carbohydrate, 563 mg sodium

STUFFED CHERRY TOMATOES

Limited Choice Plan
Makes 1 Midday or Evening Meal serving, ¼ meal; supplement as required

Using **12 cherry tomatoes,** cut a thin slice from the stem end of each. Scoop out **pulp, reserving 1 tablespoon.** Place tomato shells, cut-side down, on paper towels and let drain.

In small bowl combine reserved pulp, **2 tablespoons plus 2 teaspoons low-fat cottage cheese,** and **dash onion powder.** Spoon mixture into tomato shells; sprinkle each with **dash pepper.** Serve at once or cover and refrigerate for up to 4 hours.

Each serving is equivalent to: 1 serving Vegetables; ⅙ cup Soft Cheese.

Per serving: 39 calories, 5 g protein, 0.5 g fat, 4 g carbohydrate, 154 mg sodium

BAKED STUFFED CHERRY TOMATOES
Full Choice Plan
Makes 1 Midday or Evening Meal serving, ⅛ meal; supplement as required

Using **6 cherry tomatoes,** cut a thin slice from the stem end of each and **reserve slices.** Scoop out **pulp** and reserve. Place tomato shells, cut-side down, on paper towels and let drain.

Preheat oven to 400°F. In small bowl combine reserved pulp with **¼ ounce shredded Swiss cheese** and **1 teaspoon pickle relish.** Spoon an equal amount of mixture into each tomato shell and replace top slices. Set stuffed tomatoes on toaster-oven tray or piece of foil. Bake until cheese is bubbly, about 10 minutes. Serve hot.

Each serving is equivalent to: 1 serving Vegetables; ¼ ounce Hard Cheese; 1 serving Extras.

Per serving: 47 calories, 3 g protein, 2 g fat, 5 g carbohydrate, 57 mg sodium

BLEU CHEESE-STUFFED CHERRY TOMATOES
Full Choice Plan
Makes 1 Midday or Evening Meal serving, ¼ meal; supplement as required

Using **6 cherry tomatoes,** cut a thin slice from the stem end of each and **reserve slices.** Scoop out **pulp** and reserve. Place tomato shells, cut-side down, on paper towels and let drain.

In small bowl combine **½ ounce bleu cheese** with reserved pulp. Spoon mixture into tomato shells and replace top slices. Serve at once or cover and refrigerate for up to 4 hours.

Each serving is equivalent to: 1 serving Vegetables; ½ ounce Hard Cheese.

Per serving: 63 calories, 4 g protein, 4 g fat, 3 g carbohydrate, 200 mg sodium

STUFFED ZUCCHINI ROUNDS
Full Choice Plan
Makes 2 or 4 Midday or Evening Meal servings, ¼ or ⅛ meal each; supplement as required

Zucchini rounds can be prepared ahead of time and refrigerated until ready to bake.

2 medium zucchini, about 6 ounces each	**1 ounce Swiss cheese, shredded**
3 tablespoons seasoned dried bread crumbs	**2 teaspoons minced onion**
	¼ teaspoon each oregano leaves and salt

1. In deep 9-inch skillet place zucchini in water to cover; bring to a boil. Reduce heat and simmer 5 minutes. Drain and place in cold water until zucchini are cool enough to handle.
2. Cut each zucchini in half lengthwise; remove and reserve pulp. Place each shell, cut-side down, on a paper towel and let drain.
3. Finely chop pulp and transfer to a sieve; using the back of a spoon, press out moisture.
4. Preheat oven to 400°F. In bowl combine chopped pulp with remaining ingredients. Stuff each zucchini shell with ¼ of the pulp mixture.
5. Form 2 whole zucchini by placing the halves from each together and securing with toothpicks. Cut each zucchini into 6 rounds, each about 1 inch thick, and place, cut-side down, on nonstick baking sheet.
6. Bake until stuffing bubbles, 15 to 20 minutes.
7. Turn oven control to broil and broil until tops are crisp, about 1 minute. Serve hot, 6 or 3 rounds per portion.

Each ¼-meal serving is equivalent to: 2⅖ servings Vegetables; ½ serving Bread; ½ ounce Hard Cheese; 1 teaspoon Limited Vegetables.

Per serving: 123 calories, 7 g protein, 5 g fat, 14 g carbohydrate, 380 mg sodium

Each ⅛-meal serving is equivalent to: 1⅕ servings Vegetables; ¼ serving Bread; ¼ ounce Hard Cheese; ½ teaspoon Limited Vegetables.

Per serving: 61 calories, 4 g protein, 2 g fat, 7 g carbohydrate, 88 mg sodium

BAKED MACARONI AND CHEESE LOAF

Full Choice Plan
Makes 2 Midday or Evening Meal servings

1⅓ cups cooked enriched elbow
    macaroni
3 ounces sharp Cheddar cheese,
    shredded

½ cup evaporated skimmed milk
1 large egg, beaten
1 tablespoon chopped chives
Dash each salt and pepper

Garnish
Chopped fresh parsley

Preheat oven to 350°F. In medium bowl combine all ingredients except garnish. Spray a 7⅜ x 3⅝ x 2¼-inch loaf pan with nonstick cooking spray and transfer macaroni mixture to pan. Place loaf pan into larger baking pan; pour boiling water into larger pan to a depth of about 1 inch. Bake until loaf has set, 25 to 30 minutes. Remove loaf pan from water bath and let rest for 5 minutes. Unmold loaf by inverting pan onto serving platter. Serve garnished with parsley.

Each serving is equivalent to: 1 serving Bread Substitutes; 1½ ounces Hard Cheese; ½ serving Milk; ½ Egg.

Per serving: 369 calories, 22 g protein, 17 g fat, 30 g carbohydrate, 439 mg sodium

CHEESE "BURGERS"
Full Choice Plan
Makes 2 Midday or Evening Meal servings, 2 "burgers" each

⅔ cup cottage cheese
1 ounce sharp Cheddar cheese, shredded
1 large egg
1 tablespoon chopped chives
¼ teaspoon salt
Dash each pepper and paprika

¼ cup plus 2 tablespoons seasoned dried bread crumbs, divided
1 medium tomato, sliced
8 iceberg or romaine lettuce leaves
1 tablespoon plus 1 teaspoon ketchup

Preheat oven to 350°F. In medium bowl combine all ingredients except bread crumbs, tomato, lettuce, and ketchup; using an electric mixer, beat at high speed until well mixed. Stir in ¼ cup bread crumbs.
Divide mixture into 4 portions and roll each into a ball. Roll balls in the remaining 2 tablespoons bread crumbs. Transfer balls to nonstick baking sheet and flatten each slightly with palm of hand. Sprinkle an equal amount of any remaining bread crumbs onto each "burger."
Bake "burgers" until golden brown and slightly puffed, 15 to 20 minutes. Serve each portion with half of the tomato slices, 4 lettuce leaves, and 2 teaspoons ketchup.
Each serving is equivalent to: ⅓ cup Soft Cheese; ½ ounce Hard Cheese; ½ Egg; 1 serving Bread; 2 servings Vegetables; 1 serving Extras.

Per serving: 283 calories, 20 g protein, 12 g fat, 24 g carbohydrate, 961 mg sodium

Variation: Use Swiss instead of Cheddar cheese.

Per serving: 279 calories, 20 g protein, 11 g fat, 25 g carbohydrate, 910 mg sodium

CHEESE PUFF
Limited Choice Plan
Makes 2 Midday or Evening Meal servings, ¾ meal each; supplement as required

⅓ cup low-fat cottage cheese
1 ounce low-fat American cheese
1 egg, separated

¼ teaspoon pepper
¼ teaspoon powdered mustard
Dash ground red pepper

1. Preheat oven to 375°F. Spray two 10-ounce custard cups or individual soufflé dishes with nonstick cooking spray.
2. In blender container combine cottage cheese, American cheese, egg yolk, and seasonings; process until smooth, scraping food down from sides of container with a narrow rubber scraper. Pour mixture into small bowl.
3. In another small bowl beat egg white until stiff but not dry. Using rubber scraper, blend about ⅓ of egg white into cheese mixture. Fold in remaining egg white.
4. Spoon mixture into prepared cups or dishes. Bake on lowest rack in oven until golden brown, 20 to 25 minutes.
Each serving is equivalent to: ⅙ cup Soft Cheese; ½ ounce Hard Cheese; ½ Egg.

Per serving: 94 calories, 11 g protein, 4 g fat, 2 g carbohydrate, 409 mg sodium

CHEESE TIMBALES
Full Choice Plan
Makes 4 Midday or Evening Meal servings

1 tablespoon plus 1 teaspoon margarine	1 teaspoon prepared brown mustard
1 tablespoon plus 1 teaspoon enriched all-purpose flour	½ teaspoon salt
1 cup skim milk	⅛ teaspoon white pepper
4 ounces sharp Cheddar cheese, shredded	Dash each ground red pepper and Worcestershire sauce
	4 eggs, beaten
	¼ cup chopped onion

Preheat oven to 350°F. In 1-quart saucepan heat margarine until bubbly; add flour and cook, stirring constantly, for 3 minutes (*do not allow mixture to brown*). Remove pan from heat. Using a wire whisk, slowly stir in milk, stirring until smooth. Cook over medium heat, stirring constantly, until slightly thickened, about 3 minutes. Remove from heat and add cheese, mustard, salt, white and red peppers, and Worcestershire sauce; beat with whisk until smooth. Stir in eggs and beat until smooth. Add chopped onion and stir to combine.

Spray four 6-ounce custard cups with nonstick cooking spray; pour ¼ of egg mixture into each. Place cups in baking pan and pour water into pan to within 1 inch of rim of cups. Bake until firm, 25 to 30 minutes.

Each serving is equivalent to: 1 serving Fats; 1 serving Extras; ¼ serving Milk; 1 ounce Hard Cheese; 1 Egg; 1 tablespoon Limited Vegetables.

Per serving: 264 calories, 16 g protein, 19 g fat, 7 g carbohydrate, 604 mg sodium

EGGPLANT MEXICANA
Full Choice Plan
Makes 4 Midday or Evening Meal servings

Delicious served with a mixed green salad.

1 large eggplant (about 1½ pounds), cut crosswise into ½-inch-thick rounds	8 pitted black olives, sliced
	½ teaspoon ground cumin
	¼ teaspoon garlic powder
2 cups tomato sauce	8 ounces sharp Cheddar cheese, shredded
¼ cup peeled and chopped canned green chilies*	½ cup plain unflavored yogurt
¼ cup thinly sliced scallions (green onions)	

Garnish
Parsley sprigs

On a 10 x 15-inch nonstick baking sheet arrange eggplant slices in a single layer. Bake at 450°F. until soft, about 20 minutes.

While eggplant is baking, in a 1½-quart saucepan combine tomato sauce, chilies, scallions, olives, cumin, and garlic powder; simmer for 10 minutes.

Line the bottom of a shallow 1½-quart casserole with a single layer of half of the eggplant slices; spread half the sauce over the eggplant and sprinkle with half of the cheese; repeat layers, ending with cheese. Bake at 350°F. until hot and bubbly, about 25 minutes. Serve each portion topped with 2 tablespoons yogurt and garnished with parsley.

Each serving is equivalent to: 2⅛ servings Vegetables; 1 serving Bonus; 1 tablespoon Limited Vegetables; 1 serving Extras; 2 ounces Hard Cheese; ¼ serving Milk.

Per serving: 349 calories, 19 g protein, 22 g fat, 22 g carbohydrate, 1,020 mg sodium

Variation: Before adding first layer of eggplant, line bottom of casserole with 4 corn tortillas (6-inch diameter each). Add 1 serving Bread to equivalent listing.

Per serving: 391 calories, 20 g protein, 23 g fat, 31 g carbohydrate, 1,020 mg sodium

* Green chilies make this dish mild to moderately hot; vary the amount according to your taste—up to an additional ¼ cup chilies can be added (adjust equivalents accordingly).

EGGPLANT PARMIGIANA
Full Choice Plan
Makes 2 Midday or Evening Meal servings

1 medium eggplant (about 1 pound), cut crosswise into 8 rounds, each about ¾ inch thick
1 tablespoon plus 1 teaspoon olive oil, divided
Salt and pepper
2 tablespoons diced onion

1 garlic clove, mashed
½ cup tomato sauce
Dash oregano leaves
4 ounces mozzarella cheese, shredded*
2 teaspoons grated Parmesan cheese

Garnish
1 tablespoon chopped fresh parsley

1. Brush 1 side of each eggplant slice with ¼ teaspoon oil. Transfer slices to nonstick baking sheet, oiled-side up, and sprinkle each with dash each salt and pepper.
2. Bake at 400°F. until browned, about 10 minutes. Turn slices, brush each with ¼ teaspoon oil, and bake 10 minutes longer.
3. While eggplant is baking, in small nonstick skillet combine onion and garlic and cook until onion is tender.
4. In shallow 1-quart casserole spread 3 tablespoons tomato sauce; sprinkle sauce with oregano. Arrange eggplant in casserole, overlapping slices, and pour remaining sauce over eggplant; top with onion mixture, then cheeses.
5. Reduce oven temperature to 350°F. and bake Eggplant Parmigiana until cheese is melted and browned, 25 to 30 minutes. Serve garnished with parsley.
Each serving is equivalent to: 3 servings Vegetables; 2 servings Fats;

1 tablespoon Limited Vegetables; ½ serving Bonus; 2 ounces Hard Cheese; 1 serving Extras.

Per serving: 334 calories, 15 g protein, 23 g fat, 20 g carbohydrate, 1,059 mg sodium

* Any hard cheese may be substituted for the mozzarella in this recipe; try Cheddar or Swiss.

EGGPLANT PIE
Full Choice Plan
Makes 2 Midday or Evening Meal servings

1 large eggplant (about 1½ pounds), pared and cut lengthwise into ¼-inch-thick slices
2 ounces mozzarella cheese, shredded
2 ounces sharp Cheddar cheese, shredded

1 medium tomato, diced
½ cup each diced green bell pepper and onion
½ cup sliced mushrooms
Dash each oregano leaves and garlic powder
2 teaspoons grated Parmesan cheese

On baking sheet arrange eggplant slices in a single layer; broil, turning once, 3 to 5 minutes on each side (slices should be crisp and brown). Set oven temperature at 350°F.

In small bowl combine mozzarella and Cheddar cheeses. Arrange eggplant in a 9-inch nonstick pie pan, overlapping slices in a circular pattern. Press edges of eggplant together to resemble a pie crust. Spread vegetables evenly over eggplant and sprinkle with oregano and garlic powder. Top vegetable mixture evenly with combined cheeses, then sprinkle with Parmesan cheese. Bake until cheese is melted and browned, 20 to 25 minutes. Cut into 4 wedges and serve 2 wedges per portion.

Each serving is equivalent to: 6 servings Vegetables; 2 ounces Hard Cheese; ¼ cup Limited Vegetables; 1 serving Extras.

Per serving: 331 calories, 20 g protein, 17 g fat, 30 g carbohydrate, 334 mg sodium

TOMATO–CHEESE PIE
Full Choice Plan
Makes 4 Midday or Evening Meal servings

4 slices enriched white bread, toasted and cut into 1-inch squares
6 ounces Gruyère cheese, shredded
1 medium tomato, cut into ¼-inch-thick slices
1 tablespoon chopped scallion (green onion)

2 eggs
½ teaspoon powdered mustard
¼ teaspoon each paprika and salt
¼ teaspoon basil leaves, crushed
⅛ teaspoon pepper
1½ cups skim milk

Preheat oven to 350°F. Spray a 9-inch pie plate with nonstick cooking spray; arrange toast squares in pie plate and sprinkle with half of the cheese. Top cheese with tomato slices and chopped scallion; sprinkle with remaining cheese.

In small bowl beat eggs with mustard, paprika, salt, basil leaves, and pepper. Add milk and beat until well combined. Pour over cheese. Bake until puffy and brown, about 40 minutes.

Each serving is equivalent to: 1 serving Bread; 1½ ounces Hard Cheese; ½ serving Vegetables; ¾ teaspoon Limited Vegetables; ½ Egg; ⅜ serving Milk.

Per serving: 322 calories, 21 g protein, 18 g fat, 19 g carbohydrate, 479 mg sodium

WELSH RAREBIT

Full Choice Plan

Makes 2 Midday or Evening Meal servings

Serve with mixed green salad.

4 ounces Cheddar cheese, shredded
1 tablespoon plus 1 teaspoon
   enriched all-purpose flour
2 fluid ounces beer*
2 teaspoons margarine

½ teaspoon Worcestershire sauce
¼ teaspoon powdered mustard
Dash ground red pepper
1 English muffin, split and toasted

In 1-quart nonstick saucepan combine cheese with flour. Add remaining ingredients except English muffin; cook over low heat, stirring constantly, until cheese is melted and mixture is smooth and thick.

Place each muffin half in a shallow individual flameproof casserole; spoon half of cheese mixture over each. Broil 3 inches from source of heat until cheese is browned on top, about 1 minute.

Each serving is equivalent to: 2 ounces Hard Cheese; 2 servings Extras; ⅛ serving Occasional Substitutes; 1 serving Fats; 1 serving Bread.

Per serving: 363 calories, 17 g protein, 23 g fat, 19 g carbohydrate, 543 mg sodium

* Each serving may be accompanied by 7 fluid ounces beer. Change equivalent listing to 1 serving Occasional Substitutes and nutrition figures to 451 calories, 18 g protein, 27 g carbohydrate, 558 mg sodium.

Variation: Slice 1 medium tomato; arrange half of the slices on each muffin half, then top with cheese mixture and proceed as directed. Add 1 serving Vegetables to equivalent listing.

Per serving: 378 calories, 18 g protein, 23 g fat, 22 g carbohydrate, 545 mg sodium
With additional 7 fluid ounces beer: 466 calories, 19 g protein, 23 g fat, 30 g carbohydrate, 560 mg sodium

SWISS FONDUE

Full Choice Plan

Makes 4 Midday or Evening Meal servings

8 fluid ounces white wine
8 ounces Gruyère cheese, shredded
1 tablespoon plus 1 teaspoon
   cornstarch, dissolved in ¼ cup
   water

Dash each powdered mustard and
   ground red pepper
2 cups cut-up raw vegetables*

In fondue pot or small saucepan bring wine to a boil. Reduce heat to low, add cheese, and cook, stirring constantly, until cheese is melted and mixture is smooth. Stir in dissolved cornstarch; cook, stirring constantly, until thickened. Add mustard and pepper and stir until thoroughly combined. (If made in saucepan, pour into fondue pot for serving.) Keep hot on fondue stand over low heat.

To Serve: Let each person spear vegetables on long-handled fork and dip into fondue.

Each serving is equivalent to: ½ serving Occasional Substitutes; 2 ounces Hard Cheese; 1 serving Extras; 1 serving Vegetables.

Per serving: 304 calories, 18 g protein, 18 g fat, 7 g carbohydrate, 215 mg sodium

* As vegetable dippers, use one of the following or any combination thereof to equal 2 cups: cauliflower, cucumbers, zucchini, celery, fennel. For additional suggestions, see Crudités (page 57).

SWISS SOUFFLÉ
Full Choice Plan
Makes 2 Midday or Evening Meal servings

2 teaspoons grated Parmesan cheese
2 large eggs, separated
1 tablespoon plus 1 teaspoon
　reduced-calorie margarine
1 tablespoon plus ¾ teaspoon
　enriched all-purpose flour

½ cup skim milk, heated
2 ounces Swiss cheese, shredded
¼ teaspoon salt
⅛ teaspoon paprika
Dash white pepper
½ teaspoon cream of tartar

1. Spray two 10-ounce custard cups with nonstick cooking spray. Sprinkle 1 teaspoon Parmesan cheese into each cup, coating bottom and sides.

2. Cut 2 pieces of foil, each long enough to go around custard cup and about 4 inches wide. Wrap foil around each cup so that about 2 inches extend above rim, and secure with cellophane tape; set aside.

3. In small bowl beat egg yolks and set aside.

4. In small nonstick saucepan heat margarine, over medium heat, until bubbly; add flour and, using a wire whisk, stir until well blended. Stirring constantly, slowly pour in milk; continue to stir with whisk until sauce is smooth.

5. Stir small amount of hot sauce into beaten yolks. Slowly pour yolk mixture into remaining sauce, stirring rapidly to prevent lumping. Continuing to stir, add cheese, salt, paprika, and pepper and cook until cheese has melted and sauce is thick and smooth (*do not boil*); remove from heat.

6. Preheat oven to 325°F. In small mixing bowl beat egg whites until foamy; add cream of tartar and beat until stiff peaks form.

7. Gently fold whites into cheese mixture, ⅓ of the whites at a time. Pour half of mixture into each prepared custard cup and place in the center of the oven. Bake 25 to 30 minutes (soufflé should be set and

golden brown). Remove from oven, carefully remove foil collars, and serve immediately. Each serving is equivalent to: 1 serving Extras; 1 Egg; 1 serving Fats; ¼ serving Bread; ¼ serving Milk; 1 ounce Hard Cheese.

Per serving: 268 calories, 18 g protein, 18 g fat, 9 g carbohydrate, 568 mg sodium

Variation: Substitute shredded Cheddar cheese for the Swiss cheese.

Per serving: 275 calories, 17 g protein, 19 g fat, 8 g carbohydrate, 671 mg sodium

NOT-SO-DANISH PASTRY
Limited Choice Plan
Makes 1 Mealtime serving, 1 Morning or ½ Midday or Evening Meal; supplement as required

⅓ cup low-fat cottage cheese
1 teaspoon honey
¼ teaspoon maple extract

Dash ground nutmeg
1 slice raisin bread, toasted

In small bowl combine cottage cheese with honey, maple extract, and nutmeg. Spread mixture on toast; place toast on piece of foil or in broiler pan. Broil in toaster-oven or broiler until cheese is hot and bubbly, about 2 minutes. Each serving is equivalent to: ⅓ cup Soft Cheese; 2 servings Extras; 1 serving Bread.

Per serving: 143 calories, 11 g protein, 2 g fat, 21 g carbohydrate, 393 mg sodium

Variation: Substitute artificial sweetener to equal 1 teaspoon sugar for the honey. Reduce maple extract to ⅛ teaspoon and substitute ground cinnamon for the nutmeg. Omit Extras from equivalent listing.

Per serving: 122 calories, 11 g protein, 1 g fat, 16 g carbohydrate, 393 mg sodium

STRAWBERRY–CHEESE "DANISH"
Full Choice Plan
Makes 4 Mealtime servings, 1 Morning or ½ Midday or Evening Meal each; supplement as required

2 large eggs
½ cup plus 2 tablespoons
  enriched cake flour
1 tablespoon plus 1 teaspoon
  granulated sugar, divided
1½ teaspoons double-acting baking
  powder
Dash salt

2 tablespoons plus 2 teaspoons
  reduced-calorie margarine
¼ cup evaporated skimmed milk
⅔ cup part-skim ricotta cheese
1 tablespoon plus 1 teaspoon
  reduced-calorie strawberry spread
  (16 calories per 2 teaspoons)

1. Separate 1 egg and set aside yolk and white.
2. In bowl combine flour, 1 tablespoon sugar, the baking powder, and salt. With a pastry blender, or 2 knives used scissor-fashion, cut in margarine until mixture resembles coarse meal.
3. In another bowl combine 1 whole egg, milk, and reserved yolk; beat slightly. Add to flour mixture and blend thoroughly, forming a thin batter.
4. Preheat oven to 425°F. Spray a cookie sheet with nonstick cooking spray. Spoon batter onto prepared sheet, forming 8 "danish" and leaving a space of about 2 inches between each.
5. In small bowl beat reserved egg white until stiff peaks form.
6. In another small bowl combine cheese with remaining teaspoon sugar, then fold in beaten egg white. Spoon an equal amount of cheese mixture onto center of each "danish."
7. Bake until "danish" are golden brown and cheese is slightly puffed, 10 to 12 minutes.
8. Remove "danish" from oven and immediately top center of each with ½ teaspoon strawberry spread. Serve 2 "danish" per portion.

Each serving is equivalent to: ½ Egg; 1 serving Bread; 2 servings Extras; 1 serving Fats; ⅛ serving Milk; ⅙ cup Soft Cheese; 8 calories Specialty Foods.

Per serving: 222 calories, 10 g protein, 10 g fat, 23 g carbohydrate, 384 mg sodium

Variation: Substitute reduced-calorie orange marmalade (16 calories per 2 teaspoons) for the strawberry spread.

CHEESECAKE LOAF
Full Choice Plan
Makes 6 Mealtime servings, 1 Morning or ½ Midday or Evening Meal each; supplement as required

2 cups part-skim ricotta cheese
2 tablespoons lemon juice
1 teaspoon each vanilla and
   almond extract
½ teaspoon grated lemon peel

2 egg whites (at room temperature)
2 tablespoons confectioners' sugar
3 cups strawberries, sliced, or 1½
   cups blueberries

Preheat oven to 350°F. In medium bowl combine cheese, lemon juice, extracts, and lemon peel; using an electric mixer, beat until smooth. In small bowl, using clean beaters, beat egg whites, adding sugar gradually while beating, until whites become stiff and glossy. Fold beaten whites into cheese mixture, being careful not to overmix. Pour into a 7⅜ x 3⅝ x 2¼-inch nonstick loaf pan. Bake 40 to 45 minutes (until top is lightly browned).

Turn oven off and let cake rest in oven for 15 minutes. Remove from oven and invert pan onto plate; remove pan. Turn cake over on plate, cover lightly, and chill.

Serve with strawberries or blueberries.
Each serving is equivalent to: ⅓ cup Soft Cheese; 2⅔ servings Extras;
½ serving Fruits.

Per serving with strawberries: 164 calories, 11 g protein, 7 g fat, 14 g carbohydrate,
121 mg sodium
With blueberries: 158 calories, 11 g protein, 7 g fat, 13 g carbohydrate, 121 mg sodium

MOCHA–ALMOND CHEESECAKE
Full Choice Plan
Makes 8 Midday or Evening Meal servings, ½ meal each; supplement as required

Crust
2 slices enriched white bread,
  toasted and made into fine
  crumbs

2 teaspoons unsweetened cocoa
Artificial sweetener to equal 2
  teaspoons sugar

Filling
2⅔ cups part-skim ricotta cheese
24 ounces chocolate dietary frozen
  dessert
2 teaspoons instant coffee powder,
  dissolved in 2 tablespoons water

1 teaspoon almond extract
4 envelopes unflavored gelatin
1 cup water

To Prepare Crust: Spray a 9-inch springform pan with nonstick cooking
spray. In small bowl combine bread crumbs, cocoa, and sweetener; sprinkle
bottom and sides of pan with crumb mixture, allowing any crumbs that
do not adhere to remain in an even layer on bottom of pan.
To Prepare Filling:
1. In blender container process half of the ricotta cheese until smooth;
transfer to large bowl. Process remaining cheese and combine with first
batch in bowl.
2. Repeat Step 1 with frozen dessert, adding dessert to cheese.
3. Add dissolved coffee and extract to bowl and stir to combine.
4. In small saucepan sprinkle gelatin over water and let stand for 1
minute to soften; cook over low heat, stirring constantly, until gelatin is
completely dissolved.
5. Add dissolved gelatin to cheese-dessert mixture and stir vigorously
until thoroughly combined.
6. Pour into prepared crust and, using a spatula, spread into an even
layer. Cover and refrigerate at least 4 hours.
To Serve: Run a small knife around the edge of the cake and carefully
remove sides of springform. Serve on the pan's metal base.
Each serving is equivalent to: ¼ serving Bread; 1¼ servings Extras;
⅓ cup Soft Cheese; ½ serving Milk; 1 serving Fruits.

Per serving: 245 calories, 17 g protein, 8 g fat, 27 g carbohydrate, 206 mg sodium

NEAPOLITAN CHEESECAKE
Full Choice Plan
Makes 8 Midday or Evening Meal servings, ½ meal each; supplement as required

Crust
2 slices enriched white bread, toasted and made into fine crumbs

2 teaspoons unsweetened cocoa
Artificial sweetener to equal 2 teaspoons sugar

Layer 1
1 envelope unflavored gelatin
¼ cup water
⅔ cup part-skim ricotta cheese

6 ounces vanilla dietary frozen dessert
½ teaspoon almond extract

Layer 2
1 envelope unflavored gelatin
¼ cup water
2 teaspoons instant coffee powder

⅔ cup part-skim ricotta cheese
6 ounces chocolate dietary frozen dessert

Layer 3
1 envelope unflavored gelatin
¼ cup water
⅔ cup part-skim ricotta cheese

6 ounces strawberry dietary frozen dessert

Layer 4
1 envelope unflavored gelatin
¼ cup water
⅔ cup part-skim ricotta cheese

6 ounces maple dietary frozen dessert

To Prepare Crust: Spray a 9-inch springform pan with nonstick cooking spray. In small bowl combine bread crumbs, cocoa, and sweetener; sprinkle bottom and sides of pan with crumb mixture, reserving 1 tablespoon and allowing any crumbs that do not adhere to remain in an even layer on bottom of pan.

To Prepare Layers:
Layer 1:
1. In small saucepan sprinkle 1 envelope gelatin over ¼ cup water and allow to stand 1 minute to soften; cook over low heat, stirring constantly, until gelatin is completely dissolved.

2. In blender container process ⅔ cup ricotta cheese until smooth. Add 6 ounces vanilla frozen dessert and process until smooth. Add almond extract and dissolved gelatin and process until combined.

3. Pour into prepared crust and, using a spatula, spread into an even layer. Cover and refrigerate 15 minutes. Meanwhile, proceed with next layer.

Layer 2: Repeat Steps 1, 2, and 3 adding instant coffee to dissolved gelatin in Step 1 and, in Step 2, using chocolate frozen dessert and eliminating almond extract.

Layers 3 and 4: Repeat Steps 1, 2, and 3 using strawberry and maple frozen desserts and eliminating almond extract in Step 2.

When all layers have been completed, garnish with reserved crumbs, cover, and refrigerate for at least 4 hours.

To Serve: Run a small knife around the edge of the cake and carefully remove sides of springform. For ease of serving, serve on the pan's metal base.

Each serving is equivalent to: ¼ serving Bread; 1¼ servings Extras; ⅓ cup Soft Cheese; ½ serving Milk; 1 serving Fruits.

Per serving: 244 calories, 17 g protein, 8 g fat, 27 g carbohydrate, 205 mg sodium

STRAWBERRY–CHEESE PARFAIT
Full Choice Plan
Makes 2 Midday or Evening Meal servings, ½ meal each; supplement as required

¾ cup strawberries, divided
2 tablespoons orange juice (no sugar added)
1½ teaspoons granulated sugar, divided

⅔ cup part-skim ricotta cheese
Artificial sweetener to equal 1 teaspoon sugar
¼ teaspoon grated orange peel
¼ teaspoon vanilla extract

In small bowl crush ½ cup strawberries; slice remaining berries and set aside. Add orange juice and ½ teaspoon sugar to crushed berries and let stand 15 minutes.

In separate bowl mix cheese with sweetener, orange peel, vanilla, and remaining teaspoon sugar. Drain juice from crushed strawberries into cheese mixture and stir to combine. Add half of cheese mixture to crushed strawberries and stir well.

Spoon half of crushed strawberry mixture into each of 2 parfait glasses; top each portion with 3 or 4 strawberry slices. Spoon half of remaining cheese mixture into each glass; top each portion with half of the remaining strawberry slices. Chill for 30 minutes.

Each serving is equivalent to: ½ serving Fruits; 1½ servings Extras; ⅓ cup Soft Cheese.

Per serving: 157 calories, 10 g protein, 7 g fat, 14 g carbohydrate, 103 mg sodium

Peanut Butter

When the Weight Watchers Program was revised in 1981, peanut butter got a legal permit. This popular high-nutrition food provides an energy-giving boost. Peanuts are a staple in the Far East and Africa, and in France gourmets give peanut oil top rating. Here at home, where peanut butter sandwiches are a childhood nostalgia trip, you can use this familiar food from "soup to nuts"—in soups, crêpes, cookies, and "ice cream."

Guidelines for Using Peanut Butter (Full Choice Plan Only)

1. Amounts:

Women, Men, and Youth	Serving
Morning Meal	1 tablespoon (omit 1 serving Fats)
Midday and Evening Meals	3 tablespoons (omit 2 servings Fats)

2. Peanut Butter may be consumed at mealtime *only* and may be split with items from the Eggs, Cheese, Poultry, Veal, and Game, Meat Group, Fish, and Legumes categories.
3. Since peanut butter has a high fat content, some Fats must be omitted when it is selected (see serving chart above for amounts).
4. Commercial smooth and chunky-style peanut butters may be selected. These products may contain sugar.
5. Homemade peanut butter may be used.
6. Nuts or other commercial nut butters may *not* be substituted for peanut butter.

PEANUT BUTTER CRUMBLE
Full Choice Plan
Makes 2 Morning Meal servings

Delicious served with milk and fruit.

¾ ounce wheat germ
1 tablespoon plus ¾ teaspoon whole wheat flour
1 tablespoon plus ¾ teaspoon enriched all-purpose flour

3 tablespoons hot water
2 tablespoons smooth peanut butter
1 teaspoon granulated brown sugar

1. Preheat oven to 350°F. In small bowl combine wheat germ, whole wheat flour, and all-purpose flour.
2. In separate bowl combine water, peanut butter, and sugar and blend until smooth. Add to flour mixture, stirring to make a soft dough.
3. Place dough between 2 sheets of wax paper and roll as thin as possible.

4. Spray a baking sheet with nonstick cooking spray. Remove top sheet of wax paper and invert dough onto prepared sheet. Peel off remaining wax paper.

5. Bake until edges are slightly browned, about 15 minutes; let cool on baking sheet.

6. Crumble into small pieces and store in airtight container until ready to use.

Each serving is equivalent to: 1 serving Bread; 1 tablespoon Peanut Butter (1 serving Protein and 1 serving Fats); 1 serving Extras.

Per serving: 178 calories, 9 g protein, 9 g fat, 17 g carbohydrate, 99 mg sodium

CREAMY PEANUT BUTTER SOUP
Full Choice Plan
Makes 2 Midday or Evening Meal servings, ½ meal each; supplement as required

This recipe yields about 1 cup soup per serving.

¼ cup diced onion
1 garlic clove, minced
2 teaspoons enriched all-purpose flour
1 packet instant chicken broth and seasoning mix
1½ cups water

2 tablespoons each diced carrot and celery
3 tablespoons chunky-style peanut butter
½ cup evaporated skimmed milk
Dash each salt and white pepper
1 teaspoon chopped fresh parsley (optional)

In 1-quart nonstick saucepan combine onion and garlic and cook until onion is softened. Add flour and cook, stirring constantly, for 2 minutes longer. Add broth mix, then stir in water. Add carrot and celery and bring to a boil. Reduce heat, cover, and simmer until vegetables are tender, about 10 minutes.

Measure ½ cup of the hot liquid into a small bowl; add peanut butter and stir until smooth. Add peanut butter mixture to saucepan containing vegetables and simmer 3 minutes. Stir in milk and simmer until heated, about 2 minutes longer (*do not boil*). Season with salt and pepper and ladle into 2 soup bowls; if desired, garnish each portion with ½ teaspoon parsley.

Each serving is equivalent to: ⅛ cup Limited Vegetables; 1½ servings Extras; ¼ serving Vegetables; 1 tablespoon plus 1½ teaspoons Peanut Butter (½ serving Protein and 1 serving Fats); ½ serving Milk.

Per serving: 220 calories, 13 g protein, 12 g fat, 18 g carbohydrate, 717 mg sodium

ONION–PEANUT SAUCE
Full Choice Plan
Makes 2 or 4 Midday or Evening Meal servings, ½ or ¼ meal each; supplement as required

This recipe will yield about 1⅓ cups sauce. Serve over cooked macaroni or vegetables.

1 cup tomato juice
2 tablespoons minced onion
2 teaspoons each red wine and
tomato paste

3 tablespoons chunky-style peanut
butter*

In small nonstick saucepan combine tomato juice, onion, wine, and tomato paste; cook over low heat until mixture simmers. Add peanut butter and cook, stirring constantly, until mixture is well blended. Serve hot.

Each ½-meal serving is equivalent to: ½ serving Bonus; 1 tablespoon Limited Vegetables; 1 serving Extras; 1 tablespoon plus 1½ teaspoons Peanut Butter (½ serving Protein and 1 serving Fats).

Per serving: 176 calories, 8 g protein, 12 g fat, 11 g carbohydrate, 432 mg sodium

Each ¼-meal serving is equivalent to: ¼ serving Bonus; 1½ teaspoons Limited Vegetables; ½ serving Extras; 2¼ teaspoons Peanut Butter (¼ serving Protein and ½ serving Fats).

Per serving: 88 calories, 4 g protein, 6 g fat, 6 g carbohydrate, 216 mg sodium

* Smooth peanut butter can be substituted for the chunky-style.

PEANUT SAUCE

Full Choice Plan

Makes 2 or 4 Midday or Evening Meal servings, ½ or ¼ meal each; supplement as required

This recipe will yield about 1⅓ cups sauce. Serve over cooked noodles, rice, or vegetables.

¾ cup Chicken Broth (see page
401)
½ medium tomato, blanched,
peeled, seeded, and diced

2 tablespoons thinly sliced scallion
(green onion)
3 tablespoons smooth peanut
butter*

In small nonstick saucepan combine broth, tomato, and scallion; cook over medium heat until scallion slices are tender, about 2 minutes. Reduce heat, add peanut butter, and cook, stirring constantly, until mixture is well blended. Serve hot.

Each ½-meal serving is equivalent to: ½ serving Extras; ½ serving Vegetables; 1 tablespoon Limited Vegetables; 1 tablespoon plus 1½ teaspoons Peanut Butter (½ serving Protein and 1 serving Fats).

Per serving: 157 calories, 9 g protein, 12 g fat, 8 g carbohydrate, 160 mg sodium

Each ¼-meal serving is equivalent to: ¼ serving Extras; ¼ serving Vegetables; 1½ teaspoons Limited Vegetables; 2¼ teaspoons Peanut Butter (¼ serving Protein and ½ serving Fats).

Per serving: 78 calories, 5 g protein, 6 g fat, 4 g carbohydrate, 80 mg sodium

* Chunky-style peanut butter can be substituted for the smooth.

BROILED PEANUT BUTTER AND MARMALADE SANDWICH

Full Choice Plan
Makes 1 Midday or Evening Meal serving, ½ meal; supplement as required

Spread 1 tablespoon plus 1½ teaspoons chunky-style peanut butter on 1 slice toasted whole wheat bread and top with 2 teaspoons reduced-calorie orange marmalade (16 calories per 2 teaspoons). Place on piece of foil or in broiler pan. Broil in toaster-oven or broiler until marmalade is bubbly and lightly browned.

Each serving is equivalent to: 1 tablespoon plus 1½ teaspoons Peanut Butter (½ serving Protein and 1 serving Fats); 1 serving Bread; 16 calories Specialty Foods.

Per serving: 212 calories, 9 g protein, 13 g fat, 19 g carbohydrate, 266 mg sodium

POCKET FULL OF SURPRISES

Full Choice Plan
*Makes 4 Midday or Evening Meal servings**

2 teaspoons lime juice (no sugar added)
2 teaspoons Dijon-style mustard
1½ teaspoons honey
2 cups alfalfa sprouts
6 ounces sliced Canadian-style bacon
4 whole wheat pita breads, 1 ounce each
⅓ cup plus 2 teaspoons peanut butter, divided

1. In small metal measuring cup or other small flameproof container combine lime juice, mustard, and honey; heat, stirring constantly, until thinned.
2. In small bowl toss alfalfa sprouts with honey mixture and set aside.
3. In small nonstick skillet cook bacon, turning once, until crisp and brown on both sides. Set aside.
4. Cut halfway around edge of each pita bread and open to form a pocket. Inside each pita bread, spread one side with 1 tablespoon plus 1½ teaspoons peanut butter; top with ¼ of the alfalfa sprout mixture and ¼ of the Canadian-style bacon.

Each serving is equivalent to: ¾ serving Extras; 1 serving Vegetables; 1½ ounces Meat Group (cured); 1 serving Bread; 1 tablespoon plus 1½ teaspoons Peanut Butter (½ serving Protein and 1 serving Fats).

Per serving: 366 calories, 23 g protein, 21 g fat, 21 g carbohydrate, 1,308 mg sodium

Variation: Substitute sesame pita breads for the whole wheat pita breads.

* Men—For each serving use 2 ounces sliced Canadian-style bacon, browned. Change equivalent listing to 2 ounces Meat Group (cured).

PEANUT BUTTER–JELLY CRÊPES
Full Choice Plan
Makes 2 Midday or Evening Meal servings

3 tablespoons smooth peanut butter (at room temperature)	1 tablespoon plus 1 teaspoon reduced-calorie strawberry spread (16 calories per 2 teaspoons), divided
2 large eggs	

1. In blender container combine peanut butter and eggs and process until smooth. (Ingredients may be beaten with a fork or a wire whisk, but the blender gives a better consistency.)
2. Heat 6- or 7-inch nonstick skillet or crêpe pan over medium heat. When a drop of water sizzles in pan, pour in half of egg mixture and tilt skillet to form a thin round pancake (crêpe). Cook until brown on bottom. Loosen edges of crêpe with spatula; turn crêpe over very carefully and reduce heat to low.
3. Spoon 2 teaspoons strawberry spread across center of crêpe and heat just enough to allow spread to melt. Remove skillet from heat.
4. Using a spatula, carefully roll crêpe away from skillet handle toward opposite side, or fold in half. Transfer to warm plate.
5. Pour remaining egg mixture into skillet and repeat Steps 2 through 4.

Each serving is equivalent to: 1 tablespoon plus 1½ teaspoons Peanut Butter (½ serving Protein and 1 serving Fats); 1 Egg; 16 calories Specialty Foods.

Per serving: 236 calories, 13 g protein, 18 g fat, 9 g carbohydrate, 216 mg sodium

CHOCOLATE–NUT CAKE
Full Choice Plan
Makes 4 Midday or Evening Meal servings, ½ meal each; supplement as required*

2 envelopes (1 serving each) reduced-calorie chocolate dairy drink mix	½ cup water
¼ cup plus 1½ teaspoons chunky-style peanut butter	½ cup plus 2 tablespoons enriched all-purpose flour
1 egg	Artificial sweetener to equal 4 teaspoons sugar
1 tablespoon plus 1 teaspoon honey	1 teaspoon double-acting baking powder
1 teaspoon vanilla extract	Dash salt

1. Preheat oven to 350°F. Spray a 7⅜ x 3⅝ x 2¼-inch nonstick loaf pan with nonstick cooking spray; set aside.
2. In medium bowl combine first 5 ingredients; add water and mix well.
3. In separate bowl combine flour, sweetener, baking powder, and salt. Add to chocolate mixture, a little at a time, mixing well after each addition. Transfer to prepared loaf pan.
4. Bake about 25 minutes (a cake tester, inserted in center, should come out clean).

5. Transfer pan to wire rack and let cool for 10 to 15 minutes; remove cake from pan and let cool completely on rack.

Each serving is equivalent to: ½ serving Milk Substitutes; 1 tablespoon plus ⅜ teaspoon Peanut Butter (⅜ serving Protein and ¾ serving Fats); ¼ Egg; 2 servings Extras; 1 serving Bread.

Per serving: 362 calories, 14 g protein, 11 g fat, 52 g carbohydrate, 263 mg sodium

* Serve at same meal as Garden Luncheon Salad (see page 156), which contains ¾ Egg and ¼ ounce Hard Cheese per serving.

PEANUT–CREAM SANDWICH COOKIES
Full Choice Plan
Makes 4 Midday or Evening Meal servings, ¼ meal each; supplement as required

3 tablespoons chunky-style peanut butter
2 tablespoons plus 2 teaspoons plain unflavored yogurt

8 graham crackers (2½-inch squares)
2 teaspoons chocolate syrup

In small bowl blend peanut butter with yogurt. Carefully break each graham cracker in half. Spread ⅛ of the peanut butter mixture (about 3¾ teaspoons) on each of 8 graham cracker halves; top each with 1 of the remaining halves. Spread ¼ teaspoon chocolate syrup over top of each graham cracker sandwich. Transfer sandwiches to airtight container,* cover, and freeze for at least 2 hours. Serve 2 sandwich cookies per portion.

Each serving is equivalent to: 2¼ teaspoons Peanut Butter (¼ serving Protein and ½ serving Fats); 2 teaspoons Yogurt (¹⁄₁₂ serving Milk); 1 serving Bread; 1 serving Extras.

Per serving: 138 calories, 5 g protein, 8 g fat, 15 g carbohydrate, 173 mg sodium

* If airtight container is not available, transfer cookies to plate and cover with a tent of foil, being careful that foil does not touch cookies.

PEANUT–BANANA TREAT
Full Choice Plan
Makes 1 Midday or Evening Meal serving, ¼ meal; supplement as required

½ medium banana
2¼ teaspoons chunky-style peanut butter

½ teaspoon chocolate syrup
⅛ teaspoon shredded coconut

Peel banana half and cut in half lengthwise. Spread peanut butter on cut side of one half and top with remaining half; transfer to plate. Spread syrup over banana and sprinkle with coconut. Serve immediately.

Each serving is equivalent to: 1 serving Fruits; 2¼ teaspoons Peanut Butter (¼ serving Protein and ½ serving Fats); 1⅛ servings Extras.

Per serving: 130 calories, 4 g protein, 6 g fat, 17 g carbohydrate, 76 mg sodium

PEANUT BUTTER "ICE CREAM"

Full Choice Plan
Makes 4 Midday or Evening Meal servings, ½ meal each; supplement as required

12 ounces vanilla dietary frozen
dessert
⅓ cup plus 2 teaspoons smooth
peanut butter

4 graham crackers (2½-inch
squares), made into crumbs

1. In medium bowl allow frozen dessert to soften slightly.
2. Add peanut butter to softened dessert and blend thoroughly.
3. Fit a sheet of plastic wrap into a 3½ x 7½ x 2¼-inch loaf pan, pressing wrap as close to sides as possible and allowing ends to extend beyond rim of pan (it will probably not fit smoothly).
4. Fill lined loaf pan with frozen dessert mixture, pressing to fill corners. Tap pan gently on table to eliminate air spaces. Cover and freeze until firm.
5. Spread cracker crumbs on sheet of wax paper. Lift chilled "ice cream" block out of pan by grasping ends of plastic wrap and invert onto crumbs; peel off plastic wrap. Using your hands, press crumbs into sides and top of "ice cream" block. Wrap in moisture- and vapor-proof wrapping, return to freezer, and freeze until firm.
6. Carefully transfer "ice cream" to serving plate and cut into 8 slices, 2 slices per serving.

Each serving is equivalent to: ½ serving Milk; 1 serving Fruits; 1 tablespoon plus 1½ teaspoons Peanut Butter (½ serving Protein and 1 serving Fats); ½ serving Bread.

Per serving: 268 calories, 11 g protein, 14 g fat, 29 g carbohydrate, 263 mg sodium

Poultry, Veal, and Game

Poultry flies to the rescue of the budget when food prices soar, but with our recipes budget doesn't have to be boring. Chicken, turkey, and Cornish hens appear in casseroles, fricassees, and various continental treats. Veal, a more costly gourmet favorite, can be stretched, as in our Veal Chili or Veal and Spinach Cannelloni. For game-lovers, we offer recipes for quail, rabbit, and pheasant.

Guidelines for Using Poultry, Veal, and Game

1. Amounts (skinned and boned cooked or drained canned weight):

	Morning Meal	
	Full Choice Plan	Limited Choice Plan
Women, Men, and Youth	1 ounce	1 ounce

	Midday and Evening Meals	
	Full Choice Plan	Limited Choice Plan
Women and Youth	3 to 4 ounces	3 ounces
Men	4 to 5 ounces	4 ounces

2. Poultry, veal, and game may be consumed at mealtime *only* and may be split with items from the Eggs, Cheese, Peanut Butter (Full Choice Plan only), Meat Group, Fish, and Legumes categories.

3. The Full Choice Plan range of 3 to 4 ounces for Women and Youth (4 to 5 ounces for Men) provides flexibility. It is a way of individualizing the Food Plan to meet your specific needs.

4. Fresh, frozen, freeze-dried, canned, cured, smoked, and pressed products may be selected. *If cured or smoked products are selected, use the low end of the serving size range.*

5. Uncured and unsmoked products should *not* contain sugar; cured and smoked products may contain sugar.

6. Equate freeze-dried products to the amount of fresh used before drying.

7. Examples of poultry and game selections are: capon, chicken, Cornish hen, guinea hen, pheasant, quail, rabbit, squab, turkey, venison, wild duck, wild goose.

8. Remove skin from poultry and game before serving.

9. Whenever possible, weigh foods after cooking (except canned

products). Canned products should be well drained before weighing; do *not* consume the liquid (or broth) in which the product was packed.

10. As a "rule of thumb," for each serving of poultry, veal, or game, allow 2 ounces (for raw items) for shrinkage in cooking and an additional 2 ounces for any skin and bone; for each half serving allow 1 ounce (for raw items) for shrinkage in cooking and an additional 1 ounce for any skin and bone. If using precooked cured or smoked products or cooked items, do not allow additional ounces for shrinkage. Whole chicken, chicken parts, and Cornish hen are exceptions to this "rule" (see "What Size to Buy?," below).

11. Cooking Procedures:

A. Poultry, veal, and game may be boiled, poached, broiled, pan-broiled, baked, roasted, sautéed, or stir-fried. A measured amount of Fats may be used for broiling, pan-broiling, baking, roasting, sautéing, and stir-frying provided poultry and game have been skinned before cooking; equate Fats to the Food Plan.

B. Poultry, veal, and game may be basted during baking or roasting.

C. Veal and *skinned* poultry and game may be added, raw or cooked, to casseroles and stews.

D. Remove and discard skin of poultry and game before pan-broiling, sautéing, or stir-frying, and before adding to casseroles and stews.

E. Poultry, veal, and game may be marinated before cooking.

F. Uncooked whole poultry or game may *not* be stuffed.

G. Homemade broth may be prepared by boiling veal or *skinned* poultry or game in water to cover; vegetables and seasonings may be used. Refrigerate broth until fat congeals on top; remove and discard congealed fat. If poultry or game is boiled with the skin, do *not* consume the broth.

Chickens and Hens
What Size to Buy?

A common source of confusion is the size bird to buy for the number being served; how much meat will a chicken actually yield?

As a "rule of thumb," raw whole chicken or cut-up chicken parts will yield about 33 percent skinned cooked meat; 67 percent is bone, skin, and weight lost in cooking. Raw chicken breasts will yield about 50 percent skinned cooked meat and raw Cornish hen will yield about 40 percent skinned cooked meat. Use the following chart as a guide to purchasing birds of the appropriate size. But remember, whenever possible, weigh portions after cooking.

Whole or Cut-Up Poultry (Raw with Skin and Bone)	Approx. Yield (Skinned and Boned Cooked Meat)
7 pounds	2 pounds 5 ounces
6 pounds	2 pounds
5 pounds	1 pound 11 ounces
4½ pounds	1½ pounds
4 pounds	1 pound 5 ounces
3½ pounds	1 pound 3 ounces
3 pounds	1 pound
2½ pounds	13 ounces
2 pounds	11 ounces
1½ pounds Cornish hen	10 ounces
1¼ pounds Cornish hen	8 ounces

Chicken Breasts (Raw with Skin and Bone)	Approx. Yield (Skinned and Boned Cooked Meat)
1½ pounds	12 ounces
1 pound	8 ounces
8 ounces	4 ounces
6 ounces	3 ounces

Cooking Methods

Pan-Broiling—Remove and discard skin from chicken; if using a whole chicken, cut into pieces (or use skinned and boned chicken). Heat a nonstick skillet or spray skillet with nonstick cooking spray and heat. Add chicken parts and cook uncovered, over medium heat, until browned on all sides. Reduce heat to low and continue cooking, turning chicken frequently, until done to taste. Weigh portions.

Poaching—Prepare chicken as for pan-broiling. In shallow saucepan that is wide enough to hold chicken in one layer, bring to a boil enough water to cover chicken. Reduce heat and add chicken parts; cover pan and simmer until done to taste. White meat will cook in a shorter period of time than dark meat. Poach white meat (breast and wing portions) for 10 to 15 minutes, dark meat (leg and thigh portions) for 20 to 30 minutes (timing may vary depending upon thickness of meat and its temperature at start of cooking). If white and dark meat are to be poached at the same time, add dark meat to liquid first and poach for about 10 minutes; add white meat and poach about 10 minutes longer or until done to taste. Remove chicken from liquid and serve immediately or cool slightly, cover, and chill for later use.

If desired, poaching liquid may be reused. Cool, then cover and chill until fat congeals on top. Remove and discard congealed fat (¾ cup poaching liquid is equivalent to: 1 serving Extras).

Roasting—Place whole chicken, breast-side up, on rack in shallow roasting pan. Insert meat thermometer into center of thigh, close to body, being careful that thermometer does not touch bone (for information on meat thermometers see Meat Group, page 255). Roast uncovered, basting frequently with chicken bouillon, until chicken is tender, about 30 minutes per pound (longer for very small birds). Chicken is done when thermometer registers 180° to 185°F. (If thermometer is not used, chicken is done when drumstick twists easily in socket and if, when pierced with a fork, juices run clear.) To serve, remove and discard skin, slice chicken, and weigh portions. Equate chicken and bouillon in accordance with the Food Plan.

The following chart can be used as a guide to roasting times; actual cooking time may vary due to type of heat (gas or electric), variations in oven calibration, proportion of meat to bone, and temperature of chicken at start of roasting. The best way to ensure a properly roasted chicken is to use a meat thermometer.

Approx. Weight	Oven Temperature	Approx. Cooking Time per Pound	Approx. Total Cooking Time
1½ pounds	400°F.	40 minutes	1 hour
2 pounds	400°F.	35 minutes	1 hour 10 minutes
2½ pounds	375°F.	30 minutes	1¼ hours
3 pounds	375°F.	30 minutes	1½ hours
3½ pounds	375°F.	30 minutes	1¾ hours
4 pounds	375°F.	30 minutes	2 hours
4½ pounds	375°F.	30 minutes	2¼ hours
5 pounds	375°F.	30 minutes	2½ hours

HOT AND SOUR SOUP
Full Choice Plan
Makes 4 Midday or Evening Meal servings, ¼ meal each; supplement as required*

4 medium dried mushrooms
3 cups Chicken Broth (see page
    401)
3 ounces skinned and boned
    cooked chicken, cut into thin
    slices
½ cup drained canned sliced
    bamboo shoots
2 ounces tofu (soybean curd),
    cut into ½-inch cubes
2 tablespoons white wine vinegar

1 tablespoon soy sauce
1 tablespoon plus 1 teaspoon
    cornstarch, dissolved in 2
    tablespoons water
½ cup cooked chopped spinach
2 tablespoons chopped scallion
    (green onion)
1 teaspoon Chinese sesame oil
½ teaspoon white pepper
Dash salt

In small bowl combine mushrooms with enough water to cover. Allow to soak for 30 minutes.

Drain mushrooms; cut off and discard stems. Thinly slice caps, squeeze to remove moisture, and set aside.

In 2-quart saucepan bring Chicken Broth to a boil; add mushrooms, chicken, and bamboo shoots. Reduce heat and simmer 5 minutes, stirring occasionally. Add tofu, vinegar, and soy sauce; simmer for 1 minute longer. Bring soup to a boil and slowly stir in dissolved cornstarch. Cook, stirring constantly, until soup is slightly thickened. Add remaining ingredients and stir to blend. Pour into 4 soup bowls and serve immediately.

Each serving is equivalent to: ¾ serving Vegetables; 2 servings Extras; ¾ ounce Poultry; ½ ounce Legumes (tofu); 1½ teaspoons Limited Vegetables; ¼ serving Fats.

Per serving: 111 calories, 13 g protein, 4 g fat, 11 g carbohydrate, 423 mg sodium

* Men—Add ¼ ounce sliced cooked chicken to each soup bowl. Change equivalent listing to 1 ounce Poultry.

CHICKEN SALAD
Full Choice Plan
Makes 1 Midday or Evening Meal serving

1 teaspoon mayonnaise
1 teaspoon lemon juice
¼ teaspoon salt
Dash each pepper, thyme leaves,
    and ground sage
4 ounces skinned and boned
    cooked chicken, diced

2 tablespoons seeded and diced
    pared cucumber
1 tablespoon each diced carrot,
    celery, and red onion
1 teaspoon chopped fresh parsley
2 iceberg or romaine lettuce leaves

In small bowl combine mayonnaise, lemon juice, salt, pepper, thyme, and sage. Add remaining ingredients except lettuce and toss well. Cover and chill. Serve on lettuce leaves.

Each serving is equivalent to: 1 serving Fats; 4 ounces Poultry; 1 serving Vegetables; 1 tablespoon Limited Vegetables.

Per serving: 265 calories, 34 g protein, 12 g fat, 4 g carbohydrate, 679 mg sodium

OPEN-FACE CURRIED CHICKEN SALAD SANDWICH
Full Choice Plan
Makes 1 Midday or Evening Meal serving

1 tablespoon reduced-calorie mayonnaise
1 tablespoon plain unflavored yogurt
1 teaspoon lemon juice
⅛ teaspoon curry powder
4 ounces skinned and boned cooked chicken, diced

½ small apple, pared, cored, and diced
6 large seedless green grapes, cut into quarters
Dash each salt and white pepper
2 slices whole wheat bread, toasted

In medium bowl combine mayonnaise, yogurt, lemon juice, and curry powder. Stir in chicken, apple, and grapes; season with salt and pepper. Spread half of chicken salad on each slice of toast.

Each serving is equivalent to: 1½ servings Fats; ⅛ serving Milk; 4 ounces Poultry; 1 serving Fruits; 2 servings Bread.

Per serving: 427 calories, 39 g protein, 13 g fat, 40 g carbohydrate, 548 mg sodium

ZESTY CHICKEN SALAD
Full Choice Plan
Makes 2 Midday or Evening Meal servings

1 garlic clove, cut
¼ cup plain unflavored yogurt
¼ cup lemon juice
1 tablespoon plus 1 teaspoon mayonnaise
1 tablespoon grated Parmesan cheese
1 teaspoon mashed anchovy fillets

8 ounces skinned and boned cooked chicken, cut into ½-inch pieces
½ cup diced celery
2 tablespoons diced scallion (green onion)
Dash each salt and pepper
2 romaine or iceberg lettuce leaves

Rub a salad bowl with garlic and discard garlic clove; combine yogurt, lemon juice, mayonnaise, Parmesan cheese, and anchovy fillets in prepared bowl. Add chicken, celery, scallion, salt, and pepper. Toss well to coat. Serve on lettuce leaves.

Each serving is equivalent to: ¼ serving Milk; 2 servings Fats; 2 servings Extras; 4 ounces Poultry; ¾ serving Vegetables; 1 tablespoon Limited Vegetables.

Per serving: 335 calories, 36 g protein, 18 g fat, 7 g carbohydrate, 339 mg sodium

CHICKEN MOUSSE WITH DILL
Full Choice Plan
Makes 4 Midday or Evening Meal servings

¾ cup Chicken Broth (see
  page 401), divided
¼ cup chopped onion
8 ounces skinned and boned
  cooked chicken breasts, cut into
  pieces
¼ cup skim milk
2 tablespoons plain unflavored
  yogurt
1 envelope unflavored gelatin

1 tablespoon plus 1 teaspoon
  mayonnaise
1 tablespoon chopped fresh dill
1 tablespoon lemon juice
1 teaspoon prepared horseradish
½ teaspoon salt
⅛ teaspoon white pepper
4 large lettuce leaves
4 eggs, hard-cooked and cut into
  quarters

Garnish
4 dill sprigs

1. In blender container combine ½ cup broth and the onion; process until coarsely chopped. Add chicken, milk, and yogurt and process until smooth; set aside.
2. In small saucepan sprinkle gelatin over remaining ¼ cup broth. Cook over low heat, stirring constantly, until gelatin is completely dissolved.
3. Add dissolved gelatin, mayonnaise, chopped dill, lemon juice, horseradish, salt, and pepper to chicken mixture in blender container and process until smooth.
4. Rinse a 3½- to 4-cup mold or bowl with cold water; pour chicken mixture into mold or bowl, cover, and chill until set, 4 to 5 hours.
5. To unmold, dip the point of a small knife into warm water; with point loosen mousse around edge of mold. Dip mold, just to rim, in warm (*not hot*) water for about 10 seconds; remove from water and shake mold to loosen mousse. Invert serving platter on mold, then invert platter and mold together and gently lift off mold. Surround mousse with lettuce leaves and egg quarters; garnish with dill sprigs.

Each serving is equivalent to: ¾ serving Extras; 1 tablespoon Limited Vegetables; 2 ounces Poultry; ⅛ serving Milk; 1 serving Fats; ¼ serving Vegetables; 1 Egg.

Per serving: 238 calories, 27 g protein, 12 g fat, 5 g carbohydrate, 432 mg sodium

CREAMED CHICKEN WITH DILL
Full Choice Plan
Makes 2 Midday or Evening Meal servings

1 tablespoon plus 1 teaspoon
  margarine
1 tablespoon plus ¾ teaspoon
  enriched all-purpose flour
¾ cup Chicken Broth (see
  page 401), heated

8 ounces skinned and boned
  cooked chicken, cut into 1-inch
  pieces
1 tablespoon chopped fresh dill or
  1 teaspoon dill weed
Dash each salt and white pepper
2 tablespoons plain unflavored
  yogurt

In 1-quart saucepan heat margarine until bubbly. Add flour and cook, stirring constantly, for 2 minutes; remove from heat. Stir in broth and return to heat. Stirring constantly, simmer for 5 minutes. Add chicken and dill; simmer until chicken is heated. Season with salt and pepper. Stir in yogurt and heat (*do not boil*).

Each serving is equivalent to: 2 servings Fats; ¼ serving Bread; ½ serving Extras; 4 ounces Poultry; ⅛ serving Milk.

Per serving: 325 calories, 36 g protein, 17 g fat, 8 g carbohydrate, 270 mg sodium

CHICKEN À LA KING
Full Choice Plan
Makes 2 Midday or Evening Meal servings

2 teaspoons margarine
¼ cup diced onion
¼ cup sliced mushrooms
2 teaspoons enriched all-purpose
   flour, dissolved in 1 tablespoon
   water
1 teaspoon each salt and paprika
½ teaspoon white pepper

½ cup evaporated skimmed milk
⅓ cup plus 2 teaspoons Chicken
   Broth (see page 401)
8 ounces skinned and boned
   cooked chicken, diced
¼ cup each peas and diced
   pimientos

In 10-inch skillet heat margarine, over medium heat, until bubbly; add onion and sauté until translucent. Add mushrooms and sauté 1 minute longer. Add dissolved flour to onion mixture and cook, stirring constantly, until mixture is smooth. Stir in salt, paprika, and pepper and continue to cook until mixture bubbles. Remove from heat and stir in milk and broth. Return to heat and cook, stirring constantly, until mixture begins to boil. Reduce heat to low and stir in chicken, peas, and pimientos. Cook, stirring occasionally, until chicken and peas are thoroughly heated. Serve hot.

Each serving is equivalent to: 1 serving Fats; ¼ cup Limited Vegetables; ½ serving Vegetables; 1¼ servings Extras; ½ serving Milk; 4 ounces Poultry.

Per serving: 348 calories, 41 g protein, 13 g fat, 17 g carbohydrate, 1,331 mg sodium

Variation: Substitute 8 ounces skinned and boned cooked turkey for the chicken.

Per serving: 323 calories, 42 g protein, 10 g fat, 17 g carbohydrate, 1,318 mg sodium

BROILED CHICKEN
No Choice Plan
Makes 4 Evening Meal servings*

Cut a 2¼-pound chicken into quarters. Sprinkle with **dash each salt and pepper**. Place, skin-side down, on rack in broiler pan. Broil 6 to 9 inches

from heat source for 25 to 30 minutes; turn chicken and broil until fork-tender, 15 to 20 minutes longer. Broiling time will vary depending upon distance of chicken from heat source. Remove and discard skin before serving.
Each serving is equivalent to: 3 ounces Poultry.

Per serving: 162 calories, 25 g protein, 6 g fat, trace carbohydrate, 105 mg sodium

Variations:

1. Before broiling, season chicken with dash each garlic powder, salt, pepper, paprika, and lemon juice.

Per serving: 162 calories, 25 g protein, 6 g fat, 0.1 g carbohydrate, 105 mg sodium

2. *Limited Choice Plan*—Place chicken quarters in shallow pan (not aluminum). Combine ¼ cup Chicken Broth (see page 401), 2 tablespoons chopped fresh tarragon, and 2 teaspoons lemon juice. Pour over chicken, cover pan, and refrigerate for 1 hour; drain, reserving marinade. Broil chicken as directed. In saucepan, bring marinade to a boil; serve with chicken. Add ¹⁄₁₂ serving Extras to equivalent listing.

Per serving: 166 calories, 25 g protein, 6 g fat, 1 g carbohydrate, 108 mg sodium

3. *Limited Choice Plan*—For each serving, spread 1 teaspoon low-calorie Italian dressing (6 calories per tablespoon) over chicken before broiling. Add ⅓ serving Extras to equivalent listing. (See page 407 for Full Choice Plan adjustments.)

Per serving: 164 calories, 25 g protein, 7 g fat, 0.3 g carbohydrate, 145 mg sodium

Note: On the Full and Limited Choice Plans this recipe may be used at the Midday or Evening Meal.

* Men—Add 1 ounce skinned and sliced broiled chicken per portion. Change equivalent listing to 4 ounces Poultry.

BRAISED CHICKEN GREEK STYLE
Full Choice Plan
Makes 2 Midday or Evening Meal servings

2 teaspoons vegetable oil	2 medium tomatoes, blanched,
1½ pounds chicken parts, skinned	peeled, seeded, and chopped
¼ teaspoon salt	¼ cup Chicken Broth (see page
Dash pepper	401)
¾ cup diced onions	1 tablespoon tomato paste
1 teaspoon minced fresh garlic	2-inch piece cinnamon stick

In skillet large enough to hold chicken in 1 layer, heat oil. Add chicken parts and brown on all sides. Remove chicken to plate and sprinkle with salt and pepper.

In same skillet sauté onions with garlic until onions are lightly browned. Stir in remaining ingredients and bring mixture to a boil. Return chicken to skillet. Reduce heat, cover, and simmer for 35 minutes, basting occasionally. Remove cover and simmer until chicken is tender, about 5 minutes longer. Remove cinnamon stick before serving.

Each serving is equivalent to: 1 serving Fats; 4 ounces Poultry; ¼ cup plus 2 tablespoons Limited Vegetables; 2 servings Vegetables; 1 serving Extras.

Per serving: 323 calories, 36 g protein, 14 g fat, 15 g carbohydrate, 447 mg sodium

CHICKEN AND PEACH SAUTÉ
Full Choice Plan
Makes 2 Midday or Evening Meal servings

2 teaspoons vegetable oil
1½ pounds chicken parts, skinned
⅓ cup apple juice (no sugar added)
½ teaspoon salt
⅛ teaspoon ground cinnamon

Dash ground cloves
2 medium peaches, blanched, peeled, pitted, and sliced
2 teaspoons cornstarch, dissolved in 1 tablespoon water

Garnish
Mint leaves

In 9-inch skillet heat oil; add chicken parts and sauté until lightly browned on all sides. Add apple juice, salt, cinnamon, and cloves. Cover and cook over low heat until chicken is tender, about 20 minutes; add peaches. Stirring constantly, add dissolved cornstarch and cook until thickened, 3 to 5 minutes. Serve garnished with mint leaves.

Each serving is equivalent to: 1 serving Fats; 4 ounces Poultry; 1½ servings Fruits; 1 serving Extras.

Per serving: 334 calories, 34 g protein, 13 g fat, 22 g carbohydrate, 637 mg sodium

CHICKEN AND VEGETABLES IN ROSÉ SAUCE
Full Choice Plan
Makes 2 Midday or Evening Meal servings

1 teaspoon each vegetable oil and margarine
1½ pounds chicken parts, skinned
¼ teaspoon salt
Dash pepper
2 tablespoons diced onion

1 cup mushrooms
2 fluid ounces rosé wine
¼ cup Chicken Broth (see page 401)
¾ cup frozen artichoke hearts, partially thawed
½ cup broccoli florets, blanched

In a 9-inch skillet combine oil and margarine and heat over medium heat; add chicken parts and sauté until lightly browned on all sides. Sprinkle with salt and pepper and transfer chicken to a plate. In same skillet sauté onion until softened. Add mushrooms and sauté for 2 minutes longer. Stir in wine and broth and bring to a boil. Reduce heat to low, add chicken, cover, and simmer until almost tender, about 40 minutes. Add artichoke hearts and simmer 5 minutes longer. Stir in broccoli florets and simmer 3 more minutes.

Each serving is equivalent to: 1 serving Fats; 4 ounces Poultry; ¼ cup plus 3 tablespoons Limited Vegetables; 1½ servings Vegetables; ¼ serving Occasional Substitutes; ⅙ serving Extras.

Per serving: 323 calories, 37 g protein, 13 g fat, 10 g carbohydrate, 437 mg sodium

CHICKEN FRICASSEE
Full Choice Plan
Makes 4 Midday or Evening Meal servings

To complete this meal, serve with a mixed green salad.

½ cup plus 2 tablespoons enriched all-purpose flour, divided
2 teaspoons salt, divided
1 teaspoon pepper
3 pounds chicken parts, skinned
1 tablespoon plus 1 teaspoon margarine
2 cups onion wedges
2 cups sliced celery (1-inch pieces)
2 cups sliced carrots (½-inch-thick slices)
4 crushed peppercorns
2 bay leaves
1 quart water
2 cups sliced mushrooms
¼ cup chopped fresh parsley
Dash white pepper

1. In shallow container or on sheet of wax paper combine ½ cup plus 2 teaspoons flour with 1 teaspoon each salt and pepper.
2. Dredge chicken parts in seasoned flour and set aside.
3. In 12-inch skillet heat margarine over medium heat. Increase heat, add chicken, and brown on all sides (do not overcrowd chicken parts; brown a few pieces at a time); transfer browned chicken to a 4-quart saucepan.
4. In same skillet combine onions and celery and cook, stirring occasionally, until onions are translucent.
5. Add onion mixture, carrots, peppercorns, and bay leaves to saucepan containing chicken. Pour in water, cover, and simmer until chicken and vegetables are tender, about 30 minutes.
6. Measure out 2 tablespoons of liquid from saucepan. In small bowl dissolve remaining 1 tablespoon plus 1 teaspoon flour in liquid and stir into saucepan.
7. Add mushrooms, parsley, white pepper, and remaining teaspoon salt to saucepan; cook, stirring constantly, until mushrooms are cooked and mixture thickens, 3 to 5 minutes. Remove bay leaves and serve.

Each serving is equivalent to: 1 serving Bread; 4 ounces Poultry; 1 serving Fats; ½ cup Limited Vegetables; 3 servings Vegetables.

Per serving: 404 calories, 39 g protein, 13 g fat, 33 g carbohydrate, 1,335 mg sodium

CHICKEN GUMBO
Full Choice Plan
Makes 2 Midday or Evening Meal servings, ½ meal each; supplement as required

12 ounces chicken parts, skinned
¼ teaspoon salt
⅛ teaspoon pepper
2 teaspoons enriched all-purpose flour
1 tablespoon margarine

¼ cup chopped onion
1 cup canned crushed tomatoes
2½ cups water
¼ cup sliced okra
½ cup fresh or frozen whole-kernel corn

Sprinkle chicken with salt and pepper, then flour. In a 2-quart saucepan heat margarine until bubbly; add chicken and onion and sauté until chicken parts are browned on all sides. Stir in tomatoes; add water and okra and bring to a boil. Reduce heat, cover, and simmer for 1½ hours. Add corn and simmer 5 minutes longer.

Each serving is equivalent to: 2 ounces Poultry; 1 serving Extras; 1½ servings Fats; ¼ cup Limited Vegetables; 1 serving Vegetables; ½ serving Bread Substitutes.

Per serving: 241 calories, 20 g protein, 10 g fat, 18 g carbohydrate, 543 mg sodium

COUNTRY CAPTAIN
Full Choice Plan
Makes 2 Midday or Evening Meal servings

1½ pounds chicken parts, skinned
¼ teaspoon salt
⅛ teaspoon pepper
2 teaspoons enriched all-purpose flour
2 teaspoons vegetable oil
½ cup diced onion
¼ cup each diced carrot and green bell pepper

1 garlic clove, minced
1½ teaspoons curry powder
1½ cups chopped drained canned Italian plum tomatoes
2 tablespoons raisins
¼ cup Chicken Broth (see page 401)

Sprinkle chicken parts with salt and pepper, then flour. In a skillet large enough to hold chicken in 1 layer, heat oil. Add chicken and brown on all sides; remove chicken to a plate.

In same skillet combine onion, carrot, green pepper, and garlic; sauté until vegetables are tender but not browned. Add curry powder and stir to combine; stir in tomatoes and raisins and bring mixture to a boil. Return chicken to skillet and pour in broth. Reduce heat, cover, and simmer for 20 minutes. Remove cover and simmer until chicken is tender, 5 to 10 minutes longer.

Each serving is equivalent to: 4 ounces Poultry; 1⅙ servings Extras; 1 serving Fats; ¼ cup Limited Vegetables; 2 servings Vegetables; ½ serving Fruits.

Per serving: 367 calories, 37 g protein, 14 g fat, 25 g carbohydrate, 621 mg sodium

CHICKEN CHINESE STYLE
Full Choice Plan
Makes 2 Midday or Evening Meal servings

12 ounces skinned and boned chicken breasts, cut into 3-inch-long strips
1 tablespoon plus 1 teaspoon each soy sauce and dry sherry
2 teaspoons arrowroot
¾ cup Chicken Broth (see page 401)

2 teaspoons vegetable oil
¼ cup sliced onion
2 teaspoons minced pared ginger root
1 garlic clove, minced
1 cup diagonally sliced celery
¼ cup sliced water chestnuts

1. In small bowl combine chicken, soy sauce, and sherry and toss. Cover and refrigerate for at least 1 hour.
2. In measuring cup or small bowl dissolve arrowroot in broth and set aside.
3. In 12-inch nonstick skillet heat oil; add chicken and sauté until cooked, about 3 minutes. Using a slotted spoon, remove chicken to a plate; set aside.
4. In the same skillet sauté onion with ginger and garlic until onion is translucent. Add celery and water chestnuts; sauté until tender-crisp. Add chicken and reserved broth mixture. Cook, stirring occasionally, until sauce thickens and chicken is hot.

Each serving is equivalent to: 4 ounces Poultry; 2½ servings Extras; 1 serving Fats; ¼ cup Limited Vegetables; 1 serving Vegetables.

Per serving: 306 calories, 39 g protein, 10 g fat, 13 g carbohydrate, 1,066 mg sodium

CHICKEN ORIENTAL
Full Choice Plan
Makes 4 Midday or Evening Meal servings

1½ pounds skinned and boned chicken, thinly sliced
2 tablespoons teriyaki sauce
⅛ teaspoon grated pared ginger root
1 tablespoon plus 1 teaspoon vegetable oil
1 teaspoon minced fresh garlic
2 cups sliced mushrooms
1 tablespoon plus 1 teaspoon cornstarch

¾ cup Chicken Broth (see page 401)
2 cups broccoli (florets and thinly sliced stems), blanched
2 cups slivered carrots (2½-inch-long pieces), blanched
Dash each salt and pepper
½ cup chopped scallions (green onions)

In medium bowl combine chicken, teriyaki sauce, and ginger root; set aside.
In 12-inch nonstick skillet heat oil; add garlic and sauté briefly (*do not brown*). Add mushrooms and sauté, stirring constantly, until tender. Add chicken mixture; cook, stirring and turning, until chicken is no longer pink, about 5 minutes.
In small bowl or measuring cup stir cornstarch into broth; pour over chicken mixture. Cook over medium heat, stirring constantly, until thickened. Stir in broccoli and carrots and toss gently until heated through. Season with salt and pepper and sprinkle with scallions.
Each serving is equivalent to: 4 ounces Poultry; 1 serving Fats; 3 servings Vegetables; 1¼ servings Extras; ⅛ cup Limited Vegetables.

Per serving: 347 calories, 39 g protein, 14 g fat, 19 g carbohydrate, 486 mg sodium

CHICKEN SUKIYAKI
Limited Choice Plan
*Makes 2 Midday or Evening Meal servings**

10 ounces skinned and boned
   chicken breasts, cut into
   2 x ½-inch strips
2 teaspoons lemon juice
2 teaspoons Chinese sesame oil
1 thin slice pared ginger root
   (about 1 x ¼ inch)
½ garlic clove, minced

½ cup sliced celery
¼ cup each red bell pepper strips
   and sliced mushrooms
2 teaspoons teriyaki sauce
1 cup canned mandarin orange
   sections (no sugar added)
1 teaspoon cornstarch

In bowl combine chicken and lemon juice and toss; set aside for 5 minutes.
In a 9-inch skillet heat oil over medium heat; add ginger and garlic and cook until lightly browned. Add chicken mixture and cook until chicken strips are lightly browned. Reduce heat to low; add celery, pepper strips, mushrooms, and teriyaki sauce and simmer 8 minutes.
While chicken mixture is simmering, drain juice from 1 cup orange sections into small bowl or cup; add cornstarch and stir to dissolve.
Add juice mixture to skillet and cook over low heat, stirring occasionally, until mixture thickens. Stir in orange sections and cook just until fruit is heated. Remove and discard ginger before serving.
Each serving is equivalent to: 3 ounces Poultry; 1 serving Fats; ½ serving Vegetables; 1 serving Fruits; ½ serving Extras. (See page 407 for Full Choice Plan adjustments.)

Per serving: 287 calories, 27 g protein, 9 g fat, 24 g carbohydrate, 309 mg sodium

* Men—One serving provides ¾ of a meal. Supplement with an additional ¼ serving of Protein at the Midday or Evening Meal.

STIR-FRIED CHICKEN WITH VEGETABLES
Full Choice Plan
Makes 4 Midday or Evening Meal servings

1 cup canned pineapple chunks
(no sugar added), drain and
reserve juice
2 tablespoons each cider vinegar
and soy sauce
2 teaspoons dry sherry
1 teaspoon honey
1 teaspoon grated pared ginger root
1½ pounds skinned and boned
chicken breasts, thinly sliced

2 teaspoons cornstarch
1 tablespoon vegetable oil
1 cup diagonally sliced carrots,
blanched
1 cup broccoli florets, blanched
1 cup trimmed Chinese pea pods
(stem ends and strings removed),
blanched
1 teaspoon sesame seed, toasted

In shallow pan (not aluminum) combine juice from 1 cup canned pineapple with vinegar, soy sauce, sherry, honey, and ginger root. Add chicken;
cover and let marinate in refrigerator at least 1 hour.

Drain chicken, reserving marinade. Dissolve cornstarch in marinade
and set aside.

In 12-inch nonstick skillet heat oil; add chicken, a few pieces at a time,
stirring constantly with a wooden spoon until chicken loses pink color:
Add vegetables and sesame seed; cook, stirring constantly, until thoroughly
heated, 1 to 2 minutes. Stir in reserved marinade and cook, stirring, until
thickened. Add pineapple chunks and cook, stirring constantly, until
pineapple is heated, about 1 minute. Serve immediately.

Each serving is equivalent to: ½ serving Fruits; 1¾ servings Extras;
4 ounces Poultry; ¾ serving Fats; 1 serving Vegetables; ¼ cup Limited
Vegetables.

Per serving: 333 calories, 39 g protein, 9 g fat, 23 g carbohydrate, 775 mg sodium

TANGY STIR-FRIED CHICKEN
Limited Choice Plan
*Makes 2 Midday or Evening Meal servings**

2 teaspoons margarine
½ cup each thinly sliced carrot
and celery
10 ounces skinned and boned
chicken breasts, cut into cubes
⅓ cup lemon juice
2 tablespoons grated lemon peel

1 packet instant chicken broth and
seasoning mix, dissolved in ¾
cup hot water
1 teaspoon onion flakes
½ teaspoon chopped chives
Dash each salt and pepper
2 teaspoons cornstarch, dissolved
in 2 tablespoons water

In 2-quart saucepan heat margarine; add carrot and celery slices and cook,
stirring quickly and frequently, for 1 minute. Add chicken and continue
stir-frying for 1 minute longer. Add remaining ingredients, except corn-

starch, and stir well. Bring to a boil. Reduce heat, cover, and simmer until chicken is tender, about 20 minutes.

Drain liquid from saucepan into another small pan and bring to a boil. Add dissolved cornstarch and cook, stirring constantly, until thickened. Pour back into pan containing chicken; return pan to medium heat and stir to combine.

Each serving is equivalent to: 1 serving Fats; ½ serving Vegetables; 3 ounces Poultry; 1½ servings Extras. (See page 407 for Full Choice Plan adjustments.)

Per serving: 231 calories, 28 g protein, 8 g fat, 12 g carbohydrate, 644 mg sodium

* Men—One serving provides ¾ of a meal. Supplement with an additional ¼ serving of Protein at the Midday or Evening Meal.

INDIAN CHICKEN CURRY
Full Choice Plan
Makes 4 Midday or Evening Meal servings

1 small red apple, cored and diced
1 tablespoon lemon juice
1½ pounds skinned and boned chicken breasts
1 tablespoon plus 1 teaspoon vegetable oil
½ cup sliced celery
½ cup chopped onion
½ medium green bell pepper, seeded and cut into strips
1 garlic clove, minced
1 tablespoon plus 1 teaspoon enriched all-purpose flour

1 tablespoon curry powder, or to taste
¼ teaspoon each salt and ground ginger
1 cup Chicken Broth (see page 401)
¼ cup evaporated skimmed milk
⅓ cup plus 2 teaspoons raisins
2 cups hot cooked enriched rice
2 teaspoons shredded coconut, toasted

In small bowl combine diced apple with lemon juice and toss; set aside.

Using paper towels wipe chicken dry. In 12-inch skillet heat oil until hot but not smoking. Add chicken and sauté until lightly browned on all sides. Remove chicken from skillet, cut into 1-inch cubes, and set aside.

In same skillet combine celery, onion, green pepper, and garlic; sauté over medium heat, stirring occasionally, until vegetables are soft. Sprinkle with flour, curry powder, salt, and ginger. Cook 3 minutes, stirring constantly. Gradually stir in broth and milk; bring to a boil. Reduce heat to low, add chicken cubes, and simmer for 5 minutes. Stir in apple mixture and raisins and heat through. Serve each portion over ½ cup hot rice and garnish each with ¼ of the toasted coconut.

Each serving is equivalent to: 1 serving Fruits; 4 ounces Poultry; 1 serving Fats; ½ serving Vegetables; ⅛ cup Limited Vegetables; 2 servings Extras; ⅛ serving Milk; 1 serving Bread Substitutes.

Per serving: 457 calories, 41 g protein, 11 g fat, 49 g carbohydrate, 276 mg sodium

SESAME–CRUMB CHICKEN
Full Choice Plan
Makes 4 Midday or Evening Meal servings

This is delicious served with Hot Fruit Sauce (see page 382).

1½ ounces cornflake crumbs
⅓ cup plus 2 teaspoons seasoned
   dried bread crumbs
2 teaspoons sesame seed, crushed
Dash each salt, onion powder, and
   garlic powder

1½ pounds skinned and boned
   chicken breasts, pounded to
   ¼-inch thickness
2 tablespoons evaporated skimmed
   milk*
2 tablespoons vegetable oil

In shallow pan combine cornflake crumbs, bread crumbs, sesame seed, and seasonings. Dip chicken into milk, then into crumb mixture, coating thoroughly and using all of crumb mixture. In 9-inch skillet heat oil until hot but not smoking. Brown chicken quickly on both sides, 3 to 4 minutes per side.

Each serving is equivalent to: 1 serving Bread; 1 serving Extras; 4 ounces Poultry; 1½ teaspoons Evaporated Skimmed Milk (¹⁄₁₆ serving Milk); 1½ servings Fats.

Per serving: 353 calories, 38 g protein, 13 g fat, 17 g carbohydrate, 333 mg sodium

* In a pinch, substitute skim milk for the evaporated skimmed milk. Change equivalent listing to 1½ teaspoons Skim Milk (¹⁄₃₂ serving Milk).

ARROZ CON POLLO
Full Choice Plan
Makes 4 Midday or Evening Meal servings

1 tablespoon plus 1 teaspoon olive
   oil
3 pounds chicken parts, skinned
1 cup finely chopped onions
4 ounces uncooked regular
   long-grain enriched rice
2 cups drained canned tomatoes,
   chopped

½ cup finely chopped green bell
   pepper
2 teaspoons salt
2 garlic cloves, minced
1 teaspoon chili powder, or to taste
½ teaspoon pepper
¼ teaspoon whole saffron,
   dissolved in 2 cups boiling water

In a 12-inch nonstick skillet heat oil; add chicken and brown on all sides. Transfer to a 2½-quart casserole.

Preheat oven to 350°F. In same skillet sauté onions until translucent. Add rice and cook, stirring constantly, until browned. Add remaining ingredients and stir to combine.

Pour rice mixture over chicken in casserole; cover and bake 40 minutes. Uncover and bake until chicken is tender, about 15 minutes longer.

Each serving is equivalent to: 1 serving Fats; 4 ounces Poultry; ¼ cup Limited Vegetables; 1 serving Bread Substitutes; 1¼ servings Vegetables.

Per serving: 410 calories, 37 g protein, 14 g fat, 34 g carbohydrate, 1,343 mg sodium

CHICKEN HUNTERS' STYLE

Full Choice Plan
Makes 2 Midday or Evening Meal servings

2 teaspoons vegetable oil
12 ounces skinned and boned
chicken breasts
½ cup diced onion
2 garlic cloves, minced
1 cup sliced mushrooms
4 fluid ounces white wine
½ cup canned crushed tomatoes

1 teaspoon each oregano and basil
leaves
½ teaspoon salt
¼ teaspoon pepper
2 tablespoons chopped fresh
parsley
2 teaspoons grated Parmesan
cheese

Heat oil in 9-inch nonstick skillet; add chicken breasts and brown lightly. Remove breasts to a 1½- or 2-quart casserole. Preheat oven to 350°F.

In same skillet combine onion and garlic and sauté until onion is translucent. Add mushrooms and wine and cook until liquid is reduced by half. Stir in tomatoes, oregano, basil, salt, and pepper and cook 5 minutes, stirring occasionally.

Pour sauce over chicken breasts. Cover casserole and bake 10 minutes. Remove cover and bake until chicken is tender, about 10 minutes longer. Divide onto 2 plates and sprinkle each portion with 1 tablespoon parsley and 1 teaspoon Parmesan cheese.

Each serving is equivalent to: 1 serving Fats; 4 ounces Poultry; ¼ cup Limited Vegetables; 1½ servings Vegetables; ½ serving Occasional Substitutes; 1 serving Extras.

Per serving: 344 calories, 39 g protein, 11 g fat, 13 g carbohydrate, 749 mg sodium

ROSÉ CHICKEN

Full Choice Plan
Makes 4 Midday or Evening Meal servings

This dish reheats well; in fact, the flavor improves with standing. Reheat, uncovered, at 350°F. for 20 to 25 minutes.

1 tablespoon plus 1 teaspoon olive
oil
3 pounds chicken parts, skinned
½ cup thinly sliced onion
2 cups canned tomatoes, chopped
1 cup thinly sliced mushrooms

½ cup each red and green bell
pepper strips
½ cup chopped celery
4 fluid ounces rosé wine
2 garlic cloves, minced
1 teaspoon salt
¼ teaspoon pepper

Preheat oven to 400°F. In 9-inch skillet heat oil; add chicken parts and brown lightly on all sides. Transfer chicken to a 2½-quart casserole and set aside.

In same skillet sauté onion until translucent; spread over chicken. In medium bowl combine remaining ingredients; pour over chicken, cover casserole, and bake for 20 minutes. Uncover and bake until chicken is tender and sauce is thick, 30 to 40 minutes longer. Serve immediately or cool, cover, and refrigerate until ready to use.

Each serving is equivalent to: 1 serving Fats; 4 ounces Poultry; ⅛ cup Limited Vegetables; 2¼ servings Vegetables; ¼ serving Occasional Substitutes.

Per serving: 335 calories, 36 g protein, 14 g fat, 12 g carbohydrate, 821 mg sodium

SPICY CHICKEN IN WINE SAUCE
Full Choice Plan
Makes 4 Midday or Evening Meal servings

⅓ cup less 1 teaspoon enriched all-purpose flour
2 teaspoons tarragon leaves
1 teaspoon salt
½ teaspoon each paprika and ground ginger
3 pounds chicken parts, skinned
1 tablespoon plus 1 teaspoon vegetable oil

1 cup finely chopped onions
2 garlic cloves, minced
4 fluid ounces white wine
¼ cup Chicken Broth (see page 401)
2 tablespoons chopped fresh parsley

1. Preheat oven to 350°F. In a plastic bag combine flour, tarragon, salt, paprika, and ginger. Add chicken pieces, a few at a time, and shake to coat, being sure to use all flour mixture.
2. In 10-inch skillet heat oil; add chicken and brown well on all sides. Transfer chicken to a 1½-quart casserole.
3. In same skillet combine onions and garlic and sauté until translucent; add wine and broth. Bring to a boil and pour over chicken.
4. Bake, basting occasionally with pan juices, until tender, about 1 hour. Sprinkle with parsley before serving.

Each serving is equivalent to: ½ serving Bread; 4 ounces Poultry; 1 serving Fats; ¼ cup Limited Vegetables; ¼ serving Occasional Substitutes; 1/12 serving Extras.

Per serving: 342 calories, 35 g protein, 13 g fat, 14 g carbohydrate, 644 mg sodium

TARRAGON CHICKEN
Full Choice Plan
Makes 2 Midday or Evening Meal servings

1 teaspoon vegetable oil
1 teaspoon margarine
1½ pounds chicken parts, skinned
¼ teaspoon salt
Dash pepper
2 tablespoons diced onion

1 cup sliced mushrooms
1 tablespoon chopped fresh tarragon
2 fluid ounces dry white wine
¼ cup Chicken Broth (see page 401)

Preheat oven to 350°F. In 9-inch skillet combine oil and margarine and heat until margarine is bubbly; add chicken parts and sauté until lightly browned on all sides. Sprinkle with salt and pepper. Transfer chicken to a 1½-quart casserole.

In same skillet sauté onion until softened. Add mushrooms and tarragon and sauté for 2 minutes. Stir in wine and broth and bring to a boil. Pour mixture over chicken, cover casserole, and bake until tender, about 40 minutes.

Each serving is equivalent to: 1 serving Fats; 4 ounces Poultry; 1 table-spoon Limited Vegetables; 1 serving Vegetables; ¼ serving Occasional Substitutes; ⅙ serving Extras.

Per serving: 301 calories, 35 g protein, 13 g fat, 6 g carbohydrate, 402 mg sodium

YORKSHIRE CHICKEN
Full Choice Plan
Makes 6 Midday or Evening Meal servings

3 pounds 6 ounces chicken parts, skinned
1 teaspoon ground sage
2 teaspoons salt, divided
½ teaspoon pepper
1 cup less 1 tablespoon enriched all-purpose flour

1 teaspoon double-acting baking powder
3 eggs, beaten
1½ cups skim milk
¼ cup margarine, melted
¼ cup chopped fresh parsley

1. Preheat oven to 350°F. Heat a 10-inch nonstick skillet; add chicken parts and brown well on all sides.

2. Transfer chicken to a 2½-quart casserole that has been sprayed with nonstick cooking spray. Sprinkle with sage, 1 teaspoon salt, and the pepper.

3. In medium bowl sift together flour, baking powder, and remaining teaspoon salt. In another bowl combine eggs with milk, margarine, and parsley; stir into flour mixture and beat until smooth.

4. Pour egg mixture over chicken. Bake until egg mixture is puffed and chicken is tender, about 1 hour.

Each serving is equivalent to: 3 ounces Poultry; 1 serving Bread; ½ Egg; ¼ serving Milk; 2 servings Fats.

Per serving: 366 calories, 32 g protein, 17 g fat, 19 g carbohydrate, 1,014 mg sodium

CHICKEN ROLLS WITH CAULIFLOWER PUREE
No Choice Plan
Makes 2 Evening Meal servings*

1 cup well-drained cooked chopped spinach
2 skinned and boned chicken breasts (5 ounces each), pounded to about ¼-inch thickness

Dash each onion powder, garlic powder, and ground nutmeg
2 teaspoons vegetable oil
1 cup cooked cauliflower, reserve ¼ cup cooking liquid
Dash salt
1 tablespoon chopped fresh parsley

Spread an equal amount of spinach over each chicken breast; sprinkle with onion powder, garlic powder, and nutmeg. Roll each breast and place, seam-side down, in a 1-quart flameproof casserole. Brush each breast with an equal amount of oil. Bake at 375°F. until juices run clear when chicken is pierced with a fork, about 25 minutes.

While chicken is baking, combine cauliflower, reserved cooking liquid, and salt in blender container and process until smooth.

When chicken is done, remove from oven and spread cauliflower puree evenly over rolled breasts. Turn oven control to broil and broil chicken until puree is thoroughly heated, about 3 minutes. Serve sprinkled with parsley.

Each serving is equivalent to: 2 servings Vegetables; 3 ounces Poultry; 1 serving Fats.

Per serving: 226 calories, 31 g protein, 9 g fat, 6 g carbohydrate, 183 mg sodium

Note: On the Full and Limited Choice Plans this recipe may be used at the Midday or Evening Meal.

* Men—For each serving use a 6-ounce skinned and boned chicken breast. Change equivalent listing to 4 ounces Poultry.

COCONUT CHICKEN
Full Choice Plan
Makes 2 Midday or Evening Meal servings

Chicken
¾ ounce cornflake crumbs
Dash each garlic powder, onion powder, salt, and ground ginger

12 ounces skinned and boned chicken breasts, pounded lightly with meat mallet
½ cup canned crushed pineapple (no sugar added)

Vegetables
2 teaspoons vegetable oil
3 cups shredded green cabbage
2 medium red bell peppers, seeded and cut into thin slivers

1 cup sliced scallions (green onions)
Dash each salt and garlic powder

Topping
2 teaspoons shredded coconut, toasted

To Prepare Chicken: In shallow dish combine cornflake crumbs and seasonings. Coat chicken breasts with crumb mixture. Spray an 8 x 8-inch baking pan with nonstick cooking spray; transfer chicken breasts to prepared pan and sprinkle with any remaining crumb mixture. Bake at 375°F. until lightly browned, about 20 minutes. Remove pan from oven and spread crushed pineapple evenly over chicken. Set oven control to broil and broil chicken until pineapple is well heated, 3 to 4 minutes.

To Prepare Vegetables: During last 10 minutes that chicken is cooking, in 9-inch skillet heat oil. Add cabbage and red peppers and sauté just until cabbage is softened, 5 to 10 minutes. Add scallions, salt, and garlic powder. Cover and keep warm.

To Serve: Transfer vegetables to serving platter; top with chicken and sprinkle with coconut.

Each serving is equivalent to: ½ serving Bread; 4 ounces Poultry; ½ serving Fruits; 1 serving Fats; 5 servings Vegetables; ½ cup Limited Vegetables; 1 serving Extras.

Per serving: 411 calories, 40 g protein, 11 g fat, 39 g carbohydrate, 391 mg sodium

FRUITED CHICKEN

Limited Choice Plan
Makes 2 Midday or Evening Meal servings*

1 pound 2 ounces chicken parts
  (drumsticks and thighs), skinned
½ medium banana, peeled and
  cut into ¼-inch-thick slices
¼ teaspoon salt

⅓ cup unfermented apple cider
  (no sugar added)
½ cup applesauce (no sugar added)
¼ cup plain unflavored yogurt
Dash ground nutmeg

In a shallow 1½-quart flameproof casserole combine chicken and banana. Sprinkle with salt, then drizzle with apple cider. Cover and bake at 350°F. until chicken is tender, about 35 minutes.

Transfer pan juices and banana slices to blender container or work bowl of food processor, leaving chicken in casserole. Add applesauce, yogurt, and nutmeg to banana mixture and process until smooth; pour over chicken. Broil until chicken is golden brown.

Each serving is equivalent to: 3 ounces Poultry; 1½ servings Fruits; ¼ serving Milk.

Per serving: 262 calories, 25 g protein, 9 g fat, 20 g carbohydrate, 363 mg sodium

* Men—One serving provides ¾ of a meal. Supplement with an additional ¼ serving of Protein at the Midday or Evening Meal.

HONEY–LIME CHICKEN

Full Choice Plan
Makes 2 servings

1½ pounds chicken legs
  (drumsticks and thighs
  attached), skinned, or 1 pound
  chicken breasts, skinned and
  halved
Dash each garlic powder and salt

2 tablespoons lime juice (no sugar
  added)
2 teaspoons prepared Dijon-style
  mustard
2 teaspoons honey

1. In shallow 8 x 8-inch nonstick baking pan sprinkle chicken with garlic powder and salt.
2. Bake at 350°F. until fork pierces chicken easily, about 30 minutes.

3. In small saucepan combine lime juice, mustard, and honey; heat. Spread mixture over chicken pieces.

4. Set oven control to broil and broil chicken until lightly browned, about 5 minutes.

Each serving is equivalent to: 4 ounces Poultry; 2 servings Extras.

Per serving with chicken legs: 264 calories, 31 g protein, 11 g fat, 8 g carbohydrate, 320 mg sodium

With chicken breasts: 228 calories, 35 g protein, 5 g fat, 8 g carbohydrate, 302 mg sodium

YOGURT-GLAZED CHICKEN

Limited Choice Plan
Makes 2 Midday or Evening Meal servings*

2 tablespoons plain unflavored yogurt
1 teaspoon granulated brown sugar
1 teaspoon Worcestershire sauce
1 garlic clove, minced

Dash each salt, pepper, and hot sauce
10 ounces skinned and boned chicken breasts

1. In small bowl combine all ingredients except chicken.

2. Spray a shallow 8 x 8-inch baking pan with nonstick cooking spray. Arrange chicken in pan and top with half of the yogurt mixture.

3. Cover and bake at 350°F. until chicken is tender, about 20 minutes.

4. Remove pan from oven and spread remaining yogurt mixture over chicken.

5. Turn oven control to broil and broil chicken until lightly browned. Transfer to serving platter and spoon pan juices over chicken.

Each serving is equivalent to: ⅛ serving Milk; 1 serving Extras; 3 ounces Poultry.

Per serving: 169 calories, 27 g protein, 4 g fat, 3 g carbohydrate, 139 mg sodium

* Men—One serving provides ¾ of a meal. Supplement with an additional ¼ serving of Protein at the Midday or Evening Meal.

CHICKEN IN PEANUT SAUCE

Full Choice Plan
Makes 2 Midday or Evening Meal servings

Chicken

2 cups cauliflower florets, blanched
2 cups chopped zucchini, blanched
2 carrots (about 4 ounces each), sliced diagonally into 1-inch pieces and blanched

6 ounces skinned and boned chicken breast, cut into 1 x 2-inch strips

Sauce

¼ cup thinly sliced onion
¾ cup Chicken Broth (see page 401)

1 teaspoon teriyaki sauce
3 tablespoons chunky-style peanut butter

To Prepare Chicken: Preheat oven to 375°F. In a 1½-quart baking dish that has been sprayed with nonstick cooking spray arrange cauliflower, zucchini, and carrots; top with chicken strips. Bake until chicken is done, 15 to 20 minutes.

To Prepare Sauce: In 7- or 8-inch nonstick skillet cook onion, over medium heat, until translucent. Stir in broth and teriyaki sauce and cook, stirring constantly, until liquid comes to a boil. Reduce heat and stir in peanut butter. Cook, stirring constantly, until mixture is well blended. Remove from heat and pour over chicken and vegetables. Serve hot.

Each serving is equivalent to: 6 servings Vegetables; 2 ounces Poultry; ⅛ cup Limited Vegetables; ½ serving Extras; 1 tablespoon plus 1½ teaspoons Peanut Butter (½ serving Protein and 1 serving Fats).

Per serving: 351 calories, 32 g protein, 15 g fat, 29 g carbohydrate, 372 mg sodium

POULET BELLE (STUFFED CHICKEN ROLLS WITH WINE SAUCE)

Full Choice Plan
Makes 2 Midday or Evening Meal servings

Chicken Rolls

1 skinned and boned chicken breast, 6 ounces
1 teaspoon mashed anchovy fillets
1 garlic clove, minced
¼ teaspoon oregano leaves
Dash pepper
2 medium tomatoes, blanched, peeled, seeded, and finely chopped

2 ounces Fontina cheese, thinly sliced
2 teaspoons enriched all-purpose flour
2 tablespoons buttermilk
3 tablespoons plain dried bread crumbs
2 teaspoons vegetable oil

Sauce

2 teaspoons margarine
1 tablespoon chopped shallots
½ cup sliced mushrooms
1 tablespoon lemon juice
1 teaspoon enriched all-purpose flour

Dash each salt and pepper
¾ cup Chicken Broth (see page 401)
2 fluid ounces dry white wine

Garnish

1 tablespoon chopped fresh parsley

To Prepare Chicken Rolls: Using a meat mallet, pound chicken breast to about ¼-inch thickness; cut in half. In small bowl combine anchovies, garlic, oregano, and pepper; add tomatoes and stir to combine. Spread half of mixture on each chicken breast half; top each with 1 ounce cheese. Roll halves, tucking in ends to enclose filling. Dredge rolls in 2 teaspoons flour; dip in buttermilk, then in bread crumbs.

In small skillet that has a metal or removable handle heat oil; add chicken rolls and brown quickly on all sides. Transfer skillet to oven and bake at 375°F. until chicken is fork-tender, 15 to 20 minutes.

To Prepare Sauce: While chicken is baking, in 9-inch skillet heat margarine until bubbly; add shallots and sauté briefly. Add mushrooms and lemon juice. Cook, stirring constantly, until liquid evaporates, about 3 minutes. Sprinkle flour, salt, and pepper over vegetables and stir to combine. Add broth and wine. Cook, stirring constantly, until mixture thickens.

To Serve: Transfer chicken rolls to serving platter; pour sauce over chicken and sprinkle with parsley.

Each serving is equivalent to: 2 ounces Poultry; 2½ servings Extras; 2½ servings Vegetables; 1 ounce Hard Cheese; 1 tablespoon Buttermilk (1⁄12 serving Milk); ½ serving Bread; 2 servings Fats; 1½ teaspoons Limited Vegetables; ¼ serving Occasional Substitutes.

Per serving: 422 calories, 32 g protein, 21 g fat, 23 g carbohydrate, 287 mg sodium

CLAY-COOKED CHICKEN CASSEROLE
Full Choice Plan
Makes 2 Midday or Evening Meal servings

Cooking in wet clay dates back to the ancient Etruscans and produces unique results. Wet-clay cooking is self-basting and produces its own natural sauces, thus preserving food value and flavor. You will need an unglazed pot of very porous, highly fired clay; these are available in housewares departments. Since the pot should be totally immersed in water for at least 10 minutes prior to cooking, you can gather together and prepare all of your ingredients while the pot is soaking.

¼ cup diced onion
2 tablespoons diced celery
1½ pounds chicken parts, skinned
¼ teaspoon salt, divided
⅛ teaspoon pepper, divided
1 cup each sliced carrots and
zucchini (1-inch-thick slices)

4 ounces pared potato, quartered
1 tablespoon plus 1 teaspoon
margarine
4 fluid ounces dry white wine
½ teaspoon arrowroot
1 tablespoon water

1. Immerse clay pot in water according to manufacturer's directions.
2. Spread diced onion and celery in bottom of pot. Sprinkle chicken parts with ⅛ teaspoon salt and dash pepper and arrange over vegetables. Arrange carrots, zucchini, and potato pieces around chicken. Sprinkle with remaining salt and pepper and dot with margarine; pour wine over chicken and vegetables.

3. Cover pot and place in a cold oven. Set oven control at 450°F. and bake until chicken is tender, about 55 minutes.

4. Transfer chicken and vegetables to a serving platter and keep warm. Pour juices from pot into a small saucepan. In small cup dissolve arrowroot in water; stir into juices in saucepan and bring to a boil. Reduce heat and simmer until thickened, about 2 minutes. Pour sauce over chicken.

Each serving is equivalent to: ⅛ cup Limited Vegetables; 2⅛ servings Vegetables; 4 ounces Poultry; ½ serving Bread Substitutes; 2 servings Fats; ½ serving Occasional Substitutes; ¼ serving Extras.

Per serving: 422 calories, 36 g protein, 16 g fat, 23 g carbohydrate, 498 mg sodium

BAKED STUFFED CHICKEN LOAF
Full Choice Plan
Makes 4 Midday or Evening Meal servings

Chicken

1½ pounds skinned and boned chicken	1 teaspoon poultry seasoning
⅓ cup plus 2 teaspoons plain dried bread crumbs	½ teaspoon salt
	Dash pepper

Stuffing

1½ cups drained canned whole golden hominy	1 small red delicious apple, cored and diced
½ cup each finely diced celery and onion	2 teaspoons margarine, softened
	½ teaspoon salt
	Dash pepper

To Prepare Chicken: Using a meat grinder or food processor, grind chicken (if processor is used, grind using an on and off motion). In bowl combine ground chicken with bread crumbs, poultry seasoning, salt, and pepper; set aside.

To Prepare Stuffing: In another bowl combine all ingredients for stuffing and set aside.

To Prepare Stuffed Chicken: Preheat oven to 350°F. On a 15½ x 12-inch nonstick baking sheet form half of the chicken mixture into an oval, about 12 inches long, 8 inches wide, and ½ inch thick. Spoon stuffing mixture over oval, mounding stuffing and leaving about 1 inch uncovered all around edge of oval. Divide remaining chicken into 4 portions. Using your hands, flatten 1 portion and place over ¼ of the stuffing. Repeat procedure 3 more times, covering entire surface of stuffing. Pinch all edges together to seal; shape into a loaf, making sure there are no cracks. Place in center of oven and bake until chicken is cooked and loaf is lightly browned, about 30 minutes.

Each serving is equivalent to: 4 ounces Poultry; ½ serving Bread; ½ serving Bread Substitutes; ¼ serving Vegetables; ⅛ cup Limited Vegetables; ¼ serving Fruits; ½ serving Fats.

Per serving: 346 calories, 36 g protein, 11 g fat, 24 g carbohydrate, 751 mg sodium

Variations:
1. Substitute skinned and boned turkey for the chicken.

Per serving: 321 calories, 36 g protein, 8 g fat, 24 g carbohydrate, 737 mg sodium

2. In a small saucepan, using a wire whisk to remove lumps and blend, dissolve 1 tablespoon enriched all-purpose flour in ¾ cup Chicken Broth (see page 401). Cook over medium heat, stirring constantly, until mixture comes to a boil. Reduce heat; add dash each salt and pepper and cook, stirring occasionally, until mixture is smooth and raw flour taste is cooked out, about 2 minutes. Serve with stuffed chicken. Add 1 serving Extras to equivalent listing.

Per serving: 356 calories, 37 g protein, 11 g fat, 26 g carbohydrate, 789 mg sodium

CHEDDAR–CHICKEN MUFFINS
Full Choice Plan
Makes 2 Midday or Evening Meal servings, 2 muffins each

This is a delicious way of using up leftover chicken or turkey. These muffins can be served hot or chilled and, therefore, are ideal as a "brown-bag" lunch.

4 ounces skinned and boned cooked chicken or turkey, diced
2 ounces uncooked enriched orzo macaroni,* cooked according to package directions
1 large egg, beaten
1 ounce grated sharp Cheddar cheese

4 pimiento-stuffed green olives, chopped
2 tablespoons minced onion
1 tablespoon chopped fresh parsley
¼ teaspoon salt†
Dash pepper

Preheat oven to 375°F. Spray 4 cups of a muffin pan with nonstick cooking spray. In bowl combine all ingredients and spoon ¼ of mixture into each sprayed cup. Fill remaining cups with water. Bake until muffins are firm and golden brown, about 30 minutes.

Each serving is equivalent to: 2 ounces Poultry; 1 serving Bread Substitutes; ½ Egg; ½ ounce Hard Cheese; 1 serving Extras; 1 tablespoon Limited Vegetables.

Per serving with chicken: 323 calories, 27 g protein, 13 g fat, 23 g carbohydrate, 634 mg sodium
With turkey: 311 calories, 27 g protein, 12 g fat, 23 g carbohydrate, 628 mg sodium

Variation: Substitute 4 ounces drained canned tuna, flaked, for the chicken. Change equivalent listing to 2 ounces Fish.

Per serving: 327 calories, 27 g protein, 14 g fat, 23 g carbohydrate, 1,039 mg sodium

* Orzo macaroni is a very small, rice-shaped pasta.
† If desired, an additional ¼ teaspoon salt may be added. Add 267 mg sodium to nutrition information.

CHICKEN POT PIE
Full Choice Plan
Makes 2 Midday or Evening Meal servings

Pastry Dough
⅓ cup less 1 teaspoon enriched
  all-purpose flour
Dash salt

2 teaspoons margarine
2 tablespoons plain unflavored
  yogurt

Pie Filling
¾ cup Chicken Broth (see page
  401), at room temperature
2 teaspoons enriched all-purpose
  flour
1 cup cooked sliced carrots
½ cup drained canned or frozen
  peas

1 tablespoon chopped scallion
  (green onion)
8 ounces skinned and boned
  cooked chicken, cut into cubes
Dash each salt, pepper, and thyme
  leaves

To Prepare Pastry Dough: In mixing bowl combine flour and salt; using a pastry blender, or 2 knives used scissor-fashion, cut in margarine until mixture resembles coarse meal. Add yogurt and mix thoroughly. Form into a ball. Wrap in plastic wrap and chill at least 1 hour.

To Prepare Filling: In 1-quart saucepan combine broth and flour, stirring until flour is dissolved. Bring to a boil and add carrot slices, peas, and chopped scallion. Cook for 5 minutes, stirring occasionally. Add chicken and seasonings. Cook 5 minutes longer to blend flavors.

To Prepare Pot Pie: Divide chicken mixture into two 4½ x 1¼-inch foil tart pans or shallow individual casseroles. Preheat oven to 400°F.

Cut chilled pastry dough in half. Roll each half between 2 sheets of wax paper into a piece large enough to cover 1 pot pie (about ⅛ inch thick). Cover each pie with dough, pressing dough against inside edges of tart pan or casserole; pierce with a fork to let steam escape. Bake until crust is lightly browned, about 30 minutes.

Each serving is equivalent to: 1 serving Bread; 1 serving Fats; ⅛ serving Milk; 1½ servings Extras; 1 serving Vegetables; ¼ cup plus 1½ teaspoons Limited Vegetables; 4 ounces Poultry.

Per serving: 400 calories, 41 g protein, 13 g fat, 30 g carbohydrate, 365 mg sodium

CHICKEN BREAST EN CROÛTE
Full Choice Plan
Makes 2 Midday or Evening Meal servings

"En croûte" is the method of cooking food, particularly pâté or meat, completely encased in pastry.

Pastry Dough
See Chicken Pot Pie recipe
(page 232)

Chicken
12 ounces skinned and boned whole chicken breasts, reserve skin	Dash each salt and pepper

Filling
1 teaspoon margarine	¼ teaspoon salt
¾ cup finely chopped mushrooms	2 fluid ounces dry white wine
1 tablespoon finely chopped scallion (green onion)	¼ teaspoon Dijon-style mustard

To Prepare Pastry Dough: Combine and chill ingredients as directed in Chicken Pot Pie recipe.

To Prepare Chicken: Fold chicken breasts together, shaping them into one oblong; if necessary, tie with colorfast or undyed cotton string to hold shape. Season with salt and pepper; cover with reserved skin and place in 8 x 8-inch nonstick baking pan. Bake at 350°F. for 25 minutes. Remove from oven and allow to cool slightly; discard skin, cover chicken, and chill.

To Prepare Filling: In small nonstick skillet heat margarine until bubbly; add mushrooms, scallion, and salt. Sauté, stirring occasionally, until all liquid is evaporated, about 5 minutes. Add wine and continue to cook until vegetables resemble a smooth paste, about 3 minutes longer; stir in mustard. Remove from heat and allow to cool slightly; cover and chill.

To Prepare Chicken Breast en Croûte: Roll chilled pastry dough between 2 sheets of wax paper to about ⅛-inch thickness, forming a circle large enough to enclose chicken breast. Spread center of pastry with chilled mushroom mixture; top with chilled chicken, flat side up. Fold pastry dough over chicken to enclose and pinch edges to seal well. Turn stuffed pastry over and place in 8 x 8-inch nonstick baking pan that has been sprayed with nonstick cooking spray. Bake at 375°F. until golden, 35 to 40 minutes.

Each serving is equivalent to: 1 serving Bread; 1½ servings Fats; ⅛ serving Milk; 4 ounces Poultry; ¾ serving Vegetables; 1½ teaspoons Limited Vegetables; ¼ serving Occasional Substitutes.

Per serving: 363 calories, 39 g protein, 12 g fat, 19 g carbohydrate, 583 mg sodium

CRISPY OVEN-FRIED MEXICAN CHICKEN
Full Choice Plan
Makes 4 Midday or Evening Meal servings

1 cup mixed vegetable juice	1½ ounces cornflake crumbs
¼ teaspoon hot sauce	1 teaspoon garlic powder
2¼ pounds chicken parts, skinned	½ teaspoon each salt, pepper,
2 ounces sharp Cheddar cheese,	chili powder, paprika, oregano
finely shredded	leaves, and ground cumin

1. In large shallow pan (not aluminum) combine vegetable juice and hot sauce; add chicken parts and let marinate for 30 minutes at room temperature or cover and refrigerate for 3 hours; turn chicken frequently.
2. Drain chicken and discard marinade. Preheat oven to 375°F. Spray a baking sheet with nonstick cooking spray.
3. In a large plastic bag combine remaining ingredients. Place chicken parts, a few at a time, in bag and shake to coat chicken; transfer coated pieces to prepared baking sheet.
4. Sprinkle any remaining crumb mixture over chicken and press to adhere. Bake until chicken is tender and crisp, about 1 hour.

Each serving is equivalent to: 3 ounces Poultry; ½ ounce Hard Cheese; ½ serving Bread.

Per serving: 267 calories, 29 g protein, 11 g fat, 10 g carbohydrate, 567 mg sodium

ORANGE–GINGER CHICKEN
Full Choice Plan
Makes 2 Midday or Evening Meal servings

2 tablespoons teriyaki sauce	2 teaspoons grated pared ginger
1 tablespoon thawed frozen	root
concentrated orange juice	1 garlic clove, minced
(no sugar added)	12 ounces skinned and boned
2 teaspoons dry white wine	chicken breasts*
2 teaspoons chili sauce	

1. In a measuring cup or small bowl prepare marinade by combining all ingredients except chicken.
2. In shallow 1-quart flameproof casserole arrange chicken breasts in 1 layer. Pour marinade over chicken, cover, and refrigerate 1 hour, turning chicken occasionally.
3. Transfer chicken to a plate and set aside. Strain marinade into a small saucepan, discarding ginger and garlic. Bring marinade to a boil. Reduce heat to low and cook for 2 minutes, stirring occasionally; set aside.
4. Return chicken to casserole and broil, turning occasionally and basting with marinade, until crisp and brown, about 10 minutes.
5. Heat any remaining marinade; pour over chicken and serve.

Each serving is equivalent to: ¼ serving Fruits; 1 serving Extras; 4 ounces Poultry.

Per serving: 242 calories, 36 g protein, 5 g fat, 9 g carbohydrate, 768 mg sodium

* Skinned and boned turkey can be substituted for the chicken in this recipe.

Per serving: 218 calories, 36 g protein, 3 g fat, 9 g carbohydrate, 756 mg sodium

CORNISH HEN MARSALA
Full Choice Plan
Makes 2 Midday or Evening Meal servings

1¼-pound Cornish hen, skinned and cut into pieces
½ teaspoon salt
1 tablespoon plus ¾ teaspoon enriched all-purpose flour
1 tablespoon margarine

1 garlic clove, minced
1 cup sliced mushrooms
¾ cup Chicken Broth (see page 401)
2 fluid ounces dry Marsala wine
Dash pepper

Garnish
1 tablespoon chopped fresh parsley

Sprinkle hen with salt; dredge in flour and set aside.

In 12-inch nonstick skillet heat margarine over medium heat until bubbly; add garlic and sauté briefly, being careful not to burn. Add hen pieces to skillet and brown well on all sides. Reduce heat to low, cover skillet, and cook until hen is tender, 10 to 15 minutes. Add mushrooms and cook uncovered, stirring occasionally, about 3 minutes. Add broth, wine, and pepper; cover and simmer about 10 minutes. Serve sprinkled with parsley.

Each serving is equivalent to: 4 ounces Poultry; ¼ serving Bread; 1½ servings Fats; 1 serving Vegetables; ½ serving Extras; ¼ serving Occasional Substitutes.

Per serving: 328 calories, 37 g protein, 14 g fat, 9 g carbohydrate, 721 mg sodium

MINT-GLAZED CORNISH HEN
Full Choice Plan
Makes 2 Midday or Evening Meal servings

2 tablespoons finely chopped fresh mint leaves
2 teaspoons olive oil
2 teaspoons honey, heated
1 garlic clove, minced

1¼-pound Cornish hen, skinned and cut in half
½ teaspoon salt
2 tablespoons lemon juice

Garnish
Mint leaves

In small bowl combine chopped mint, oil, honey, and garlic. In 8 x 8-inch nonstick baking pan sprinkle both sides of hen halves with salt. Brush mint–honey mixture over entire hen and sprinkle with lemon juice. Bake, cut-side down, at 400°F. until tender, 25 to 30 minutes.

Remove baking pan from oven and baste hen with pan juices. Set oven control to broil and broil hen 3 inches from heat source until browned and crisp, about 1 minute. Garnish with mint leaves before serving.

Each serving is equivalent to: 1 serving Fats; 2 servings Extras; 4 ounces Poultry.

Per serving: 285 calories, 33 g protein, 13 g fat, 8 g carbohydrate, 636 mg sodium

ROAST CORNISH HEN WITH SPICY ORANGE SAUCE
Full Choice Plan
Makes 2 Midday or Evening Meal servings

Hen

1¼-pound Cornish hen
⅛ teaspoon white pepper

¼ cup Chicken Broth (see page 401)

Sauce

½ cup orange juice (no sugar added)
¼ cup lemon juice
2 teaspoons arrowroot, dissolved in 2 tablespoons water
1 teaspoon firmly packed dark brown sugar

Grated peel of ½ orange
Grated peel of ½ lemon
¼ cinnamon stick
1 whole clove
½ cup canned mandarin orange sections (no sugar added)
2 teaspoons chopped fresh parsley

To Prepare Hen: Sprinkle hen with pepper. Place on rack in roasting pan; roast at 350°F., basting occasionally with broth, until done, about 40 minutes.

To Prepare Sauce: In small saucepan combine juices and dissolved arrowroot; over high heat and stirring constantly, bring to a boil and cook until thickened. Reduce heat to low; add sugar, orange and lemon peels, cinnamon stick, and clove and simmer for 5 minutes. Remove and discard cinnamon stick and clove. Add orange sections to saucepan and simmer, stirring constantly, until sections are heated and coated with sauce; stir in parsley and remove from heat.

To Serve: Cut hen in half; remove and discard skin. Serve each half topped with half of the sauce.

Each serving is equivalent to: 4 ounces Poultry; 2⅙ servings Extras; 1 serving Fruits.

Per serving: 322 calories, 34 g protein, 9 g fat, 27 g carbohydrate, 104 mg sodium

BASIC ROAST TURKEY

Remove and discard any excess fat from **turkey**. Place turkey, breast-side down, on rack in shallow roasting pan. Insert meat thermometer into center of thigh, close to body, being careful that thermometer does not touch bone. Roast uncovered at 325°F. Allow about 20 minutes per pound for a bird that is under 12 pounds, and about 15 minutes per pound if over 12 pounds. Using **1½ cups Turkey Broth** (see page 402), baste turkey every 30 minutes with some of the broth. Turn turkey breast-side up for the last 15 minutes of roasting. Turkey is done when thermometer registers 180°F. Roasting time may be affected by oven calibration, type of heat, shape of turkey, proportion of bone to meat, and temperature of turkey at start of roasting. Therefore, be sure to start checking for doneness about 1 hour before end of recommended roasting time. Let stand about 15 minutes before carving (this makes carving easier). Remove and discard skin, carve turkey, and weigh portions. Equate turkey and broth in accordance with the Food Plan.

ROAST TURKEY

Limited Choice Plan
Makes about 8 Midday or Evening Meal servings

8-pound turkey	**⅛ teaspoon each pepper, thyme**
2 tablespoons lemon juice	**leaves, rosemary leaves, and**
1 teaspoon salt	**ground sage**
	¾ cup Chicken Broth (see page
	401)

1. Preheat oven to 350°F. Remove any excess fat from turkey. Dry turkey inside and out with paper towels. Sprinkle lemon juice in cavity and rub over skin of turkey; sprinkle cavity with seasonings. Close neck cavity with skewer and truss turkey.
2. Spray cooking rack with nonstick cooking spray; place in shallow roasting pan. Set turkey, breast-side up, on rack. If meat thermometer is to be used, insert into center of thigh, close to body, being careful thermometer does not touch bone. Cover turkey with a loose tent of foil. Roast for 2 hours.
3. Uncover and continue roasting, basting occasionally with broth, 30 minutes longer or until meat thermometer registers 180°F. Let turkey stand for 15 minutes before carving.
4. Remove and discard skin, carve, and weigh portions. Serve 3 ounces sliced turkey per portion.*
Each serving is equivalent to: 3 ounces Poultry; ⅛ serving Extras.

Per serving: 143 calories, 25 g protein, 4 g fat, trace carbohydrate, 63 mg sodium

* Men—Add 1 ounce sliced cooked turkey per portion. Change equivalent listing to 4 ounces Poultry.

CURRIED TURKEY
Limited Choice Plan
Makes 2 Midday or Evening Meal servings*

⅓ cup low-fat cottage cheese
¼ cup skim milk
½ teaspoon grated lemon peel
½ teaspoon curry powder†

Dash salt
4½ ounces skinned and boned
    cooked turkey, cut into thin
    strips

Garnish
1 tablespoon chopped fresh parsley

In blender container combine cheese, milk, lemon peel, curry powder, and salt and process until smooth.

Pour cheese mixture into a small saucepan. Over high heat and stirring constantly, bring to a boil. Add turkey and cook, stirring constantly, until heated through. Serve each portion sprinkled with 1½ teaspoons parsley.

Each serving is equivalent to: ⅙ cup Soft Cheese; ⅛ serving Milk; 2¼ ounces Poultry.

Per serving: 147 calories, 24 g protein, 4 g fat, 3 g carbohydrate, 278 mg sodium

* Men—Add ¾ ounce heated julienne cooked turkey to each portion of Curried Turkey. Change equivalent listing to 3 ounces Poultry.
† For those who like it hot, add up to an additional ½ teaspoon curry powder to the recipe.

STIR-FRIED TURKEY
Limited Choice Plan
Makes 1 Midday or Evening Meal serving*

1 teaspoon Chinese sesame oil
½ garlic clove, minced
5 ounces skinned and boned turkey
    breast, cut into 2 x 1-inch strips
½ cup broccoli florets, blanched

½ cup diagonally sliced carrot
    (¼-inch-thick slices), blanched
2 teaspoons soy sauce
½ teaspoon onion flakes
Dash each salt and pepper

In small skillet heat oil over high heat; add garlic, then turkey and stir-fry until turkey is browned. Reduce heat; add remaining ingredients, cover, and simmer 5 to 10 minutes. Serve immediately.

Each serving is equivalent to: 1 serving Fats; 3 ounces Poultry; 2 servings Vegetables.

Per serving: 235 calories, 30 g protein, 8 g fat, 12 g carbohydrate, 1,116 mg sodium

* Men—For each serving use 6 ounces skinned and boned turkey breast. Change equivalent listing to 4 ounces Poultry.

STUFFED TURKEY LEG
Full Choice Plan
Makes 2 Midday or Evening Meal servings

12 ounces skinned and boned turkey leg (drumstick and thigh attached)
1 tablespoon plus 1 teaspoon margarine, divided
¼ cup diced scallions (green onions)
¼ cup minced celery, divided
1 cup sliced mushrooms
¼ teaspoon salt, divided

⅛ teaspoon thyme leaves
Dash pepper
1 slice enriched white bread, made into crumbs
2 tablespoons each diced onion and carrot
¾ cup Chicken Broth (see page 401)
½ teaspoon arrowroot
1 tablespoon water

1. Between 2 sheets of wax paper, using a meat mallet, pound turkey to an even thickness. Remove wax paper and set turkey aside.
2. In 9-inch skillet heat 2 teaspoons margarine until bubbly; add scallions and 2 tablespoons celery and sauté until vegetables are softened. Add mushrooms, dash salt, thyme, and pepper and sauté for 5 minutes. Stir in bread crumbs and remove from heat.
3. Sprinkle turkey with remaining salt and spread with mushroom mixture. Roll tightly and tie roll, in several places, with colorfast or undyed cotton string.
4. In skillet or saucepan just large enough to hold turkey roll heat remaining 2 teaspoons margarine until bubbly; add turkey roll and brown lightly on all sides. Remove roll from pan and set aside.
5. Add onion, carrot, and remaining 2 tablespoons celery to same pan and sauté until softened. Return turkey roll to pan and add broth. Cover and simmer, turning roll occasionally, until turkey is tender, 50 to 55 minutes.
6. Remove turkey from pan, snip and remove strings, and keep warm. Transfer pan juices and vegetables to blender container and process until smooth; return to pan. In small cup or bowl dissolve arrowroot in water; stir into sauce. Stirring constantly, bring to a boil and cook until thickened, 1 to 2 minutes. Cut turkey roll into thick slices and serve each portion with half of the sauce.

Each serving is equivalent to: 4 ounces Poultry; 2 servings Fats; 3 tablespoons Limited Vegetables; 1⅓ servings Vegetables; ½ serving Bread; ¾ serving Extras.

Per serving: 343 calories, 37 g protein, 16 g fat, 13 g carbohydrate, 550 mg sodium

TURKEY LEG JARDINIÈRE
Full Choice Plan
Makes 2 Midday or Evening Meal servings

12 ounces skinned and boned
turkey leg (drumstick and thigh
attached)
1 teaspoon Worcestershire sauce
⅛ teaspoon salt
Dash each pepper, thyme leaves,
and ground sage
12 carrot sticks, each about
3 inches x ½ inch

12 celery sticks, each about
3 inches x ½ inch
1 teaspoon enriched all-purpose
flour
1 teaspoon margarine
1 teaspoon olive oil
2 fluid ounces dry red wine
¾ cup Chicken Broth (see page
401)
½ bay leaf

1. Between 2 sheets of wax paper, using a meat mallet, pound turkey to an even thickness. Remove wax paper and sprinkle meat with Worcestershire sauce, salt, pepper, thyme leaves, and sage; set aside.

2. In small saucepan, in lightly salted boiling water, blanch carrot sticks for 3 minutes. Using a slotted spoon, remove carrots and set aside. Add celery sticks to water and blanch for 2 minutes; drain.

3. Refresh vegetables under running cold water and drain on paper towels.

4. Arrange vegetable sticks crosswise over turkey; roll tightly and tie, in several places, with colorfast or undyed cotton string. Sprinkle roll with flour.

5. In skillet or saucepan just large enough to hold turkey roll combine margarine and oil and heat; add turkey roll and brown lightly on all sides. Add wine and bring to a boil. Add chicken broth and bay leaf, cover, and simmer until meat is tender, 50 to 55 minutes.

6. Remove roll from pan; snip and remove strings. Cut roll into thick slices. Strain pan juices and serve with turkey roll.

Each serving is equivalent to: 4 ounces Poultry; 1½ servings Vegetables; 1 serving Extras; 1 serving Fats; ¼ serving Occasional Substitutes.

Per serving: 311 calories, 36 g protein, 12 g fat, 10 g carbohydrate, 323 mg sodium

POTTED TURKEY BURGERS
Full Choice Plan
Makes 2 Midday or Evening Meal servings

12 ounces ground turkey
¾ cup Chicken Broth (see
page 401), divided
1 slice enriched white bread, made
into crumbs
1 tablespoon chopped scallion
(green onion)
1 tablespoon chopped fresh parsley,
divided

½ teaspoon salt
⅛ teaspoon pepper
1 tablespoon margarine
1 teaspoon enriched all-purpose
flour
½ teaspoon Dijon-style mustard
⅛ teaspoon Worcestershire sauce

In medium bowl combine turkey, 2 tablespoons broth, bread crumbs, scallion, 2 teaspoons parsley, salt, and pepper; form into 4 patties. In medium skillet heat margarine until bubbly; add patties and cook until done, about 5 minutes on each side. Remove to a platter and keep warm. Stir flour into the drippings in skillet; stirring constantly, cook for 2 minutes. Stir in remaining broth and bring to a simmer. Add mustard and Worcestershire sauce and simmer, stirring constantly, until sauce has thickened. Pour over patties and sprinkle with remaining teaspoon parsley.

Each serving is equivalent to: 4 ounces Poultry; 1 serving Extras; ½ serving Bread; 1½ teaspoons Limited Vegetables; 1½ servings Fats.

Per serving: 288 calories, 37 g protein, 12 g fat, 9 g carbohydrate, 797 mg sodium

TURKEY HASH
Limited Choice Plan
Makes 2 Midday or Evening Meal servings*

2 teaspoons vegetable oil
1 garlic clove, minced
10 ounces ground turkey
½ cup diced celery
1 teaspoon each salt and onion
  powder

⅛ teaspoon ground thyme
Dash pepper
1 teaspoon browning sauce, diluted
  in 1 tablespoon water
1 medium tomato, diced

In 9-inch skillet heat oil over medium heat; add garlic and sauté stirring constantly, until lightly browned. Add turkey, celery, and seasonings; sauté, stirring constantly, just until turkey is no longer pink and celery is tender. Stir diluted browning sauce into turkey mixture. Reduce heat and add tomato; cover and simmer for 5 minutes.

Each serving is equivalent to: 1 serving Fats; 3 ounces Poultry; 1 serving Vegetables. (See page 407 for Full Choice Plan adjustments.)

Per serving: 216 calories, 26 g protein, 9 g fat, 7 g carbohydrate, 1,178 mg sodium

* Men—One serving provides ¾ of a meal. Supplement with an additional ¼ serving of Protein at the Midday or Evening Meal.

TURKEY LOAF
Full Choice Plan
Makes 4 Midday or Evening Meal servings

1½ pounds ground turkey
1 cup each diced celery, onions,
  and red bell peppers
⅓ cup plus 2 teaspoons plain dried
  bread crumbs

½ teaspoon each thyme leaves and
  salt
⅛ teaspoon pepper

Preheat oven to 350°F. In medium bowl combine all ingredients thoroughly. Transfer mixture to nonstick baking sheet and shape into a loaf. Bake until crisp and browned, about 30 minutes (do not overbake or turkey will dry out).

Each serving is equivalent to: 4 ounces Poultry; 1 serving Vegetables; ¼ cup Limited Vegetables; ½ serving Bread.

Per serving: 263 calories, 36 g protein, 6 g fat, 15 g carbohydrate, 472 mg sodium

TURKEY–TARRAGON BAKE
Full Choice Plan
Makes 4 Midday or Evening Meal servings

1 cup skim milk
2 slices enriched white bread, made into fine crumbs
12 ounces ground turkey
4 ounces Swiss cheese, shredded
2 egg whites
1 teaspoon salt
⅛ teaspoon each pepper, ground mace, and ground red pepper

½ cup plain unflavored yogurt
¼ cup chopped fresh parsley
1 tablespoon chopped fresh tarragon or 1 teaspoon dried tarragon leaves
Tomato–Herb Velouté
(see page 378)

1. In small nonstick saucepan combine milk and bread crumbs; cook over high heat, stirring constantly, until very thick, about 3 minutes.
2. Spoon onto a plate, cover, and refrigerate until well chilled, about 30 minutes.
3. Preheat oven to 350°F. In work bowl of food processor combine turkey, cheese, egg whites, salt, pepper, mace, and red pepper; process until very smooth. Add yogurt, parsley, tarragon, and chilled bread crumb mixture; process until combined.
4. Spray four 1¼-cup baking dishes with nonstick cooking spray; spoon ¼ of mixture into each prepared dish and, using a spatula that has been dipped in cold water, smooth tops.
5. Cover dishes with foil and set in baking pan; pour water into pan to about halfway up the sides of dishes. Bake until firm, 30 to 40 minutes.
6. Let stand for a few seconds, then unmold. Serve immediately with Tomato–Herb Velouté.

Each serving is equivalent to: ½ serving Milk; ½ serving Bread; 2 ounces Poultry; 1 ounce Hard Cheese; 1 serving Extras; Tomato–Herb Velouté (see page 378).

Per serving: 331 calories, 32 g protein, 16 g fat, 15 g carbohydrate, 909 mg sodium

Variation: *Turkey Quenelles*—Follow Steps 1, 2, and 3, but do not preheat oven. Spoon turkey mixture into a pastry bag that has been fitted with plain tube. Pipe puffs (about 1-inch diameter each) into a 10- or 12-inch skillet. Slowly pour enough boiling water into skillet to cover puffs. Poach, simmering gently, until quenelles float to the top. Serve with Tomato–Herb Velouté.

Veal

Most of the cooking tips that apply to beef and lamb are also applicable to veal (see Meat Group, page 255). However, because of its lack of fat and large proportion of connective tissue, veal can easily toughen and dry; it should be checked carefully during cooking.

Seasoning Tips—Veal is the most delicate of meats, with a subtle flavor and texture. A variety of herbs and spices go well with its bland flavor. Try sprinkling chops or a roast with one or two of your favorites from the following list, or experiment with one that you've never tried before. By just a change of seasoning, you can create an entire new taste.

Basil	Oregano	Saffron
Celery seed	Paprika	Sage
Chervil	Parsley	Salt
Chives	Pepper	Savory
Marjoram	Powdered mustard	Thyme
Nutmeg	Rosemary	

Basic Roasting Procedure—Roast veal uncovered, on rack in roasting pan, at a constant oven temperature of 300° to 325°F. As for chicken, the following chart is merely a guide. A meat thermometer is the best indication of when the roast is done (for information on meat thermometers see Meat Group, page 255). Veal is cooked when the internal temperature registers 170°F.

Cut	Approx. Weight	Approx. Cooking Time per Pound
Leg	5 to 8 pounds	25 to 35 minutes
Loin	4 to 6 pounds	30 to 35 minutes
Rib (rack)	3 to 5 pounds	35 to 40 minutes
Boneless shoulder	4 to 6 pounds	40 to 45 minutes

CREAMED VEAL AND CABBAGE
Full Choice Plan
Makes 2 servings

1 tablespoon margarine
1 cup sliced onions
1 garlic clove, minced
1 cup julienne-cut carrots
3 cups shredded green cabbage
8 ounces thinly sliced cooked veal
2 tablespoons plus 1½ teaspoons
  enriched all-purpose flour

¾ cup Chicken Broth (see page 401)
½ cup skim milk
1 tablespoon chopped fresh parsley
½ teaspoon salt
Dash white pepper

In 9-inch skillet heat margarine until bubbly; add onions and garlic and sauté, over low heat, until onions are translucent. Add carrots and sauté 3 minutes longer. Add cabbage and cook, stirring constantly, until cabbage begins to soften, about 10 minutes. Add veal. In small bowl dissolve flour in broth. Stirring constantly, slowly pour flour mixture into veal mixture and cook until thickened, about 3 minutes. Add remaining ingredients and heat thoroughly (*do not boil*).

Each serving is equivalent to: 1½ servings Fats; ½ cup Limited Vegetables; 4 servings Vegetables; 4 ounces Veal; ½ serving Bread; ½ serving Extras; ¼ serving Milk.

Per serving: 472 calories, 41 g protein, 21 g fat, 33 g carbohydrate, 766 mg sodium

VEAL-SALAD MOLD

Full Choice Plan
Makes 2 Midday or Evening Meal servings

This is an excellent way to use up leftover veal. It is equally as delicious using chicken or turkey.

1 envelope unflavored gelatin
1 teaspoon salt
1 cup boiling water
1 cup plain unflavored yogurt
½ teaspoon cider vinegar
1 to 2 drops hot sauce
8 ounces finely diced cooked veal

¼ cup diced pimientos
2 tablespoons thinly sliced scallion (green onion), green portion only
Dash pepper
4 iceberg or romaine lettuce leaves

Garnish
Dill sprigs

1. In medium heatproof bowl combine gelatin and salt. Add boiling water and stir until gelatin is completely dissolved.
2. In small bowl combine yogurt, vinegar, and hot sauce; add to dissolved gelatin. Cover and refrigerate until mixture is the consistency of unbeaten egg whites, about 15 minutes.
3. In bowl combine veal, pimientos, scallion slices, and pepper; add to chilled gelatin mixture.
4. Spray a 4-cup mold with nonstick cooking spray; transfer veal mixture to prepared mold. Cover and refrigerate until firm, about 1 hour.
5. Unmold onto serving platter, surround with lettuce, and garnish with dill sprigs (see Chicken Mousse with Dill, page 211, for unmolding directions).

Each serving is equivalent to: 1 serving Extras; 1 serving Milk; 4 ounces Veal; ¾ serving Vegetables; 1 tablespoon Limited Vegetables.

Per serving: 358 calories, 39 g protein, 18 g fat, 8 g carbohydrate, 1,193 mg sodium

SAUTÉED VEAL CHOPS
Limited Choice Plan
*Makes 2 Midday or Evening Meal servings**

In 10-inch nonstick skillet heat **2 teaspoons margarine** until bubbly; add two **7-ounce veal chops** and cook over medium-high heat for about 4 minutes on each side. Season with **dash each salt and pepper** and serve immediately.
Each serving is equivalent to: 1 serving Fats; 3 ounces Veal.

Per serving: 233 calories, 22 g protein, 15 g fat, 0.1 g carbohydrate, 164 mg sodium

Variation: Along with salt and pepper, sprinkle veal chops with 2 teaspoons lemon juice and dash garlic powder.

* Men—For each serving use an 8-ounce veal chop. Change equivalent listing to 4 ounces Veal.

VEAL ROULADEN
Full Choice Plan
Makes 2 Midday or Evening Meal servings

¼ cup finely diced onion
1 tablespoon plus 1½ teaspoons plain dried bread crumbs
1 teaspoon imitation bacon bits, crushed
2 veal cutlets, 6 ounces each
2 teaspoons prepared brown mustard

1 medium dill pickle, cut lengthwise into quarters
2 teaspoons margarine
¾ cup Chicken Broth (see page 401)
2 teaspoons enriched all-purpose flour

1. In small nonstick skillet cook onion, over medium heat, until translucent.
2. In small bowl combine cooked onion with bread crumbs and bacon bits; set aside.
3. Between 2 sheets of wax paper, using a meat mallet, pound veal to about ¼-inch thickness.
4. Carefully remove paper and spread 1 teaspoon mustard on each cutlet, then sprinkle each with half of the crumb mixture. Place 2 pickle quarters at narrow end of each cutlet; roll to enclose filling and secure with toothpicks.
5. In skillet used for onions heat margarine, over medium heat, until bubbly; add veal rolls and brown on all sides. Reduce heat to low; add broth and simmer until veal is done, about 15 minutes. Using a slotted spoon, remove rolls to serving platter; keep warm.
6. Measure 1 tablespoon of pan juices into small cup; add flour and stir to dissolve. Stirring constantly, add flour mixture to juices remaining

in skillet and cook until sauce is smooth and thickened, 1 to 2 minutes. Pour over veal and serve.

Each serving is equivalent to: ⅛ cup Limited Vegetables; ¼ serving Bread; 2 servings Extras; 4 ounces Veal; 1 serving Vegetables; 1 serving Fats.

Per serving: 335 calories, 35 g protein, 17 g fat, 10 g carbohydrate, 732 mg sodium

VEAL AND PEPPERS
Full Choice Plan
Makes 4 Midday or Evening Meal servings

1½ pounds boneless veal, cut into 1-inch cubes
4 fluid ounces white wine
2 teaspoons margarine, divided
1 cup sliced onions
1 cup sliced mushrooms
1 garlic clove, minced

1 cup drained canned tomatoes, coarsely chopped
1 teaspoon salt
¼ teaspoon pepper
½ cup each red and green bell pepper strips
2 tablespoons chopped fresh parsley

1. Spray 12-inch nonstick skillet with nonstick cooking spray. Add half the veal and brown well on all sides; transfer to 2-quart saucepan and repeat with remaining veal.

2. Add wine to same skillet and bring to a boil; using a wooden spoon, scrape down browned particles clinging to sides of pan. Pour wine mixture over veal.

3. In same skillet heat 1 teaspoon margarine until bubbly. Add onions and sauté until translucent; add to saucepan.

4. Add remaining teaspoon margarine to skillet. Add mushrooms and garlic and sauté 2 minutes; set aside.

5. Add tomatoes, salt, and pepper to saucepan; cover and simmer over low heat for 45 minutes.

6. Add pepper strips and reserved mushroom mixture to saucepan and continue simmering until veal and peppers are tender, about 15 minutes. Serve sprinkled with parsley.

Each serving is equivalent to: 4 ounces Veal; ¼ serving Occasional Substitutes; ½ serving Fats; ¼ cup Limited Vegetables; 1½ servings Vegetables.

Per serving: 354 calories, 34 g protein, 17 g fat, 11 g carbohydrate, 707 mg sodium

VEAL MARENGO

Full Choice Plan
Makes 4 Midday or Evening Meal servings

1 tablespoon plus 1 teaspoon olive oil
1½ pounds boneless veal, cut into 1-inch cubes
½ cup finely chopped onion
1 tablespoon plus 1 teaspoon enriched all-purpose flour
4 fluid ounces white wine
¼ cup tomato paste

2 cups sliced mushrooms
1 cup water
Bouquet garni (2 parsley sprigs, 1 celery rib, and 1 bay leaf, tied together with colorfast or undyed cotton string)
1 teaspoon salt
½ teaspoon thyme leaves
¼ teaspoon pepper

Garnish
2 tablespoons chopped fresh parsley

Preheat oven to 325°F. In 10-inch skillet heat oil; add veal cubes and brown lightly on all sides. Transfer meat to a 2-quart casserole.

In same skillet sauté onion until lightly browned. Sprinkle flour over onion and stir with wooden spoon to coat. Add wine and tomato paste; stirring constantly, bring to a boil. Add remaining ingredients except chopped parsley. Return to a boil and pour over veal.

Cover casserole and bake for 30 minutes. Uncover and continue to bake until veal is tender, 30 to 40 minutes. Remove and discard bouquet garni and sprinkle with chopped parsley before serving.

Each serving is equivalent to: 1 serving Fats; 4 ounces Veal; ⅛ cup Limited Vegetables; 1 serving Extras; ¼ serving Occasional Substitutes; ¼ serving Bonus; 1 serving Vegetables.

Per serving: 376 calories, 34 g protein, 19 g fat, 10 g carbohydrate, 733 mg sodium

VEAL MEATBALLS

Full Choice Plan
Makes 2 Midday or Evening Meal servings

1 teaspoon margarine
¼ cup minced onion
1 garlic clove, minced
10 ounces ground veal
1 egg
3 tablespoons seasoned dried bread crumbs
1 tablespoon water
¼ teaspoon salt

⅛ teaspoon white pepper
1 teaspoon olive oil
1 cup tomato sauce
1 tablespoon plus 1 teaspoon red wine
¼ teaspoon oregano leaves
Dash each onion powder and garlic powder

Heat margarine in small nonstick skillet until bubbly; add onion and garlic and sauté until soft but not brown. In small bowl combine onion mixture, veal, egg, bread crumbs, water, salt, and white pepper; mix well. Form mixture into 8 meatballs.

Heat oil in 9-inch nonstick skillet; add meatballs and cook, turning occasionally, until browned. Add remaining ingredients; cover and simmer 20 to 25 minutes.

Each serving is equivalent to: 1 serving Fats; ⅛ cup Limited Vegetables; 3 ounces Veal; ½ Egg; ½ serving Bread; 1 serving Bonus; 1 serving Extras.

Per serving: 375 calories, 30 g protein, 19 g fat, 19 g carbohydrate, 1,032 mg sodium

VEAL PATTIES
Full Choice Plan
Makes 2 Midday or Evening Meal servings

2 teaspoons margarine, divided
¼ cup each minced onion and celery
10 ounces ground veal
1 egg
6 saltines, crushed and moistened with 2 tablespoons water
¼ teaspoon salt

Dash each thyme leaves and white pepper
1 teaspoon enriched all-purpose flour
⅓ cup plus 2 teaspoons Chicken Broth (see page 401)
¼ cup drained canned mushrooms

1. In small nonstick skillet heat 1 teaspoon margarine until bubbly; add onion and celery and sauté until vegetables are soft but not brown.

2. In bowl combine half the onion mixture, veal, egg, saltines, salt, thyme, and white pepper; mix well.

3. Shape veal mixture into 4 patties; sprinkle each with ¼ teaspoon flour.

4. In 10-inch nonstick skillet heat remaining teaspoon margarine; add veal patties and brown on both sides.

5. Add broth, mushrooms, and remaining onion mixture. Cover and simmer 20 to 25 minutes.

Each serving is equivalent to: 1 serving Fats; ⅛ cup Limited Vegetables; ½ serving Vegetables; 3 ounces Veal; ½ Egg; ½ serving Bread; ¾ serving Extras.

Per serving: 336 calories, 30 g protein, 19 g fat, 12 g carbohydrate, 639 mg sodium

QUICK VEAL CHILI FOR TWO
Full Choice Plan
Makes 2 Midday or Evening Meal servings*

2 teaspoons vegetable oil
½ cup each chopped onion and green bell pepper
1 teaspoon minced fresh garlic or ¼ teaspoon garlic powder
10 ounces gound veal
1½ teaspoons chili powder

½ teaspoon each oregano leaves and ground cumin
Dash each salt and hot sauce
½ cup canned crushed tomatoes
1 tablespoon plus 1 teaspoon tomato paste
3 ounces drained canned pinto beans

1. In medium saucepan heat oil; add onion, green pepper, and garlic or garlic powder; sauté until onion is translucent, about 5 minutes.
2. Add veal, chili powder, oregano, cumin, salt, and hot sauce; stirring constantly to break up veal, cook until veal loses its pink color, about 3 minutes.
3. Add crushed tomatoes and tomato paste; cook, stirring occasionally, about 5 minutes longer.
4. Stir in beans and cook until heated, about 5 minutes.

Each serving is equivalent to: 1 serving Fats; ¼ cup Limited Vegetables; 1 serving Vegetables; 3 ounces Veal; 1 serving Extras; 1½ ounces Legumes.

Per serving: 330 calories, 28 g protein, 17 g fat, 18 g carbohydrate, 302 mg sodium (estimated)

* Men—Add ½ ounce heated pinto beans to each portion of Quick Veal Chili. Change equivalent listing to 2 ounces Legumes.

VEAL CHILI
Full Choice Plan
Makes 4 Midday or Evening Meal servings

1 tablespoon plus 1 teaspoon vegetable oil	2 teaspoons chili powder, or to taste
1 cup minced onions	1 teaspoon ground cumin
4 garlic cloves, minced	½ teaspoon salt
1½ pounds ground veal	½ teaspoon hot sauce, or to taste
1 cup each minced celery and green bell peppers	¼ teaspoon pepper
1 cup canned crushed tomatoes	12 ounces drained canned red kidney beans, rinsed
1 cup mixed vegetable juice	

In 4-quart saucepan heat vegetable oil; add onions and garlic and sauté until onions are translucent, about 5 minutes. Add ground veal and sauté until browned, stirring constantly to break up veal. Stir in remaining ingredients except kidney beans and bring to a boil. Reduce heat, cover, and simmer for 30 minutes.

Stir kidney beans into veal mixture and cook until heated, about 5 minutes. While beans are heating, warm 4 soup bowls. Serve chili in heated bowls.

Each serving is equivalent to: 1 serving Fats; ¼ cup Limited Vegetables; 4 ounces Veal; 1½ servings Vegetables; ¼ serving Bonus; 1 serving Bread Substitutes.

Per serving: 447 calories, 39 g protein, 20 g fat, 27 g carbohydrate, 869 mg sodium (estimated)

Variation: *Beef Chili*—Substitute 1 pound cooked ground beef (rare) for the ground veal.

Per serving: 486 calories, 39 g protein, 25 g fat, 27 g carbohydrate, 889 mg sodium (estimated)

VEAL-STUFFED CABBAGE LEAVES IN WINE SAUCE

Full Choice Plan
Makes 2 Midday or Evening Meal servings

¼ cup minced shallots
10 ounces ground veal
1 egg, lightly beaten with 1
  tablespoon water
3 tablespoons seasoned dried bread
  crumbs
¼ teaspoon salt
Dash each white pepper and
  ground nutmeg

4 medium green cabbage leaves,
  blanched
½ cup tomato sauce
⅓ cup plus 2 teaspoons Chicken
  Broth (see page 401)
2 tablespoons plus 2 teaspoons dry
  red wine
Dash each garlic powder and onion
  powder

1. In 7-inch nonstick skillet cook shallots until softened.
2. In medium bowl combine cooked shallots, veal, egg, bread crumbs, salt, pepper, and nutmeg; mix well.
3. Remove about 1 inch from core end of each blanched cabbage leaf. Place ¼ of meat mixture in center of each leaf; roll tightly, tucking in sides to enclose filling. Place filled leaves seam-side down in 7-inch nonstick skillet.
4. In small bowl combine tomato sauce, broth, wine, and garlic and onion powders; pour over rolls.
5. Bring to a boil and cook 10 minutes. Reduce heat to low, cover, and simmer until tender, about 25 minutes.

Each serving is equivalent to: ⅛ cup Limited Vegetables; 3 ounces Veal; ½ Egg; ½ serving Bread; 1 serving Vegetables; ½ serving Bonus; 2¼ servings Extras.

Per serving: 340 calories, 31 g protein, 15 g fat, 19 g carbohydrate, 728 mg sodium

VEAL-STUFFED ZUCCHINI BOATS

Full Choice Plan
Makes 2 Midday or Evening Meal servings

2 medium zucchini, about 5 ounces
  each
1 teaspoon olive oil
2 tablespoons each diced celery and
  onion
1 garlic clove, minced
1 tablespoon chopped fresh parsley
1 teaspoon chopped fresh basil or
  ¼ teaspoon dried basil leaves

1 teaspoon oregano leaves, divided
½ teaspoon salt
6 ounces ground veal*
2 ounces mozzarella cheese,
  shredded
2 teaspoons enriched all-purpose
  flour
¼ cup tomato sauce
Dash pepper

1. Preheat oven to 350°F. Cut each zucchini in half lengthwise and scoop out pulp, leaving 4 firm zucchini shells; set shells aside.
2. Chop pulp and set aside.
3. In 8- or 9-inch skillet heat oil; add celery, onion, garlic, and reserved pulp and cook until onion is translucent. Remove from heat and add

parsley, basil, ½ teaspoon oregano, and salt. Add veal and mix thoroughly to combine.

4. Spoon ¼ of mixture into each reserved zucchini shell and transfer stuffed shells to an 8 x 8-inch baking pan.

5. Bake until meat is no longer pink and zucchini shells are tender, 25 to 30 minutes.

6. Sprinkle each zucchini boat with ½ ounce shredded cheese and continue to bake until cheese is melted.

7. Turn oven control to broil and broil until cheese is lightly browned, about 2 minutes.

8. Remove pan from broiler. Transfer zucchini boats to serving platter and keep warm. Drain liquid from baking pan into small saucepan. Add flour to saucepan and stir with wire whisk until flour is dissolved and mixture is smooth.

9. Stir in tomato sauce, remaining ½ teaspoon oregano, and pepper and cook, over medium heat, until mixture thickens and is thoroughly heated. Pour sauce over zucchini boats and serve immediately.

Each serving is equivalent to: 2⅛ servings Vegetables; ½ serving Fats; 1 tablespoon Limited Vegetables; 2 ounces Veal; 1 ounce Hard Cheese; 1 serving Extras; ¼ serving Bonus.

Per serving: 289 calories, 24 g protein, 16 g fat, 12 g carbohydrate, 832 mg sodium

* Ground turkey may be substituted for the veal in this recipe.

Per serving: 251 calories, 25 g protein, 12 g fat, 12 g carbohydrate, 846 mg sodium

VEAL AND SPINACH CANNELLONI
Full Choice Plan
Makes 2 Midday or Evening Meal servings

Crêpes
½ cup skim milk
1 egg

⅓ cup less 1 teaspoon enriched
   all-purpose flour
Dash salt

Filling
2 teaspoons margarine
1 tablespoon minced shallots
1 teaspoon minced fresh garlic
10 ounces ground veal
1 cup sliced mushrooms

1 cup well-drained cooked chopped
   spinach
1 cup tomato sauce, divided
Dash each salt, pepper, and
   ground nutmeg

Topping
2 teaspoons grated Parmesan
   cheese

To Prepare Crêpes: In blender container combine milk and egg; turn motor on and quickly turn off. Add flour and salt and process until smooth. Let batter stand 15 to 20 minutes.

Heat small nonstick omelet pan or skillet; pour in ¼ of the batter and quickly move pan from side to side so that batter covers entire bottom of pan. Cook until underside is dry. Using a pancake turner, carefully turn crêpe over; cook other side briefly. Slide onto dish. Repeat procedure 3 more times, making 4 crêpes.

To Prepare Filling: In medium skillet heat margarine until bubbly; add shallots and garlic and sauté until shallots are translucent, about 3 minutes. Add veal and cook, stirring constantly, until mixture is finely crumbled, about 5 minutes. Add mushrooms and spinach. Stirring constantly, cook 5 minutes longer. Add ¼ cup tomato sauce, salt, pepper, and nutmeg and stir to combine.

To Prepare Cannelloni: Spoon ¼ of the filling onto center of each crêpe; roll crêpes to enclose filling. In 2-quart casserole place crêpes seamside down; top with remaining sauce and sprinkle with Parmesan cheese. Bake at 400°F. until thoroughly heated and bubbly, about 25 minutes.

Each serving is equivalent to: ¼ serving Milk; ½ Egg; 1 serving Bread; 1 serving Fats; 1½ teaspoons Limited Vegetables; 3 ounces Veal; 2 servings Vegetables; 1 serving Bonus; 1 serving Extras.

Per serving: 453 calories, 37 g protein, 19 g fat, 33 g carbohydrate, 955 mg sodium

Game

RABBIT SALAD
Full Choice Plan
Makes 2 Midday or Evening Meal servings

8 ounces boned cooked rabbit, diced
¼ cup diagonally sliced celery
¼ cup diced pimientos
2 tablespoons diced onion
2 teaspoons chopped capers

1 teaspoon each olive oil and mayonnaise
¼ teaspoon each salt and cider vinegar
Dash each paprika and pepper
2 drops hot sauce
6 iceberg or romaine lettuce leaves

Garnish
2 parsley sprigs

In bowl combine all ingredients except lettuce and parsley; cover and chill at least 30 minutes.

To Serve: Arrange 3 lettuce leaves on each of 2 salad plates; mound half of salad on each portion of lettuce and garnish each with a parsley sprig.

Each serving is equivalent to: 4 ounces Game; 1¼ servings Vegetables; 1 tablespoon Limited Vegetables; 1 serving Fats.

Per serving: 299 calories, 34 g protein, 16 g fat, 4 g carbohydrate, 430 mg sodium

RABBIT CASSEROLE
Full Choice Plan
Makes 2 Midday or Evening Meal servings

Serve with cooked enriched noodles or rice.

2 teaspoons margarine
2 teaspoons imitation bacon bits
12 ounces boned rabbit, cut into 1-inch cubes
1 cup each diced onions and green bell peppers
2 medium tomatoes, blanched, peeled, seeded, and chopped

1 garlic clove, minced
1 teaspoon salt
½ teaspoon each crushed marjoram and thyme leaves
Dash pepper
1 cup sliced mushrooms
4 fluid ounces dry white wine

1. Preheat oven to 350°F. In 9-inch nonstick skillet melt margarine over medium heat; stirring constantly, add bacon bits and cook 1 minute. Using a slotted spoon, remove bacon bits and set aside.
2. Increase heat, add rabbit cubes, and brown on all sides; transfer to a 1-quart casserole.
3. In the same skillet combine onions and green peppers and cook until onions are translucent. Add tomatoes and seasonings and cook until a sauce-like consistency. Stir in mushrooms and wine; cook 1 to 2 minutes longer.
4. Pour mixture over rabbit; cover casserole and bake until rabbit is tender, about 45 minutes.
5. Sprinkle rabbit mixture with reserved bacon bits and serve hot.

Each serving is equivalent to: 1 serving Fats; 1 serving Extras; 4 ounces Game; ½ cup Limited Vegetables; 4 servings Vegetables; ½ serving Occasional Substitutes.

Per serving: 429 calories, 39 g protein, 16 g fat, 23 g carbohydrate, 1,291 mg sodium

PHEASANT CASSEROLE
Full Choice Plan
Makes 4 Midday or Evening Meal servings

1 tablespoon plus 1 teaspoon margarine
2 small apples, pared, cored, and cut into cubes
2 pounds pheasant parts, skinned
⅔ cup apple juice (no sugar added)
1 lemon, thinly sliced

1 lime, thinly sliced
1 teaspoon salt
¼ teaspoon pepper
2 teaspoons arrowroot
1 tablespoon water
1 tablespoon chopped fresh parsley

1. Preheat oven to 350°F. In 9-inch nonstick skillet heat margarine until bubbly. Add apples and sauté until lightly browned; transfer apples to a 1-quart casserole.
2. In same skillet brown pheasant parts and transfer to casserole; pour apple juice over pheasant, top with lemon and lime slices, and sprinkle with salt and pepper.

3. Cover casserole and bake until pheasant is tender, about 1 hour.

4. In small cup or bowl dissolve arrowroot in water. Drain juices from casserole into small saucepan and bring to a boil. Stirring constantly, add dissolved arrowroot and cook until sauce is thickened. Pour sauce over pheasant and sprinkle with parsley.

Each serving is equivalent to: 1 serving Fats; 1 serving Fruits; 4 ounces Game; ½ serving Extras.

Per serving: 209 calories, 21 g protein, 7 g fat, 18 g carbohydrate, 616 mg sodium

QUAIL NEW ORLEANS
Full Choice Plan
*Makes 2 Midday or Evening Meal servings**

4 quail (about 3½ ounces each), skinned	1 tablespoon finely chopped shallots
1 tablespoon plus 1 teaspoon enriched all-purpose flour	½ cup sliced mushrooms
1 teaspoon salt	2 medium tomatoes, blanched, peeled, seeded, and chopped
¼ teaspoon pepper	4 fluid ounces white wine
1 tablespoon plus 1 teaspoon olive oil	¼ cup Chicken Broth (see page 401)

1. Using butcher's twine, tie wings of each quail to body and tie legs together.

2. In large plastic bag combine flour, salt, and pepper. Place 1 quail in bag and shake to coat; repeat with remaining 3 quail.

3. In 10-inch skillet heat oil; add quail and brown well on all sides. Remove quail from pan and set aside.

4. In same skillet sauté shallots for 1 minute; add mushrooms and sauté 1 minute longer. Stir in tomatoes, wine, and broth and bring to a boil.

5. Return quail to skillet. Reduce heat to low, cover skillet, and cook until quail are tender, 20 to 25 minutes.

Each serving is equivalent to: 3 ounces Game; 2⅙ servings Extras; 2 servings Fats; 1½ teaspoons Limited Vegetables; 2½ servings Vegetables; ½ serving Occasional Substitutes.

Per serving: 372 calories, 34 g protein, 16 g fat, 13 g carbohydrate, 1,160 mg sodium

* Men—One serving provides ¾ of a meal. Supplement with an additional ¼ serving of Protein at the Midday or Evening Meal.

Meat Group

Trim pennies as well as pounds by learning how to make less meat go a longer way. Many Oriental dishes, like Japanese Beef Teriyaki or Sweet 'n' Tangy Pork Sauté, stretch meat through skillful blending with vegetables. Even ground meat becomes exotic when combined with eggplant and spices to make Moussaka. Variety meats also offer tastiness and good nutrition at a low cost.

Guidelines for Using Meat Group Items

1. Amounts (trimmed and boned cooked or drained canned weight):

	Morning Meal	
	Full Choice Plan	Limited Choice Plan
Women, Men, and Youth	1 ounce	1 ounce

	Midday and Evening Meals	
	Full Choice Plan	Limited Choice Plan
Women and Youth	3 to 4 ounces	3 ounces
Men	4 to 5 ounces	4 ounces

2. Meat Group selections may be consumed at mealtime *only* and may be split with items from the Eggs, Cheese, Peanut Butter (Full Choice Plan only), Poultry, Veal, and Game, Fish, and Legumes categories.

3. Meat Group items may be selected *up to* 3 times weekly on the Full Choice Plan, once weekly on the Limited Choice Plan. If split with items from the above categories, the meal *must* still be considered one of the weekly Meat Group meals.

4. The Full Choice Plan range of 3 to 4 ounces for Women and Youth (4 to 5 ounces for Men) provides flexibility. It is a way of individualizing the Food Plan to meet your specific needs.

5. Fresh, frozen, freeze-dried, canned, cured, smoked, and pressed products may be selected. *If cured or smoked products are selected, use the low end of the serving size range.*

6. Uncured and unsmoked products should *not* contain sugar; cured and smoked products may contain sugar.

7. Equate freeze-dried products to the amount of fresh used before drying.

8. The following items may be used as Meat Group selections. Those in italics are for the Full Choice Plan only and should *not* be used with the Limited Choice Plan. The other items may be used on both plans.

beef	organ meats:
beefalo	gizzards
bologna	hearts
Canadian-style bacon	kidneys
frankfurters	sweetbreads
ham	tripe
knockwurst	pork
lamb	*sausages*
liverwurst	tongue

9. Bologna, frankfurters, knockwurst, and sausages may contain a combination of beef, turkey, chicken, pork, and veal (Full Choice Plan only).

10. Raw meat may be consumed if permitted by local health agencies. However, care should be taken since raw meat may contain salmonella, a bacteria that causes intestinal upsets.

11. Use lean meat and remove any visible fat before eating.

12. Whenever possible, weigh food after cooking (except canned items). Canned products should be well drained before weighing; do *not* consume the liquid (or broth) in which the product was packed.

13. As a "rule of thumb," for each serving of a Meat Group item, allow 2 ounces (for raw items) for shrinkage in cooking and an additional 2 ounces for any bone; for each half serving, allow 1 ounce (for raw items) for shrinkage in cooking and an additional 1 ounce for any bone. If using "fully cooked" ham, boiled ham, Canadian-style bacon, frankfurters, knockwurst, precooked sausages, liverwurst, bologna, or a cooked item, or if consuming raw meat, do *not* allow additional ounces for shrinkage. Tripe is an exception to this "rule of thumb." One pound uncooked tripe will yield about 8 ounces cooked tripe.

14. Cooking Procedures:

    A. Trim away as much visible fat as possible before cooking.

    B. Raw Meat Group selections (except organ meats) should be broiled, baked, or roasted, on a rack, or boiled. Pan juices from broiling, baking, and roasting may *not* be consumed. Organ meats may be handled in the same manner as veal (see Poultry, Veal, and Game, page 203).

    C. Raw ground meat may be combined with Vegetables, Bread, Bread Substitutes, and items from the Optional category and broiled or baked, on a rack, or boiled. Equate items used to the Food Plan.

    D. Only cooked Meat Group selections (except organ meats)

may be pan-broiled, sautéed, stir-fried, or added to casseroles and stews. A measured amount of Fats may be used for pan-broiling, sautéing, stir-frying, and in casseroles and stews. Equate Fats to the Food Plan. Organ meats may be handled in the same manner as veal.

E. Meat Group selections may be marinated before cooking; only items from the Vegetables and Optional categories may be used. If the marinade is discarded, it does not have to be equated to the Food Plan; if consumed, equate to the Food Plan.

F. Uncooked Meat Group selections may *not* be stuffed.

G. Homemade broth may be prepared by boiling Meat Group selections in water to cover; vegetables and seasonings may be used. Refrigerate broth until fat congeals on top; remove and discard congealed fat.

Tips for Cooking Beef, Lamb, and Pork

Although some cuts of meat are more tender than others, any cut can be made tender if cooked properly. Slow cooking will break down the muscle fibers in stringy, tough cuts, making them tender, juicy, and delicious.

Tender cuts of meat are usually best when cooked by dry heat, such as roasting and broiling. Less tender cuts will become more tender when cooked by moist heat, such as simmering in liquid.

Seasonings—The hearty flavor of meat needs little or no seasoning to be delicious, but a sprinkling of herbs and spices can make even the most choice cut a new culinary experience. The following list indicates the seasonings that go well with beef, pork, and lamb. Sprinkle one or two on your next roast or chop and make the ordinary *extra*ordinary!

Spice	Beef	Pork	Lamb
Saffron			x
Sage	x	x	x
Salt	x	x	x
Savory	x	x	x
Tarragon	x		
Thyme	x	x	x

Broiling—Trim away any excess fat and place meat on rack in broiler pan. There is no need to preheat the broiler, but it may be preheated if desired. Depending upon thickness, broil meat 2 to 5 inches from heat source (broil ¾- to 1-inch-thick cuts 2 to 3 inches from heat; 1- to 2-inch-thick cuts 3 to 5 inches from heat). Broil until top is brown and meat is approximately half done; then, if desired, season *cooked* side. (Do not salt meat before broiling; salt tends to draw moisture from within to the cut surface and this delays browning. Since browning is an indication of doneness, delayed browning could result in overcooked meat.) Turn meat over and broil until other side is brown and meat is done to taste. Season other side if desired.

Cooking in Liquid—Place meat in a large pot or kettle and add enough water to cover. By entirely covering the meat with water, uniform cooking is assured; it is not necessary to turn the meat. Add vegetables and seasonings to the liquid as desired; they will add flavor to the meat. Bring liquid just to a boil. Reduce heat, cover, and simmer until meat is tender. *Do not boil,* as this tends to shrink the meat, make it dry, detract from its flavor and texture, and make it difficult to slice. When meat is tender, remove it from the liquid. If desired, cooking liquid may be reused. Cool, then strain to remove solids. Cover and chill until fat congeals on top; remove and discard congealed fat (¾ cup liquid is equivalent to: 1 serving Extras).

Roasting—Trim excess fat off meat, then season if desired. (Roasts may be seasoned before, during, or after cooking. Remember that salt will penetrate only ¼ to ½ inch of the meat, so do not overseason.) Place meat on rack in shallow roasting pan. *Add no water and do not cover.* There is usually no need to preheat an oven for roasting. Roast meat at temperatures indicated on the charts on pp. 262–265.

Due to many variables, timing on the roasting charts is approximate; using a meat thermometer will take the guesswork out of roasting all kinds of meat and assure you of having a roast done the way you like it. The thermometer should be durable with clearly marked, easy-to-read temperatures. There are two types that can be purchased. One is inserted into a large muscle of the roast, not touching bone, before the meat is placed in the oven. It registers the temperature as the meat cooks. The other type, which was developed for use in a microwave oven, gives an instant reading when inserted.

It is inserted and removed periodically during the time that the meat is roasting. An easy way to test the accuracy of a thermometer is to place the bulb in boiling water. It should register 212°F.; if it registers higher or lower, the thermometer can still be used as long as the variance is taken into consideration.

A roast continues to cook by retained heat after it has been removed from the oven. Therefore, remove it when the thermometer registers about 5°F. below the desired temperature. Then let it stand for about 15 to 20 minutes; the cooking process will be completed and, additionally, carving will be easier.

See pages 262–265 for Roasting Charts.

OLD-FASHIONED POT ROAST
Full Choice Plan
Makes 4 Midday or Evening Meal servings

1½ pounds bottom round of beef
1 tablespoon plus 1 teaspoon
   vegetable oil
1 cup each sliced onions and celery
2 cups mixed vegetable juice
1 cup sliced carrots
1 cup drained canned tomatoes,
   coarsely chopped
2 tablespoons Worcestershire sauce
2 teaspoons salt
4 bay leaves
¼ teaspoon pepper
4 pared potatoes, 4 ounces each
½ cup water
1 tablespoon plus 1 teaspoon
   enriched all-purpose flour

Garnish
2 tablespoons chopped fresh parsley

1. Preheat oven to 375°F. On rack in roasting pan roast beef until rare, about 30 minutes.
2. In 5-quart Dutch oven heat vegetable oil; add onions and celery and sauté until onions are translucent.
3. Add vegetable juice, carrots, tomatoes, Worcestershire sauce, salt, bay leaves, and pepper; bring to a boil. Add beef and baste with sauce. Cover and simmer for 1½ hours.
4. Add potatoes; cover and continue simmering until potatoes are fork-tender, about 25 minutes.
5. In measuring cup or small bowl combine water and flour and stir to dissolve. Remove bay leaves from pot roast and slowly stir dissolved flour into sauce. Simmer uncovered, stirring constantly, until sauce is thickened, about 3 minutes. Serve sprinkled with parsley.

Each serving is equivalent to: 4 ounces Meat Group; 1 serving Fats; ¼ cup Limited Vegetables: 1½ servings Vegetables; ½ serving Bonus; 1 serving Bread Substitutes; 1 serving Extras.

Per serving: 427 calories, 41 g protein, 12 g fat, 37 g carbohydrate, 1,538 mg sodium

Roasting Chart for Beef

Cut	Approx. Weight (in pounds)	Oven Temperature (constant)	Approx. Cooking Time (minutes per pound)	Internal Temperature (when removed from oven)
Rib,* bone in	6 to 8	300° to 325°F.	23 to 25 27 to 30 32 to 35	Rare—140°F. Medium—160°F. Well—170°F.
	4 to 6	300° to 325°F.	26 to 32 34 to 38 40 to 42	Rare—140°F. Medium—160°F. Well—170°F.
Rib, boned, rolled, and tied	5 to 7	300° to 325°F.	32 38 48	Rare—140°F. Medium—160°F. Well—170°F.
Rib eye (delmonico)	4 to 6	350°F.	18 to 20 20 to 22 22 to 24	Rare—140°F. Medium—160°F. Well—170°F.
Whole tenderloin	4 to 6	425°F.	45 to 60†	Rare—140°F.
Half tenderloin	2 to 3	425°F.	35 to 40†	Rare—140°F.
Boneless rump, rolled (high quality)	4 to 6	300° to 325°F.	25 to 30 25 to 30 25 to 30	Rare—150°F. Medium—160°F. Well—170°F.
Tip (high quality)	3½ to 4	300° to 325°F.	35 to 40 35 to 40 35 to 40	Rare—140°F. Medium—160°F. Well—170°F.
	4 to 6	300° to 325°F.	30 to 35 30 to 35 30 to 35	Rare—140°F. Medium—160°F. Well—170°F.

Roasting Chart for Lamb

Cut	Approx. Weight (in pounds)	Oven Temperature (constant)	Approx. Cooking Time (minutes per pound)	Internal Temperature (when removed from oven)
Leg: Bone in	7 to 9	325°F.	15 to 20 20 to 25 25 to 30	Rare—140°F. Medium—160°F. Well—170°F.
Boneless	5 to 7	325°F.	25 to 30 30 to 35 35 to 40	Rare—140°F. Medium—160°F. Well—170°F.
Shoulder: Bone in	4 to 6	300° to 325°F.	15 to 20 20 to 25 25 to 30	Rare—140°F. Medium—160°F. Well—170°F.
Boneless	4 to 6	325°F.	30 to 35 35 to 40 40 to 45	Rare—140°F. Medium—160°F. Well—170°F.
Rib: Rib roast	1½ to 2½	375°F.	30 to 35 35 to 40 40 to 45	Rare—140°F. Medium—160°F. Well—170°F.
Crown roast (unstuffed)	2 to 3	375°F.	15 to 20 25 to 30 30 to 35	Rare—140°F. Medium—160°F. Well—170°F.

Roasting Chart for Fresh Pork

Cut	Approx. Weight (in pounds)	Oven Temperature (constant)	Approx. Cooking Time (minutes per pound)	Internal Temperature (when removed from oven)
Loin:				
Center	3 to 5	325°F.	30 to 35	170°F.
Half	5 to 7	325°F.	35 to 40	170°F.
Blade and sirloin	3 to 4	325°F.	40 to 45	170°F.
Boneless double	3 to 5	325°F.	35 to 45	170°F.
Arm picnic shoulder:				
Bone in	5 to 8	325°F.	30 to 35	170°F.
Boneless	3 to 5	325°F.	35 to 40	170°F.
Blade (Boston) shoulder	4 to 6	325°F.	40 to 45	170°F.
Leg (fresh ham):				
Whole (bone in)	12 to 16	325°F.	22 to 26	170°F.
Whole (boneless)	10 to 14	325°F.	24 to 28	170°F.
Half (bone in)	5 to 8	325°F.	35 to 40	170°F.

Roasting Chart for Smoked Pork

Cut	Approx. Weight (in pounds)	Oven Temperature (constant)	Approx. Cooking Time (minutes per pound)	Internal Temperature (when removed from oven)
Ham (cook-before-eating):				
Whole	10 to 14	300° to 325°F.	18 to 20	160°F.
Half	5 to 7	300° to 325°F.	22 to 25	160°F.
Shank and rump portion	3 to 4	300° to 325°F.	35 to 40	160°F.
Ham (fully cooked):				
Whole	10 to 14	325°F.	15 to 18	140°F.
Half	5 to 7	325°F.	18 to 24	140°F.
Arm picnic shoulder	5 to 8	300° to 325°F.	35	170°F.
Shoulder roll	2 to 3	300° to 325°F.	35 to 40	170°F.
Canadian-style bacon	2 to 4	325°F.	35 to 40	160°F.

COUNTRY BEEF STEAK
Limited Choice Plan
Makes 1 Midday or Evening Meal serving*

1 thin beef top or bottom round
   steak, 5 ounces
1 teaspoon vegetable oil
½ cup drained canned tomatoes,
   chopped
½ cup each sliced celery and
   mushrooms

¼ cup diced green bell pepper
1 garlic clove, minced
½ cup mixed vegetable juice
2 teaspoons onion flakes
⅛ teaspoon pepper
Dash salt

Garnish
1 tablespoon chopped fresh parsley

Preheat broiler. On rack in broiler pan broil steak, turning once, until rare, about 5 minutes.

While steak is broiling, in 1-quart saucepan heat oil; add tomatoes, celery, mushrooms, green pepper, and garlic and sauté for 3 minutes. Add vegetable juice, onion flakes, pepper, and salt and bring to a boil. Add steak; spoon vegetable mixture over meat. Cover pan and simmer until meat is tender, about 45 minutes. Serve sprinkled with chopped parsley.

Each serving is equivalent to: 3 ounces Meat Group; 1 serving Fats; 2½ servings Vegetables; ⅔ serving Bonus. (See page 407 for Full Choice Plan adjustments.)

Per serving: 287 calories, 31 g protein, 11 g fat, 18 g carbohydrate, 678 mg sodium

* Men—For each serving use a 6-ounce steak. Change equivalent listing to 4 ounces Meat Group.

JAPANESE BEEF TERIYAKI
Limited Choice Plan
Makes 1 Midday or Evening Meal serving*

1 beef top or bottom round steak,
   5 ounces
½ cup water
1 tablespoon onion flakes

1 tablespoon minced pared ginger
   root
1 tablespoon soy sauce
1 teaspoon Worcestershire sauce
1 garlic clove

Place steak in shallow pan (not aluminum). In blender container combine remaining ingredients and process until smooth; pour over steak. Cover pan and refrigerate for at least 1 hour.

Preheat broiler. Transfer steak to rack in broiler pan and drain marinade into small saucepan. Broil steak, turning once, until done to taste.

While steak is broiling, bring marinade to a boil. Reduce heat and simmer for 5 minutes. Slice steak diagonally across the grain and serve with heated marinade.

Each serving is equivalent to: 3 ounces Meat Group.

Per serving: 193 calories, 28 g protein, 6 g fat, 5 g carbohydrate, 1,397 mg sodium

* Men—For each serving use a 6-ounce steak. Change equivalent listing to 4 ounces Meat Group.

BEEF WITH PEPPERS AND SNOW PEAS
Full Choice Plan
Makes 2 Midday or Evening Meal servings

2 teaspoons vegetable oil
1 tablespoon minced pared ginger root
1 garlic clove, minced
1 cup thinly sliced red bell pepper strips
¾ cup trimmed snow peas (stem ends and strings removed)

½ cup sliced mushrooms
¼ cup sliced scallions (green onions)
8 ounces broiled flank steak, thinly sliced diagonally across the grain
2 tablespoons soy sauce

In 12-inch nonstick skillet heat oil; add ginger and garlic and sauté until garlic is golden. Add pepper strips, snow peas, mushrooms, and scallions and sauté until tender-crisp. Add steak and cook, stirring constantly, until heated through. Add soy sauce and stir to combine.

Each serving is equivalent to: 1 serving Fats; 1½ servings Vegetables; ½ cup Limited Vegetables; 4 ounces Meat Group.

Per serving: 342 calories, 39 g protein, 14 g fat, 16 g carbohydrate, 1,409 mg sodium

Variation: If more sauce is desired, dissolve 2 teaspoons cornstarch in ¾ cup Chicken Broth (see page 401). Add to skillet with soy sauce and cook, stirring constantly, until thickened. Add 1½ servings Extras to equivalent listing.

Per serving: 357 calories, 41 g protein, 14 g fat, 20 g carbohydrate, 1,409 mg sodium

MARINATED FLANK STEAK WITH HONEY–PINEAPPLE SAUCE
Full Choice Plan
Makes 2 Midday or Evening Meal servings

Be sure to plan ahead since this steak should be marinated overnight.

Marinade and Steak
½ cup diced onion
½ cup sliced green bell pepper
4 fluid ounces dry sherry
⅓ cup apple juice (no sugar added)
¼ cup teriyaki sauce
2 teaspoons soy sauce

2 garlic cloves, sliced
2 small slices pared ginger root or ¼ teaspoon gound ginger
½ teaspoon powdered mustard
12 ounces flank steak

Sauce
½ cup canned crushed pineapple (no sugar added)
2 teaspoons cornstarch

1 teaspoon honey
2 teaspoons vegetable oil

To Prepare Marinated Steak: Combine first 9 ingredients in shallow pan (not aluminum) large enough to hold steak; add steak, cover, and refrigerate overnight, turning steak occasionally.

Remove meat from marinade and place on rack in broiler pan. Strain marinade and reserve liquid and vegetables; discard garlic and ginger. Broil steak 2 to 3 inches from heat source, turning once, until medium-rare, about 4 minutes on each side.

To Prepare Sauce: In small bowl combine pineapple, cornstarch, and honey, stirring to dissolve cornstarch; set aside.

In small skillet heat oil; add reserved vegetables and sauté briefly, about 3 minutes. Add reserved marinade liquid and bring to a boil. Stirring constantly, add pineapple mixture and cook until thickened.

To Serve: Slice flank steak diagonally across the grain into ½-inch-thick strips. Pour sauce over steak.

Each serving is equivalent to: ¼ cup Limited Vegetables; ½ serving Vegetables; ½ serving Occasional Substitutes; 1 serving Fruits; 4 ounces Meat Group; 2 servings Extras; 1 serving Fats.

Per serving: 488 calories, 38 g protein, 14 g fat, 38 g carbohydrate, 1,714 mg sodium

PEPPER STEAK WITH MUSHROOMS

Full Choice Plan
Makes 4 Midday or Evening Meal servings

¾ cup Chicken Broth (see page 401)
2 tablespoons plus 2 teaspoons dry sherry
2 teaspoons arrowroot, dissolved in 1 tablespoon water
1 tablespoon plus 1 teaspoon vegetable oil

4 garlic cloves, crushed
4 slices pared ginger root
1 cup sliced mushrooms
1 cup green bell pepper strips
½ cup each sliced onion and drained canned water chestnuts
1 pound broiled flank steak, thinly sliced diagonally across the grain

1. In 2-cup measure or small bowl combine broth, sherry, and dissolved arrowroot; set aside.
2. Heat oil in 12-inch nonstick skillet; add garlic and ginger and sauté until lightly browned. Remove and discard garlic pieces and ginger slices.
3. To same skillet add mushrooms, pepper strips, onion, and water chestnuts; cook, stirring quickly and frequently, until tender-crisp, about 3 minutes.
4. Stirring constantly, add reserved broth mixture to skillet and cook until thickened.
5. Add steak and cook until thoroughly heated.

Each serving is equivalent to: 1¾ servings Extras; 1 serving Fats; 1 serving Vegetables; ¼ cup Limited Vegetables; 4 ounces Meat Group.

Per serving: 320 calories, 37 g protein, 13 g fat, 10 g carbohydrate, 80 mg sodium

BEEF BOURGUIGNON
Full Choice Plan
Makes 2 Midday or Evening Meal servings

12 ounces boneless chuck, cut into
    2-inch cubes
2 teaspoons margarine
½ cup sliced onion
½ teaspoon minced fresh garlic
2 teaspoons enriched all-purpose
    flour
¾ cup Beef Broth (see page 401)

4 fluid ounces red Burgundy wine
2 teaspoons tomato paste
Bouquet garni (celery, bay leaf,
    peppercorns, and parsley sprigs,
    tied in cheesecloth)
1 teaspoon salt
1 cup sliced carrots
1 cup sliced mushrooms

On rack in broiler pan broil chuck 2 to 4 inches from heat source, turning once, until browned on all sides, about 5 minutes per side.

While meat is browning, in 2-quart saucepan heat margarine until bubbly; add onion and garlic and sauté until onion is translucent. Sprinkle flour over onion and stir to combine. Add broth, wine, tomato paste, bouquet garni, and salt. Stir in broiled beef and bring to a boil. Reduce heat, cover, and simmer until meat is fork-tender, about 1½ hours.

Add carrots and mushrooms and cook until carrots are tender, about 20 minutes longer. Remove and discard bouquet garni. Serve immediately or freeze for future use.

Each serving is equivalent to: 4 ounces Meat Group; 1 serving Fats; ¼ cup Limited Vegetables; 2 servings Extras; ½ serving Occasional Substitutes; 2 servings Vegetables.

Per serving: 396 calories, 37 g protein, 15 g fat, 17 g carbohydrate, 1,266 mg sodium

BEEF STEW
Limited Choice Plan
Makes 2 Midday or Evening Meal servings*

10 ounces boneless beef for stew,
    cut into 1-inch cubes
2 teaspoons vegetable oil
1 teaspoon minced fresh garlic
1 cup water
2 medium tomatoes, blanched,
    peeled, seeded, and chopped

½ cup diced celery
½ teaspoon each onion powder
    and salt
1 bay leaf
Dash each thyme leaves and
    ground pepper
½ cup sliced carrot

On rack in broiler pan broil beef 2 to 4 inches from heat source, turning once, until browned on all sides, about 5 minutes per side.

While meat is browning, in 1½-quart saucepan heat oil; add garlic and sauté briefly (*do not brown*). Add water, tomatoes, celery, and seasonings and bring mixture to a boil. Add broiled beef. Reduce heat, cover, and simmer until meat is fork-tender, about 1½ hours. Stir in carrot and cook until slices are tender-crisp, about 15 minutes longer.

Each serving is equivalent to: 3 ounces Meat Group; 1 serving Fats; 2½ servings Vegetables. (See page 407 for Full Choice Plan adjustments.)

Per serving: 276 calories, 28 g protein, 13 g fat, 12 g carbohydrate, 638 mg sodium

* Men—One serving provides ¾ of a meal. Supplement with an additional ¼ serving of protein at the Midday or Evening Meal.

"BEEF STROGANOFF"

Full Choice Plan
Makes 2 Midday or Evening Meal servings

12 ounces beef tenderloin, cut into
   1-inch-thick slices
1 tablespoon margarine
2 tablespoons minced onion
¼ teaspoon minced fresh garlic
1 cup thinly sliced mushrooms
1 tablespoon plus ¾ teaspoon
   enriched all-purpose flour

¾ cup Beef Broth (see page 401)
2 teaspoons tomato paste
½ cup plain unflavored yogurt
Dash freshly ground pepper
1 tablespoon chopped fresh parsley
1 cup cooked enriched noodles or
   rice, hot

On rack in broiler pan broil tenderloin slices 2 to 4 inches from heat source, turning once, until browned on all sides, about 5 minutes per side.

While meat is browning, in 9-inch skillet heat margarine until bubbly; add onion and garlic and sauté until onion is translucent, about 2 minutes. Add mushrooms and, stirring occasionally, cook 3 minutes longer. Sprinkle flour over mushrooms and stir until thoroughly combined. Stirring constantly, add broth and tomato paste and cook until slightly thickened. Remove from heat; stir in yogurt, pepper, and parsley. Add broiled meat and cook just until heated (*do not boil*). Serve over hot noodles or rice.

Each serving is equivalent to: 4 ounces Meat Group; 1½ servings Fats; 1 tablespoon Limited Vegetables; 1 serving Vegetables; ¼ serving Bread; 1 serving Extras; ½ serving Milk; 1 serving Bread Substitutes.

Per serving with noodles: 502 calories, 40 g protein, 24 g fat, 30 g carbohydrate, 228 mg
   sodium
With rice: 515 calories, 38 g protein, 23 g fat, 36 g carbohydrate, 226 mg sodium

CHUCKBURGER

Limited Choice Plan
*Makes 1 Midday or Evening Meal serving**

5 ounces ground chuck
1 tablespoon chopped fresh parsley
¼ teaspoon each basil and oregano
   leaves

Dash each garlic powder and
   pepper

In small bowl combine all ingredients. Shape into a patty. On rack in broiler pan broil patty, turning once, about 7 minutes or until done to taste.

Each serving is equivalent to: 3 ounces Meat Group.

Per serving: 187 calories, 26 g protein, 8 g fat, 1 g carbohydrate, 47 mg sodium

* Men—One serving provides ¾ of a meal. Supplement with an additional ¼ serving of Protein at the Midday or Evening Meal.

HOT AND SPICY MEAT SAUCE
Full Choice Plan
Makes 4 Midday or Evening Meal servings

Delicious served over pasta.

1 tablespoon plus 1 teaspoon
  vegetable oil
1 cup diced onions
2 garlic cloves, minced
½ cup finely chopped celery
1 pound cooked ground beef,
  crumbled
3 cups water
2 cups tomato puree
2 medium canned tomatoes, pureed
3 tablespoons Worcestershire sauce

1 tablespoon plus 1 teaspoon
  granulated brown sugar
1 tablespoon minced fresh parsley
2 teaspoons paprika
2 bay leaves
1 teaspoon chili powder, or to taste
½ teaspoon each salt and oregano
  leaves
¼ teaspoon each thyme leaves,
  pepper, and ground cinnamon

Garnish
Chopped fresh parsley

In 4-quart saucepan heat oil; add onions and garlic and sauté until onions are translucent. Add celery and sauté 1 minute longer. Add remaining ingredients except garnish. Simmer until thick, about 2 hours.

Remove bay leaves and garnish with parsley before serving. Serve hot.

Each serving is equivalent to: 1 serving Fats; ¼ cup Limited Vegetables; 1¼ servings Vegetables; 4 ounces Meat Group; 1 serving Bonus; 2 servings Extras.

Per serving: 400 calories, 35 g protein, 18 g fat, 24 g carbohydrate, 911 mg sodium

MEATBALL STEW
Limited Choice Plan
*Makes 2 Midday or Evening Meal servings**

10 ounces ground beef
1 slice enriched white bread, made
  into crumbs
1 tablespoon chopped fresh parsley
1 tablespoon each plain unflavored
  yogurt and Worcestershire sauce
½ teaspoon each onion flakes and
  marjoram leaves
Pepper
2 teaspoons margarine

¾ cup sliced carrots (¼-inch-thick
  slices)
½ cup chopped celery
1 bay leaf, broken in half
¼ cup sliced mushrooms
1 packet instant beef broth and
  seasoning mix
2 teaspoons enriched all-purpose
  flour
½ cup water
Dash salt

1. In small bowl thoroughly combine ground beef, bread crumbs, parsley, yogurt, Worcestershire sauce, onion flakes, marjoram, and dash pepper; shape into 12 small meatballs.

2. Arrange meatballs on rack in broiler pan and broil 6 inches from heat source, turning once, until browned.

3. In 1½-quart saucepan melt margarine over medium heat. Add carrots, celery, and bay leaf and stir to coat vegetables with margarine; cover and cook until vegetables are tender, 3 to 5 minutes.

4. Add meatballs, mushrooms, and broth mix and stir to combine; cover and simmer for 5 minutes.

5. In measuring cup or small bowl dissolve flour in water; add salt and dash pepper and add to stew. Cook uncovered, stirring constantly, until mixture thickens. Remove bay leaf and serve.

Each serving is equivalent to: 3 ounces Meat Group; ½ serving Bread; 1½ teaspoons Yogurt (¹⁄₁₆ serving Milk); 1 serving Fats; 1 serving Vegetables; 1½ servings Extras. (See page 407 for Full Choice Plan adjustments.)

Per serving: 305 calories, 27 g protein, 14 g fat, 16 g carbohydrate, 661 mg sodium

* Men—One serving provides ¾ of a meal. Supplement with an additional ¼ serving of Protein at the Midday or Evening Meal.

MEAT LOAF
Full Choice Plan
Makes 2 Midday or Evening Meal servings

12 ounces ground beef
1 medium tomato, blanched,
    peeled, and diced
⅓ cup plus 2 teaspoons plain dried
    bread crumbs
2 tablespoons each minced green
    bell pepper, celery, and onion

1 tablespoon chopped fresh basil or
    1 teaspoon dried basil leaves
1 tablespoon chopped fresh parsley
    or 1 teaspoon parsley flakes
2 teaspoons imitation bacon bits,
    crushed
1 garlic clove, minced
Dash each salt and pepper

Preheat oven to 350°F. In bowl thoroughly combine all ingredients; shape into a loaf. Place loaf on rack in baking pan and bake until browned (about 20 minutes) or until done to taste.

Each serving is equivalent to: 4 ounces Meat Group; 1¼ servings Vegetables; 1 serving Bread; 1 tablespoon Limited Vegetables; 1 serving Extras.

Per serving: 361 calories, 36 g protein, 14 g fat, 21 g carbohydrate, 395 mg sodium

BARBECUED LAMB
Limited Choice Plan
*Makes 2 Midday or Evening Meal servings**

½ cup lemon juice
2 teaspoons chili sauce
1¼ teaspoons grated orange peel
1 teaspoon Worcestershire sauce
¾ teaspoon grated lemon peel

½ teaspoon granulated sugar
½ teaspoon honey
1 garlic clove, minced
10 ounces boneless lamb, cut into
    1-inch cubes

In medium bowl combine all ingredients except lamb; add cubes and toss to coat well. Cover and refrigerate at least 1 hour, turning lamb occasionally. Transfer meat to rack in broiler pan, reserving marinade; broil for 6 minutes. Turn cubes and brush with marinade; broil 6 minutes longer or until done to taste.

Each serving is equivalent to: 1½ servings Extras; 3 ounces Meat Group.

Per serving: 211 calories, 23 g protein, 9 g fat, 10 g carbohydrate, 134 mg sodium

* Men—One serving provides ¾ of a meal. Supplement with an additional ¼ serving of Protein at the Midday or Evening Meal.

HOT HONEYED LAMB STEAKS
Full Choice Plan
Makes 2 Midday or Evening Meal servings

1 tablespoon plus 1 teaspoon reduced-calorie apricot spread (16 calories per 2 teaspoons)	1 teaspoon teriyaki sauce
1 teaspoon Dijon-style mustard	½ garlic clove, finely mashed to form paste
1 teaspoon honey	1 pound lamb steaks

In small bowl thoroughly combine all ingredients except lamb steaks. On rack in broiler pan broil steaks 2 to 5 inches from heat source (depending on thickness of steaks; thinner steaks should be closer to heat) for 1 to 2 minutes. Brush with half the mustard-honey mixture; broil 5 to 7 minutes longer. Turn steaks over and broil 1 to 2 minutes. Brush with remaining mustard-honey mixture; broil 5 to 7 minutes longer or until done to taste.

Each serving is equivalent to: 16 calories Specialty Foods; 1 serving Extras; 4 ounces Meat Group.

Per serving: 248 calories, 30 g protein, 11 g fat, 4 g carbohydrate, 204 mg sodium

LAMB ZINGARA
Full Choice Plan
Makes 2 Midday or Evening Meal servings

1 tablespoon olive or vegetable oil	2 teaspoons tomato paste
½ cup sliced onion	½ teaspoon rosemary leaves, ground
1 teaspoon minced fresh garlic	2 fluid ounces dry vermouth
½ cup frozen artichoke hearts	½ teaspoon salt
¾ cup Chicken Broth (see page 401)	Dash freshly ground pepper
½ cup blanched, peeled, seeded, and chopped tomatoes	1 pound lamb loin chops

Garnish
1 tablespoon chopped fresh parsley

In 9-inch skillet heat oil; add onion and garlic and sauté until onion slices are translucent. Add artichoke hearts, cover, and cook over medium heat for 5 minutes. Add broth, tomatoes, tomato paste, and rosemary; cover and simmer, stirring occasionally, for about 10 minutes. Add vermouth, salt, and pepper and cook uncovered, over medium heat, until mixture thickens slightly.

While vegetable sauce is cooking, on rack in broiler pan broil chops 2 to 5 inches from heat source (depending on thickness of chops; thinner chops should be closer to heat) for 6 to 9 minutes on each side or until done to taste. Transfer to warm serving platter, top with vegetable sauce, and sprinkle with parsley.

Each serving is equivalent to: 1½ servings Fats; ½ cup Limited Vegetables; 1 serving Extras; ½ serving Vegetables; ¼ serving Occasional Substitutes; 4 ounces Meat Group.

Per serving: 354 calories, 36 g protein, 16 g fat, 11 g carbohydrate, 691 mg sodium

MOUSSAKA
Full Choice Plan
Makes 2 Midday or Evening Meal servings

Vegetables and Lamb

2 cups sliced pared eggplant
　(½-inch-thick slices)
1 teaspoon salt, divided
1 teaspoon olive oil
½ cup diced onion
1 garlic clove, minced
½ cup drained canned tomatoes,
　chopped

1 tablespoon chopped fresh parsley
2 teaspoons dry red wine
½ teaspoon ground allspice
Dash pepper
8 ounces cooked ground lamb,
　crumbled

Sauce

2 teaspoons margarine
2 teaspoons enriched all-purpose
　flour

¼ cup skim milk

Topping

1 teaspoon grated Parmesan cheese　Dash ground nutmeg

To Prepare Vegetables and Lamb: Place eggplant slices on paper towels; sprinkle with ½ teaspoon salt and let stand about 30 minutes.

Pat eggplant dry. In 9-inch nonstick skillet brown slices on both sides; set eggplant aside. In same skillet heat oil; add onion and garlic and sauté until onion is golden. Add tomatoes, parsley, wine, allspice, pepper, and remaining ½ teaspoon salt and cook, stirring occasionally, until moisture evaporates; stir in lamb and remove from heat.

Preheat oven to 350°F. In 1½-quart casserole layer half the eggplant slices, then half the meat mixture; repeat layers.

To Prepare Sauce: In small nonstick saucepan heat margarine until bubbly; add flour and cook, stirring constantly, 1 minute. Gradually stir in milk; continue to stir and cook until sauce is smooth and thickened.

To Bake: Pour sauce over meat mixture and sprinkle with cheese and nutmeg. Bake until heated and top is golden brown, about 30 minutes.

Each serving is equivalent to: 2½ servings Vegetables; 1½ servings Fats; ¼ cup Limited Vegetables; 2 servings Extras; 4 ounces Meat Group; ⅛ serving Milk.

Per serving: 373 calories, 35 g protein, 18 g fat, 17 g carbohydrate, 1,044 mg sodium

Variations:

1. Substitute cooked ground beef for the lamb.

Per serving: 389 calories, 35 g protein, 20 g fat, 17 g carbohydrate, 1,044 mg sodium

2. Reduce lamb to 4 ounces and prepare vegetables and lamb as directed. Add 2 ounces shredded hard cheese to sauce at same time as milk. Bake as directed. Add 1 ounce Hard Cheese to equivalent listing and reduce Meat Group to 2 ounces.

Per serving: 371 calories, 27 g protein, 22 g fat, 17 g carbohydrate, 1,182 mg sodium

3. Reduce lamb to 4 ounces and prepare vegetables, lamb, and sauce as directed. In small bowl beat 2 large eggs. Stir small amount of sauce into eggs, then stir egg mixture into sauce; cook until heated. Bake as directed. Add 1 Egg to equivalent listing and reduce Meat Group to 2 ounces.

Per serving: 336 calories, 26 g protein, 18 g fat, 17 g carbohydrate, 1,075 mg sodium

LAMB-STUFFED YELLOW SQUASH
Limited Choice Plan
Makes 1 Midday or Evening Meal serving*

5 ounces ground lamb
¾ cup mixed vegetable juice, divided
1 teaspoon onion flakes, reconstituted in 1 tablespoon hot water

½ teaspoon mint flakes
⅛ teaspoon each ground coriander, cardamom, and pepper
Dash salt
1 yellow crookneck squash, about 5 ounces

1. Preheat broiler. Form ground lamb into a patty. On rack in broiler pan broil lamb, turning once, until rare, about 5 minutes.
2. Transfer meat to small bowl and, using a fork, crumble. Add 2 tablespoons juice and the seasonings and mix to combine; set aside.
3. Using a sharp knife, cut a thin slice off each end of squash; discard slices. Using an apple corer, remove pulp from center of squash, reserving pulp and leaving a cylindrical opening in shell about ¾ inch in diameter.

4. Chop pulp and transfer to a bowl; add remaining vegetable juice and stir to combine.

5. Using a small spoon, pack as much meat mixture as possible into squash shell. Combine remaining meat mixture with pulp-juice mixture.

6. Place stuffed squash in shallow 8 x 8-inch casserole and spoon pulp-juice mixture over squash. Bake at 350°F. until squash is tender, about 45 minutes.

7. Remove squash from casserole and, using a serrated knife, cut cross-wise into ¼-inch-thick slices. Top sauce remaining in casserole with slices and serve.

Each serving is equivalent to: 3 ounces Meat Group; 1 serving Bonus; 2 servings Vegetables. (See page 407 for Full Choice Plan adjustments.)

Per serving: 234 calories, 26 g protein, 9 g fat, 13 g carbohydrate, 548 mg sodium

* Men—One serving provides ¾ of a meal. Supplement with an additional ¼ serving of Protein at the Midday or Evening Meal.

TANGY LAMB PATTY

Full Choice Plan
Makes 1 Midday or Evening Meal serving

2 tablespoons diced onion
6 ounces ground lamb
1 tablespoon chopped fresh parsley

1 teaspoon Worcestershire sauce
½ teaspoon soy sauce
⅛ teaspoon pepper

Heat a small nonstick skillet; add onion and cook, stirring constantly, until lightly browned. In small bowl mix browned onion with remaining ingredients and shape into a patty. On rack in broiler pan broil patty, turning once, about 7 minutes or until done to taste.

Each serving is equivalent to: ⅛ cup Limited Vegetables; 4 ounces Meat Group.

Per serving: 230 calories, 33 g protein, 9 g fat, 3 g carbohydrate, 304 mg sodium

GLAZED ROAST LOIN OF PORK

Full Choice Plan
Makes 6 Midday or Evening Meal servings

3-pound pork center loin roast
Dash salt
1 tablespoon vegetable oil
2 garlic cloves, minced
3 medium peaches, blanched, peeled, pitted, and sliced

6 fluid ounces dry sherry
¼ cup reduced-calorie apricot spread (16 calories per 2 teaspoons)
1 tablespoon teriyaki sauce
1 tablespoon granulated sugar

Set pork loin on rack in roasting pan and sprinkle with salt. Insert meat thermometer into center of roast, being careful thermometer does not touch bone. Roast at 325°F. until thermometer registers 170°F., about 1½ hours. Remove pan from oven.

In 1-quart saucepan heat oil; add garlic and sauté briefly. Add remaining ingredients and bring to a boil. Reduce heat and simmer until sauce is thickened, about 5 minutes. Spread over pork and return meat to oven; roast until sauce is bubbly and pork is glazed, about 5 minutes.

Each serving is equivalent to: 4 ounces Meat Group; ½ serving Fats; ½ serving Fruits; ¼ serving Occasional Substitutes; 16 calories Specialty Foods; 1 serving Extras.

Per serving: 407 calories, 34 g protein, 19 g fat, 17 g carbohydrate, 249 mg sodium

BRAISED PORK CHOPS WITH CARAWAY SEED
Full Choice Plan
Makes 1 Midday or Evening Meal serving

2 pork chops, 4 ounces each	¼ teaspoon caraway seed
1 teaspoon margarine	Dash pepper
½ cup sliced onion	½ cup water
¼ teaspoon salt	

1. On rack in broiler pan broil pork chops, turning once, until well browned.
2. In skillet just large enough to hold chops in 1 layer, heat margarine until bubbly; add onion and sauté until softened.
3. Arrange pork chops over onion slices and sprinkle with salt, caraway seed, and pepper. Sauté pork, turning once, until onion slices are browned, 3 to 4 minutes on each side.
4. Add water and bring to a boil. Reduce heat; cover and simmer, turning chops every 15 minutes, until meat is tender, about 45 minutes.

Each serving is equivalent to: 4 ounces Meat Group; 1 serving Fats; ½ cup Limited Vegetables; ½ serving Extras.

Per serving: 356 calories, 35 g protein, 20 g fat, 8 g carbohydrate, 672 mg sodium

STUFFED PORK CHOPS
Full Choice Plan
Makes 2 Midday or Evening Meal servings

2 pork loin chops, 8 ounces each	½ small apple, cored and finely diced
2 teaspoons prepared mustard, divided	2 tablespoons finely diced onion
Dash each salt and pepper	1 teaspoon ground savory

Preheat oven to 325°F. Cut a pocket in side of each chop. Brush ½ teaspoon mustard over each side of both chops and sprinkle with salt and pepper. Place on rack in 8 x 8-inch baking pan and bake until thoroughly cooked, 15 to 20 minutes.

While chops are baking, in small nonstick skillet combine remaining ingredients; cook over medium heat until apple is soft. Spoon half of hot apple mixture into pocket of each chop and serve immediately.

Each serving is equivalent to: 4 ounces Meat Group; ¼ serving Fruits; 1 tablespoon Limited Vegetables.

Per serving: 314 calories, 34 g protein, 17 g fat, 6 g carbohydrate, 213 mg sodium

PORK AND CHINESE CABBAGE IN ORANGE SAUCE

Limited Choice Plan
*Makes 2 Midday or Evening Meal servings**

1 cup orange juice (no sugar added)
1 cup shredded Chinese cabbage
1 tablespoon cider vinegar
2 teaspoons reduced-calorie apricot spread (16 calories per 2 teaspoons)
1 teaspoon granulated brown sugar
1 teaspoon arrowroot, dissolved in 1 tablespoon water
6 ounces broiled pork cubes (1-inch cubes)

In 1-quart saucepan bring orange juice to a boil. Add cabbage, vinegar, apricot spread, and sugar. Cook, stirring occasionally, until cabbage is slightly softened. Add dissolved arrowroot and cook, stirring constantly, until mixture is thickened. Stir in pork and cook until heated.

Each serving is equivalent to: 1 serving Fruits; 2⅓ servings Extras; 3 ounces Meat Group. (See page 407 for Full Choice Plan adjustments.)

Per serving: 304 calories, 26 g protein, 12 g fat, 21 g carbohydrate, 72 mg sodium

* Men—One serving provides ¾ of a meal. Supplement with an additional ¼ serving of Protein at the Midday or Evening Meal.

SPICY PORK AND MUSHROOMS

Limited Choice Plan
*Makes 2 Midday or Evening Meal servings**

1 teaspoon margarine
1 cup sliced mushrooms
¾ cup mixed vegetable juice
¼ cup diced green bell pepper
1 tablespoon onion flakes
1 teaspoon basil leaves
½ teaspoon Worcestershire sauce
⅛ teaspoon pepper
Dash each salt and hot sauce
6 ounces broiled pork cubes (1-inch cubes)

In 1-quart saucepan heat margarine until bubbly; add mushrooms and sauté about 3 minutes. Add remaining ingredients except pork and bring to a boil. Reduce heat and simmer for 3 minutes. Stir in pork and cook until heated.

Each serving is equivalent to: ½ serving Fats; 1¼ servings Vegetables; ½ serving Bonus; 3 ounces Meat Group. (See page 407 for Full Choice Plan adjustments.)

Per serving: 270 calories, 27 g protein, 14 g fat, 7 g carbohydrate, 338 mg sodium

* Men—One serving provides ¾ of a meal. Supplement with an additional ¼ serving of Protein at the Midday or Evening Meal.

SWEET AND SOUR PORK
Limited Choice Plan
Makes 2 Midday or Evening Meal servings*

¾ cup Chicken Broth (see page 401)
6 ounces broiled pork cubes (1-inch cubes)
1 medium tomato, cut into 8 wedges
¼ cup grated carrot
¼ cup green bell pepper strips

1 tablespoon grated orange peel
1 tablespoon cider vinegar
Artificial sweetener to equal 1 teaspoon sugar
1 teaspoon arrowroot, dissolved in 1 tablespoon water
½ cup canned mandarin orange sections (no sugar added)

In 1½-quart saucepan bring broth to a boil. Add remaining ingredients except arrowroot and orange sections and simmer for 5 minutes. Add dissolved arrowroot and cook, stirring constantly, until mixture is slightly thickened. Stir in orange sections and cook just until heated.

Each serving is equivalent to: 1 serving Extras; 3 ounces Meat Group; 1½ servings Vegetables; ½ serving Fruits.

Per serving: 296 calories, 28 g protein, 12 g fat, 19 g carbohydrate, 85 mg sodium

* Men—One serving provides ¾ of a meal. Supplement with an additional ¼ serving of Protein at the Midday or Evening Meal.

PORK AND APPLES IN "CREAM"
Full Choice Plan
Makes 2 Midday or Evening Meal servings

2 teaspoons margarine
1 small apple, pared, cored, and sliced
¼ cup sliced onion
1 teaspoon granulated brown sugar
⅓ cup apple juice (no sugar added)
2 fluid ounces dry sherry

2 teaspoons enriched all-purpose flour
¼ cup evaporated skimmed milk
¼ cup skim milk
½ teaspoon salt
Dash white pepper
8 ounces sliced cooked pork

In 9-inch skillet heat margarine until bubbly; add apple, onion, and brown sugar and sauté until onion is translucent. Pour in apple juice and sherry and bring to a boil. Reduce heat and simmer for about 3 minutes (apples should remain firm). Sprinkle flour over mixture and stir to combine. Add milks, salt, and pepper and cook, stirring constantly, until slightly thickened (*do not boil*). Add pork slices and simmer until thoroughly heated.

Each serving is equivalent to: 1 serving Fats; 1 serving Fruits; ⅛ cup Limited Vegetables; 2 servings Extras; ¼ serving Occasional Substitutes; ⅜ serving Milk; 4 ounces Meat Group.

Per serving: 471 calories, 38 g protein, 20 g fat, 26 g carbohydrate, 721 mg sodium

PORK SPRING ROLLS
Full Choice Plan
Makes 2 Midday or Evening Meal servings

Crêpes
⅓ cup less 1 teaspoon enriched all-purpose flour
1 egg

Dash salt
⅓ cup water

Filling
1 tablespoon plus 1 teaspoon vegetable oil, divided
½ teaspoon minced fresh garlic
1 cup shredded green cabbage
½ cup each sliced mushrooms and scallions (green onions)
1 tablespoon teriyaki sauce
2 teaspoons soy sauce

2 teaspoons cornstarch, dissolved in 1 tablespoon water
1 packet instant chicken broth and seasoning mix
6 ounces boned cooked pork, shredded
Dash each ground ginger and hot sauce

To Prepare Crêpes: In blender container combine flour, egg, and salt; add water and process until smooth. Set aside and let batter stand for 20 minutes.

Heat 6- or 7-inch nonstick omelet pan. Pour ¼ of the batter (about ¼ cup) into pan and quickly tilt pan to coat entire bottom. Cook until underside of crêpe is dry; carefully turn and briefly cook other side. Slide crêpe onto plate. Repeat procedure 3 more times, making 4 crêpes.

To Prepare Filling: In 9-inch skillet heat 2 teaspoons oil; add garlic and sauté briefly (*do not brown*). Add cabbage and cook, stirring constantly, until cabbage is soft, about 4 minutes. Add mushrooms, scallions, teriyaki sauce, and soy sauce; cook, stirring occasionally, about 3 minutes. Stirring constantly, add dissolved cornstarch and cook until thickened. Sprinkle mixture with broth mix, then add pork, ginger, and hot sauce and stir to combine; cook until pork is heated.

To Prepare Spring Rolls: Spoon ¼ of filling mixture onto center of each crêpe; fold over sides of crêpe, forming an envelope to enclose filling. In 9-inch nonstick skillet heat remaining 2 teaspoons oil. Add pork rolls, seam-side down, and cook until browned on all sides, turning carefully.

Each serving is equivalent to: 1 serving Bread; ½ Egg; 2 servings Fats; 1½ servings Vegetables; ¼ cup Limited Vegetables; 1½ servings Extras; 3 ounces Meat Group.

Per serving: 468 calories, 33 g protein, 25 g fat, 27 g carbohydrate, 1,336 mg sodium

SWEET 'N' TANGY PORK SAUTÉ
Full Choice Plan
Makes 4 Midday or Evening Meal servings

8 fluid ounces beer
1 tablespoon Dijon-style mustard
1½ teaspoons grated orange peel
1 teaspoon salt
¼ teaspoon Worcestershire sauce
1 garlic clove, minced
1 pound julienne-cut cooked pork
(¼-inch-thick strips)
1 tablespoon plus 1 teaspoon
vegetable oil
½ cup chopped onion
½ medium green bell pepper,
seeded and cut into 1-inch
squares

½ medium red bell pepper, seeded
and cut into 1-inch squares
1 tablespoon plus 1 teaspoon
cornstarch, dissolved in 1
tablespoon water
½ cup canned pineapple chunks
(no sugar added)
8 canned apricot halves with ¼
cup juice (no sugar added)
2 cups cooked enriched rice, hot
1 small orange, peeled and
sectioned

In bowl combine beer, mustard, orange peel, salt, Worcestershire sauce, and garlic. Add pork; cover and let marinate in refrigerator for 30 minutes, turning occasionally.

In 12-inch skillet heat oil. Add onion and green and red peppers; sauté until onion is translucent. Add pork and marinade; bring to a boil. Add dissolved cornstarch and cook, stirring constantly, until mixture thickens slightly. Stir in pineapple and apricots and heat. Serve over rice and garnish with orange sections.

Each serving is equivalent to: ¼ serving Occasional Substitutes; 4 ounces Meat Group; 1 serving Fats; ⅛ cup Limited Vegetables; ½ serving Vegetables; 1 serving Extras; 1 serving Fruits; 1 serving Bread Substitutes.

Per serving: 553 calories, 37 g protein, 21 g fat, 48 g carbohydrate, 741 mg sodium

BAKED CANNED HAM
Limited Choice Plan
Makes 8 Midday or Evening Meal servings*

Excellent for a buffet party; or freeze leftovers for use at another time. Delicious served with Hot Fruit Sauce (see page 382).

1 canned ham, 2 pounds   **10 cloves (optional)**

Preheat oven to 325°F. Remove and discard gelatinous broth clinging to ham and trim away any excess fat. Cut 1½ pounds of ham into thin slices (any remaining ham can be frozen for use at another time). Place slices back together in shape of ham and tie with colorfast or undyed cotton string. Set ham in shallow baking pan; stud with cloves if desired. Cover lightly with foil and bake until thoroughly heated, 35 to 40 minutes.†
Serve hot or chilled.

Each serving is equivalent to: 3 ounces Meat Group (cured).

Per serving: 159 calories, 22 g protein, 7 g fat, trace carbohydrate, 770 mg sodium

* Men—One serving provides ¾ of a meal. Supplement with an additional ¼ serving of Protein at the Midday or Evening Meal.
† If ham is not sliced before baking, bake for 50 to 60 minutes.

BAKED GLAZED HAM
Limited Choice Plan
Makes 8 Midday or Evening Meal servings*

1 canned ham, 2 pounds	½ teaspoon ground ginger
1 tablespoon plus 2 teaspoons each reduced-calorie orange marmalade and apricot spread (16 calories per 2 teaspoons)	Dash ground cloves

Prepare ham as directed in Baked Canned Ham recipe (see page 281), but bake for 25 minutes.

In small bowl combine remaining ingredients. Spoon mixture over ham and bake, uncovered, until thoroughly heated, about 10 minutes longer. Turn oven control to broil and broil ham, 3 inches from heat source, until glaze is browned, about 1 minute. Serve hot.

Each serving is equivalent to: 3 ounces Meat Group (cured); 1 serving Extras. (See page 407 for Full Choice Plan adjustments.)

Per serving: 175 calories, 22 g protein, 7 g fat, 4 g carbohydrate, 770 mg sodium

* Men—One serving provides ¾ of a meal. Supplement with an additional ¼ serving of Protein at the Midday or Evening Meal.

TROPICAL HAM BAKE
Limited Choice Plan
Makes 1 Midday or Evening Meal serving*

½ medium banana, peeled and cut lengthwise into 4 thin slices	½ teaspoon granulated brown sugar
1 teaspoon lemon juice	1 teaspoon shredded coconut
3 ounces boned "fully cooked" ham steak	

Preheat oven to 325°F. In bowl sprinkle banana slices with lemon juice. Place ham steak in individual shallow casserole. Arrange banana slices over ham; sprinkle with brown sugar and top with coconut. Bake until banana and coconut are browned, 15 to 20 minutes.

Each serving is equivalent to: 1 serving Fruits; 3 ounces Meat Group (cured); 2 servings Extras.

Per serving: 227 calories, 22 g protein, 8 g fat, 17 g carbohydrate, 772 mg sodium

* Men—For each serving use 4 ounces boned "fully cooked" ham steak. Change equivalent listing to 4 ounces Meat Group (cured).

HAM CHOW MEIN
Full Choice Plan
Makes 2 Midday or Evening Meal servings*

2 teaspoons peanut or vegetable oil
½ cup thinly sliced onion
½ cup sliced green or red bell
  pepper (thin strips)
½ teaspoon minced fresh garlic
4 cups thinly sliced Chinese
  cabbage
½ cup thinly sliced mushrooms
2 teaspoons teriyaki sauce

1 packet instant chicken broth and
  seasoning mix
Dash each salt, pepper, and
  powdered mustard
6 ounces sliced boiled ham (thin
  strips)
¼ cup water
1 teaspoon cornstarch
1 teaspoon granulated brown sugar

1. In 12-inch skillet heat oil; add onion, green or red pepper, and garlic. Sauté just until pepper softens.
2. Add cabbage, mushrooms, teriyaki sauce, broth mix, salt, pepper, and mustard; sauté until vegetables are tender-crisp, about 5 minutes.
3. Add ham and cook, stirring occasionally, until thoroughly heated, about 3 minutes.
4. In small bowl combine water, cornstarch, and sugar, stirring to dissolve cornstarch. Add to ham mixture and cook, stirring constantly, until thickened.

Each serving is equivalent to: 1 serving Fats; ¼ cup Limited Vegetables; 5 servings Vegetables; 2 servings Extras; 3 ounces Meat Group (cured).

Per serving: 275 calories, 26 g protein, 12 g fat, 16 g carbohydrate, 1,498 mg sodium

* Men—One serving provides ¾ of a meal. Supplement with an additional ¼ serving of Protein at the Midday or Evening Meal.

OPEN-FACE HAM SALAD SANDWICH
Full Choice Plan
Makes 1 Midday or Evening Meal serving*

1 tablespoon reduced-calorie
  mayonnaise
1 teaspoon finely chopped scallion
  (green onion)
1 teaspoon chopped capers

½ teaspoon ketchup
3 ounces diced boiled ham
2 tablespoons chopped dill pickle
1 slice whole wheat bread

Garnish
2 thin slices dill pickle (about ⅛
  medium pickle)

In small bowl combine mayonnaise, scallion, capers, and ketchup. Add ham and chopped dill pickle; stir to combine. Spread ham salad on bread and garnish with 2 pickle slices.

Each serving is equivalent to: 1½ servings Fats; 1 teaspoon Limited Vegetables; ¼ serving Extras; 3 ounces Meat Group (cured); ½ serving Vegetables; 1 serving Bread.

Per serving: 256 calories, 24 g protein, 11 g fat, 15 g carbohydrate, 1,343 mg sodium

* Men—One serving provides ¾ of a meal. Supplement with an additional ¼ serving of Protein at the Midday or Evening Meal.

HAM HASH
Full Choice Plan
Makes 2 Midday or Evening Meal servings*

2 tablespoons each diced onion
  and green bell pepper
8 ounces peeled cooked potatoes,
  diced

6 ounces ground boiled ham
Dash ground cinnamon

In 8-inch nonstick skillet combine onion and pepper and cook, stirring occasionally, until tender. Add potatoes, ham, and cinnamon and cook until all ingredients are heated through. Serve hot.

Each serving is equivalent to: 1 tablespoon Limited Vegetables; ⅛ serving Vegetables; 1 serving Bread Substitutes; 3 ounces Meat Group (cured).

Per serving: 239 calories, 24 g protein, 8 g fat, 18 g carbohydrate, 775 mg sodium

* Men—One serving provides ¾ of a meal. Supplement with an additional ¼ serving of Protein at the Midday or Evening Meal.

Variation: Reduce ham to 3 ounces. Cook ingredients as directed above, then make 2 wells in hash. Break 1 large egg into a small bowl. Carefully slide egg into 1 of the wells; repeat with another egg and second well. Cover skillet and cook, over low heat, until eggs are done. Add 1 Egg to equivalent listing and reduce Meat Group to 1½ ounces.

Per serving: 239 calories, 19 g protein, 9 g fat, 18 g carbohydrate, 459 mg sodium

* Men—One serving provides ⅞ of a meal. Supplement with an additional ⅛ serving of Protein at the Midday or Evening Meal.

HAM SPREAD
Full Choice Plan
Makes 1 Midday or Evening Meal serving*

In bowl combine **3 ounces ground boiled ham, 1 teaspoon pickle relish, and 1 teaspoon mayonnaise**; mix well. Cover and chill.

Each serving is equivalent to: 3 ounces Meat Group (cured); 1 serving Extras; 1 serving Fats.

Per serving : 200 calories, 22 g protein, 11 g fat, 2 g carbohydrate, 834 mg sodium

* Men—One serving provides ¾ of a meal. Supplement with an additional ¼ serving of Protein at the Midday or Evening Meal.

SPICY HAM 'N' BEAN BAKE
Limited Choice Plan
Makes 4 Midday or Evening Meal servings*

12 ounces cooked dry lima beans†
6 ounces coarsely ground boiled ham
1 cup canned crushed tomatoes
1 tablespoon onion flakes
1¼ teaspoons chili powder
¼ teaspoon each pepper and garlic powder
⅛ teaspoon salt
4 ounces low-fat American cheese, shredded

Preheat oven to 350°F. In medium bowl combine all ingredients except cheese. Transfer to 1-quart casserole and top with shredded cheese. Bake until thoroughly heated and cheese is melted, about 35 minutes.

Each serving is equivalent to: 1 serving Bread Substitutes; 1½ ounces Meat Group (cured); ½ serving Vegetables; 1 ounce Hard Cheese.

Per serving: 245 calories, 24 g protein, 6 g fat, 23 g carbohydrate, 992 mg sodium

* Men—Add ¼ ounce shredded low-fat American cheese to each portion of Spicy Ham 'n' Bean Bake.
† Drained canned lima beans may be substituted for the cooked dry beans in this recipe. Change nutrition information to 229 calories, 23 g protein, 6 g fat, 20 g carbohydrate, 1,191 mg sodium (estimated).

BAKED CANADIAN BACON WITH BEANS
Full Choice Plan
Makes 2 Midday or Evening Meal servings*

1 medium tomato, blanched, peeled, seeded, and diced
2 tablespoons diced onion
1 teaspoon each granulated brown sugar and cider vinegar
½ teaspoon dark molasses
1 cinnamon stick, 2 inches long
1 garlic clove, minced
Dash Worcestershire sauce
6 ounces drained canned small pink beans
6 ounces sliced Canadian-style bacon

Preheat oven to 350°F. In small skillet combine all ingredients except beans and bacon; cook over medium heat until moisture has evaporated. Remove from heat and stir in beans.

Line 1-quart casserole with bacon slices; top with bean mixture. Bake until all ingredients are thoroughly heated, about 15 minutes. Serve hot.

Each serving is equivalent to: 1 serving Vegetables; 1 tablespoon Limited Vegetables; 1½ servings Extras; 1 serving Bread Substitutes; 3 ounces Meat Group (cured).

Per serving: 364 calories, 30 g protein, 16 g fat, 26 g carbohydrate, 2,184 mg sodium (estimated)

* Men—One serving provides ¾ of a meal. Supplement with an additional ¼ serving of Protein at the Midday or Evening Meal.

BOILED TONGUE
Full Choice Plan
Makes about 6 Midday or Evening Meal servings

1 fresh beef tongue (about 2¾ pounds),* washed and drained	3 garlic cloves, crushed
	2 parsley sprigs
3 quarts water	1½ teaspoons salt
2 medium tomatoes, quartered	½ teaspoon thyme leaves
2 large carrots, pared	6 whole peppercorns
1 large onion, quartered	3 whole cloves
2 celery ribs	2 bay leaves

Place tongue in 5- or 6-quart saucepan; add remaining ingredients and bring to a boil. Reduce heat, cover, and simmer until tongue is fork-tender, 2½ to 3 hours. Allow meat to cool in broth.

Remove tongue from broth, reserving broth.† On underside of tongue, slit skin lengthwise from root to tip and peel off skin. Cut off root end, any small bones, and gristle. Starting at large end, thinly slice diagonally across the grain. Serve hot or chilled, 4 ounces sliced tongue per portion.

Each serving is equivalent to: 4 ounces Meat Group.

Per serving: 277 calories, 24 g protein, 19 g fat, 0.5 g carbohydrate, 69 mg sodium

* A fresh 2¾-pound beef tongue will yield about 1½ pounds cooked meat.
† Cover and chill broth until fat congeals on surface. Remove and discard fat. Strain broth and reserve; use in Tongue Provençale recipe (see page 287). Three-fourths cup Broth is equivalent to 1 serving Extras.

CHILLED TONGUE WITH HORSERADISH SAUCE
Full Choice Plan
Makes 2 Midday or Evening Meal servings

½ cup plain unflavored yogurt	1 teaspoon minced shallots or onion
1 tablespoon prepared horseradish	
1 tablespoon chopped fresh parsley	¼ teaspoon granulated sugar
2 teaspoons Dijon-style mustard	8 ounces sliced cooked fresh beef tongue, chilled

In small bowl combine all ingredients except tongue. Arrange tongue on serving platter and serve with sauce.

Each serving is equivalent to: ½ serving Milk; ½ teaspoon Limited Vegetables; ¼ serving Extras; 4 ounces Meat Group.

Per serving: 324 calories, 27 g protein, 21 g fat, 5 g carbohydrate, 252 mg sodium

TONGUE PROVENÇALE
Full Choice Plan
Makes 4 Midday or Evening Meal servings

1 tablespoon plus 1 teaspoon
  margarine
1 tablespoon minced shallots
1 cup sliced mushrooms
2 teaspoons enriched all-purpose
  flour
4 fluid ounces dry white wine
1 medium tomato, blanched,
  peeled, seeded, and chopped

¾ cup beef tongue broth (see
  Boiled Tongue, page 286)*
Dash each salt and freshly ground
  pepper
1 pound sliced cooked fresh beef
  tongue
1 tablespoon chopped fresh parsley

1. In 9-inch skillet heat margarine until bubbly; add shallots and sauté briefly (about 1 minute).
2. Add mushrooms and cook, stirring occasionally, until liquid evaporates, about 3 minutes. Sprinkle flour over mushrooms and stir to combine.
3. Add wine and cook, stirring constantly, until slightly thickened, about 2 minutes.
4. Stir in tomato, broth, salt, and pepper and bring to a boil. Reduce heat and simmer, stirring occasionally, for 3 minutes.
5. Add tongue, turning each slice in tomato mixture to coat evenly; simmer just until tongue is thoroughly heated. Serve sprinkled with parsley.

Each serving is equivalent to: 1 serving Fats; ¾ teaspoon Limited Vegetables; 1 serving Vegetables; ¾ serving Extras; ¼ serving Occasional Substitutes; 4 ounces Meat Group.

Per serving: 357 calories, 26 g protein, 23 g fat, 6 g carbohydrate, 154 mg sodium

* If beef tongue broth is not available, Beef Broth (see p. 401) may be substituted.

LAMB KIDNEYS IN MUSHROOM SAUCE
Full Choice Plan
Makes 2 Midday or Evening Meal servings

2 teaspoons margarine, divided
½ cup finely chopped onion
½ cup sliced mushrooms
12 ounces trimmed lamb kidneys
  (tubes and fat removed), cut
  into quarters
2 teaspoons enriched all-purpose
  flour
⅛ teaspoon pepper

1 packet instant beef broth and
  seasoning mix, dissolved in
  ¼ cup hot water
1 tablespoon plus 1 teaspoon dry
  sherry
2 slices enriched white bread,
  toasted and cut diagonally into
  halves
2 teaspoons chopped fresh parsley

1. Preheat oven to 350°F. In 8-inch skillet heat 1 teaspoon margarine until bubbly; add onion and sauté until translucent. Add mushrooms and continue cooking until lightly browned. Transfer mushroom mixture to 1-quart casserole.

2. In small bowl sprinkle kidneys with flour and pepper; using a fork, toss to coat.

3. In same skillet heat remaining teaspoon margarine until bubbly; add kidneys and sauté until lightly browned. Arrange over mushroom mixture in casserole.

4. Pour dissolved broth mix over ingredients in casserole and stir to combine; cover and bake until kidneys are tender, about 45 minutes.

5. Stir in sherry. Place 2 toast triangles on each of 2 plates; spoon half of kidney mixture over each portion of toast and sprinkle with parsley.

Each serving is equivalent to: 1 serving Fats; ¼ cup Limited Vegetables; ½ serving Vegetables; 4 ounces Meat Group; 2½ servings Extras; 1 serving Bread.

Per serving: 325 calories, 33 g protein, 10 g fat, 22 g carbohydrate, 884 mg sodium

BOLOGNA–VEGETABLE KABOBS

Full Choice Plan
*Makes 1 Midday or Evening Meal serving**

3-ounce piece bologna, cut into
  1-inch cubes
½ medium tomato, cut into
  wedges
¼ cup onion wedges

2 teaspoons thawed frozen
  concentrated pineapple juice
  (no sugar added)
½ teaspoon water
⅛ teaspoon powdered mustard
1 frankfurter roll (2 ounces), split
  and toasted

Preheat broiler. Onto a skewer thread bologna cubes and tomato and onion wedges, alternating ingredients. Transfer skewer to broiler pan and broil until meat is browned, about 5 minutes.

While kabobs are broiling, in small bowl combine juice, water, and mustard. Remove bologna and vegetables from skewer onto roll; brush with pineapple sauce and serve immediately.

Each serving is equivalent to: 3 ounces Meat Group (cured); 1 serving Vegetables; ¼ cup Limited Vegetables; ½ serving Fruits; 2 servings Bread.

Per serving: 492 calories, 16 g protein, 28 g fat, 45 g carbohydrate, 1,160 mg sodium

* Men—For each serving use a 4-ounce piece bologna. Change equivalent listing to 4 ounces Meat Group (cured).

GRILLED BOLOGNA STACK

Full Choice Plan
*Makes 1 Midday or Evening Meal serving**

3-ounce piece bologna
1 teaspoon prepared brown
  mustard, divided
½ teaspoon pickle relish

½ teaspoon granulated brown
  sugar
½ teaspoon water
1 hamburger roll (2 ounces), cut
  in half and toasted

1. Preheat broiler. Cut bologna in half crosswise, forming 2 slices.
2. Spread 1 bologna slice with ½ teaspoon each mustard and relish; top with second slice.
3. In small bowl combine brown sugar, water, and remaining ½ teaspoon mustard; brush over meat.
4. Place bologna stack in small shallow foil pan and broil until lightly browned, about 2½ minutes. Turn stack over, baste with pan juices, and broil until other side is lightly browned, about 2½ minutes longer. Serve bologna stack on roll, topped with any remaining pan juices.

Each serving is equivalent to: 3 ounces Meat Group (cured); 1½ servings Extras; 2 servings Bread.

Per serving: 455 calories, 15 g protein, 28 g fat, 36 g carbohydrate, 1,223 mg sodium

* Men—For each serving use a 4-ounce piece bologna. Change equivalent listing to 4 ounces Meat Group (cured).

CHEESE DOG

Full Choice Plan
*Makes 1 Midday or Evening Meal serving**

1 refrigerated buttermilk flaky biscuit (unbaked), 1 ounce
1½ ounces frankfurter
1 ounce hard cheese, shredded
1 teaspoon pickle relish
1 teaspoon prepared brown mustard

1. Preheat oven to 350°F. Between 2 sheets of wax paper roll biscuit dough into a circle, about 6 inches in diameter; carefully remove paper.
2. Set frankfurter in center of dough and top with cheese. Fold dough around frankfurter and cheese to enclose.
3. Place Cheese Dog, seam-side up, on baking sheet; at open ends, pinch up bottom portion of dough so that cheese does not melt onto baking sheet. Bake until biscuit is golden brown and cheese is melted, about 15 minutes.
4. In small cup combine relish and mustard; serve with Cheese Dog.

Each serving is equivalent to: 1 serving Bread; 1½ ounces Meat Group (cured); 1 ounce Hard Cheese; 1 serving Extras.

Per serving: 344 calories, 14 g protein, 24 g fat, 17 g carbohydrate, 1,033 mg sodium

* Men—For each serving use 2 ounces frankfurter. Change equivalent listing to 2 ounces Meat Group (cured).

FRANKFURTER "PIZZA"

Full Choice Plan
*Makes 1 Midday or Evening Meal serving**

¼ cup tomato sauce
⅛ teaspoon basil leaves
Dash garlic powder
1 English muffin, split and toasted
1½ ounces frankfurter, thinly sliced lengthwise
1 ounce mozzarella cheese, shredded

In small bowl mix tomato sauce with basil and garlic powder. Place muffin halves on piece of foil or in broiler pan. Spread ¼ of the sauce mixture on each half; top each with half of the frankfurter slices, then half of remaining sauce mixture, and half of the cheese. Broil until cheese is melted.†

Each serving is equivalent to: ½ serving Bonus; 2 servings Bread; 1½ ounces Meat Group (cured); 1 ounce Hard Cheese.

Per serving: 362 calories, 15 g protein, 20 g fat, 30 g carbohydrate, 1,113 mg sodium

* Men—For each serving use 2 ounces frankfurter. Change equivalent listing to 2 ounces Meat Group (cured).
† This can be broiled in a conventional broiler or toaster-oven.

QUICK SKILLET FRANKS 'N' VEGETABLES
Full Choice Plan
Makes 2 Midday or Evening Meal servings

2 teaspoons vegetable oil
½ cup each sliced onion and carrot
½ cup thinly sliced green bell pepper
1 small garlic clove, minced, or ⅛ teaspoon garlic powder
1 cup shredded green cabbage

6 ounces frankfurters, cut crosswise into ¼-inch-thick slices
¼ cup prepared instant chicken broth mix (at room temperature)
1 teaspoon cornstarch
1 teaspoon soy sauce

In 9- or 10-inch nonstick skillet heat oil. Add onion, carrot, green pepper, and garlic or garlic powder; sauté until onion is translucent, about 5 minutes. Stir in cabbage. Reduce heat, cover, and cook, stirring occasionally, until cabbage is soft, about 10 minutes. Add frankfurters and cook until thoroughly heated.

In measuring cup combine broth and cornstarch, stirring well to dissolve; add soy sauce and pour over frankfurter mixture. Cook, stirring constantly, until slightly thickened.

Each serving is equivalent to: 1 serving Fats; ¼ cup Limited Vegetables; 2 servings Vegetables; 3 ounces Meat Group (cured); ⅔ serving Extras.

Per serving: 371 calories, 12 g protein, 30 g fat, 15 g carbohydrate, 1,343 mg sodium

* Men—One serving provides ¾ of a meal. Supplement with an additional ¼ serving of Protein at the Midday or Evening Meal.

LIVERWURST SALAD SANDWICH
Full Choice Plan
Makes 1 Midday or Evening Meal serving

3 ounces liverwurst
1 tablespoon minced celery
2 teaspoons minced dill pickle
2 teaspoons reduced-calorie mayonnaise

Dash pepper
2 slices whole wheat bread, toasted
2 iceberg or romaine lettuce leaves

In small bowl, using a fork, mash liverwurst. Add celery, pickle, mayonnaise, and pepper; mix well. Spread half of liverwurst mixture on each slice of toast; cover 1 slice with lettuce leaves and top with remaining slice to form a sandwich. Cut diagonally into triangles.

Each serving is equivalent to: 3 ounces Meat Group (cured); ⅔ serving Vegetables; 1 serving Fats; 2 servings Bread.

Per serving: 415 calories, 17 g protein, 28 g fat, 26 g carbohydrate, 1,326 mg sodium

* Men—One serving provides ¾ of a meal. Supplement with an additional ¼ serving of Protein at the Midday or Evening Meal.

SAUSAGE-STUFFED PEPPERS
Full Choice Plan
*Makes 2 Midday or Evening Meal servings**

2 medium green bell peppers
½ cup chopped onion
½ cup canned crushed tomatoes
4 fluid ounces dry red wine
½ teaspoon each oregano and basil leaves

½ teaspoon salt
6 ounces cooked beef or veal sausage, crumbled
2 teaspoons grated Parmesan cheese

1. Cut top off each green pepper. Remove and discard seeds; set peppers aside.
2. Preheat oven to 350°F. In 8-inch nonstick skillet cook onion, stirring occasionally, until lightly browned.
3. Add tomatoes, wine, oregano, basil, and salt and stir to combine; bring to a boil.
4. Reduce heat and add sausage; simmer for 1 minute.
5. Set green peppers upright in baking pan just large enough to hold them. Fill each with half of the sausage mixture and sprinkle with 1 teaspoon Parmesan cheese. Pour water into baking pan to a depth of 1 inch.
6. Bake until peppers are fork-tender, about 30 minutes.

Each serving is equivalent to: 2½ servings Vegetables; ¼ cup Limited Vegetables; ½ serving Occasional Substitutes; 3 ounces Meat Group (cured); 1 serving Extras.

Per serving: 380 calories, 13 g protein, 26 g fat, 15 g carbohydrate, 1,536 mg sodium

* Men—One serving provides ¾ of a meal. Supplement with an additional ¼ serving of Protein at the Midday or Evening Meal.

Liver

There's no reason to hear cries of "Oh, no, not liver," for this high-nutrition, low-cost variety meat can be one of the tastiest entrées imaginable, whether you let it substitute for beef in "Stroganoff" or tuck it appetizingly into "shells." Even ordinary liver-and-onions takes on new appeal when sautéed with tomatoes or stir-fried with broccoli. And for those who ordinarily won't eat liver, offer a sweet and sour version of chicken livers.

Guidelines for Using Liver

1. Amounts (trimmed cooked weight):

	Midday or Evening Meal	
	Full Choice Plan	Limited Choice Plan
Women and Youth	3 to 4 ounces	3 ounces
Men	4 to 5 ounces	4 ounces

2. Liver should be consumed at the Midday or Evening Meal *only* and may *not* be split.

3. Select liver once a week; if liver is not tolerated, ask your physician whether you require an iron supplement.

4. The Full Choice Plan range of 3 to 4 ounces for Women and Youth (4 to 5 ounces for Men) provides flexibility. It is a way of individualizing the Food Plan to meet your specific needs.

5. Beef, calf, chicken, lamb, pork, or turkey liver may be selected.

6. To aid in the absorption of iron, an asterisked fruit should be consumed at the same meal as liver (see Fruit Servings, page 29).

7. As a "rule of thumb," for each serving of liver, allow 2 ounces (for raw liver) for shrinkage in cooking.

8. Cooking Procedures:
   A. Liver may be boiled, poached, broiled, pan-broiled, baked, sautéed, or stir-fried. A measured amount of Fats may be used for broiling, pan-broiling, baking, sautéing, and stir-frying; equate Fats to the Food Plan.
   B. Liver may be added, raw or cooked, to casseroles and stews.
   C. Liver may be marinated before cooking.
   D. Uncooked liver may be stuffed.

BROILED LIVER
Limited Choice Plan
Midday or Evening Meal

Slice liver ½- to ¾-inch thick. Preheat broiler; place liver on rack in broiler pan and broil 3 to 4 inches from heat source, turning once, until liver is browned on outside but still pink inside, or done to taste, 2 to 4 minutes on each side. Serve 3 ounces cooked liver per portion for Women and Youths; 4 ounces cooked liver per portion for Men.

Per 3-ounce serving with beef liver: 195 calories, 22 g protein, 9 g fat, 5 g carbohydrate, 156 mg sodium
With calf liver: 222 calories, 25 g protein, 11 g fat, 3 g carbohydrate, 100 mg sodium

Variation: If desired, spread cooked liver with a measured amount of margarine. Adjust equivalent listing accordingly.

Per ½ teaspoon margarine: Add 17 calories, 2 g fat, and 23 mg sodium to nutrition figures.

BEEF LIVER WITH ONIONS AND TOMATOES
Full Choice Plan
Makes 2 Midday or Evening Meal servings

2 teaspoons margarine
12 ounces beef liver, cut into
   3 x 1-inch strips
1 cup thinly sliced onions

2 medium tomatoes, blanched,
   peeled, and cut into wedges
2 teaspoons dry red wine
1 teaspoon salt
¼ teaspoon pepper

Garnish
Chopped fresh parsley

In 12-inch nonstick skillet heat margarine, over medium heat, until bubbly. Increase heat, add liver and onions and sauté, stirring occasionally, until liver is browned and onions are tender, about 5 minutes. Reduce heat, add remaining ingredients except parsley, and simmer until tomatoes are thoroughly heated. Serve garnished with chopped parsley.

Each serving is equivalent to: 1 serving Fats; 4 ounces Liver; ½ cup Limited Vegetables; 2 servings Vegetables; ½ serving Extras.

Per serving: 360 calories, 33 g protein, 16 g fat, 20 g carbohydrate, 1,340 mg sodium

LIVER ROSEMARY
Full Choice Plan
Makes 2 Midday or Evening Meal servings

2 teaspoons vegetable oil
1 cup sliced mushrooms
½ cup sliced green bell pepper
   (thin strips)
½ cup julienne-cut carrot
½ teaspoon minced fresh garlic
12 ounces calf liver, cut into
   1-inch-wide strips

2 medium tomatoes, blanched,
   peeled, seeded, and chopped
½ cup Chicken Broth (see page
   401)
2 teaspoons enriched all-purpose
   flour
¼ teaspoon rosemary leaves,
   crushed
Dash each salt and pepper

Garnish
1 tablespoon chopped fresh parsley

In 9-inch skillet heat oil; add mushrooms, green pepper, carrot, and garlic and sauté until vegetables are tender-crisp, about 5 minutes. Add liver

and cook, stirring quickly, until all pink has disappeared, about 5 minutes. Add remaining ingredients except parsley. Cook, stirring constantly, until sauce is thickened. Serve sprinkled with parsley.
Each serving is equivalent to: 1 serving Fats; 4 servings Vegetables; 4 ounces Liver; 1⅓ servings Extras.

Per serving: 414 calories, 38 g protein, 20 g fat, 21 g carbohydrate, 235 mg sodium

PIQUANT CALF LIVER
Full Choice Plan
Makes 2 Midday or Evening Meal servings

½ cup plain unflavored yogurt	12 ounces calf liver, cut into
½ teaspoon Dijon-style mustard	½-inch-wide strips
¼ teaspoon Worcestershire sauce	2 teaspoons enriched all-purpose
2 teaspoons margarine	flour
½ cup diced onion	⅛ teaspoon thyme leaves
	Dash each pepper and salt

1. In small bowl combine yogurt, mustard, and Worcestershire sauce; set aside.
2. In 9-inch skillet heat margarine until bubbly; add onion and sauté until softened.
3. Add liver and sprinkle with flour; add thyme and pepper and sauté, over medium-high heat, until liver strips are browned outside but still pink within, about 5 minutes.
4. Reduce heat to low and stir in yogurt mixture. Heat but *do not boil.* Season wiith salt.
Each serving is equivalent to: ½ serving Milk; 1 serving Fats; ¼ cup Limited Vegetables; 4 ounces Liver; 1 serving Extras.

Per serving: 392 calories, 36 g protein, 21 g fat, 13 g carbohydrate, 310 mg sodium

STUFFED LIVER
Full Choice Plan
Makes 2 Midday or Evening Meal servings

1 tablespoon margarine, divided	½ teaspoon salt
½ cup sliced onion	Dash each ground sage, nutmeg,
¼ cup minced celery	and white pepper
½ teaspoon minced fresh garlic	½ cup cooked enriched rice
2 fluid ounces dry sherry	2 slices calf liver, 6 ounces each
1 small apple, pared, cored, and	2 tablespoons buttermilk
diced	3 tablespoons plain dried bread
1 tablespoon raisins	crumbs

1. In 9-inch skillet heat 2 teaspoons margarine until bubbly; add onion, celery, and garlic and sauté until onion is translucent, about 5 minutes.
2. Add sherry, then apple, raisins, and seasonings; cover and cook, stirring occasionally, until most of liquid evaporates, about 5 minutes. Add rice and stir to combine; remove from heat and set aside.

3. Dip each slice of liver into buttermilk, coating both sides, then into bread crumbs, being sure to use all crumbs.

4. Spray an 8 x 8-inch baking pan with nonstick cooking spray. Place 1 slice of breaded liver in pan; top with stuffing mixture, then second liver slice. Secure with toothpicks (some stuffing may fall into pan). Dot liver with remaining 1 teaspoon margarine.

5. Bake at 375°F. until liver is slightly pink inside when pierced with a fork, about 20 minutes.

Each serving is equivalent to: 1½ servings Fats; ¼ cup Limited Vegetables; ¼ serving Vegetables; ¼ serving Occasional Substitutes; ¾ serving Fruits; ½ serving Bread Substitutes; 4 ounces Liver; 1 tablespoon Buttermilk (½2 serving Milk); ½ serving Bread.

Per serving: 549 calories, 37 g protein, 22 g fat, 43 g carbohydrate, 852 mg sodium

CHICKEN LIVERS CREOLE
Full Choice Plan
Makes 2 Midday or Evening Meal servings

12 ounces chicken livers	1 garlic clove, minced
2 teaspoons enriched all-purpose flour	½ cup sliced green bell pepper
	1 medium tomato, cut into 8 wedges
Dash paprika	
2 teaspoons margarine	2 teaspoons white wine
½ cup diced onion	Dash salt

Using paper towels, dry chicken livers. In small bowl combine flour and paprika; dredge livers in flour mixture and set aside.

In 9-inch skillet heat margarine until bubbly; add onion and garlic and sauté until softened. Add livers and sauté, over medium-high heat, for 3 minutes. Add green pepper and sauté for 2 minutes longer. Add tomato and wine and sauté until just heated through. Season with salt.

Each serving is equivalent to: 4 ounces Liver; 1½ servings Extras; 1 serving Fats; ¼ cup Limited Vegetables; 1½ servings Vegetables.

Per serving: 276 calories, 32 g protein, 9 g fat, 15 g carbohydrate, 190 mg sodium

CHICKEN LIVERS "STROGANOFF"
Limited Choice Plan
*Makes 2 Midday or Evening Meal servings**

2 teaspoons margarine	1 teaspoon enriched all-purpose flour
10 ounces chicken livers	
2 cups sliced mushrooms	2 tablespoons plain unflavored yogurt
1 packet instant onion broth and seasoning mix	2 slices enriched white bread, toasted and cut into 4 triangles each
¼ teaspoon each paprika and salt	
Dash pepper	
1 tablespoon water	

Garnish
2 tablespoons chopped fresh parsley

1. In small skillet heat margarine until bubbly.
2. Add chicken livers, mushrooms, broth mix, paprika, salt, and pepper; cover and cook for 5 minutes, stirring occasionally.
3. In small cup combine water and flour, stirring to dissolve. Stir dissolved flour into liver mixture. Stirring constantly, cook over medium heat until mixture thickens.
4. Remove skillet from heat and stir in yogurt.
5. Arrange 4 toast triangles on each of 2 plates; spoon half of the liver mixture over each portion of toast. Sprinkle each serving with 1 tablespoon parsley.
   Each serving is equivalent to: 1 serving Fats; 3 ounces Liver; 2 servings Vegetables; 1 serving Extras; ⅛ serving Milk; 1 serving Bread.

Per serving: 277 calories, 28 g protein, 9 g fat, 20 g carbohydrate, 883 mg sodium

* Men—Add 1 ounce cooked chicken livers to each portion of Chicken Livers "Stroganoff." Change equivalent listing to 4 ounces Liver.

MUSTARD SEED CHICKEN LIVERS
Full Choice Plan
Makes 1 Midday or Evening Meal serving

6 ounces chicken livers
1 teaspoon enriched all-purpose flour
1 teaspoon margarine
2 tablespoons chopped scallion (green onion)

1 tablespoon mustard seed
2 fluid ounces dry white wine
¼ cup Chicken Broth (see page 401)
Dash each salt and pepper

1. Using paper towels, dry chicken livers; sprinkle with flour.
2. In 9-inch skillet heat margarine until bubbly; add livers and sauté until browned but still pink inside, about 3 minutes. Using a slotted spoon, remove livers to a dish and keep warm.
3. Add scallions and mustard seed to same skillet and sauté until seeds begin to pop.
4. Stir in wine and broth and bring to a boil. Reduce heat and simmer for 2 minutes.
5. Add livers, salt, and pepper to skillet and cook until livers are heated through.
   Each serving is equivalent to: 4 ounces Liver; 1⅓ servings Extras; 1 serving Fats; ⅛ cup Limited Vegetables; ½ serving Occasional Substitutes.

Per serving: 342 calories, 35 g protein, 12 g fat, 14 g carbohydrate, 255 mg sodium

SAUTÉED CHICKEN LIVERS 'N' MUSHROOMS
Full Choice Plan
Makes 1 Midday or Evening Meal serving

6 ounces chicken livers
1 teaspoon enriched all-purpose flour
1 teaspoon margarine
2 tablespoons chopped scallion (green onion)
1 cup sliced mushrooms
⅛ teaspoon thyme leaves

Salt and pepper
¼ cup Chicken Broth (see page 401)
2 teaspoons dry sherry
2 tablespoons evaporated skimmed milk
1 teaspoon chopped fresh parsley
1 slice enriched white bread, toasted and cut into 4 triangles

Using paper towels, dry chicken livers; sprinkle with flour. In 9-inch skillet heat margarine until bubbly; add livers and sauté until browned on outside but still pink within, 2 to 3 minutes. Transfer livers to a bowl and set aside.

In same skillet sauté scallion until softened. Add mushrooms, thyme, and dash each salt and pepper; sauté for 2 minutes. Add broth and sherry and bring mixture to a boil. Add milk and cook 1 minute longer. Add livers to skillet and cook, over low heat, until livers are heated through. Season with dash each salt and pepper. Sprinkle with parsley before serving and serve with toast triangles.

Each serving is equivalent to: 4 ounces Liver; 2⅓ servings Extras; 1 serving Fats; ⅛ cup Limited Vegetables; 2 servings Vegetables; ¼ serving Milk; 1 serving Bread.

Per serving: 364 calories, 38 g protein, 10 g fat, 28 g carbohydrate, 547 mg sodium

STIR-FRIED LIVER AND VEGETABLES
No Choice Plan
Makes 2 Evening Meal servings*

10 ounces chicken livers
1 tablespoon soy sauce
¼ teaspoon ground ginger
¼ teaspoon onion powder
Dash artificial sweetener

1½ teaspoons peanut oil
½ teaspoon Chinese sesame oil
1 garlic clove, crushed
1 cup sliced mushrooms
1 cup cooked broccoli florets

In small bowl combine livers, soy sauce, ginger, onion powder, and sweetener; set aside.

In 9-inch skillet heat peanut and sesame oils; add garlic and sauté until lightly browned. Remove and discard garlic. Add mushrooms to skillet and sauté about 3 minutes. Add liver and soy mixture; cook, stirring quickly and frequently, until liver is no longer pink, about 5 minutes. Add broccoli and stir gently until thoroughly heated.

Each serving is equivalent to: 3 ounces Liver; 1 serving Fats; 2 servings Vegetables.

Per serving: 225 calories, 27 g protein, 9 g fat, 10 g carbohydrate, 736 mg sodium

Note: On the Full and Limited Choice Plans this recipe may be used at the Midday or Evening Meal.

* Men—Add 1 ounce cooked chicken livers to each portion of Stir-Fried Liver and Vegetables. Change equivalent listing to 4 ounces Liver.

SWEET 'N' SOUR CHICKEN LIVERS
Full Choice Plan
Makes 2 Midday or Evening Meal servings

1 teaspoon Chinese sesame oil
12 ounces chicken livers
¼ cup diced green bell pepper
¼ cup thinly sliced scallions
   (green onions)
½ cup canned pineapple chunks
   (no sugar added)

1 tablespoon each rice vinegar and
   teriyaki sauce
1½ teaspoons granulated brown
   sugar
1 teaspoon cornstarch

1. In 9-inch skillet heat oil over medium heat. Increase heat to high, add livers, green pepper, and scallions and cook, stirring constantly, until livers are browned; remove from heat and set aside.
2. Drain juice from ½ cup pineapple into small bowl and reserve.
3. In small saucepan combine pineapple chunks, vinegar, teriyaki sauce, and sugar; heat.
4. While fruit is heating, dissolve cornstarch in reserved pineapple juice; add to heated fruit and cook, stirring constantly, until mixture is thickened.
5. Pour fruit mixture over liver mixture in skillet; return skillet to medium heat and cook for 1 minute.

Each serving is equivalent to: ½ serving Fats; 4 ounces Liver; ¼ serving Vegetables; ⅛ cup Limited Vegetables; ½ serving Fruits; 2 servings Extras.

Per serving: 282 calories, 31 g protein, 7 g fat, 22 g carbohydrate, 376 mg sodium

BREADED CHICKEN LIVERS WITH SAUTÉED ONIONS
Full Choice Plan
Makes 2 Midday or Evening Meal servings

½ cup plus 1 tablespoon plain
   dried bread crumbs
1 tablespoon plus 1 teaspoon grated
   Parmesan cheese
1 tablespoon chopped fresh parsley
½ teaspoon oregano leaves

¼ teaspoon garlic powder
Dash each salt and pepper
12 ounces chicken livers
3 tablespoons buttermilk
2 teaspoons margarine
1 cup sliced onions

1. In shallow dish combine bread crumbs, cheese, parsley, oregano, garlic, salt, and pepper.
2. Dip livers, 1 at a time, into buttermilk, then into crumb mixture;

place on baking sheet that has been sprayed with nonstick cooking spray. Sprinkle any remaining crumbs evenly over livers.

3. Bake at 350°F. until lightly browned, 15 to 20 minutes.

4. While livers are baking, in 9-inch nonstick skillet heat margarine until bubbly; add onions and sauté until golden. Serve with breaded livers.

Each serving is equivalent to: 1½ servings Bread; 2 servings Extras; 4 ounces Liver; ⅛ serving Milk; 1 serving Fats; ½ cup Limited Vegetables.

Per serving: 397 calories, 37 g protein, 11 g fat, 34 g carbohydrate, 492 mg sodium

LIVER-STUFFED SHELLS

Full Choice Plan
Makes 2 Midday or Evening Meal servings

2 ounces uncooked enriched jumbo macaroni shells
12 ounces chicken livers
1 tablespoon minced onion
½ teaspoon minced fresh garlic
1 tablespoon plus 1 teaspoon red wine

¼ teaspoon each oregano leaves, basil leaves, and salt
½ cup tomato sauce
2 teaspoons grated Parmesan cheese
Dash ground nutmeg

Garnish
Chopped fresh parsley

1. In 2-quart saucepan combine 1 quart water and ½ teaspoon salt; bring to a boil. Add shells, return to a boil, and cook 5 minutes; drain and set aside.

2. In small nonstick skillet combine livers, onion, and garlic and cook, over high heat, until livers are done. Remove from heat and allow to cool.

3. Transfer liver mixture to work bowl of food processor and, using an on-off motion, process until finely chopped (*do not puree*). Add wine, oregano, basil, and salt and stir to combine.

4. Preheat oven to 350°F. Stuff each shell with an equal amount of liver mixture. Spread 2 tablespoons tomato sauce on bottom of 1-quart casserole; arrange shells in casserole and spoon an equal amount of remaining sauce over each shell.

5. In small bowl combine cheese and nutmeg; sprinkle an equal amount over each shell.

6. Bake until thoroughly heated and cheese is lightly browned, about 20 minutes. Garnish with parsley.

Each serving is equivalent to: 1 serving Bread Substitutes; 4 ounces Liver; 1½ teaspoons Limited Vegetables; 2 servings Extras; ½ serving Bonus.

Per serving: 332 calories, 35 g protein, 6 g fat, 30 g carbohydrate, 666 mg sodium

Fish

Our recipes will help you make a culinary splash as you set sail for new taste experiences by discovering the many ways to prepare fish. You need not be limited to just a few kinds of fish. Try substituting in various dishes; just be careful to use the same kind of fish as the original—either a delicately or a strongly flavored one. Remember, for the best taste, fish should be fresh and never overcooked.

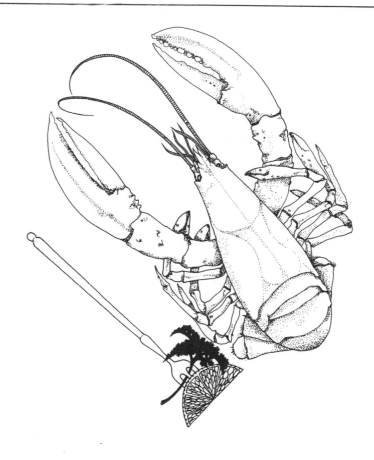

Guidelines for Using Fish

1. Amounts (boned cooked, shelled cooked, or drained canned weight):

	Morning Meal	
	Full Choice Plan	Limited Choice Plan
Women, Men, and Youth	1 ounce	1 ounce

	Midday and Evening Meals	
	Full Choice Plan	Limited Choice Plan
Women and Youth	3 to 4 ounces	3 ounces
Men	4 to 5 ounces	4 ounces

2. Fish should be consumed at mealtime *only* and may be split with items from the Eggs, Cheese, Peanut Butter (Full Choice Plan only), Poultry, Veal, and Game, Meat Group, and Legumes categories.

3. Select Fish meals *at least* 3 times weekly; if fish is split with items from the above categories, or consumed at the Morning Meal, it may *not* be counted as a Fish meal. Fish should be eaten often during the week, since it's low in calories and the fat that it contains is polyunsaturated.

4. The Full Choice Plan range of 3 to 4 ounces for Women and Youth (4 to 5 ounces for Men) provides flexibility. It is a way of individualizing the Food Plan to meet your specific needs.

5. On the Full Choice Plan, fresh, frozen, freeze-dried, canned, cured, smoked, and pressed products may be selected. *If cured or smoked products are selected, use the low end of the serving size range.*

On the Limited Choice Plan, select *only* fresh, frozen, or canned fish. Do *not* use freeze-dried, cured, smoked, or pressed products.

6. On the Full Choice Plan, canned fish may be packed in vegetable oils permitted on the Food Plan, tomato sauce, water, gelatin, broth, or mustard sauce.

On the Limited Choice Plan, canned fish *must* be packed in water.

305

7. Cured and smoked products may contain sugar.

8. Equate freeze-dried products to the amount of fresh used before drying.

9. On the Full Choice Plan, all fish are permitted except eel; do *not* use fish roe.

On the Limited Choice Plan, *only* the following fish may be selected:

clams	red snapper
cod	sardines
crab	scallops
haddock	shrimp
halibut	sole
perch	tuna

10. Raw fish may be consumed if permitted by local government agencies.

11. On the Full Choice Plan, frogs legs may be used and counted as a Fish meal.

12. Whenever possible, weigh fish after cooking (except canned fish). Canned fish should be well drained before weighing; do not consume the liquid, broth, or sauce in which the fish was packed.

13. As a "rule of thumb," for each serving of fish, allow 2 ounces (for raw items) for shrinkage in cooking and an additional 2 ounces for any bone; for each half serving, allow 1 ounce (for raw items) for shrinkage in cooking and an additional 1 ounce for any bone. If using cured or smoked fish or a cooked item, or if consuming raw fish, do not allow additional ounces for shrinkage.

Clams, lobsters, mussels, oysters, scallops, and shrimp are exceptions to this "rule of thumb." Equate as follows:

A. 12 small clams, oysters, scallops, or shrimp, raw or cooked, equate to 4 ounces Fish.

B. A drained chowder clam will yield about 2 to 2¼ ounces raw fish.

C. A 1½-pound lobster will yield about 6 ounces cooked lobster meat; a 6-ounce lobster tail will yield about 3 ounces cooked lobster meat.

D. Approximately 20 mussels will yield about 4 ounces cooked fish.

14. Cooking Procedures:

A. Fish may be boiled, poached, broiled, pan-broiled, baked, sautéed, or stir-fried. Measured amounts of Fats may be used for broiling, pan-broiling, baking, sautéing, and stir-frying; equate Fats to the Food Plan.

B. Fish may be added, raw or cooked, to casseroles and stews.
C. Fish may be marinated before cooking.
D. Uncooked fish may be stuffed.
E. Homemade broth may be prepared by boiling fish in water to cover; vegetables and seasonings may be used. Broth does *not* have to be refrigerated before consuming.

Tips for Cooking Finfish

Timing is an essential element to consider when preparing fish. Fish is done when the flesh is opaque, flakes easily, and falls away from the bones. Overcooking dries out the flesh and makes it tough.

To determine approximate cooking times, measure fish fillet or steak at the thickest part; allow 10 minutes cooking time per inch of thickness. Proportionately shorten cooking time for fish that are less than 1 inch thick. Double cooking time if fish is being cooked frozen (allow 20 minutes per inch of thickness). An additional 5 minutes per inch should be added if fish is being cooked in foil or sauce. However, these are approximate cooking times; fish should always be tested for doneness during preparation.

Remember, fish is delicate and should be handled gently before and during preparation.

Seasonings—A good combination for almost any type of fish is paprika, white pepper, onion powder, and garlic powder. For convenience, this combination can be prepared in advance and kept in a salt shaker. For variety, also try lemon juice and fresh parsley; they will add flavor to any fish.

Baking—This is one of the easiest methods of cooking fish. Season fish as desired; transfer to baking pan just large enough to hold fish in 1 layer. Bake uncovered at 350°F. until fish flakes easily at the touch of a fork. This method is suggested for dressed fish, fillets, and steaks. As an interesting alternative, place lemon slices in baking pan, then top with fish. The lemon will add flavor and prevent the fish from sticking to the pan.

Broiling—Season fish as desired and arrange in a single layer in broiler pan. Broil 3 to 4 inches from heat source until fish flakes easily when tested with a fork, 10 to 15 minutes depending on thickness. As a rule, fish fillets do not need to be turned; the heat of the pan will cook the underside adequately. Thicker pieces, such as pan-dressed fish and thick steaks, should be turned halfway through cooking time.

Poaching—Use a large shallow skillet (or fish poacher) wide enough to hold fish in a single layer. Place fish on piece of double-thick cheesecloth that is large enough so that the ends of cloth extend slightly over edges of skillet (or place on tray of poacher). Set cheesecloth in skillet (or tray in poaching pan) and barely cover fish with liquid, such as lightly salted water, Fish Broth (see page 402), or water seasoned with spices and herbs. Cover skillet (or poacher) and simmer until fish flakes easily, 5 to 10 minutes. Remove fish by grasping extended ends of cheesecloth and lifting (or lift tray from poaching pan). When fish is done, the poaching liquid may be reduced and thickened to make a tasty sauce for the fish. Poached fish may be served as is, with a sauce, or chilled and flaked in cold dishes.

Steaming—Use a steam cooker or a deep pan with a tight-fitting cover and a steaming rack that will keep fish from touching the water. Use plain water or water seasoned with various spices and/or herbs. Heat water to a boil; place fish on rack and cover pan. Steam until fish flakes easily when tested with a fork. Steamed fish may be served in the same manner as poached fish.

Tips for Preparing Shellfish

Clams

Clams in the shell must be alive with their valves (shells) tightly closed when purchased. If refrigerated at 40°F., they will stay alive for several days.

To Clean—Clams ingest large quantities of sand and therefore must be thoroughly cleansed. Place them in a salt solution (⅓ cup salt to 1 gallon water), to which 1 cup cornmeal has been added, for several hours (seawater may be substituted but do not use freshwater without salt). Discard any hardshell clams that do not close, and any softshell clams that do not constrict their necks when touched; this indicates that they are dead.

To Prepare—Clams can be eaten raw with lemon juice or seafood cocktail sauce, or steamed. To prepare, scrub clams with stiff brush under running cold water to remove any surface dirt and foreign matter clinging to shells.

If clams are to be eaten raw, shuck as directed below and serve on the half shell.

To steam, place clams in clam steamer or deep pot that has a tight-fitting cover; pour in about 1 to 2 inches water. Cover tightly and steam until clams on top just barely open. Do not overcook, as prolonged steaming will toughen clams.

To Shuck—Grasp clam firmly with hinge part of shell in palm of hand. Insert flat-bladed shucking knife between the valves. Move blade around to sever the muscle at the hinge and free clam from top and bottom shells. Hint: Place unshucked clams in ice for 1 hour or in freezer for 30 minutes; the shells will open more easily.

Mussels

Like clams, mussels in the shell must be alive when purchased. However, mussels will "gape" when exposed to temperature changes. To test for freshness, hold mussel between thumb and forefinger and press laterally, as though sliding the shells across one another. If the shells move, the mussel is not fresh; a live mussel will remain rigid. Mussels are usually cooked and served in their shells.

To Prepare—Using a wire brush or plastic pot scrubber, thoroughly scrub each mussel under running cold water to remove the byssus (beard) as well as any surface dirt clinging to shells. Discard any that are open. Steam as for clams, stirring once to help mussels open. After cooking, discard any mussels that have not opened.

Oysters

If purchased in the shell, shells must be tightly closed; if shucked, liquor should be clear. If the natural juice is milky, do not use the oysters. Raw oysters are usually served on the half shell, well chilled; serve with lemon juice or seafood cocktail sauce.

To Shuck—Discard any oysters that are open. Thoroughly rinse oysters in running cold water. Hold oyster firmly with hinge part of shell in palm of hand. Push the blade of a thick oyster knife between the shells near the hinge. Run the knife around until muscle holding valves together is cut. Open oyster and remove any bits of shell that may be clinging to muscle. Placing unshucked oysters in ice, as for clams, will make shucking easier.

Shrimp

Shrimp can be purchased fresh, frozen, and canned. Fresh shrimp should be firm and smell fresh. A stale shrimp has an offensive ammonia odor. If there's one bad shrimp in a box, they're probably all bad.

To Prepare—Place whole, unshelled, fresh shrimp in saucepan with water to cover and shrimp spice (if shrimp spice is not available, a mixture of peppercorns, bay leaf, dill sprig, and lemon juice can be used). Partially cover pan and bring water to a rolling boil. When steam escapes from under cover, immediately turn off heat. Cover pan fully and, using potholders, carefully drain off liquid; let stand, covered, for 10 to 15 minutes (or, do not drain, but let shrimp stand in water, removed from heat, just until pink, 3 to 5 minutes). Let cool, then shell and devein as directed below (if desired, shrimp may be shelled and deveined before cooking). It's very easy to toughen shrimp by overcooking. The above method helps to produce firm but tender shrimp. Serve with lemon juice or seafood cocktail sauce.

If using frozen shelled and deveined shrimp, do not thaw before boiling.

If shrimp are to be cooked, then cooked again with additional ingredients, boil just until shrimp turn pink but are not quite opaque. Cooking twice toughens shrimp just as overcooking does; usually heating semiboiled shrimp in sauce will be sufficient to finish cooking them.

For dishes that take a long time to cook, use raw fresh shrimp or thawed and drained frozen raw shrimp.

To Shell and Devein—Hold tail end of shrimp in one hand. Slip thumb of other hand under the shell, between the feelers, and lift off shell segments. Then, firmly hold tail in one hand and gently pull shrimp free of remaining shell, making sure to keep tail meat intact.

To devein a shelled cooked shrimp, pull a narrow strip off back (outside curve) of shrimp, peeling strip down to tail. Using a small, pointed knife, remove and discard the vein.

To devein a shelled raw shrimp, using small, pointed knife, cut lengthwise along back (outside curve), deep enough just to expose vein but not cut all the way through, about ⅛ inch; remove and discard vein.

To Butterfly—Shell and devein raw shrimp, leaving tail "feathers" attached. Cut lengthwise along back down to tail, as deep as possible without cutting through to other side. Spread shrimp open so that it lies flat.

Lobsters

As with other shellfish, it's important that lobsters be fresh. A fresh lobster will be active in the holding tank, the more active the better. Avoid those that appear listless, which though probably safe to eat, may have been in the tank for several weeks; lobsters in captivity are not fed and their meat gradually shrinks away from the shell. When choosing a live lobster, pick it up near its head; its tail should curl under and it should feel heavy for its size.

Although smaller lobsters tend to be more popular, size is actually no indication of tenderness. A very large lobster can be just as tender and flavorful as a one-pounder.

The spiny lobster, also known as crawfish, is usually sold in tail form. It can be purchased with or without its shell, fresh, frozen, and precooked. Live spiny lobsters are extremely rare in the markets; frozen are more readily available, but, depending on freezing facilities and transportation, there is considerable variation in quality.

Lobsterettes or "Danish lobsters," although not marketed in the United States in live form, generally do not suffer any quality loss. They can be purchased whole and in tail form, fresh and frozen.

To Prepare Whole Live Lobsters—Boiling is the easiest method of cooking. Into large saucepot measure enough water to cover lobsters; add 1 tablespoon salt for each quart of water. Cover pot and bring water to a rolling boil. Drop lobsters, head first, into water. Return water to a boil, then allow about 10 minutes cooking time for one 1-pound lobster and an additional 3 minutes for each additional 1-pound lobster. As a "rule of thumb," begin timing from the second boiling and cook an individual lobster according to the following table:

Weight of One Lobster	Time (from second boiling)
1 to 1¼ pounds	10 to 12 minutes
1½ to 2 pounds	15 to 18 minutes
2½ to 5 pounds	20 to 25 minutes
6 to 10 pounds	25 to 35 minutes

To split cooked lobster—Holding lobster with head away from you, insert large, sharp knife at the point where tail and body are joined and cut toward tail; turn lobster around so that head is facing you and cut toward head. Split lobster into halves and remove sand sack from head. Serve with lemon juice and melted margarine.

To Prepare Spiny Lobster Tails

Piggyback lobster tail—Holding the tail with fan away from you and using scissors, cut upper shell down center, leaving fan intact; do not remove undershell. Lift uncooked meat through slit so that it rests on the shell. Brush with lemon juice and margarine and broil 6 inches from heat source just until tender.

Butterfly lobster tail—Cut upper shell all the way through tail and press halves apart. Brush and broil as above.

Fancut lobster tail—Cut off undershell, leaving tail fan intact. Boil just until tender. Serve with lemon juice and melted margarine.

FISH CHOWDER
Full Choice Plan
Makes 2 Midday or Evening Meal servings, about 2½ cups each

1 tablespoon plus 1 teaspoon
  reduced-calorie margarine
2 tablespoons plus 1½ teaspoons
  enriched all-purpose flour
1½ cups Fish Broth (see page
  402),* heated
8 ounces pared and thinly sliced
  potatoes
1 cup thinly sliced carrots
½ cup diced onion

½ cup water
½ teaspoon salt
Dash each ground thyme and white
  pepper
12 ounces codfish fillets or other
  bland white fish fillets, cut into
  2-inch pieces
½ cup evaporated skimmed milk,
  heated

1. In 2-quart saucepan heat margarine, over medium heat, until bubbly.
2. Remove pan from heat and stir in flour until dissolved.
3. Return to heat and, using a wire whisk, slowly stir in warm broth. Cook, stirring constantly, until mixture is smooth and thickened.
4. Add remaining ingredients except fish and milk. Reduce heat, cover, and simmer until vegetables are tender but not soft, about 15 minutes.
5. Add fish and milk, stirring to combine; cover and simmer until fish flakes easily at the touch of a fork, about 5 minutes.

Each serving is equivalent to: 1 serving Fats; ½ serving Bread; 1 serving Extras; 1 serving Bread Substitutes; 1 serving Vegetables; ¼ cup Limited Vegetables; 4 ounces Fish; ½ serving Milk.

Per serving: 391 calories, 41 g protein, 5 g fat, 45 g carbohydrate, 872 mg sodium

* Water may be substituted for the Fish Broth; omit Extras from equivalent listing.

Per serving: 379 calories, 39 g protein, 5 g fat, 44 g carbohydrate, 858 mg sodium

MANHATTAN CLAM CHOWDER
Full Choice Plan
Makes 4 Midday or Evening Meal servings

To complete the meal, serve with a mixed green salad.

1 tablespoon plus 1 teaspoon margarine
1 cup diced onions
1 tablespoon plus 1 teaspoon imitation bacon bits
8 ounces pared potatoes, cut into cubes
2 cups blanched, peeled, and crushed very ripe tomatoes*
2 cups diced carrots
2 cups bottled clam juice
1 cup diced celery
1 cup boiling water
2 teaspoons salt
1 teaspoon thyme leaves
Dash pepper
1½ pounds shucked and chopped chowder clams
2 tablespoons chopped fresh parsley
40 oyster crackers

In 4-quart saucepan heat margarine until bubbly; add onions and bacon bits and cook until onions are translucent. Add remaining ingredients except clams, parsley, and crackers and bring to a boil. Reduce heat and simmer for 1 hour. Add chopped clams and parsley and bring to a boil. Reduce heat and simmer 5 minutes longer. Serve each portion with 10 oyster crackers.

Each serving is equivalent to: 1 serving Fats; ¼ cup Limited Vegetables; 1 serving Extras; ½ serving Bread Substitutes; 2½ servings Vegetables; ½ serving Bonus; 4 ounces Fish; ½ serving Bread.

Per serving: 344 calories, 27 g protein, 7 g fat, 43 g carbohydrate, 2,193 mg sodium

* 2 cups canned crushed tomatoes can be substituted.

Per serving: 347 calories, 27 g protein, 7 g fat, 44 g carbohydrate, 2,346 mg sodium

BAKED STUFFED FISH
Limited Choice Plan
Makes 2 Midday or Evening Meal servings*

2 teaspoons vegetable or olive oil
¼ cup each chopped mushrooms and zucchini
½ slice enriched white bread, toasted and made into coarse crumbs
¼ cup lemon juice, divided

Dash each rosemary leaves, salt, and pepper
2 fish fillets (cod, haddock, or scrod), 5 ounces each
½ medium tomato, blanched, peeled, and sliced

Preheat oven to 375°F. In small skillet heat oil; add mushrooms and zucchini and sauté until tender. Add bread crumbs, 2 tablespoons lemon juice, and the seasonings and stir to combine; remove from heat.

Spray shallow baking dish, large enough to hold fillets flat, with nonstick cooking spray; arrange fillets in dish. Spread stuffing mixture over fillets; top with tomato slices and sprinkle with remaining 2 tablespoons lemon juice. Bake until fish flakes easily at the touch of a fork, 15 to 20 minutes.

Each serving is equivalent to: 1 serving Fats; 1 serving Vegetables; ¼ serving Bread; 3 ounces Fish.

Per serving with cod or scrod: 188 calories, 26 g protein, 5 g fat, 8 g carbohydrate, 196 mg sodium
With haddock: 189 calories, 27 g protein, 5 g fat, 8 g carbohydrate, 183 mg sodium

* Men—For each serving use a 6-ounce fish fillet. Change equivalent listing to 4 ounces Fish.

CODFISH BAKE
Limited Choice Plan
Makes 1 Midday or Evening Meal serving*

5 ounces thawed frozen codfish fillets
¼ cup sliced mushrooms
½ cup canned crushed tomatoes
1 tablespoon chopped fresh parsley

1 teaspoon lemon juice
½ garlic clove, minced
Dash each thyme leaves, salt, and pepper

Preheat oven to 375°F. Spray an individual shallow baking dish, large enough to hold codfish flat, with nonstick cooking spray. Set fillets in dish and top with mushrooms.

In cup or small bowl combine remaining ingredients; pour over fish. Bake until fish flakes easily at the touch of a fork, 15 to 20 minutes.

Each serving is equivalent to: 3 ounces Fish; 1½ servings Vegetables.

Per serving: 146 calories, 27 g protein, 1 g fat, 7 g carbohydrate, 389 mg sodium

* Men—For each serving use 6 ounces codfish fillets. Change equivalent listing to 4 ounces Fish.

CODFISH CAKES
Full Choice Plan
Makes 2 Midday or Evening Meal servings

12 saltines
6 ounces boned cooked codfish
1 egg
¼ cup lemon juice

2 tablespoons chopped fresh parsley
⅛ teaspoon each salt and pepper
2 teaspoons vegetable oil

Garnish
4 lemon wedges

In work bowl of food processor process saltines until finely crumbed. Add remaining ingredients except oil and lemon wedges and process until well combined. Form mixture into 4 round patties.

In 9-inch skillet heat oil; add fish cakes and cook, turning once, until browned on both sides. Serve with lemon wedges.

Each serving is equivalent to: 1 serving Bread; 3 ounces Fish; ½ Egg; 1 serving Fats.

Per serving: 313 calories, 29 g protein, 14 g fat, 16 g carbohydrate, 468 mg sodium

CODFISH GRATINÉE
Full Choice Plan
Makes 1 Midday or Evening Meal serving

5 ounces thawed frozen codfish
   fillets
¼ cup evaporated skimmed milk

½ ounce shredded sharp Cheddar
   cheese
¼ teaspoon pepper

1. Preheat oven to 375°F. Spray individual shallow flameproof casserole, large enough to hold fillets flat, with nonstick cooking spray. Arrange codfish in casserole.

2. In small saucepan combine milk, cheese, and pepper; cook over medium heat, stirring constantly, until cheese melts.

3. Pour sauce over fish and bake until fish flakes easily at the touch of a fork, 15 to 20 minutes.

4. Turn oven control to broil and broil fish until sauce bubbles and is slightly browned.

Each serving is equivalent to: 3 ounces Fish; ½ serving Milk; ½ ounce Hard Cheese.

Per serving: 219 calories, 33 g protein, 5 g fat, 8 g carbohydrate, 261 mg sodium

COD SUPREME
Full Choice Plan
Makes 2 Midday or Evening Meal servings

12 ounces cod or haddock fillets
2 fluid ounces white wine
½ cup chopped asparagus
½ cup drained canned tomatoes, chopped
¼ cup sliced mushrooms
2 teaspoons enriched all-purpose flour, dissolved in 2 tablespoons water

⅛ teaspoon salt
Dash white pepper
½ cup evaporated skimmed milk
2 slices enriched white bread, toasted and cut into small cubes
2 teaspoons grated Parmesan cheese

Garnish
1 tablespoon chopped fresh parsley

1. Preheat oven to 400°F. Spray a 1½-quart casserole with nonstick cooking spray; arrange fillets in casserole and pour wine over fish. Cover and bake for 6 minutes.
2. Remove casserole from oven and reduce oven temperature to 350°F. Drain accumulated juices in casserole into 1-quart saucepan. Cover casserole and set aside.
3. Add vegetables to saucepan and cook, over high heat, until liquid is reduced by half. Add dissolved flour, salt, and pepper; stirring constantly, cook over high heat until thickened. Add milk and cook just until heated (*do not boil*).
4. Pour vegetable mixture over fish; top with bread cubes and sprinkle with cheese. Bake, uncovered, until cheese is melted and fish is heated, about 10 minutes. Sprinkle with chopped parsley.

Each serving is equivalent to: 4 ounces Fish; ¼ serving Occasional Substitutes; 1¼ servings Vegetables; 2 servings Extras; ½ serving Milk; 1 serving Bread.

Per serving with cod: 312 calories, 40 g protein, 2 g fat, 27 g carbohydrate, 563 mg sodium
With haddock: 313 calories, 41 g protein, 2 g fat, 27 g carbohydrate, 546 mg sodium

MANDARIN CODFISH
Limited Choice Plan
Makes 1 Midday or Evening Meal serving*

5 ounces thawed frozen codfish fillets
¼ cup canned mandarin orange sections (no sugar added), drain and reserve juice

1 teaspoon lemon juice
½ teaspoon granulated brown sugar
½ teaspoon each Worcestershire sauce and soy sauce

Preheat oven to 375°F. Spray a shallow baking pan, large enough to hold fillets flat, with nonstick cooking spray; place codfish in pan. Arrange mandarin orange sections over the fish.

In small bowl combine reserved juice and remaining ingredients; pour over fish. Cover pan with foil and bake until fish flakes easily when tested with a fork, about 15 minutes.

Each serving is equivalent to: 3 ounces Fish; ½ serving Fruits; 1 serving Extras.

Per serving: 161 calories, 25 g protein, 0.5 g fat, 12 g carbohydrate, 321 mg sodium

* Men—For each serving use 6 ounces codfish fillets. Change equivalent listing to 4 ounces Fish.

CREOLE FISH BAKE
Limited Choice Plan
Makes 1 Midday or Evening Meal serving*

5 ounces flounder fillets
1 teaspoon vegetable oil
¼ cup diced green bell pepper
1 teaspoon onion flakes
¼ garlic clove, minced

¼ medium tomato, diced
1 teaspoon lemon juice
¼ teaspoon salt
½ bay leaf
Dash pepper

Preheat oven to 350°F. Spray a casserole that is just large enough to hold fillets flat with nonstick cooking spray; place fish in casserole and set aside.

In small skillet heat oil; add green pepper, onion flakes, and garlic and sauté until pepper is soft. Add remaining ingredients and simmer for 1 minute.

Pour vegetable mixture over fish and bake until fish flakes easily at the touch of a fork, about 15 minutes.

Each serving is equivalent to: 3 ounces Fish; 1 serving Fats; 1 serving Vegetables.

Per serving: 176 calories, 25 g protein, 6 g fat, 5 g carbohydrate, 655 mg sodium

* Men—For each serving use 6 ounces flounder fillets. Change equivalent listing to 4 ounces Fish.

FISH CUPS
Full Choice Plan
Makes 2 Midday or Evening Meal servings, 2 cups each

12 ounces flounder fillets
Dash each salt and pepper
½ cup chopped mushrooms
2 tablespoons chopped scallion
  (green onion)
1 medium tomato, blanched,
  peeled, and diced

2 slices enriched white bread,
  toasted and cut into cubes
2 tablespoons chopped fresh parsley
1 tablespoon margarine, melted
1 tablespoon lemon juice
¼ teaspoon paprika

Garnish
Lemon wedges and parsley sprigs

1. Season fillets with salt and pepper.
2. Spray 4 muffin pan cups (2½-inch diameter each) with nonstick cooking spray; fit 3 ounces of fish into each, overlapping ends of fillet to form a cup. Set aside.
3. In small nonstick skillet combine mushrooms and diced scallion; cook over medium heat until tender.
4. Preheat oven to 375°F. In small bowl combine cooked vegetables with remaining ingredients except garnish. Spoon ¼ of vegetable mixture into each fish-lined muffin pan cup; fill remaining muffin pan cups with water.
5. Bake until fish flakes easily at the touch of a fork, 15 to 20 minutes. Using 2 serving spoons, transfer Fish Cups to serving platter. Garnish with lemon wedges and parsley sprigs.

Each serving is equivalent to: 4 ounces Fish; 1½ servings Vegetables; 1 tablespoon Limited Vegetables; 1 serving Bread; 1½ servings Fats.

Per serving: 275 calories, 32 g protein, 8 g fat, 18 g carbohydrate, 389 mg sodium

FLOUNDER CHINESE STYLE
Full Choice Plan
Makes 2 Midday or Evening Meal servings

1¼-pound whole flounder,* dressed with head removed
¼ teaspoon salt
¼ cup Chicken Broth (see page 401)
1 tablespoon plus ¼ teaspoon soy sauce, divided
1 tablespoon chopped scallion (green onion)
1 tablespoon dry sherry
½ teaspoon minced pared ginger root
2 teaspoons peanut oil
1 cup sliced mushrooms
½ cup each thinly sliced green and red bell pepper
½ cup drained canned bamboo shoots, cut into thin strips
2 garlic cloves, minced
1 tablespoon water
1 teaspoon cornstarch

1. Preheat oven to 400°F. Rinse flounder under running cold water; pat dry with paper towels.
2. Using a sharp knife, cut 4 parallel diagonal slashes, each about ½ inch deep, through skin on both sides of flounder. Sprinkle fish with salt.
3. Line baking pan, just large enough to hold fish flat, with foil and place flounder in pan.
4. In measuring cup or small bowl combine broth, 1 tablespoon soy sauce, scallion, sherry, and ginger; pour over fish.
5. Cover pan with foil and bake 10 minutes. Remove foil and bake, basting twice, until fish flakes easily when tested with a fork, about 10 minutes longer.
6. While fish is baking, in small skillet heat oil; add mushrooms, peppers, bamboo shoots, and garlic and sauté until vegetables are tender-crisp.

7. Using 2 pancake turners, carefully remove flounder from baking pan to large platter; keep warm. Pour liquid remaining in pan into skillet containing vegetable mixture; bring to a boil. In a small cup combine water and cornstarch and stir to dissolve. Add dissolved cornstarch and remaining ¼ teaspoon soy sauce to vegetable mixture; cook, stirring constantly, until thickened. Pour over fish and serve.

Each serving is equivalent to: 4 ounces Fish; 1½ servings Extras; 1½ teaspoons Limited Vegetables; 1 serving Fats; 2½ servings Vegetables.

Per serving: 244 calories, 33 g protein, 6 g fat, 13 g carbohydrate, 1,143 mg sodium

* A 1¼-pound flounder will yield about 8 ounces cooked fish.

LEMON MERINGUE FLOUNDER
Full Choice Plan
Makes 2 Midday or Evening Meal servings

12 ounces flounder fillets*
Dash each salt and pepper
2 tablespoons lemon juice

1 egg white (at room temperature)
2 teaspoons mayonnaise
1 teaspoon pickle relish

Preheat oven to 400°F. Season fish with salt and pepper and place in shallow nonstick baking pan large enough to hold fillets flat; bake until fish flakes easily at the touch of a fork, 10 to 15 minutes. Remove from oven and sprinkle with lemon juice.

In small bowl beat egg white until stiff peaks form. In small cup or bowl combine mayonnaise and relish and gently fold into beaten egg white. Spread mixture over fish and broil 6 inches from heat source until browned, about 1 minute.

Each serving is equivalent to: 4 ounces Fish; 1½ servings Extras; 1 serving Fats.

Per serving: 184 calories, 30 g protein, 5 g fat, 2 g carbohydrate, 268 mg sodium

* Any white-fleshed fish may be substituted for the flounder.

STIR-FRIED FISH WITH PEPPER SAUCE
Limited Choice Plan
*Makes 2 Midday or Evening Meal servings**

2 teaspoons vegetable oil
2 teaspoons finely chopped pared
   ginger root
¼ teaspoon finely chopped fresh
   garlic
Dash crushed red pepper
10 ounces firm white-fleshed fish
   fillets, cut into 1½-inch pieces

2 medium celery ribs, thinly sliced
½ cup shredded lettuce
¼ cup water
1 tablespoon plus 1 teaspoon chili
   sauce
2 teaspoons soy sauce

Heat wok or 10-inch skillet over high heat for about 30 seconds; add oil to pan and swirl until hot but not smoking. Add ginger, garlic, and pepper and stir-fry for about 20 seconds. Add fish and celery and stir-fry for 1 minute. Add lettuce and stir-fry until fish flakes easily when tested with a fork, about 1 minute. Add remaining ingredients and stir to heat through.

Each serving is equivalent to: 1 serving Fats; 3 ounces Fish; 1 serving Extras. (See page 407 for Full Choice Plan adjustments.)

Per serving: 286 calories, 28 g protein, 17 g fat, 5 g carbohydrate, 709 mg sodium

* Men—One serving provides ¾ of a meal. Supplement with an additional ¼ serving of Protein at the Midday or Evening Meal.

CURRIED HADDOCK
Full Choice Plan
Makes 2 Midday or Evening Meal servings

2 teaspoons margarine	1 tablespoon raisins
½ cup diced onion	1 teaspoon curry powder
½ medium red delicious apple, cored and diced	½ teaspoon salt
	12 ounces haddock fillets*

Preheat oven to 350°F. In small skillet melt margarine over medium heat; add onion, apple, raisins, curry, and salt and cook, stirring occasionally, until apples are soft.

Spray a shallow 1-quart casserole with nonstick cooking spray; arrange fillets in casserole and top with onion mixture. Bake until fish flakes easily at the touch of a fork, 15 to 20 minutes.

Each serving is equivalent to: 1 serving Fats; ¼ cup Limited Vegetables; ½ serving Fruits; 4 ounces Fish.

Per serving: 232 calories, 32 g protein, 5 g fat, 16 g carbohydrate, 692 mg sodium

* Any white-fleshed fish may be substituted for the haddock.

HADDOCK SALAD PIE
Full Choice Plan
Makes 2 Midday or Evening Meal servings

2 refrigerated buttermilk flaky biscuits (unbaked), 1 ounce each	1 tablespoon minced scallion (green onion)
¼ teaspoon coarsely ground pepper	1 teaspoon lemon juice
Dash oregano leaves	¼ cup plain unflavored yogurt
8 ounces cooked haddock fillets, flaked	1 tablespoon plus 1 teaspoon reduced-calorie mayonnaise
¼ cup diced celery	1 teaspoon Dijon-style mustard
1 tablespoon diced green bell pepper	⅛ teaspoon Worcestershire sauce
	Dash each salt and white pepper
	1 medium tomato, cut into 8 wedges

Garnish
Parsley sprigs

1. Preheat oven to 400°F. On sheet of wax paper sprinkle biscuit dough with coarsely ground pepper and oregano; knead until combined.
2. Form dough into a ball. Between 2 sheets of wax paper roll dough into a circle, about 7 inches in diameter.
3. Spray 6-inch pie pan with nonstick cooking spray; line pan with dough. Using a fork, prick dough in several places. Bake until lightly browned, 7 to 8 minutes.
4. Let pie shell cool in pan for 5 minutes. Carefully remove shell from pan and set on wire rack to cool completely.
5. In bowl combine haddock, celery, green pepper, scallion, and lemon juice.
6. In small bowl mix together yogurt, mayonnaise, mustard, and Worcestershire sauce; pour over fish mixture and toss lightly to combine. Add salt and pepper.
7. Gently spoon fish salad into baked pie shell. Garnish with tomato wedges and parsley sprigs.

Each serving is equivalent to: 1 serving Bread; 4 ounces Fish; 1⅓ servings Vegetables; 1½ teaspoons Limited Vegetables; ¼ serving Milk; 1 serving Fats.

Per serving: 281 calories, 35 g protein, 5 g fat, 21 g carbohydrate, 621 mg sodium

MARINATED FISH GREEK STYLE
Full Choice Plan
Makes 2 Midday or Evening Meal servings

1 cup tomato sauce	2 teaspoons enriched all-purpose
¼ cup lemon juice, divided	flour
1 tablespoon plus 1 teaspoon	⅛ teaspoon salt
white wine	Dash pepper
2 garlic cloves, minced	12 ounces haddock or cod fillets,
1 teaspoon granulated sugar	cut into 1-inch cubes
½ teaspoon rosemary leaves	2 teaspoons olive oil

1. In small saucepan combine tomato sauce, 3 tablespoons lemon juice, and the wine, garlic, sugar, and rosemary. Cover and simmer 10 minutes.
2. While sauce is simmering, on a plate or sheet of wax paper combine flour with salt and pepper. Dredge fish cubes in flour mixture to coat.
3. In 9-inch nonstick skillet heat oil; add fish cubes and sauté, turning to brown on all sides, until cooked, 6 to 8 minutes.
4. Transfer fish to shallow container (not aluminum); pour tomato sauce over cubes and allow to cool. Cover and refrigerate overnight.
5. Remove from refrigerator about 30 minutes before serving. Add remaining tablespoon lemon juice just before serving.

Each serving is equivalent to: 1 serving Bonus; 3 servings Extras; 4 ounces Fish; 1 serving Fats.

Per serving with haddock: 254 calories, 33 g protein, 5 g fat, 16 g carbohydrate, 835 mg sodium
With cod: 252 calories, 32 g protein, 6 g fat, 16 g carbohydrate, 850 mg sodium

HALIBUT PORTUGUESE STYLE
Full Choice Plan
Makes 2 Midday or Evening Meal servings

1 tablespoon olive oil, divided
¼ cup diced onion
1 garlic clove, minced
½ cup diced green bell pepper
1 cup canned plum tomatoes,
    drained and chopped (reserve
    liquid)

2 fluid ounces white wine
4 pitted black olives, sliced
1 teaspoon enriched all-purpose
    flour
Dash each salt and pepper
1 boned halibut steak, 12 ounces

Garnish
2 teaspoons chopped fresh parsley

1. In 1-quart saucepan heat 1 teaspoon oil; add onion and garlic and sauté until onion is softened. Add green pepper and sauté for 3 minutes longer.
2. Add tomatoes with reserved liquid, wine, and olives; cover and simmer, stirring occasionally, for 10 minutes.
3. In small cup mix flour with salt and pepper; sprinkle both sides of halibut steak with flour mixture.
4. In 9-inch skillet heat remaining 2 teaspoons oil. Add fish and sauté until one side is golden brown, 3 to 4 minutes; turn and brown other side.
5. Spoon vegetable mixture over fish and simmer until fish flakes easily when tested with a fork and vegetables are hot, about 3 minutes. Sprinkle with parsley before serving.

Each serving is equivalent to: 1½ servings Fats; ⅛ cup Limited Vegetables; 1½ servings Vegetables; ¼ serving Occasional Substitutes; 1½ servings Extras; 4 ounces Fish.

Per serving: 321 calories, 38 g protein, 11 g fat, 12 g carbohydrate, 381 mg sodium

HALIBUT STEAK WITH HERBED "BUTTER"
Limited Choice Plan
Makes 1 Midday or Evening Meal serving*

1 boned halibut steak, 5 ounces
    (½ inch thick)
½ teaspoon vegetable oil
1 teaspoon water
1 teaspoon reduced-calorie
    margarine
1 tablespoon chopped fresh parsley,
    divided

¼ teaspoon chervil leaves
¼ teaspoon prepared brown
    mustard
Dash each salt and pepper
1 teaspoon lemon juice
1 lemon wedge

Preheat oven to 375°F. Spray shallow baking dish, just large enough to hold halibut steak snuggly, with nonstick cooking spray. Place fish steak in dish and brush with oil, then water. Cover with foil and bake until fish flakes easily when tested with a fork, 15 to 20 minutes.

While halibut is baking, in small bowl cream margarine with 1 teaspoon parsley and the chervil, mustard, salt, and pepper; slowly blend in lemon juice. Cover and chill.

When fish is done, remove foil and top with margarine mixture; return to oven and bake until margarine is melted. Dip lemon wedge in remaining 2 teaspoons chopped parsley and serve alongside fish.

Each serving is equivalent to: 3 ounces Fish; 1 serving Fats.

Per serving: 187 calories, 30 g protein, 6 g fat, 3 g carbohydrate, 267 mg sodium

* Men—For each serving use a 6-ounce boned halibut steak. Change equivalent listing to 4 ounces Fish.

BAKED RED SNAPPER WITH ARTICHOKE STUFFING
Full Choice Plan
Makes 6 Midday or Evening Meal servings

1 tablespoon vegetable oil
¾ cup finely chopped onions
1½ cups frozen artichoke hearts, thawed and chopped
3 slices enriched white bread, toasted and made into fine crumbs

¼ cup chopped fresh parsley
¼ cup lemon juice
1 teaspoon salt
½ teaspoon pepper
1 red snapper, 3 pounds dressed with head and tail left on
1 cup mixed vegetable juice

Preheat oven to 350°F. In 9-inch skillet heat oil; add onions and sauté until translucent. Add artichoke hearts and sauté 3 minutes longer. Stir in bread crumbs, parsley, lemon juice, salt, and pepper; remove from heat and allow mixture to cool slightly.

Stuff fish with onion mixture, using toothpicks or wooden skewers to close cavity. Spray a baking dish that is large enough to hold fish flat with nonstick cooking spray; transfer stuffed snapper to dish and pour juice over fish. Bake, basting frequently with pan juices, until fish flakes easily at the touch of a fork, 40 to 50 minutes.

Each serving is equivalent to: ½ serving Fats; ¼ cup plus 2 tablespoons Limited Vegetables; ½ serving Bread; 4 ounces Fish; ⅙ serving Bonus.

Per serving: 210 calories, 30 g protein, 4 g fat, 12 g carbohydrate, 609 mg sodium

SNAPPER AREGANATA
Full Choice Plan
Makes 2 Midday or Evening Meal servings

⅓ cup plus 2 teaspoons seasoned dried bread crumbs
2 tablespoons chopped fresh parsley
1 tablespoon plus 1 teaspoon grated Parmesan cheese
¼ teaspoon each oregano leaves and garlic powder

12 ounces red or pink snapper fillets
Dash each salt and pepper
2 tablespoons buttermilk
1 tablespoon plus 1 teaspoon vegetable oil

Garnish
Lemon wedges

1. In shallow dish combine bread crumbs, parsley, cheese, oregano leaves, and garlic powder; set aside.
2. Sprinkle fillets with salt and pepper.
3. Place buttermilk in shallow dish; dip fillets in buttermilk, then into crumb mixture, being sure to use up all milk and crumbs.
4. In 9-inch nonstick skillet heat oil; add fish and cook, turning once, until fillets are browned on both sides and flake easily when tested with a fork. Serve with lemon wedges.

Each serving is equivalent to: 1 serving Bread; 2 servings Extras; 4 ounces Fish; 1 tablespoon Buttermilk (½₂ serving Milk); 2 servings Fats.

Per serving: 344 calories, 38 g protein, 13 g fat, 16 g carbohydrate, 404 mg sodium

SALMON IN RED WINE SAUCE
Full Choice Plan
Makes 2 Midday or Evening Meal servings

4 fluid ounces red wine	⅛ teaspoon thyme leaves
2 tablespoons sliced shallots	2 salmon steaks, 8 ounces each
½ bay leaf	2 teaspoons margarine
1 parsley sprig	1 tablespoon chopped fresh parsley

1. In small saucepan combine wine, shallots, bay leaf, parsley, and thyme and bring to a boil. Reduce heat, cover, and simmer for 20 minutes.
2. Strain sauce into a bowl and set aside; discard solids.
3. Preheat oven to 375°F. Place salmon steaks in nonstick baking pan just large enough to hold them snugly in 1 layer. Spoon 1 tablespoon wine sauce over each steak, reserving remaining sauce.
4. Cover pan and bake until fish flakes easily when tested with a fork, 15 to 20 minutes.
5. While fish is baking, return remaining sauce to saucepan and bring to a boil; cook until reduced by half.
6. When fish is done, reheat sauce; remove from heat and stir in margarine and parsley.
7. Using a pancake turner, transfer salmon steaks to warmed serving platter; spoon sauce over salmon and serve.

Each serving is equivalent to: ½ serving Occasional Substitutes; 1 tablespoon Limited Vegetables; 4 ounces Fish; 1 serving Fats.

Per serving: 462 calories, 39 g protein, 27 g fat, 5 g carbohydrate, 176 mg sodium

SALMON VERTE
Full Choice Plan
Makes 2 Midday or Evening Meal servings

2 teaspoons olive oil
1 tablespoon minced shallots
1 garlic clove, minced
½ cup cooked chopped asparagus
½ teaspoon salt, divided
¼ teaspoon white pepper, divided

2 teaspoons mayonnaise
¼ teaspoon Dijon-style mustard
1 salmon fillet, 12 ounces
2 fluid ounces dry white wine
2 teaspoons grated Parmesan
  cheese

1. In 9-inch skillet heat oil; add shallots and garlic and sauté until shallots are translucent, being careful not to burn garlic.
2. Transfer shallot mixture to blender container. Add asparagus, ¼ teaspoon salt, and ⅛ teaspoon pepper and process until smooth; set aside.
3. Preheat oven to 400°F. In small bowl combine mayonnaise and mustard; spread on fillet and sprinkle with remaining ¼ teaspoon salt and ⅛ teaspoon pepper.
4. Transfer salmon to 8 x 8-inch nonstick baking pan; add wine and bake until fish flakes easily when tested with a fork, about 15 minutes (exact timing will depend upon thickness of fillet).
5. Remove pan from oven and turn oven control to broil. Spread asparagus puree over fish and sprinkle with cheese. Broil just until heated through.

Each serving is equivalent to: 2 servings Fats; 1½ teaspoons Limited Vegetables; ½ serving Vegetables; 4 ounces Fish; ¼ serving Occasional Substitutes; 1 serving Extras.

Per serving: 494 calories, 41 g protein, 32 g fat, 5 g carbohydrate, 743 mg sodium

SCROD FLORENTINE
Full Choice Plan
Makes 2 Midday or Evening Meal servings

This dish may be prepared with fresh or frozen fish. If frozen fish is used, reduce salt to ¼ teaspoon.

12 ounces scrod fillets
½ teaspoon salt, divided
1 teaspoon margarine
½ garlic clove, minced
1 cup well-drained cooked
  chopped spinach

1 tablespoon plus 1 teaspoon white
  wine
1 tablespoon lemon juice
Dash pepper

Preheat oven to 350°F. Spray a shallow 1-quart casserole with nonstick cooking spray; arrange fillets in casserole and sprinkle with ¼ teaspoon salt. Bake until fish flakes easily when tested with a fork, 10 to 12 minutes.

While fish is baking, in small nonstick skillet heat margarine until bubbly; add garlic and sauté briefly but do not brown. Add spinach, wine, lemon juice, pepper, and remaining ¼ teaspoon salt. Cook 2 to 3 minutes.

When fish is done, spoon spinach mixture over fillets; return to oven and bake until heated, 3 to 5 minutes.

Each serving is equivalent to: 4 ounces Fish; ½ serving Fats; 1 serving Vegetables; 1 serving Extras.

Per serving: 182 calories, 33 g protein, 3 g fat, 5 g carbohydrate, 725 mg sodium
With ¼ tsp. salt: 182 calories, 33 g protein, 3 g fat, 5 g carbohydrate, 457 mg sodium

BAKED BREADED FISH FILLETS
Limited Choice Plan
Makes 1 Midday or Evening Meal serving*

5 ounces fish fillets (sole, halibut, or flounder)
½ slice enriched white bread, toasted and made into coarse crumbs
1 tablespoon lemon juice
1 teaspoon chopped fresh parsley

⅛ teaspoon pepper
Dash each salt, paprika, and thyme leaves
1 tablespoon evaporated skimmed milk
1 teaspoon margarine

Garnish
1 lemon wedge

1. Preheat oven to 450°F. Spray shallow oven-to-table baking dish, large enough to hold fillets flat, with nonstick cooking spray; place fillets in dish.
2. In small bowl combine bread crumbs, lemon juice, parsley, and seasonings.
3. Brush fillets with milk and pat crumb mixture over fillets; pour any remaining milk over crumbs.
4. Bake until fish flakes easily when tested with a fork, about 5 minutes (exact timing will depend upon thickness of fillets).
5. Remove baking dish from oven and top fish with margarine; return to oven and bake until margarine is melted. Serve garnished with lemon wedge.

Each serving is equivalent to: 3 ounces Fish; ½ serving Bread; ⅛ serving Milk; 1 serving Fats.

Per serving with sole or flounder: 195 calories, 26 g protein, 5 g fat, 9 g carbohydrate, 362 mg sodium
With halibut: 225 calories, 32 g protein, 6 g fat, 9 g carbohydrate, 328 mg sodium

* Men—For each serving use 6 ounces fish fillets. Change equivalent listing to 4 ounces Fish.

FILLET OF SOLE FLORENTINE
Limited Choice Plan
Makes 2 Midday or Evening Meal servings*

1 cup well-drained cooked chopped spinach	2 tablespoons lemon juice, divided
2 sole fillets, 5 ounces each	½ garlic clove, crushed
1 tablespoon plus 1 teaspoon margarine, divided	1 cup sliced mushrooms
	½ teaspoon salt
	Dash white pepper

Garnish
1 tablespoon chopped fresh parsley

1. Preheat oven to 375°F. Spread ½ cup spinach over each fillet; roll fillets to enclose filling. Spray a 1-quart casserole with nonstick cooking spray and place fish rolls, seam-side down, in casserole.
2. Spread 1 teaspoon margarine over each fillet and sprinkle each with 1½ teaspoons lemon juice.
3. Cover casserole and bake for 15 minutes.
4. While fish is baking, in small skillet heat remaining 2 teaspoons margarine until bubbly; add garlic and sauté until golden. Remove and discard garlic. Add mushrooms, salt, pepper, and remaining tablespoon lemon juice to skillet and stir to combine.
5. Top fish fillets in casserole with mushroom mixture. Return casserole to oven and bake, uncovered, until fish flakes easily at the touch of a fork, about 5 minutes. Sprinkle with chopped parsley before serving.
  Each serving is equivalent to: 2 servings Vegetables; 3 ounces Fish; 2 servings Fats.

Per serving: 216 calories, 28 g protein, 9 g fat, 6 g carbohydrate, 788 mg sodium

* Men—For each serving use a 6-ounce sole fillet. Change equivalent listing to 4 ounces Fish.

ITALIAN PACKETS OF SOLE
Full Choice Plan
Makes 2 Midday or Evening Meal servings

2 grey or lemon sole fillets, 6 ounces each	1 tablespoon plus 1 teaspoon white wine
2 teaspoons vegetable oil	¼ teaspoon salt
2 teaspoons minced fresh garlic	⅛ teaspoon pepper
½ cup drained canned tomatoes, chopped	2 teaspoons mashed drained canned anchovy fillets
2 tablespoons chopped fresh parsley	

1. Preheat oven to 350°F. Place each fillet on 12 x 12-inch sheet of foil and set aside.
2. In small nonstick skillet heat oil; add garlic and sauté until golden.

3. Add tomatoes, parsley, wine, salt, and pepper; cook over medium heat, stirring occasionally, for 5 minutes. Stir in mashed anchovy fillets and cook 3 minutes longer; allow to cool slightly.

4. Spoon half of tomato mixture onto half of each fillet; from a narrow end, fold fish in half, covering sauce.

5. To form 2 foil packets, bring 2 long sides of foil together above each fillet and fold over and down tight against fish, then press out air and mold foil to fish; fold short ends up and over, press out air, and crimp ends.

6. Place packets in 8 x 8-inch baking pan and bake for 25 minutes (fish should flake easily when tested with a fork).

Each serving is equivalent to: 4 ounces Fish; 1 serving Fats; ½ serving Vegetables; 2 servings Extras.

Per serving: 214 calories, 31 g protein, 7 g fat, 4 g carbohydrate, 532 mg sodium

TIMBALES OF SOLE
Full Choice Plan
Makes 2 Midday or Evening Meal servings

Timbales

2 sole fillets, 6 ounces each	2 teaspoons white wine
½ cup chopped mushrooms	1 teaspoon chopped fresh dill
1 slice enriched white bread,	½ teaspoon salt
made into crumbs	⅛ teaspoon white pepper
1 tablespoon chopped fresh parsley	

Sauce

½ cup tomato sauce	½ teaspoon chopped fresh dill
2 teaspoons white wine	¼ teaspoon salt
1 teaspoon chopped fresh parsley	Dash pepper

To Prepare Timbales: Preheat oven to 350°F. Cut each fillet in half lengthwise. Roll each half fillet lengthwise and fit each roll into a 2½-inch diameter muffin pan cup, forming a well in center; set aside.

In small mixing bowl combine mushrooms, bread crumbs, parsley, wine, dill, salt, and pepper. Spoon ¼ of mixture into well in center of each fish roll. Fill remaining muffin pan cups with water. Cover pan with foil and bake until fish flakes easily when tested with a fork, 12 to 18 minutes. While fish is baking, prepare sauce.

To Prepare Sauce: In small saucepan combine all ingredients for sauce and bring to a boil. Reduce heat and simmer for 10 minutes.

To Serve: Carefully drain water from muffin pan. Invert a plate on top of pan and invert pan and plate together; gently lift off pan. Using a pancake turner, carefully transfer timbales to serving platter; top with hot tomato sauce.

Each serving is equivalent to: 4 ounces Fish; ½ serving Vegetables; ½ serving Bread; 1 serving Extras; ½ serving Bonus.

Per serving: 202 calories, 31 g protein, 2 g fat, 12 g carbohydrate, 1,298 mg sodium

WHITEFISH DIABLE
Full Choice Plan
Makes 2 Midday or Evening Meal servings

1 whitefish fillet (12 ounces),
  cut in half
2 teaspoons lemon juice, divided
Dash pepper
⅛ teaspoon salt
2 teaspoons margarine
1 teaspoon Dijon-style mustard

2 teaspoons white wine
1 teaspoon capers
½ teaspoon grated lemon peel
¼ teaspoon Worcestershire sauce
2 teaspoons chopped fresh
  parsley

Sprinkle whitefish with 1 teaspoon lemon juice and the pepper. Spray rack of broiler pan with nonstick cooking spray. Transfer fish to rack and broil until fish flakes easily when tested with a fork, about 5 minutes. Sprinkle whitefish with salt, transfer to serving platter, and keep warm.

In small skillet heat margarine until bubbly; stir in mustard. Add wine, capers, lemon peel, Worcestershire sauce, and remaining teaspoon lemon juice; bring to a boil. Add parsley and pour over fish.

Each serving is equivalent to: 4 ounces Fish; 1 serving Fats; ½ serving Extras.

Per serving: 308 calories, 32 g protein, 18 g fat, 1 g carbohydrate, 385 mg sodium

WHITEFISH PIQUANTE
Full Choice Plan
Makes 2 Midday or Evening Meal servings

2 teaspoons enriched all-purpose
  flour
⅛ teaspoon salt
Dash pepper
1 whitefish fillet (12 ounces),
  cut in half

2 teaspoons olive oil
2 teaspoons margarine
2 teaspoons lemon juice
2 teaspoons each chopped capers
  and chopped fresh parsley
½ teaspoon grated lemon peel

In small cup or bowl combine flour, salt, and pepper. Sprinkle both sides of each fillet half with flour mixture. In skillet just large enough to hold fish flat, heat oil; add fish and cook until underside is browned, about 3 minutes. Using a pancake turner, carefully turn fish; cook until other side is browned and fish flakes easily when tested with a fork. Remove to serving platter and keep warm.

In small skillet heat margarine until bubbly; stir in lemon juice, capers, parsley, and lemon peel. Cook for 1 minute; pour over fish and serve.

Each serving is equivalent to: 1 serving Extras; 4 ounces Fish; 2 servings Fats.

Per serving: 351 calories, 33 g protein, 22 g fat, 3 g carbohydrate, 346 mg sodium

CLAM CASSEROLE
Limited Choice Plan
Makes 1 Midday or Evening Meal serving*

9 small clams, shucked and minced
⅓ cup diced green bell pepper
2 tablespoons plus 2 teaspoons diced pimiento
1 teaspoon lemon juice
¼ garlic clove, minced

Dash hot sauce
1 slice enriched white bread, toasted and made into crumbs
2 teaspoons reduced-calorie margarine

Preheat oven to 450°F. In small bowl combine all ingredients except crumbs and margarine; transfer to shallow 1-cup casserole.

In small bowl combine crumbs with margarine; sprinkle over clam mixture. Bake until crumb topping is browned and crisp, 8 to 10 minutes.

Each serving is equivalent to: 3 ounces Fish; 1 serving Vegetables; 1 serving Bread; 1 serving Fats.

Per serving: 345 calories, 34 g protein, 7 g fat, 33 g carbohydrate, 809 mg sodium

* Men—For each serving use 12 small clams. Change equivalent listing to 4 ounces Fish.

STUFFED CLAMS AREGANATA
Full Choice Plan
Makes 4 Midday or Evening Meal servings, 3 stuffed clams each

12 chowder clams
2 very ripe medium tomatoes, chopped
½ cup chopped mushrooms
⅓ cup plus 2 teaspoons seasoned dried bread crumbs

2 tablespoons minced onion
1 tablespoon plus 1 teaspoon olive oil
2 teaspoons grated Parmesan cheese
1 teaspoon oregano leaves
1 garlic clove, mashed

1. Shuck clams and reserve shells.
2. Preheat oven to 400°F. Weigh 1½ pounds clams; chop coarsely and place in bowl. Add remaining ingredients and mix thoroughly.
3. Fill each shell with ¹⁄₁₂ of clam mixture.
4. Transfer shells to baking sheet and bake until stuffing is browned and crisp, about 20 minutes.

Each serving is equivalent to: 4 ounces Fish; 1¼ servings Vegetables; ½ serving Bread; 1½ teaspoons Limited Vegetables; 1 serving Fats; ½ serving Extras.

Per serving: 242 calories, 22 g protein, 7 g fat, 22 g carbohydrate, 441 mg sodium

CRAB MEAT SALAD
Limited Choice Plan
Makes 2 Midday or Evening Meal servings*

Use fresh, frozen, or drained canned water-packed crab meat.

1 medium celery rib, finely diced
2 tablespoons rice vinegar
1 tablespoon plus 1 teaspoon chili sauce
1 tablespoon diced pimiento
2 teaspoons prepared horseradish
2 teaspoons lemon juice

1 teaspoon prepared brown mustard
¼ teaspoon minced fresh garlic
Dash each salt, pepper, and hot sauce
6 ounces cooked crab meat
2 iceberg or romaine lettuce leaves

In small bowl combine all ingredients except crab meat and lettuce. Add crab meat and toss to combine. Cover and refrigerate for at least 1 hour. Serve on lettuce leaves.

Each serving is equivalent to: 1 serving Extras; 1½ teaspoons Vegetables; 3 ounces Fish. (See page 407 for Full Choice Plan adjustments.)

Per serving with fresh or frozen crab meat: 104 calories, 16 g protein, 2 g fat, 6 g carbohydrate, 448 mg sodium
With canned crab meat: 111 calories, 16 g protein, 3 g fat, 7 g carbohydrate, 1,299 mg sodium

Variation: Substitute 6 ounces boned cooked fish for the crab meat.

Per serving: 137 calories, 24 g protein, 1 g fat, 6 g carbohydrate, 380 mg sodium

* Men—Add 1 ounce chilled cooked crab meat or boned cooked fish to each portion of salad. Change equivalent listing to 4 ounces Fish.

COQUILLES ST. JACQUES
Full Choice Plan
Makes 2 Midday or Evening Meal servings

1 tablespoon plus 1 teaspoon margarine
1 tablespoon minced shallots
1 cup sliced mushrooms
1 tablespoon lemon juice
2 fluid ounces dry white wine
12 ounces bay scallops
1 tablespoon plus ¾ teaspoon enriched all-purpose flour

½ cup skim milk
2 tablespoons chopped fresh parsley
Dash each salt and white pepper
1 tablespoon plus 1½ teaspoons plain dried bread crumbs
2 teaspoons grated Parmesan cheese

Preheat oven to 375°F. In 9-inch skillet heat margarine until bubbly; add shallots and sauté briefly. Add mushrooms and lemon juice; cook over high heat until most of liquid evaporates, about 3 minutes. Add wine and cook, stirring occasionally, for 3 minutes longer. Add scallops and cook just until tender, about 5 minutes. Sprinkle with flour, stirring quickly to dissolve. Add milk, parsley, salt, and pepper. Reduce heat and cook, stirring constantly, until thickened.

Divide mixture into 4 scallop shells or two 1½- or 2-cup au gratin dishes. Sprinkle each with an equal amount of crumbs, then cheese. Bake until top is browned, about 10 minutes.

Each serving is equivalent to: 2 servings Fats; 1½ teaspoons Limited Vegetables; 1 serving Vegetables; ¼ serving Occasional Substitutes; 4 ounces Fish; ½ serving Bread; ¼ serving Milk; 1 serving Extras.

Per serving: 490 calories, 36 g protein, 9 g fat, 57 g carbohydrate, 697 mg sodium

BEER-COOKED SHRIMP WITH SPICY YOGURT DIP
Full Choice Plan
Makes 2 Midday or Evening Meal servings

Shrimp cooked in beer are usually served unshelled; they may be shelled if desired, but the tails should be left on so that they are easier to pick up.

Shrimp

12 fluid ounces light beer	1 bay leaf
1 tablespoon onion flakes	1 whole clove
4 peppercorns	24 small unshelled shrimp

Yogurt Dip

½ cup plain unflavored yogurt	1 teaspoon prepared horseradish
1 tablespoon plus 1 teaspoon reduced-calorie mayonnaise	1 teaspoon chopped capers
1 tablespoon plus 1 teaspoon chili sauce	¼ teaspoon Worcestershire sauce
	2 to 3 drops hot sauce

To Prepare Shrimp: In 1-quart saucepan combine first 5 ingredients; bring to a boil and cook for 5 minutes. Add shrimp, remove from heat, and let stand until shrimp turn pink, 3 to 5 minutes; drain. Cover and chill.

To Prepare Dip: Combine all ingredients for dip in small bowl; mix well and serve with chilled shrimp.

Each serving is equivalent to: ½ serving Occasional Substitutes; 4 ounces Fish; ½ serving Milk; 1 serving Fats; 1 serving Extras.

Per serving: 280 calories, 34 g protein, 5 g fat, 13 g carbohydrate, 509 mg sodium

GARLIC SHRIMP IN WINE
Full Choice Plan
Makes 2 Midday or Evening Meal servings

1 teaspoon vegetable oil
12 ounces shelled and deveined
    shrimp
1 garlic clove, crushed
2 teaspoons dry white wine
Dash each salt and pepper

3 tablespoons seasoned dried bread
    crumbs
2 teaspoons wheat germ
1 tablespoon reduced-calorie
    margarine, melted

Garnish
2 lemon wedges and 2 parsley
    sprigs

1. In small skillet heat oil; add shrimp and garlic and sauté, stirring constantly, until shrimp turn pink, 3 to 5 minutes.
2. Remove and discard garlic. Add wine, salt, and pepper to skillet and cook, stirring constantly, for 1 minute. Divide shrimp mixture into two 6-ounce custard cups.
3. In small bowl combine bread crumbs and wheat germ; add melted margarine and stir until thoroughly combined. Sprinkle half of crumb mixture over each portion of shrimp.
4. Broil 6 inches from heat source until crumbs are evenly browned. Garnish each portion with a lemon wedge and parsley sprig.

Each serving is equivalent to: 1¼ servings Fats; 4 ounces Fish; 1½ servings Extras; ½ serving Bread.

Per serving: 254 calories, 33 g protein, 7 g fat, 12 g carbohydrate, 446 mg sodium

SHRIMP CREOLE
Full Choice Plan
Makes 4 Midday or Evening Meal servings

2 teaspoons vegetable oil
½ cup diced onion
1 garlic clove, minced
1 medium green bell pepper,
    seeded and cut into 1-inch
    squares
1 cup sliced mushrooms
½ cup chopped celery

1 cup canned plum tomatoes,
    drained and chopped (reserve
    liquid)
¾ cup Fish Broth (see page 402)
1 bay leaf
Dash pepper
1½ pounds shelled and deveined
    shrimp

Garnish
1 tablespoon chopped fresh parsley

In 2-quart saucepan heat oil; add onion and garlic and sauté until onion is softened. Add green pepper, mushrooms, and celery and sauté 5 minutes longer. Add tomatoes, reserved liquid, broth, bay leaf, and pepper; cover and simmer for 20 minutes, stirring occasionally. Stir in shrimp and continue simmering until shrimp turn pink, 3 to 5 minutes. Serve garnished with chopped parsley.

Each serving is equivalent to: ½ serving Fats; ⅛ cup Limited Vegetables; 1¾ servings Vegetables; ¼ serving Extras; 4 ounces Fish.

Per serving: 215 calories, 33 g protein, 4 g fat, 10 g carbohydrate, 347 mg sodium

Variation: Substitute ¾ cup bottled clam juice for the Fish Broth. Add ³⁄₁₆ serving Bonus to equivalent listing and omit Extras.

Per serving: 220 calories, 34 g protein, 4 g fat, 11 g carbohydrate, 524 mg sodium

SHRIMP "CUTLETS" WITH DIPPING SAUCE
Limited Choice Plan
*Makes 2 Midday or Evening Meal servings**

The size of shrimp is generally indicated by the approximate number of shrimp per pound. For this recipe use 16-20s.

Marinade and Shrimp
2 tablespoons each soy sauce and lemon juice
1 tablespoon water
2 garlic cloves, crushed
½ teaspoon minced pared ginger root or ⅛ teaspoon ground ginger

½ teaspoon prepared brown mustard
Dash sherry extract (optional)
14 ounces large shrimp

Sauce
½ cup canned sliced peaches (no sugar added), pureed
1 tablespoon plus 1 teaspoon reduced-calorie apricot spread (16 calories per 2 teaspoons)

2 teaspoons soy sauce
2 teaspoons rice vinegar or white vinegar
Dash each garlic powder and artificial sweetener (optional)

For Breading and Cooking
2 slices enriched white bread, toasted and made into crumbs

1 tablespoon plus 1 teaspoon peanut or vegetable oil

To Prepare Marinade: In shallow 2-quart casserole combine all ingredients for marinade and set aside.

To Prepare Shrimp: Shell, devein, and butterfly shrimp, removing tail shell (see page 310 for method); using paper towels, pat dry. Between 2 sheets of wax paper, using a meat mallet, pound each shrimp lightly to form a "cutlet." Transfer "cutlets" to casserole containing marinade, turning each to coat evenly; set aside for 10 minutes. While shrimp are marinating, prepare sauce.

To Prepare Sauce: In small saucepan combine all ingredients for sauce and bring to a boil. Reduce heat and simmer for 10 minutes, stirring occasionally to prevent sticking. Keep warm while cooking shrimp.

To Cook Shrimp: Spread crumbs on sheet of wax paper; press each shrimp into crumbs, turning to coat both sides. In 9-inch skillet heat oil;

add shrimp in a single layer and sprinkle with any remaining bread crumbs. Cook, turning once, until browned on both sides. Serve with warm sauce.

Each serving is equivalent to: 3 ounces Fish; ½ serving Fruits; 1⅗ servings Extras; 1 serving Bread; 2 servings Fats. (See page 407 for Full Choice Plan adjustments.)

Per serving: 334 calories, 30 g protein, 11 g fat, 28 g carbohydrate, 2,103 mg sodium

* Men—One serving provides ¾ of a meal. Supplement with an additional ¼ serving of Protein at the Midday or Evening Meal.

SHRIMP KABOBS

Limited Choice Plan
Makes 1 Midday or Evening Meal serving*

2 tablespoons lemon juice
2 teaspoons soy sauce
1 teaspoon onion flakes
5 ounces shelled and devcined shrimp

½ medium tomato, cut into 4 wedges
¼ medium green bell pepper, cut into 1-inch squares

In small bowl combine lemon juice, soy sauce, and onion flakes; add shrimp and toss to coat. Cover and refrigerate for at least 1 hour.

Onto a skewer thread shrimp, tomato wedges, and pepper squares, alternating ingredients; reserve marinade. Transfer skewer to broiler pan; broil, turning once and basting often with reserved marinade, until shrimp are firm, about 5 minutes.

Each serving is the equivalent to: 3 ounces Fish; 1½ servings Vegetables.

Per serving: 168 calories, 28 g protein, 2 g fat, 11 g carbohydrate, 1,091 mg sodium

* Men—For each serving use 6 ounces shelled and deveined shrimp. Change equivalent listing to 4 ounces Fish.

SHRIMP SCAMPI

Full Choice Plan
Makes 2 Midday or Evening Meal servings

The best size shrimp for this recipe are under 10s or 16–20s.

12 ounces shelled and deveined jumbo or large shrimp (tails left on)
1 tablespoon plus 1 teaspoon enriched all-purpose flour
2 teaspoons olive oil

½ teaspoon minced fresh garlic
2 fluid ounces dry white wine
2 teaspoons lemon juice
½ teaspoon salt
Dash white pepper

Garnish
2 tablespoons chopped fresh parsley and 1 twisted lemon slice

Dredge shrimp in flour and set aside. In 9-inch skillet heat oil; add garlic and sauté until golden. Add shrimp to skillet and sauté, turning occasionally, until shrimp begin to turn pink, about 3 minutes. Add wine and bring to a boil; cook for 1 minute. Stir in lemon juice, salt, and pepper and remove from heat. Garnish with parsley and lemon slice before serving.

Each serving is equivalent to: 4 ounces Fish; 2 servings Extras; 1 serving Fats; ¼ serving Occasional Substitutes.

Per serving: 245 calories, 32 g protein, 6 g fat, 9 g carbohydrate, 779 mg sodium

STIR-FRIED GINGER SHRIMP

Full Choice Plan
Makes 4 Midday or Evening Meal servings

¼ cup white wine
2 tablespoons soy sauce
¾ teaspoon ground ginger
1 garlic clove, minced
1½ pounds shelled and deveined shrimp
1 tablespoon plus 1 teaspoon vegetable oil

1 medium red bell pepper, seeded and cut into strips
½ cup trimmed Chinese pea pods (stem ends and strings removed)
½ cup drained canned sliced bamboo shoots
¼ cup drained canned water chestnuts, sliced
2 cups cooked enriched rice, hot

In small bowl combine wine, soy sauce, ginger, and garlic. Add shrimp; cover and let marinate in refrigerator for 1 hour.

Drain shrimp and reserve marinade. Heat oil in wok or 12-inch skillet; add shrimp and stir-fry until pink, about 2 minutes. Remove shrimp and set aside. Add red pepper, pea pods, bamboo shoots, and water chestnuts to wok; stir-fry until pepper is tender-crisp, about 3 minutes. Add reserved marinade and shrimp to wok; toss to combine and heat through. Serve each portion over ½ cup hot rice.

Each serving is equivalent to: 1½ servings Extras; 4 ounces Fish; 1 serving Fats; ¾ serving Vegetables; 3 tablespoons Limited Vegetables; 1 serving Bread Substitutes.

Per serving: 357 calories, 35 g protein, 6 g fat, 36 g carbohydrate, 909 mg sodium

CALAMARI (SQUID) SALAD

Full Choice Plan
Makes 2 Midday or Evening Meal servings

1½ pounds cleaned squid*
½ lemon
1 cup diced celery
½ cup thinly sliced red onion
3 tablespoons lemon juice
2 tablespoons chopped fresh parsley
2 tablespoons drained capers

1 tablespoon olive oil
4 pitted black olives, cut into halves
1 garlic clove, minced
½ teaspoon each oregano leaves and salt
Dash freshly ground pepper

Garnish
2 lemon wedges

Remove tentacles from each squid; turn body section (mantle) inside out, wash thoroughly to remove all grit, and return to right side. Cut mantles into bite-size pieces; place tentacles and mantle pieces in small saucepan. Add lemon and water to cover; bring to a boil. Reduce heat, cover, and cook until squid are tender, about 20 minutes; drain, cover, and chill.

In salad bowl combine remaining ingredients except lemon wedges. Weigh 8 ounces chilled squid;* add to salad and toss to combine. Serve garnished with lemon wedges.

Each serving is equivalent to: 4 ounces Fish; 1 serving Vegetables; ¼ cup Limited Vegetables; 1½ servings Fats; 1 serving Extras.

Per serving: 405 calories, 58 g protein, 12 g fat, 17 g carbohydrate, 1,151 mg sodium

* 1½ pounds cleaned squid will yield 8 to 12 ounces boiled seafood.

STEWED SQUID
Full Choice Plan
Makes 2 Midday or Evening Meal servings

1 pound cleaned squid*	1 teaspoon salt
1 tablespoon olive oil	Dash pepper
½ cup chopped onion	½ cup frozen or drained canned
2 small garlic cloves, minced	peas
1 cup chopped fresh or drained	2 fluid ounces dry white wine
canned tomatoes	2 tablespoons chopped fresh
1 tablespoon chopped fresh basil	parsley
or 1 teaspoon dried basil leaves	

1. Remove tentacles from each squid and set aside; turn body section (mantle) inside-out, wash thoroughly to remove all grit, and return to right side. Cut mantles into bite-size pieces and set aside.
2. In 2-quart saucepan heat oil; add onion and garlic and sauté until onion is translucent.
3. Add tentacles and mantle pieces and cook, stirring occasionally, for about 10 minutes.
4. Add tomatoes, basil, salt, and pepper and bring to a boil. Reduce heat, cover, and simmer just until squid are fork-tender, about 20 minutes.
5. Stir in peas, wine, and parsley and cook 5 minutes longer. Serve immediately or freeze for use at another time.

Each serving is equivalent to: 4 ounces Fish; 1½ servings Fats; ½ cup Limited Vegetables; 1 serving Vegetables; ¼ serving Occasional Substitutes.

Per serving with fresh tomato and frozen peas: 351 calories, 42 g protein, 10 g fat, 20 g carbohydrate, 1,305 mg sodium
With fresh tomato and canned peas: 357 calories, 41 g protein, 10 g fat, 21 g carbohydrate, 1,348 mg sodium
With canned tomato and frozen peas: 354 calories, 42 g protein, 10 g fat, 20 g carbohydrate, 1,458 mg sodium
With canned tomato and canned peas: 360 calories, 41 g protein, 10 g fat, 22 g carbohydrate, 1,501 mg sodium

* One pound cleaned squid will yield about 8 ounces stewed seafood.

STUFFED SQUID
Full Choice Plan
Makes 2 Midday or Evening Meal servings

12 ounces cleaned squid*
⅓ cup plus 2 teaspoons seasoned
  dried bread crumbs
1 large egg, beaten
1 tablespoon minced onion
1 garlic clove, minced
½ teaspoon salt

¼ teaspoon each oregano leaves
  and pepper
½ cup tomato sauce
2 teaspoons dry red wine
2 teaspoons grated Parmesan
  cheese

Garnish
1 tablespoon chopped fresh parsley

1. Remove tentacles from each squid; turn body section (mantle) inside-out, wash thoroughly to remove all grit, and return to right side.
2. Preheat oven to 375°F. Cut tentacles into small pieces. In small bowl combine tentacles with bread crumbs, egg, onion, and seasonings.
3. Stuff each squid with an equal amount of crumb mixture and secure open end with toothpicks. Transfer stuffed squid to shallow 1-quart casserole.
4. In small bowl combine tomato sauce and wine; pour over stuffed squid.
5. Cover casserole and bake for 30 minutes.
6. Sprinkle squid with cheese and bake, uncovered, until sauce reduces slightly and cheese is golden, 10 to 15 minutes. Garnish with parsley.

Each serving is equivalent to: 3 ounces Fish; 1 serving Bread; ½ Egg; 1½ teaspoons Limited Vegetables; ½ serving Bonus; 1½ servings Extras.

Per serving: 296 calories, 35 g protein, 6 g fat, 23 g carbohydrate, 1,170 mg sodium

* 12 ounces cleaned squid will yield about 6 ounces baked seafood.

CRAB IN WINE
Full Choice Plan
Makes 2 Midday or Evening Meal servings

2 teaspoons margarine
¼ cup each diced onion and red
  bell pepper
1 garlic clove, minced

4 fluid ounces dry white wine
8 ounces drained canned crab meat
1 tablespoon chopped fresh parsley

Garnish
Lemon wedges and parsley sprigs

In small skillet heat margarine, over medium heat, until bubbly; add onion, pepper, and garlic and cook until onion is translucent. Add wine and bring to a boil; cook for 1 to 2 minutes. Add crab meat and chopped parsley and cook, stirring constantly, until thoroughly heated, 1 to 2 minutes. Garnish with lemon wedges and parsley sprigs.

Each serving is equivalent to: 1 serving Fats; ⅛ cup Limited Vegetables; ¼ serving Vegetables; ½ serving Occasional Substitutes; 4 ounces Fish.

Per serving: 214 calories, 21 g protein, 7 g fat, 8 g carbohydrate, 1,187 mg sodium

CRAB SALAD ISLAND STYLE
Full Choice Plan
Makes 2 Midday or Evening Meal servings

8 ounces drained canned crab meat, flaked
½ medium banana, peeled and sliced
½ cup canned pineapple chunks (no sugar added)
2 tablespoons thinly sliced scallion (green onion)
1 tablespoon each diced red bell pepper and celery

Dash each salt and pepper
2 tablespoons plain unflavored yogurt
2 teaspoons mayonnaise
8 iceberg or romaine lettuce leaves
2 teaspoons shredded coconut, toasted

In medium bowl combine first 6 ingredients. In measuring cup or small bowl combine yogurt and mayonnaise; add to crab mixture, stirring until thoroughly combined. Arrange lettuce leaves on serving platter, top with crab mixture, and sprinkle with coconut.

Each serving is equivalent to: 4 ounces Fish; 1 serving Fruits; 1 tablespoon Limited Vegetables; 1⅛ servings Vegetables; ⅛ serving Milk; 1 serving Fats; 1 serving Extras.

Per serving: 236 calories, 21 g protein, 8 g fat, 21 g carbohydrate, 1,241 mg sodium

Variation: Substitute 8 ounces drained canned shrimp or tuna for the crab meat.

Per serving with shrimp: 253 calories, 29 g protein, 6 g fat, 21 g carbohydrate, 266 mg sodium
With tuna: 345 calories, 34 g protein, 14 g fat, 20 g carbohydrate, 1,014 mg sodium

CRAB TORTE
Full Choice Plan
Makes 2 Midday or Evening Meal servings

Crêpes
1 egg
½ cup skim milk

⅓ cup less 1 teaspoon enriched all-purpose flour
Dash salt

Filling

1 tablespoon plus 1 teaspoon margarine	1½ cups skim milk
¼ cup minced shallots	6 ounces frozen or drained canned crab meat
¼ cup minced red bell pepper	2 fluid ounces dry sherry
1 cup chopped mushrooms	Dash each salt and white pepper
2 tablespoons plus 1½ teaspoons enriched all-purpose flour	

Topping
2 teaspoons grated Parmesan
cheese

To Prepare Crêpes: In blender container combine egg and milk; turn motor on and off quickly. Add flour and salt and process until smooth. Let batter stand 15 to 20 minutes.

Heat small nonstick omelet pan or skillet; pour in ¼ of the batter and quickly move pan from side to side so that batter covers entire bottom of pan. Cook until underside of crêpe is dry. Using a pancake turner, carefully turn crêpe over; cook other side briefly. Slide crêpe onto a plate. Repeat procedure 3 more times, making 4 crêpes.

To Prepare Filling: In medium skillet heat margarine until bubbly; add shallots and red pepper and sauté just until vegetables are soft. Add mushrooms and cook, stirring occasionally, about 5 minutes. Sprinkle vegetables with flour, stirring quickly to dissolve. Stirring constantly, add milk and cook over low heat until slightly thickened, about 5 minutes. Add remaining ingredients for filling and cook until thoroughly heated, about 3 minutes longer.

To Prepare Torte: Place 1 crêpe in an oven-to-table 8-inch round baking dish. Spread ⅓ of crab mixture over crêpe. Repeat layers, ending with a crêpe. Sprinkle with cheese and bake at 350°F. for 20 minutes.

Each serving is equivalent to: ½ Egg; 1 serving Milk; 1½ servings Bread; 2 servings Fats; ⅛ cup Limited Vegetables; 1¼ servings Vegetables; 3 ounces Fish; ¼ serving Occasional Substitutes; 1 serving Extras.

Per serving with frozen crab: 461 calories, 32 g protein, 13 g fat, 44 g carbohydrate, 603 mg sodium
With canned crab: 468 calories, 32 g protein, 14 g fat, 45 g carbohydrate, 1,275 mg sodium

SALMON SOUFFLÉ

Full Choice Plan
Makes 2 Midday or Evening Meal servings

2 teaspoons grated Parmesan cheese	2 ounces skinned and boned drained canned salmon, flaked
1 tablespoon plus 1 teaspoon reduced-calorie margarine	1 ounce sharp Cheddar cheese, shredded
1 tablespoon plus ¾ teaspoon enriched all-purpose flour	1 teaspoon Worcestershire sauce
½ cup skim milk, heated	¼ teaspoon salt
2 large eggs, separated	⅛ teaspoon paprika
	Dash white pepper
	½ teaspoon cream of tartar

Garnish
2 lemon wedges and 2 parsley sprigs

1. Preheat oven to 325°F. Spray two 10-ounce soufflé dishes with nonstick cooking spray. Sprinkle 1 teaspoon Parmesan cheese into each dish, coating bottom and sides; set aside.
2. In small nonstick skillet heat margarine, over medium heat, until bubbly; using a wooden spoon, gradually stir in flour. Stirring constantly, gradually add milk and cook until sauce is smooth and slightly thickened.
3. In small bowl beat egg yolks lightly; stir in a small amount of the sauce. Slowly pour egg mixture into sauce remaining in skillet, stirring rapidly to prevent lumping.
4. Add salmon, cheese, Worcestershire sauce, salt, paprika, and pepper to sauce. Stirring constantly, cook until cheese is melted and mixture is smooth and thick. Remove from heat.
5. In another bowl beat egg whites with cream of tartar until stiff peaks form.
6. Fold beaten whites, ⅓ at a time, into salmon mixture. Pour half of mixture into each prepared soufflé dish and place on a baking sheet.
7. Bake in middle of center oven rack for 30 to 35 minutes (soufflés should be golden brown). Garnish each with lemon and parsley and serve immediately.

Each serving is equivalent to: 1 serving Extras; 1 serving Fats; ¼ serving Bread; ¼ serving Milk; 1 Egg; 1 ounce Fish; ½ ounce Hard Cheese.

Per serving: 263 calories, 21 g protein, 16 g fat, 8 g carbohydrate, 686 mg sodium

OPEN-FACE TANGY SARDINE SANDWICH
Full Choice Plan
Makes 1 Midday or Evening Meal serving

4 ounces drained canned skinless and boneless sardines
1 tablespoon minced dill pickle
1 tablespoon reduced-calorie mayonnaise
1 teaspoon minced onion
¼ teaspoon Dijon-style mustard
⅛ teaspoon lemon juice
1 slice enriched white bread
1 iceberg or romaine lettuce leaf

In small bowl, using a fork, mash sardines; add pickle, mayonnaise, onion, mustard, and lemon juice and mix well. Spread sardine mixture on bread and top with lettuce leaf.

Each serving is equivalent to: 4 ounces Fish; ⅓ serving Vegetables; 1½ serving Fats; 1 teaspoon Limited Vegetables; 1 serving Bread.

Per serving: 332 calories, 29 g protein, 16 g fat, 15 g carbohydrate, 1,299 mg sodium

SHRIMP FRITTERS
Full Choice Plan
Makes 2 Midday or Evening Meal servings, 2 fritters each

6 ounces drained canned shrimp, mashed
1 tablespoon each finely diced onion, celery, and green bell pepper
1 tablespoon lemon juice

⅛ teaspoon oregano leaves
Dash each salt and pepper
1 large egg, beaten
2 tablespoons plus 1½ teaspoons enriched all-purpose flour
2 teaspoons vegetable oil

Garnish
Lemon wedges and parsley sprigs

In small bowl combine shrimp, vegetables, lemon juice, and seasonings. Stir egg into shrimp mixture, then blend in flour. Shape mixture into 4 equal patties (patties will be moist).

In small nonstick skillet heat oil; add patties and cook over high heat until crisp and brown on bottom; turn and brown other side. Reduce heat to medium and cook 5 minutes longer on each side. Serve garnished with lemon wedges and parsley sprigs.

Each serving is equivalent to: 3 ounces Fish; 1½ teaspoons Limited Vegetables; ⅛ serving Vegetables; ½ Egg; ½ serving Bread; 1 serving Fats.

Per serving: 222 calories, 25 g protein, 9 g fat, 10 g carbohydrate, 224 mg sodium

EGGPLANT–TUNA SALAD
Limited Choice Plan
Makes 2 Midday or Evening Meal servings*

Dressing
1 cup canned crushed tomatoes
2 teaspoons olive oil
½ teaspoon minced fresh garlic
½ packet instant onion broth and seasoning mix

¼ teaspoon each basil and oregano leaves
Dash crushed red pepper

Salad
1 cup cubed pared eggplant (¾-inch cubes)
6 ounces drained canned tuna (water-packed), flaked

Dash each salt and pepper
2 iceberg or romaine lettuce leaves

To Prepare Dressing: In small saucepan combine all ingredients for dressing; bring to a boil. Reduce heat and simmer, stirring occasionally, for 10 minutes.

To Prepare Salad: On baking sheet arrange eggplant cubes in 1 layer and broil, turning once, until tender, about 8 minutes. In small bowl combine tuna, eggplant, and dressing. Refrigerate for at least 24 hours.

To Serve: Season salad with salt and pepper and serve on lettuce leaves.
Each serving is equivalent to: 2 servings Vegetables; 1 serving Fats;
¼ serving Extras; 3 ounces Fish. (See page 407 for Full Choice Plan adjustments.)

Per serving: 193 calories, 26 g protein, 6 g fat, 9 g carbohydrate, 1,158 mg sodium

* Men—Add 1 ounce flaked tuna to each portion of salad. Change equivalent
listing to 4 ounces Fish.

OPEN-FACE GRILLED TUNA 'N' CHEESE SANDWICH
Full Choice Plan
Makes 1 Midday or Evening Meal serving

2 teaspoons reduced-calorie
   mayonnaise
¼ teaspoon each Dijon-style
   mustard and lemon juice
2 ounces drained canned tuna,
   flaked
2 teaspoons minced celery

1 slice enriched white or whole
   wheat bread, lightly toasted
¼ medium dill pickle, thinly
   sliced (about 4 slices)
1 ounce sharp Cheddar cheese,
   thinly sliced

In small bowl combine mayonnaise, mustard, and lemon juice; stir in
tuna and celery. Cover toast with pickle slices, then tuna mixture; top with
cheese. Transfer to sheet of foil or toaster-oven tray and broil until cheese
is melted.
Each serving is equivalent to: 1 serving Fats; 2 ounces Fish; ½ serving
Vegetables; 1 serving Bread; 1 ounce Hard Cheese.

Per serving: 318 calories, 26 g protein, 17 g fat, 15 g carbohydrate, 1,270 mg sodium

PUFFED OPEN-FACE TUNA SANDWICH
Full Choice Plan
Makes 2 Midday or Evening Meal servings, ½ meal each; supplement as required

1 tablespoon mayonnaise
1 tablespoon finely chopped
   scallion (green onion)
1 teaspoon chopped capers
½ teaspoon each Dijon-style
   mustard and lemon juice

4 ounces drained canned tuna,
   flaked
1 egg white (at room temperature)
Dash salt
4 slices whole wheat bread,
   lightly toasted

1. In medium bowl mix together mayonnaise, chopped scallion, capers,
mustard, and lemon juice; stir in tuna.
2. In small bowl combine egg white with salt and beat until stiff peaks
form.
3. Fold beaten white into tuna mixture.
4. Spread ¼ of mixture on each slice of bread and transfer to broiler
pan; broil until puffed, 2 to 3 minutes.*

Each serving is equivalent to: 1½ servings Fats; 1½ teaspoons Limited Vegetables; 2 ounces Fish; 1 serving Extras; 2 servings Bread.

Per serving: 283 calories, 23 g protein, 12 g fat, 23 g carbohydrate, 896 mg sodium

* This can be broiled in a conventional broiler or toaster-oven.

TUNA BOWL SURPRISE
Full Choice Plan
Makes 4 Midday or Evening Meal servings

The pastry in this recipe can be prepared ahead and refrigerated for several days or frozen for about a week. Wrap in plastic wrap before storing.

Pastry "Bowl"
2 tablespoons plus 2 teaspoons reduced-calorie margarine
¼ teaspoon salt
½ cup water

⅓ cup less 1 teaspoon enriched all-purpose flour
2 large eggs

Filling
8 iceberg or romaine lettuce leaves
8 tomato slices (each about ¼ inch thick)
12 ounces drained canned tuna
2 tablespoons each diced celery and onion

1 tablespoon plus 1 teaspoon mayonnaise
¼ teaspoon salt
Dash pepper
8 green bell pepper rings

To Prepare Pastry "Bowl": Preheat oven to 400°F. In small saucepan combine margarine and salt; add water and bring to a boil. Reduce heat and add flour all at once, stirring constantly until mixture forms a ball; remove from heat. Using an electric mixer, beat in eggs, 1 at a time, beating after each addition until mixture is smooth.

Spray an 8- or 9-inch glass pie plate with nonstick cooking spray. Spread dough over bottom of pie plate but not up sides. Bake until puffed and golden brown, about 30 minutes. Remove pastry from plate and place on wire rack to cool. Use cooled pastry immediately or wrap in plastic wrap and store (if stored, bring to room temperature before using).

To Prepare Filling and Serve: Just before serving, line pastry "bowl" with lettuce leaves and top lettuce with tomato slices. In separate bowl combine remaining ingredients except pepper rings; spread mixture evenly over tomato slices. Garnish with green pepper rings. To serve, cut pastry "bowl" into quarters.

Each serving is equivalent to: 2 servings Fats; ½ serving Bread; ½ Egg; 1½ servings Vegetables; 3 ounces Fish; 1½ teaspoons Limited Vegetables.

Per serving: 331 calories, 30 g protein, 18 g fat, 13 g carbohydrate, 1,116 mg sodium

Variations:

1. Substitute 12 ounces shelled and deveined cooked shrimp or skinned and boned drained canned salmon for the tuna.

Per serving with shrimp: 263 calories, 26 g protein, 12 g fat, 13 g carbohydrate, 555 mg sodium
With salmon: 292 calories, 28 g protein, 15 g fat, 13 g carbohydrate, 746 mg sodium

2. Substitute 12 ounces diced skinned cooked chicken or turkey for the tuna. Add 3 ounces Poultry to equivalent listing and omit Fish.

Per serving with chicken: 326 calories, 30 g protein, 17 g fat, 13 g carbohydrate, 509 mg sodium
With turkey: 307 calories, 30 g protein, 15 g fat, 13 g carbohydrate, 499 mg sodium

3. Substitute 6 hard-cooked eggs, diced, for the tuna. Change equivalent listing to 2 Eggs and omit Fish.

Per serving: 283 calories, 14 g protein, 19 g fat, 13 g carbohydrate, 540 mg sodium

TUNA–CHEESE GRILL
Limited Choice Plan
Makes 1 Midday or Evening Meal serving*

1 slice whole wheat bread, toasted
1 teaspoon reduced-calorie margarine
¼ medium tomato, sliced
1½ ounces drained canned tuna (water-packed), flaked

1 teaspoon reduced-calorie mayonnaise
½ teaspoon Dijon-style mustard
⅛ teaspoon salt
Dash pepper
1 ounce low-fat American cheese

Spread 1 side of toast with margarine and place, margarine-side down, on small baking sheet or piece of foil. Arrange tomato slices on toast and set aside.

In small bowl combine remaining ingredients except cheese; spoon mixture over tomato slices and top with cheese. Broil 3 inches from heat source until cheese melts and is lightly browned, 3 to 5 minutes.†

Each serving is equivalent to: 1 serving Bread; 1 serving Fats; ½ serving Vegetables; 1½ ounces Fish; 1 ounce Hard Cheese.

Per serving: 198 calories, 22 g protein, 6 g fat, 15 g carbohydrate, 1,367 mg sodium

* Men—For each serving use 2 ounces flaked tuna. Change equivalent listing to 4 ounces Fish.
† This can be broiled in a conventional broiler or toaster-oven.

TUNA MUFFIN
Full Choice Plan
Makes 1 Midday or Evening Meal serving

4 ounces drained canned tuna, flaked
2 teaspoons reduced-calorie mayonnaise

2 teaspoons pickle relish
1 refrigerated buttermilk flaky biscuit (unbaked), 1 ounce

1. Preheat oven to 350°F. In bowl combine first 3 ingredients and set aside.
2. Between 2 sheets of wax paper roll biscuit dough into a circle, about 6 inches in diameter.
3. Spray 6-ounce custard cup with nonstick cooking spray and line with biscuit dough.
4. Using the tines of a fork, gently press top edge of dough around top edge of custard cup; fill with tuna mixture.
5. Bake until biscuit is golden brown, about 20 minutes.

Each serving is equivalent to: 4 ounces Fish; 1 serving Fats; 2 servings Extras; 1 serving Bread.

Per serving: 342 calories, 35 g protein, 13 g fat, 18 g carbohydrate, 1,325 mg sodium

Variation: Substitute 4 ounces drained canned shrimp, crab meat, or skinned and boned salmon, or any flaked cooked white-fleshed fish for the tuna.

Per serving with shrimp: 250 calories, 30 g protein, 5 g fat, 19 g carbohydrate, 577 mg sodium
With crab meat: 233 calories, 22 g protein, 7 g fat, 20 g carbohydrate, 1,552 mg sodium
With salmon: 290 calories, 32 g protein, 10 g fat, 18 g carbohydrate, 832 mg sodium
With flounder: 348 calories, 36 g protein, 13 g fat, 18 g carbohydrate, 687 mg sodium

TUNA SALAD
No Choice Plan
Makes 1 Midday Meal serving*

¼ cup each finely diced celery and carrot
2 teaspoons lemon juice
2 teaspoons reduced-calorie mayonnaise
½ teaspoon each onion flakes and prepared brown mustard
¼ teaspoon salt
Dash pepper
3 ounces drained canned white-meat tuna (water-packed), flaked
2 iceberg or romaine lettuce leaves

In small bowl combine all ingredients except tuna and lettuce and let stand at room temperature for 15 minutes. Add tuna and mix well. If mixture is too dry, add 1 to 2 tablespoons water. Serve tuna salad on lettuce leaves.

Each serving is equivalent to: ½ serving Vegetables; 1 serving Fats; 3 ounces Fish. (See page 407 for Full Choice Plan adjustments.)

Per serving: 157 calories, 25 g protein, 3 g fat, 7 g carbohydrate, 1,409 mg sodium

Note: On the Full and Limited Choice Plans this recipe may be used at the Midday or Evening Meal.

* Men—Add 1 ounce flaked tuna to each portion of salad. Change equivalent listing to 4 ounces Fish.

TUNA SALAD SANDWICH
Full Choice Plan
Makes 1 Midday or Evening Meal serving

1 tablespoon reduced-calorie
  mayonnaise
½ teaspoon ketchup
⅛ teaspoon lemon juice
4 ounces drained canned tuna,
  flaked

2 teaspoons minced celery
1 teaspoon minced scallion (green
  onion)
Dash white pepper
2 slices enriched white bread,
  toasted

In small bowl mix together mayonnaise, ketchup, and lemon juice; add remaining ingredients except bread and stir to combine. Spread tuna salad on 1 slice toast; top with remaining slice to form a sandwich. Cut diagonally into triangles.

Each serving is equivalent to: 1½ servings Fats; ¼ serving Extras; 4 ounces Fish; 2 teaspoons Vegetables; 1 teaspoon Limited Vegetables; 2 servings Bread.

Per serving: 389 calories, 37 g protein, 14 g fat, 27 g carbohydrate, 1,255 mg sodium

TUNA-STUFFED TOMATO
Full Choice Plan
Makes 1 Midday or Evening Meal serving

1 tomato (about 6 ounces)
Dash salt
2 teaspoons finely diced onion
1 teaspoon finely diced celery
½ teaspoon Worcestershire sauce

¼ teaspoon thyme leaves
Dash pepper
4 ounces drained canned tuna
1 tablespoon plus 1½ teaspoons
  seasoned dried bread crumbs

Garnish
Parsley sprigs

1. Cut slice off top of tomato; remove and discard core, reserving slice.
2. Scoop out and reserve tomato pulp; sprinkle inside of tomato shell with salt and place, cut-side down, on paper towel to drain.
3. Chop pulp and transfer to small nonstick skillet. Add onion, celery, Worcestershire sauce, thyme, and pepper and cook over medium heat stirring occasionally, until all liquid evaporates.
4. Remove skillet from heat; add tuna and bread crumbs and mix well.
5. Preheat oven to 350°F. Spoon tuna mixture into tomato shell, packing firmly and mounding but being careful not to split tomato; top with reserved tomato slice.
6. Spray 6-ounce custard cup with nonstick cooking spray; set stuffed tomato into cup. Bake until stuffing appears firm and tomato skin starts to peel, about 20 minutes. Garnish with parsley before serving.

Each serving is equivalent to: 2½ servings Vegetables; 2 teaspoons Limited Vegetables; 4 ounces Fish; ½ serving Bread.

Per serving: 298 calories, 36 g protein, 10 g fat, 15 g carbohydrate, 1,117 mg sodium

Variations:
1. Substitute 4 ounces skinned and boned drained canned salmon for the tuna.

Per serving: 246 calories, 33 g protein, 7 g fat, 15 g carbohydrate, 623 mg sodium

2. Reduce fish to 2 ounces and, before baking, top stuffing with 1 ounce shredded Cheddar cheese. Proceed as directed. Add 1 ounce Hard Cheese to equivalent listing and reduce Fish to 2 ounces.

Per serving: 301 calories, 26 g protein, 15 g fat, 15 g carbohydrate, 839 mg sodium

3. Reduce fish to 2 ounces and bake as directed but reduce baking time by 5 minutes. Remove tomato slice; top stuffing with 1 poached egg and replace tomato slice. Garnish with parsley and serve. Add 1 Egg to equivalent listing and reduce Fish to 2 ounces.

Per serving: 262 calories, 25 g protein, 11 g fat, 15 g carbohydrate, 804 mg sodium

TUNA TACOS
Full Choice Plan
Makes 2 Midday or Evening Meal servings

2 teaspoons vegetable oil	4 ounces drained canned tuna,
½ cup sliced onion	flaked
2 garlic cloves, minced	2 corn tortillas (6-inch diameter
½ cup chopped tomatoes	each)
½ cup tomato sauce	2 ounces Cheddar cheese,
Dash each oregano leaves, salt,	shredded
pepper, and hot sauce	½ cup shredded lettuce

In 9-inch skillet heat oil; add onion and garlic and sauté until onion slices are translucent, about 5 minutes. Add tomatoes, tomato sauce, oregano, salt, pepper, and hot sauce. Cook, stirring occasionally, for 5 minutes. Stir in tuna and cook until heated through.

On baking sheet bake tortillas at 300°F. for 5 minutes. Remove from oven and immediately fold each tortilla to form a pocket. Fill each pocket with half of the tuna mixture. Top each portion of tuna with 1 ounce cheese and ¼ cup lettuce.

Each serving is equivalent to: 1 serving Fats; ¼ cup Limited Vegetables; 1 serving Vegetables; ½ serving Bonus; 2 ounces Fish; 1 serving Bread; 1 ounce Hard Cheese.

Per serving: 362 calories, 27 g protein, 20 g fat, 21 g carbohydrate, 997 mg sodium

Variation: Just before serving, top each Tuna Taco with 1 tablespoon plain unflavored yogurt. Add ⅛ serving Milk to equivalent listing.

Per serving: 371 calories, 27 g protein, 20 g fat, 22 g carbohydrate, 1,004 mg sodium

TUNA TURNOVER
Full Choice Plan
Makes 1 Midday or Evening Meal serving

1 refrigerated buttermilk flaky
   biscuit (unbaked), 1 ounce
2 ounces drained canned tuna,
   flaked

1 ounce Cheddar cheese, shredded
2 pimiento-stuffed green olives,
   chopped

1. Preheat oven to 350°F. Between 2 sheets of wax paper roll biscuit dough into a circle, about 6 inches in diameter.
2. In small bowl combine remaining ingredients, mixing well.
3. Mound tuna mixture onto half of biscuit circle but do not cover edge; fold remaining biscuit half over filling and, using the tines of a fork, press edges together to seal. Transfer turnover to baking sheet.
4. Bake until turnover is golden brown, 10 to 12 minutes.

Each serving is equivalent to: 1 serving Bread; 2 ounces Fish; 1 ounce Hard Cheese; 1 serving Extras.

Per serving: 319 calories, 26 g protein, 17 g fat, 14 g carbohydrate, 1,163 mg sodium

Variation: Substitute 2 ounces drained canned shrimp, crab meat, or skinned and boned salmon for the tuna.

Per serving with shrimp: 273 calories, 23 g protein, 13 g fat, 14 g carbohydrate, 789 mg
   sodium
With crab meat: 264 calories, 19 g protein, 14 g fat, 14 g carbohydrate, 1,276 mg sodium
With salmon: 292 calories, 24 g protein, 16 g fat, 14 g carbohydrate, 916 mg sodium

Legumes

This nourishing food group, valued since biblical times, includes dry beans, peas, lentils, and tofu—the "chameleon" of legumes because it takes on the taste of whatever it's combined with. Modern-day nutrition-wise cooks know that legumes are economical and protein-rich. They are very versatile, too, appearing on menus from first course to last—from warming soups like Navy Bean to cooling desserts like Fruited Tofu or Tofu "Cheesecake."

Guidelines for Using Legumes (Full and Limited Choice Plans)

1. Amounts (drained cooked weight):

| | Morning Meal | | |
	Beans, Lentils, and Peas	Tofu (Soybean Curd)	Tempeh (Fermented Soybean Cake)
Women and Youth	3 ounces	4 ounces	1½ ounces
Men	4 ounces	5 ounces	2 ounces

| | Midday and Evening Meals | | |
	Beans, Lentils, and Peas	Tofu (Soybean Curd)	Tempeh (Fermented Soybean Cake)
Women and Youth	6 ounces	8 ounces	3 ounces
Men	8 ounces	10 ounces	4 ounces

2. Legumes may be consumed at mealtime *only* and may be split with items from the Eggs, Cheese, Peanut Butter (Full Choice Plan only), Poultry, Veal, and Game, and Meat Group categories.

3. To increase the protein quality of the meal, Legume meals should be planned to include poultry, meat, fish, egg, cheese, milk, a Bread item, or grain from the Bread Substitutes category.

4. Ranges are not given for Legumes since the serving sizes reflect the amounts necessary for adequate protein intake.

5. Select fresh, frozen, canned, or dry legumes, packed without sugar.

6. Do *not* use textured vegetable protein products.

7. The following items may be used as Legumes selections:

beans:
  black (turtle or black turtle)
  broad
  chick-peas (garbanzo beans)
  fava
  great northern
  kidney:
    red
    white (cannellini beans)
  lima:
    large (butter)
    small (baby)
  navy (pea beans)
  pigeon
  pink
  pinto
  red
  Roman
  soy
  white

lentils

peas:
  black-eyed (cow peas)
  split (green and yellow)

tempeh (fermented soybean cake)

tofu (soybean curd)

8. Whenever possible, weigh legumes after cooking (except canned legumes). Cooked and canned legumes should be well drained before weighing; the liquid may be consumed.

9. As a "rule of thumb," 2 ounces of dry beans, lentils, or peas will yield 6 ounces cooked legumes.

10. Cooking Procedures—see below.

Tips for Preparing Dry Legumes
Beans

Beans must be soaked before cooking in order to replace the water lost in the drying process. Before soaking, sort beans carefully and discard any foreign particles or broken or discolored beans. Place beans in colander or strainer and rinse under running cold water until water runs clear. To soak, use one of the following methods:

Quick-Soak Method—In saucepan generously cover sorted and rinsed beans with water (for 8 ounces of beans use 3 cups to 1 quart water). Bring to a boil and cook for 2 minutes; remove from heat and let stand for about 1 hour.* Drain and cook as directed (soaking liquid may be used for cooking).

* Increase soaking and cooking times at high altitudes or if using hard water.

Overnight-Soak Method—In large container generously cover sorted and rinsed beans with cold water (for 8 ounces of beans use 3 cups to 1 quart water). Let stand overnight or at least 6 hours.* Drain and cook as directed (soaking liquid may be used for cooking).

Alternate-Soak Method—Many people experience digestive discomfort from beans. In an effort to minimize or eliminate this problem, new methods of preparation are under investigation. It has been indicated that beans soaked according to the following method produce up to 50 percent less gas than beans soaked the traditional way:

Follow the Quick-Soak Method above but cook for 3 minutes; let stand for about 1 hour,* then pour off soak water and rinse beans well. Cook as directed (do not use soaking liquid for cooking).

To Cook Soaked Beans—During cooking, beans will expand 2½ to 3 times their original size, so be sure to use a pan large enough to accommodate them. Place soaked beans in saucepan and add enough salted water to cover beans by about 1 inch (use 1 teaspoon salt per 8 ounces beans); bring to a boil. Reduce heat, partially cover, and simmer (simmering helps keep skins from bursting) until beans are tender, usually 1½ to 2 hours,* adding additional hot water if liquid reduces. Stir occasionally during the cooking process to help prevent sticking. Beans are done when they are tender but still hold their shape. Drain before weighing. Cooked beans freeze well, so cook enough to have extra servings on hand.

Lentils

Unlike other legumes, lentils do not need to be soaked before cooking. Therefore, they are generally ready to be eaten in much less time than beans and whole dry peas. Sort and rinse lentils. To cook, in saucepan generously cover lentils with salted water (for 1 pound of lentils use about 1½ quarts water and 2 teaspoons salt); bring to a boil. Reduce heat and simmer until tender, 20 to 30 minutes. Drain before weighing.

Peas

Dry peas are available whole and split, and come in green and yellow varieties. Generally, as there is only a slight difference in flavor, green peas can be substituted for the yellow, and vice versa. Prepare, soak, and cook dry *whole* peas following the same methods

* Increase soaking and cooking times at high altitudes or if using hard water.

given for beans; prepare and cook dry *split* peas following the same method given for lentils.

Chick-peas are actually garbanzo beans and should be prepared in the same manner as other dry beans.

LENTIL SOUP
Full Choice Plan
Makes 2 Midday or Evening Meal servings,* about 2 cups each

4 ounces uncooked lentils
3 cups water
½ cup each diced onion, carrot, and celery
½ cup tomato juice
2 teaspoons olive oil

1 garlic clove, minced
½ teaspoon salt
Dash pepper
2 teaspoons chopped fresh parsley
2 teaspoons grated Parmesan cheese (optional)

Sort and rinse lentils. In 1½- to 2-quart saucepan combine lentils and water. Add vegetables, tomato juice, oil, and garlic; bring to a boil. Reduce heat, cover, and simmer until lentils are tender, about 45 minutes. Add salt and pepper. Serve sprinkled with parsley and, if desired, cheese.

Each serving is equivalent to: 6 ounces Legumes; ¼ cup Limited Vegetables; 1 serving Vegetables; ¼ serving Bonus; 1 serving Fats; 1 serving Extras (optional).

Per serving: 281 calories, 16 g protein, 6 g fat, 45 g carbohydrate, 730 mg sodium
With Parmesan cheese: 289 calories, 17 g protein, 6 g fat, 45 g carbohydrate, 762 mg sodium

* Men—One serving provides ¾ of a meal. Supplement with an additional ¼ serving of Protein at the Midday or Evening Meal.

MINESTRONE SOUP
Full Choice Plan
Makes 2 Midday or Evening Meal servings, ½ meal each;* supplement as required

This recipe yields about 2 cups per serving.

2 teaspoons olive oil
2 cups shredded green cabbage
½ cup sliced onion
2 teaspoons minced fresh garlic
1½ cups Beef Broth (see page 401)
1 cup chopped canned tomatoes
1 cup water
½ cup each sliced carrot and celery
6 ounces drained canned white kidney beans (cannellini beans)

½ cup diced zucchini
1 tablespoon chopped fresh basil or 2 teaspoons dried basil leaves
½ teaspoon salt
Dash pepper
⅔ cup cooked enriched small macaroni shells or elbow macaroni
1 tablespoon chopped fresh parsley
2 teaspoons grated Parmesan cheese

In 2½- to 3-quart saucepan heat oil; add cabbage, onion, and garlic and cook over medium heat, stirring occasionally, about 10 minutes. Add broth, tomatoes, water, carrot, and celery; cook 15 to 20 minutes longer.

Add beans, zucchini, basil, salt, and pepper and simmer until vegetables are tender, about 15 minutes. Add macaroni and cook until heated. Sprinkle with parsley and cheese before serving.

Each serving is equivalent to: 1 serving Fats; 4½ servings Vegetables; ¼ cup Limited Vegetables; 2 servings Extras; 3 ounces Legumes; ½ serving Bread Substitutes.

Per serving: 304 calories, 14 g protein, 7 g fat, 51 g carbohydrate, 815 mg sodium (estimated)

* Men—Add 1 ounce heated drained canned white kidney beans to each portion of soup. Change equivalent listing to 4 ounces Legumes.

NAVY BEAN SOUP
Limited Choice Plan
Makes 2 Midday or Evening Meal servings, ½ meal each; supplement as required*
This recipe yields about 1¼ cups soup per serving.

½ cup each finely diced carrot and celery
1 tablespoon onion flakes
½ teaspoon minced fresh garlic
1½ cups boiling water
¾ cup tomato juice

6 ounces cooked navy (pea) beans
2 teaspoons olive oil
Dash each salt and pepper
1 tablespoon chopped fresh parsley
2 teaspoons grated Parmesan cheese

In 1½- to 2-quart saucepan combine carrot, celery, onion flakes, and garlic; add water and tomato juice and bring to a boil. Reduce heat and simmer until vegetables are tender, about 15 minutes. Add beans, oil, salt, and pepper; cook until thoroughly heated, about 5 minutes longer. Serve sprinkled with parsley and cheese.

Each serving is equivalent to: ½ serving Vegetables; ½ serving Bonus; 3 ounces Legumes; 1 serving Fats; 1 serving Extras. (See page 407 for Full Choice Plan adjustments.)

Per serving: 186 calories, 9 g protein, 6 g fat, 27 g carbohydrate, 334 mg sodium (estimated)

* Men—Add 1 ounce heated drained canned navy (pea) beans to each portion of soup. Change equivalent listing to 4 ounces Legumes.

QUICK THREE-BEAN SOUP
Full Choice Plan
Makes 4 Midday or Evening Meal servings, about 1¼ cups each*

12 ounces drained canned red kidney beans, reserve liquid
6 ounces drained canned chick-peas (garbanzo beans), reserve liquid
6 ounces drained canned small white beans, reserve liquid

2 cups frozen Italian green beans
2 medium tomatoes, diced
1 cup diced zucchini
2 tablespoons diced onion
1 garlic clove, minced
½ teaspoon basil leaves
Dash each salt and pepper

In 2-quart saucepan combine 1 cup liquid reserved from canned legumes with remaining ingredients; bring to a boil. Reduce heat and simmer until vegetables are tender, 10 to 15 minutes.

Each serving is equivalent to: 6 ounces Legumes; 2½ servings Vegetables; 1½ teaspoons Limited Vegetables.

Per serving: 252 calories, 15 g protein, 2 g fat, 46 g carbohydrate, 415 mg sodium (estimated)

* Men—One serving provides ¾ of a meal. Supplement with an additional ¼ serving of Protein at the Midday or Evening Meal.

SPLIT PEA SOUP
Full Choice Plan
Makes 2 Midday or Evening Meal servings,* about 1½ cups each

4 ounces uncooked green split peas
1 quart water
½ cup each chopped onion, carrot, and celery
2 packets instant chicken broth and seasoning mix

1 whole clove
1 small bay leaf
Dash each salt and pepper
2 teaspoons imitation bacon bits

1. Sort and rinse peas.
2. In 2-quart saucepan combine all ingredients except salt, pepper, and bacon bits; bring to a boil. Reduce heat and simmer until peas are soft, about 45 minutes.
3. Cool slightly; remove and discard clove and bay leaf. Pour 1½ cups soup into blender container or work bowl of food processor and process just until vegetables are finely chopped (*do not puree*). Transfer mixture to a 1½-quart bowl.
4. Repeat Step 3 with remaining soup, 1½ cups at a time, until all soup has been processed.
5. Pour soup back into saucepan and heat. Stir in salt and pepper. Serve each portion sprinkled with 1 teaspoon bacon bits.

Each serving is equivalent to: 6 ounces Legumes; ¼ cup Limited Vegetables; 1 serving Vegetables; 2 servings Extras.

Per serving: 251 calories, 17 g protein, 1 g fat, 46 g carbohydrate, 1,070 mg sodium

* Men—One serving provides ¾ of a meal. Supplement with an additional ¼ serving of Protein at the Midday or Evening Meal.

BEAN 'N' CHEESE SALAD
Limited Choice Plan
Makes 1 Midday or Evening Meal serving*

3 ounces drained canned small white beans
½ cup cooked sliced carrot
½ cup sliced yellow summer squash or zucchini, blanched
1 ounce low-fat hard cheese, cut into strips

2 tablespoons plain unflavored yogurt
2 tablespoons lemon juice
1 teaspoon onion flakes
½ teaspoon basil leaves
Dash each salt and white pepper
2 iceberg or romaine lettuce leaves

Garnish
1 radish, thinly sliced

In bowl combine all ingredients except lettuce and garnish; toss well. Cover and chill at least 1 hour. Toss again before serving. Serve on lettuce leaves and garnish with radish slices.

Each serving is equivalent to: 3 ounces Legumes; 2 servings Vegetables; 1 ounce Hard Cheese; ¼ serving Milk. (See page 407 for Full Choice Plan adjustments.)

Per serving: 213 calories, 16 g protein, 4 g fat, 32 g carbohydrate, 623 mg sodium (estimated)

* Men—Add 1 ounce chilled drained canned small white beans to each portion of salad. Change equivalent listing to 4 ounces Legumes.

MARINATED CHICK-PEAS
Full Choice Plan
Makes 4 Midday or Evening Meal servings, ½ meal each;* supplement as required

12 ounces drained canned chick-peas (garbanzo beans)
2 tablespoons red wine vinegar
2 teaspoons minced onion
1 teaspoon minced fresh basil
   or ¼ teaspoon dried basil leaves

1 teaspoon olive oil
1 garlic clove, minced
½ teaspoon salt
Dash pepper

Place chick-peas in medium bowl and set aside. In measuring cup or small bowl combine remaining ingredients; pour over chick-peas and toss gently to coat. Refrigerate for at least 4 hours before serving.

Each serving is equivalent to: 3 ounces Legumes; ½ teaspoon Limited Vegetables; ¼ serving Fats.

Per serving: 116 calories, 6 g protein, 3 g fat, 18 g carbohydrate, 278 mg sodium (estimated)

* Men—Add 1 ounce chilled drained canned chick-peas to each portion of Marinated Chick-Peas. Change equivalent listing to 4 ounces Legumes.

QUICK GARBANZO BEAN SALAD
Limited Choice Plan
Makes 2 Midday or Evening Meal servings, ½ meal each;* supplement as required

6 ounces drained canned chick-peas (garbanzo beans)
½ cup each chopped celery, tomato, and pared cucumber
2 tablespoons wine vinegar
1 tablespoon lemon juice
1 tablespoon chopped fresh parsley
2 teaspoons olive or vegetable oil

½ teaspoon minced fresh garlic or ⅛ teaspoon garlic powder
¼ teaspoon prepared brown mustard
Dash each salt, pepper, and oregano leaves
Dash artificial sweetener (optional)

In 1-quart bowl combine all ingredients. Cover and chill, tossing occasionally.

Each serving is equivalent to: 3 ounces Legumes; 1 serving Vegetables; 1 serving Fats. (See page 407 for Full Choice Plan adjustments.)

Per serving: 172 calories, 7 g protein, 6 g fat, 24 g carbohydrate, 123 mg sodium (estimated)

* Men—Add 1 ounce chilled drained canned chick-peas to each portion of salad. Change equivalent listing to 4 ounces Legumes.

SPECKLED BUTTER BEAN SALAD

Full Choice Plan
Makes 2 Midday or Evening Meal servings, ½ meal each;* supplement as required

6 ounces cooked frozen speckled
    butter beans (cooked according
    to package directions)
½ cup shredded carrot
¼ cup thinly sliced scallions
    (green onions)
2 tablespoons chopped fresh
    parsley

2 tablespoons lemon juice
2 teaspoons vegetable oil
1 teaspoon salt
1 garlic clove, minced
⅛ teaspoon pepper
4 cups spinach leaves, torn

In bowl combine all ingredients except spinach. Cover and chill for about 1 hour.

Line a serving bowl with spinach; toss chilled bean mixture and spoon onto spinach.

Each serving is equivalent to: 3 ounces Legumes; 4½ servings Vegetables; ⅛ cup Limited Vegetables; 1 serving Fats.

Per serving: 211 calories, 11 g protein, 6 g fat, 32 g carbohydrate, 1,196 mg sodium

* Men—Add 1 ounce chilled cooked speckled butter beans to each portion of salad. Change equivalent listing to 4 ounces Legumes.

MEXICAN-STYLE BEAN DIP

Full Choice Plan
Makes 4 Midday or Evening Meal servings*

12 ounces drained canned pink
    beans, reserve 2 tablespoons
    liquid
1 medium garlic clove, crushed

¼ teaspoon each chili powder
    and ground cumin
4 ounces sharp Cheddar cheese,
    shredded
2 tablespoons vegetable oil

In blender container or work bowl of food processor combine beans, reserved 2 tablespoons liquid, garlic, chili powder, and cumin; process until smooth.

Transfer bean mixture to 1-quart saucepan; add cheese and cook over low heat, stirring constantly, until cheese is melted. Stir in oil and serve.

Each serving is equivalent to: 3 ounces Legumes; 1 ounce Hard Cheese; 1½ servings Fats.

Per serving: 284 calories, 14 g protein, 17 g fat, 20 g carbohydrate, 254 mg sodium (estimated)

* Men—One serving provides ⅞ of a meal. Supplement with an additional ⅛ serving of Protein at the Midday or Evening Meal.

SPICY BEAN SPREAD
Full Choice Plan
Makes 1 Midday or Evening Meal serving*

6 ounces drained canned pinto beans, reserve 1 tablespoon liquid
2 tablespoons parsley sprigs
2 tablespoons chopped onion
2 teaspoons lemon juice
1 teaspoon sesame seed, toasted

1 teaspoon each olive oil and mayonnaise
¼ teaspoon each basil leaves and chopped fresh garlic
⅛ teaspoon ground cumin
Dash ground coriander
Dash each salt and pepper

In blender container or work bowl of food processor combine reserved liquid with remaining ingredients except salt and pepper; process until smooth. Transfer mixture to a bowl and season with salt and pepper.

Each serving is equivalent to: 6 ounces Legumes; ⅛ cup Limited Vegetables; 2 servings Extras; 2 servings Fats.

Per serving: 305 calories, 14 g protein, 11 g fat, 41 g carbohydrate, 168 mg sodium (estimated)

* Men—One serving provides ¾ of a meal. Supplement with an additional ¼ serving of Protein at the Midday or Evening Meal.

BROCCOLI–CHICK CASSEROLE
Limited Choice Plan
Makes 2 Midday or Evening Meal servings*

6 ounces drained canned chick-peas (garbanzo beans)
½ cup drained canned pimientos, diced
2 teaspoons onion flakes
¼ teaspoon each salt and garlic powder
Dash pepper

3½ cups broccoli florets, blanched
2 ounces low-fat American cheese, cut into strips
2 teaspoons margarine
2 slices enriched white bread, toasted and made into crumbs
2 teaspoons grated Parmesan cheese

Preheat oven to 350°F. In bowl combine chick-peas, pimientos, onion flakes, salt, garlic powder, and pepper. Spray an oblong 1- or 1½-quart casserole with nonstick cooking spray; arrange broccoli in casserole and spread chick-pea mixture over florets. Top with American cheese and set aside.

In small skillet melt margarine; add bread crumbs and stir until crumbs absorb margarine. Remove from heat, add Parmesan cheese, and toss to combine. Sprinkle crumb mixture evenly over American cheese. Bake until cheese melts and casserole is thoroughly heated, 25 to 30 minutes.

Each serving is equivalent to: 3 ounces Legumes; 4 servings Vegetables; 1 ounce Hard Cheese; 1 serving Fats; 1 serving Bread; 1 serving Extras.

Per serving: 357 calories, 25 g protein, 10 g fat, 49 g carbohydrate, 979 mg sodium (estimated)

* Men—One serving provides ⅞ of a meal. Supplement with an additional ⅛ serving of Protein at the Midday or Evening Meal.

KIDNEY BEANS CREOLE
Limited Choice Plan
*Makes 1 Midday or Evening Meal serving**

6 ounces drained canned red kidney beans
½ cup canned crushed tomatoes
⅓ cup plus 2 teaspoons mixed vegetable juice

¼ cup each diced celery and green bell pepper
1 tablespoon onion flakes
⅛ teaspoon each powdered mustard and garlic powder
Dash each salt and pepper

Preheat oven to 350°F. In small bowl combine all ingredients. Transfer to shallow 1-quart casserole. Cover and bake for 30 minutes; uncover and bake 15 minutes longer.

Each serving is equivalent to: 6 ounces Legumes; 1½ servings Vegetables; ½ serving Bonus. (See page 407 for Full Choice Plan adjustments.)

Per serving: 261 calories, 16 g protein, 1 g fat, 49 g carbohydrate, 517 mg sodium (estimated)

* Men—One serving provides ¾ of a meal. Supplement with an additional ¼ serving of Protein at the Midday or Evening Meal.

VEGETARIAN ZUCCHINI CASSEROLE
Full Choice Plan
*Makes 1 Midday or Evening Meal serving**

2 medium zucchini, about 5 ounces each
3 ounces drained canned red kidney beans
¼ cup cooked enriched rice
1 tablespoon finely diced carrot
1 tablespoon chopped scallion (green onion), green portion only

¼ teaspoon salt
Dash each oregano leaves and pepper
1 ounce sharp Cheddar cheese, shredded
2 teaspoons reduced-calorie margarine
1 tablespoon plus 1½ teaspoons plain dried bread crumbs

Garnish
Chopped fresh parsley

1. In deep 9-inch skillet bring to a boil enough water to cover zucchini. Add zucchini and cook for 5 minutes; remove from water and cool.
2. Cut each zucchini in half lengthwise and scoop out pulp, reserving shells. Set shells, cut-side down, on paper towels to drain.
3. Transfer pulp to a sieve and, using the back of a spoon, press to remove moisture.
4. Mince pulp and, in bowl, combine with beans, rice, vegetables, and seasonings.
5. Preheat oven to 350°F. Stuff each zucchini shell with ¼ of bean mixture and place in shallow 1-quart casserole; sprinkle with cheese and set aside.
6. In small skillet melt margarine; add bread crumbs and cook, stirring constantly, until crumbs absorb margarine and are browned, about 3 minutes.
7. Sprinkle each stuffed zucchini half with ¼ of the crumb mixture and bake for 20 to 25 minutes. Garnish with parsley before serving.

Each serving is equivalent to: 4⅛ servings Vegetables; 3 ounces Legumes; ½ serving Bread Substitutes; 1 tablespoon Limited Vegetables; 1 ounce Hard Cheese; 1 serving Fats; ½ serving Bread.

Per serving: 395 calories, 19 g protein, 14 g fat, 49 g carbohydrate, 88 mg sodium (estimated)

* Men—For each serving use 1¼ ounces shredded Cheddar cheese. Change equivalent listing to 1¼ ounces Hard Cheese.

EGGPLANT ROLLS
Limited Choice Plan
Makes 2 Midday or Evening Meal servings*

Delicious with a mixed green salad.

1 small eggplant, about 12 ounces
6 ounces drained canned chick-
   peas (garbanzo beans), mashed
½ cup finely diced broccoli stems,
   blanched
⅓ cup low-fat cottage cheese
1 tablespoon chopped fresh parsley
1 teaspoon onion flakes

Dash each salt, pepper, and garlic
   powder
½ cup canned crushed tomatoes
2 teaspoons grated Parmesan
   cheese
1 ounce low-fat American cheese,
   shredded

1. Preheat oven to 400°F. Cut stem and very thin slice from top of eggplant, then cut eggplant in half lengthwise; starting from cut side and slicing lengthwise, cut three ¼-inch-thick slices (about 1 ounce each) from each half. Reserve remaining eggplant for use at another time.
2. On nonstick baking sheet bake eggplant slices for 10 minutes on each side; remove from oven and let cool slightly. Reduce oven temperature to 350°F.

3. While eggplant is cooling, in bowl combine chick-peas, broccoli, cottage cheese, parsley, and seasonings; mix thoroughly.

4. Spread ⅙ of bean mixture (about 1 heaping tablespoon) on each eggplant slice and starting from narrow end, roll slice to enclose filling. Place rolls, seam-side down, in shallow 1-quart casserole; top with crushed tomatoes and sprinkle with Parmesan cheese.

5. Bake Eggplant Rolls for 30 minutes. Sprinkle with American cheese and continue baking until cheese is melted.

Each serving is equivalent to: 2⅛ servings Vegetables; 3 ounces Legumes; ⅙ cup Soft Cheese; 1 serving Extras; ½ ounce Hard Cheese.

Per serving: 210 calories, 18 g protein, 4 g fat, 29 g carbohydrate, 566 mg sodium (estimated)

* Men—One serving provides ⅞ of a meal. Supplement with an additional ⅛ serving of Protein at the Midday or Evening Meal.

STUFFED LETTUCE LEAVES
Limited Choice Plan
Makes 1 Midday or Evening Meal serving*

3 iceberg lettuce leaves	⅛ teaspoon salt
3 ounces drained canned white	Dash ground red pepper (optional)
kidney beans (cannellini beans)	½ cup canned crushed tomatoes
2 tablespoons plus 2 teaspoons	1 teaspoon grated Parmesan
low-fat cottage cheese	cheese
1 teaspoon onion flakes	½ ounce low-fat American cheese,
½ teaspoon oregano leaves	cut into strips

1. Rinse lettuce leaves but do not dry; with water still clinging to leaves, place on paper towel and chill in freezer for 10 minutes (this softens the leaves, making them easy to roll).

2. Preheat oven to 400°F. In small bowl combine beans, cottage cheese, onion flakes, oregano, salt, and red pepper if desired.

3. Spoon ⅓ of bean mixture onto center of each lettuce leaf; fold sides of leaf over mixture and, starting from core end, roll to enclose filling.

4. Place stuffed leaves, seam-side down, in 1¾-cup casserole; top with tomatoes and bake for 30 minutes.

5. Remove casserole from oven; sprinkle stuffed leaves with Parmesan cheese, then top with American cheese. Return to oven and bake until cheese is melted and golden brown.

Each serving is equivalent to: 3 ounces Legumes; ⅙ cup Soft Cheese; 1 serving Vegetables; 1 serving Extras; ½ ounce Hard Cheese. (See page 407 for Full Choice Plan adjustments.)

Per serving: 190 calories, 17 g protein, 3 g fat, 26 g carbohydrate, 852 mg sodium (estimated)

* Men—For each serving use ¾ ounce low-fat American cheese. Change equivalent listing to ¾ ounce Hard Cheese.

TEMPEH (FERMENTED SOYBEAN CAKE)

Tempeh is a popular Indonesian food, usually made from soybeans (although tempeh is occasionally made from seeds, cereal grains, and other legumes, the product used in this book is made from soybeans). Its flavor, meatlike texture, convenience, and versatility make it suitable for many Western-style recipes.

Presently in limited distribution in the United States, tempeh's popularity is growing. It can be purchased in health food stores in some areas; if not yet available in your area, you will probably begin to notice it in the near future.

Store tempeh in a plastic bag, plastic wrap, or airtight container in the refrigerator (below 40°F.) for 2 to 3 days.

TEMPEH MARINARA
Full Choice Plan
Makes 4 Midday or Evening Meal servings*

¼ cup reduced-calorie margarine
¼ cup chopped onion
1 small garlic clove, minced
12 ounces tempeh (fermented soybean cake), cut into 1-inch-wide strips
2 cups chopped canned tomatoes
½ cup tomato puree
½ teaspoon each basil leaves and salt
¼ teaspoon each pepper and oregano leaves

In 9-inch nonstick skillet heat margarine until bubbly; add onion and garlic and sauté until onion is tender. Add tempeh and sauté until lightly browned on all sides. Stir in remaining ingredients. Reduce heat, cover, and simmer about 15 minutes to blend flavors.

Each serving is equivalent to: 1½ servings Fats; 1 tablespoon Limited Vegetables; 3 ounces Legumes (tempeh); 1 serving Vegetables; ¼ serving Bonus.

Per serving: 268 calories, 19 g protein, 16 g fat, 15 g carbohydrate, 689 mg sodium

* Men—One serving provides ¾ of a meal. Supplement with an additional ¼ serving of Protein at the Midday or Evening Meal.

TEMPEH–VEGETABLE PATTIES
Full Choice Plan
Makes 2 Midday or Evening Meal servings, 1¼ meals each*

1 tablespoon vegetable oil, divided
¼ cup diced scallions (green onions)
6 ounces tempeh (fermented soybean cake), crumbled
1 small garlic clove, minced
1½ medium carrots, cut into pieces
¼ cup cut green beans
1 medium celery rib, cut into pieces

3 tablespoons plain dried bread crumbs, divided
1 large egg
1½ teaspoons Worcestershire sauce
¼ teaspoon salt
⅛ teaspoon pepper
Sweet Mustard Sauce (see page 381)

1. In small skillet heat 1 teaspoon oil; add scallions and sauté for 2 minutes. Add tempeh and garlic and sauté until lightly browned; transfer to medium bowl and set aside.
2. In work bowl of food processor, using the grating disk, grate carrots and green beans. Transfer vegetables to bowl containing tempeh mixture.
3. Grate celery and transfer to a sieve; using the back of a spoon, squeeze out liquid and add celery to bowl.
4. Add 2 tablespoons bread crumbs and the egg, Worcestershire sauce, salt, and pepper to tempeh mixture; mix well and form into 4 patties.
5. On a sheet of wax paper spread remaining tablespoon bread crumbs; coat both sides of each patty with crumbs, being sure to use all of the crumbs. Transfer to a plate, cover, and chill for 30 minutes.
6. In 9-inch skillet heat remaining 2 teaspoons oil; add patties and sauté, turning once, until browned on both sides. Serve with Sweet Mustard Sauce.

Each serving is equivalent to: 1½ servings Fats; ⅛ cup Limited Vegetables; 3 ounces Legumes (tempeh); 2 servings Vegetables; ½ serving Bread; ½ Egg; Sweet Mustard Sauce (see page 381).

Per serving: 387 calories, 24 g protein, 21 g fat, 26 g carbohydrate, 659 mg sodium

* Omit ¼ serving of Protein at the Midday or Evening Meal. Men—One serving provides 1 Midday or Evening Meal serving; do not omit Protein at either meal.

TOFU (SOYBEAN CURD)
Tofu, a cheeselike product made from the liquid extracted from soybeans, has much the same nutritional importance to people of the Orient as dairy products, eggs, poultry, and meat have to people of the Western world. Over the years, tofu's popularity in the West has been growing; note its appearance in many supermarkets and grocery stores, as well as in various cookbooks.

As is evidenced by the recipes that follow, tofu is quite versatile and can easily be used in many types of dishes. It is relatively bland and takes on the flavor of the foods with which it is combined.

Store tofu in water to cover, in a covered container in the refrigerator, for up to 1 week. To maintain freshness, change the water daily.

GRILLED TOFU AND CHEESE SANDWICH
Full Choice Plan
Makes 1 Midday or Evening Meal serving*

¼ teaspoon Dijon-style mustard†
1 slice rye bread
4 ounces thinly sliced tofu
  (soybean curd)
½ teaspoon teriyaki or soy sauce

1 tablespoon thinly sliced scallion
  (green onion)
4 thin tomato slices
1 ounce sharp Cheddar cheese,
  shredded

Spread mustard on bread; top with tofu slices and sprinkle tofu with teriyaki or soy sauce. Top tofu with scallion, then tomato slices and shredded cheese. Place on piece of foil or in broiler pan and broil about 5 inches from heat source until cheese melts and is golden brown, 3 to 5 minutes.

Each serving is equivalent to: 1 serving Bread; 4 ounces Legumes (tofu); 1 tablespoon Limited Vegetables; ½ serving Vegetables; 1 ounce Hard Cheese.

Per serving: 271 calories, 19 g protein, 15 g fat, 19 g carbohydrate, 462 mg sodium

* Men—For each serving use 5 ounces thinly sliced tofu. Change equivalent listing to 5 ounces Legumes (tofu).

† If you like a spicy treat, increase mustard to ½ teaspoon. Add 1 calorie and 16 mg sodium to nutrition figures.

VEGETABLE–TOFU STIR-FRY
Full Choice Plan
Makes 4 Midday or Evening Meal servings, ½ meal each;* supplement as required

2 tablespoons plus 2 teaspoons dry
  sherry
2 teaspoons cornstarch
1 tablespoon soy sauce
1 teaspoon each granulated sugar
  and salt
½ teaspoon grated pared ginger
  root
1 tablespoon plus 1 teaspoon
  vegetable oil

1 pound tofu (soybean curd), cut
  into ½-inch cubes
1 cup diagonally sliced carrots,
  blanched
1 cup diagonally sliced zucchini
1 cup diced mushrooms
1 cup trimmed Chinese pea pods
  (stem ends and strings removed)
½ cup sliced scallions (green
  onions)

1. In small bowl combine sherry and cornstarch and stir to dissolve; stir in soy sauce, sugar, salt, and ginger root and set aside.

2. In 12-inch nonstick skillet or wok heat oil; add tofu and cook, stirring quickly and frequently, for 2 to 3 minutes. Remove tofu from skillet and set aside.

3. Add carrots to skillet and stir-fry for 3 minutes; add remaining vegetables and continue to stir-fry until vegetables are tender-crisp, 4 to 5 minutes longer.

4. Stir in sherry mixture and cook, stirring constantly, until thickened.

5. Return tofu to skillet. Cook until tofu is heated through, 2 to 3 minutes.

Each serving is equivalent to: 2 servings Extras; 1 serving Fats; 4 ounces Legumes (tofu); 1½ servings Vegetables; ¼ cup plus 2 tablespoons Limited Vegetables.

Per serving: 195 calories, 12 g protein, 10 g fat, 16 g carbohydrate, 895 mg sodium

* Men—Add 1 ounce heated tofu cubes to each portion of Vegetable–Tofu Stir-Fry. Change equivalent listing to 5 ounces Legumes (tofu).

FRUITED TOFU DESSERT

Limited Choice Plan
Makes 1 Midday or Evening Meal serving, ¼ meal; supplement as required*

½ medium banana, peeled and
   sliced
1½ teaspoons lemon juice,
   divided
2 ounces tofu (soybean curd)

1 tablespoon thawed frozen
   concentrated orange juice
   (no sugar added)
½ teaspoon honey
¼ teaspoon vanilla extract

1. In small bowl toss banana slices with ½ teaspoon lemon juice and set aside.

2. In blender container or work bowl of food processor combine tofu, orange juice, remaining 1 teaspoon lemon juice, honey, and vanilla and process until smooth.

3. Stop motor and, using a rubber scraper, scrape mixture down from sides of container; process to combine.

4. Pour half of tofu mixture into a dessert dish; top with half of the banana slices and repeat layers. Serve immediately or cover and refrigerate until ready to use.

Each serving is equivalent to: 1½ servings Fruits; 2 ounces Legumes (tofu); 1 serving Extras.

Per serving: 139 calories, 6 g protein, 3 g fat, 25 g carbohydrate, 5 mg sodium

* Men—For each serving use 2½ ounces tofu. Change equivalent listing to 2½ ounces Legumes (tofu).

TOFU "CHEESECAKE"

Full Choice Plan
Makes 8 Midday or Evening Meal servings, ¼ meal each;* supplement as required

Crust

16 graham crackers (2½-inch
   squares), made into fine crumbs

⅓ cup reduced-calorie margarine,
   melted

Filling

1 pound tofu (soybean curd)
½ cup canned crushed pineapple
   (no sugar added)
¼ cup thawed frozen
   concentrated orange juice
   (no sugar added)

1 tablespoon vanilla extract
1 tablespoon honey
2 teaspoons cornstarch
1 teaspoon lemon juice

Topping

1 medium kiwi fruit, pared and cut
   into thin slices

To Prepare Crust: Preheat oven to 325°F. In bowl combine graham cracker crumbs with margarine and mix thoroughly. Using the back of a spoon, press crumb mixture over bottom and up sides of a 9-inch glass pie plate. Bake until crisp and brown, about 15 minutes. Transfer pie plate to wire rack to cool.

To Prepare Filling: In work bowl of food processor or blender container process tofu until creamy. Add pineapple, orange juice, vanilla, and honey and process until smooth. In small cup add cornstarch to lemon juice and stir to dissolve; add to tofu mixture and process until smooth and thoroughly blended. Pour into prepared pie crust and bake at 325°F. for 40 to 45 minutes. Transfer to wire rack to cool.

To Serve: When cool, garnish with kiwi slices, cover lightly, and refrigerate for at least 30 minutes.

Each serving is equivalent to: 1 serving Bread; 1 serving Fats; 2 ounces Legumes (tofu); ½ serving Fruits; 1 serving Extras.

Per serving: 177 calories, 6 g protein, 7 g fat, 22 g carbohydrate, 190 mg sodium

* Men—One serving provides ⅕ of a meal. Supplement with an additional 4 ounces boned cooked meat or fish or skinned and boned cooked poultry, or 8 ounces tofu, at the Midday or Evening Meal.

Sauces and Dressings

A superb sauce or salad dressing can transform the most basic dish into a gourmet treat. We've adapted some of the world's classic sauces so you can serve them in slim style. And when it comes to dressings and dips, we include a surprise ingredient in our recipes—combining apple with a vinaigrette or blending mint with yogurt.

Fat selections supply polyunsaturated fatty acids and Vitamin E.

Guidelines for Using Fats (Full and Limited Choice Plans)

1. Amounts:
Women, Men, and Youth—3 servings daily.
2. Fat servings may be consumed at any time and may be mixed-and-matched (e.g., 2 teaspoons reduced-calorie margarine at the Morning Meal, 1 teaspoon vegetable oil at the Evening Meal, and 1 teaspoon margarine at the Evening Snack).
3. The following items may be used as Fats selections:

Selections	One Serving
margarine, liquid vegetable oil	1 level teaspoon
margarine, reduced-calorie, liquid vegetable oil	2 level teaspoons
mayonnaise, commercial and homemade	1 level teaspoon
mayonnaise, reduced-calorie	2 level teaspoons
vegetable oil:	1 teaspoon
safflower	
sunflower	
soybean	
corn	
cottonseed	
sesame	
peanut	
rapeseed (canola)	
olive	
pumpkin seed	
rice	
walnut	
wheat germ	

4. Homemade mayonnaise may be prepared using any standard recipe.
5. Mayonnaise products that are labeled "imitation" or "diet" may also be used; serving size is the same as for reduced-calorie mayonnaise.
6. The vegetable oils above are listed in order of their polyunsaturated fatty acid content, from high to low. Polyunsaturated fats provide an essential nutrient, linoleic acid.

7. Nonstick cooking sprays are allowed in amounts not exceeding 10 calories per day. These do not take the place of daily Fats servings.

8. Cooking Procedures:

A. Fats may be used to broil, pan-broil, bake, roast, sauté, and stir-fry provided specific guidelines for other foods are followed (e.g., poultry and game must be skinned; Meat Group items must be cooked first; etc.).

B. Measured amounts of Fats may be used as part of a marinade (do not use with poultry and game that have not been skinned or with uncooked Meat Group items); all of the marinade *must* be consumed and equated to the Food Plan. Therefore, all pan juices from cooked foods that have been marinated in Fats *must* be consumed.

HOMEMADE MAYONNAISE
No Choice Plan
Yields about 1¼ cups

This works best when all ingredients are at room temperature.

1 cup vegetable oil, divided	½ teaspoon salt
1 egg	¼ teaspoon powdered mustard
1 tablespoon lemon juice	Dash white pepper
1 tablespoon white vinegar	

In blender container combine ¼ cup oil and the egg, lemon juice, vinegar, salt, mustard, and pepper; process until smooth. With blender running, remove insert from blender cap and add remaining ¾ cup oil *very slowly* in a steady stream. After all oil has been added, stop motor and, using a rubber scraper, scrape down any mixture from sides of container. Process again until all oil is combined.

1 teaspoon mayonnaise is equivalent to: 1 serving Fats.

Per 1-teaspoon serving: 34 calories, 0.1 g protein, 4 g fat, 0.1 g carbohydrate, 19 mg sodium

Variation: Substitute cider vinegar or garlic vinegar for the white vinegar and, before processing, add ⅛ teaspoon each onion powder, basil leaves, oregano leaves, and parsley flakes.

Per 1-teaspoon serving: 35 calories, 0.1 g protein, 4 g fat, 0.1 g carbohydrate, 19 mg sodium

"SOUR CREAM"
Full Choice Plan
Makes 2 servings

Great on baked potatoes or a mixed green salad.

2 tablespoons part-skim ricotta cheese	2 teaspoons lemon juice
1 tablespoon buttermilk	Dash each salt and white pepper

In blender container combine all ingredients and process on low speed until smooth.

Each serving is equivalent to: 1½ servings Extras; 1½ teaspoons Buttermilk (1/24 serving Milk).

Per serving: 26 calories, 2 g protein, 1 g fat, 2 g carbohydrate, 92 mg sodium

Variation: Add dash Worcestershire sauce before processing. Process as directed, then stir in 1 tablespoon chopped chives.

Per serving: 28 calories, 2 g protein, 1 g fat, 2 g carbohydrate, 94 mg sodium

BASIC BROWN SAUCE
Full Choice Plan
Makes 4 or 8 servings, about 6 or 3 tablespoons each

2 tablespoons margarine
2 tablespoons enriched all-purpose flour
¼ cup each diced carrot and celery
¼ cup diced onion
2 cups water
¼ cup tomato puree

2 packets instant beef broth and seasoning mix
2 bay leaves
1 garlic clove
⅛ teaspoon pepper
Pinch thyme leaves

1. In medium saucepan heat margarine, over medium heat, until bubbly; add flour and cook, stirring constantly, for 3 minutes.
2. Add carrot, celery, and onion and continue to stir and cook until vegetables are lightly browned, about 5 minutes; remove from heat and stir in remaining ingredients.
3. Return pan to heat and bring mixture to a boil. Reduce heat and simmer, stirring occasionally, for 45 minutes.
4. Allow mixture to cool slightly, then remove and discard bay leaves. Transfer sauce to blender container; process until smooth.

Each 6-tablespoon serving is equivalent to: 1½ servings Fats; 2 servings Extras; ¼ serving Vegetables; 1 tablespoon Limited Vegetables; ⅛ serving Bonus.

Per serving: 87 calories, 2 g protein, 6 g fat, 8 g carbohydrate, 516 mg sodium

Each 3-tablespoon serving is equivalent to: ¾ serving Fats; 1 serving Extras; ⅛ serving Vegetables; 1½ teaspoons Limited Vegetables; 1½ teaspoons Tomato Puree (1/16 serving Bonus).

Per serving: 44 calories, 1 g protein, 3 g fat, 4 g carbohydrate, 258 mg sodium

BASIC WHITE SAUCE (BÉCHAMEL)
Limited Choice Plan
Makes 4 or 8 servings, about ½ or ¼ cup each

2 tablespoons margarine
2 tablespoons plus 2 teaspoons enriched all-purpose flour
2 cups skim milk, heated

⅛ teaspoon salt
Dash white pepper
Dash ground nutmeg (optional)

In small saucepan heat margarine until bubbly. Add flour and cook over low heat, stirring constantly, for 3 minutes; remove from heat. Using a small wire whisk, gradually stir in heated milk and continue to stir until mixture is smooth. Add salt, pepper, and, if desired, nutmeg. Cook over medium heat, stirring constantly, until thickened. Reduce heat as low as possible and cook, stirring occasionally, for 15 minutes longer.

Each ½-cup serving is equivalent to: 1½ servings Fats; 2 servings Extras; ½ serving Milk.

Per serving: 114 calories, 5 g protein, 6 g fat, 10 g carbohydrate, 201 mg sodium

Each ¼-cup serving is equivalent to: ¾ serving Fats; 1 serving Extras; ¼ serving Milk.

Per serving: 57 calories, 2 g protein, 3 g fat, 5 g carbohydrate, 101 mg sodium

CURRY SAUCE
Full Choice Plan
Makes 4 servings

1 tablespoon plus 1 teaspoon margarine	2 teaspoons curry powder
2 tablespoons minced onion	1½ cups skim milk, heated
2 tablespoons enriched all-purpose flour	⅛ teaspoon salt
	Dash white pepper

In small saucepan heat margarine until bubbly; add onion and sauté until softened. Add flour and cook over low heat, stirring constantly, for 3 minutes. Add curry powder and continue to stir and cook for 1 minute longer; remove from heat. Using a small wire whisk, gradually stir in heated milk, stirring until mixture is smooth. Add salt and pepper and cook over low heat, stirring frequently, for 10 minutes.

Each serving is equivalent to: 1 serving Fats; 1½ teaspoons Limited Vegetables; 1½ servings Extras; ⅜ serving Milk.

Per serving: 87 calories, 4 g protein, 4 g fat, 9 g carbohydrate, 164 mg sodium

CHEESE SAUCE
Full Choice Plan
Makes 4 Midday or Evening Meal servings, ¼ meal each; supplement as required

This sauce is delicious served over cooked cauliflower, broccoli, asparagus, or potato. Top cooked vegetable with sauce, then broil until lightly browned.

2 tablespoons margarine	2 ounces Gruyère or other hard cheese, shredded
2 tablespoons enriched all-purpose flour	¼ teaspoon salt
1 cup skim milk	Dash each white and ground red pepper

1. In small saucepan heat margarine, over medium heat, until bubbly. Add flour and cook, stirring constantly, for 2 minutes; set aside.
2. In another small saucepan heat milk just to the boiling point; remove from heat.
3. Add flour mixture to milk, a little at a time, beating well with wire whisk after each addition.
4. Cook over medium heat, stirring constantly, until thickened. Add cheese, salt, and peppers and continue to stir and cook until cheese is melted. Reduce heat as low as possible and cook, stirring occasionally, for 30 minutes.

Each serving is equivalent to: 1½ servings Fats; 1½ servings Extras; ¼ serving Milk; ½ ounce Hard Cheese.

Per serving: 146 calories, 7 g protein, 10 g fat, 6 g carbohydrate, 281 mg sodium

QUICK AND EASY CHEESE SAUCE
Full Choice Plan
Makes 2 Midday or Evening Meal servings, ½ meal each; supplement as required

Delicious over cooked vegetables, pasta, or rice. This recipe yields about ¼ cup sauce per serving.

½ cup evaporated skimmed milk	Dash each Worcestershire sauce,
2 ounces sharp Cheddar cheese,	hot sauce, salt, and pepper
shredded	

In small saucepan heat milk to just below the boiling point. Remove pan from heat and stir in remaining ingredients. Cook over low heat, stirring constantly, until cheese is melted.

Each serving is equivalent to: ½ serving Milk; 1 ounce Hard Cheese.

Per serving: 164 calories, 12 g protein, 10 g fat, 8 g carbohydrate, 315 mg sodium

PESTO CHEESE SAUCE
Full Choice Plan
Makes 2 Midday or Evening Meal servings, ¼ meal each; supplement as required

Serve over cooked spaghetti. This recipe yields about ¼ cup sauce per serving.

2 cups firmly packed fresh basil	½ teaspoon salt
leaves, chopped	⅛ teaspoon pepper
1 tablespoon plus 1 teaspoon	1 garlic clove, minced
olive oil	1 ounce grated Parmesan cheese

In blender container combine all ingredients except cheese and process until smooth, stopping motor when necessary to scrape mixture down from sides of container. Transfer sauce to small bowl and stir in cheese;

serve immediately or cover and refrigerate. When ready to use, bring to room temperature.

Each serving is equivalent to: 2 servings Fats; ½ ounce Hard Cheese.

Per serving: 195 calories, 9 g protein, 14 g fat, 12 g carbohydrate, 808 mg sodium

SAUCE VELOUTÉ
Limited Choice Plan
Makes 4 servings, about 3 tablespoons each

1 tablespoon plus 1 teaspoon margarine
1 tablespoon plus 1 teaspoon enriched all-purpose flour

¾ cup Chicken Broth (see page 401)
⅛ teaspoon salt
Dash white pepper

In small saucepan heat margarine until bubbly. Add flour and cook over low heat, stirring constantly, for 2 minutes; set aside.

In another saucepan bring broth to a boil; remove from heat. Add margarine mixture, a little at a time, beating well with a wire whisk after each addition. Cook over medium heat, stirring constantly, until thickened. Season with salt and pepper. Reduce heat as low as possible and continue cooking for 15 minutes longer, stirring occasionally.

Each serving is equivalent to: 1 serving Fats; 1¼ servings Extras.

Per serving: 47 calories, 1 g protein, 4 g fat, 3 g carbohydrate, 120 mg sodium

Variation: *Tomato–Herb Velouté (Full Choice Plan)*—Before serving, stir 1½ teaspoons chopped fresh parsley and ½ teaspoon tomato paste into sauce. Change equivalent listing to 1⅓ servings Extras.

Per serving: 47 calories, 1 g protein, 4 g fat, 3 g carbohydrate, 126 mg sodium

GRAVY
Limited Choice Plan
Makes 4 servings, about 3 tablespoons each

Serve with chicken or turkey.

½ cup diced carrot
½ cup chopped celery leaves

1½ cups Chicken Broth (see page 401), divided
2 teaspoons arrowroot

1. Preheat oven to 400°F. In 7-inch nonstick skillet that has a metal or removable handle combine carrot and celery leaves; bake, stirring every 5 minutes, until vegetables are browned, 20 to 25 minutes.

2. In small bowl combine 2 tablespoons broth and arrowroot and stir to dissolve.

3. Remove skillet from oven and stir in dissolved arrowroot and remaining broth; place over medium heat and bring to a boil. Reduce heat and simmer for 5 minutes; cool slightly.

4. Pour mixture into blender container and process until smooth.

5. Return gravy to skillet and heat.

Each serving is equivalent to: ¼ serving Vegetables; 1 serving Extras. (See page 407 for Full Choice Plan adjustments.)

Per serving: 19 calories, 2 g protein, 0.1 g fat, 5 g carbohydrate, 37 mg sodium

CREOLE SAUCE
Full Choice Plan
Makes 4 servings, about ½ cup each

2 teaspoons vegetable oil
½ cup diced onion
1 garlic clove, minced
1 cup diced green bell pepper
1 cup sliced mushrooms
½ cup chopped celery
1 cup canned plum tomatoes,
    drained and chopped (reserve
    liquid)

¾ cup Beef Broth (see page 401)
1 bay leaf
1 tablespoon chopped fresh parsley
¼ teaspoon salt
Dash pepper

In 1½-quart saucepan heat oil; add onion and garlic and sauté until onion is softened. Add green pepper, mushrooms, and celery and sauté for 5 minutes. Add tomatoes, reserved liquid, broth, and bay leaf; cover and simmer for 20 minutes, stirring occasionally. Stir in parsley, salt, and pepper; remove bay leaf before serving.

Each serving is equivalent to: ½ serving Fats; ⅛ cup Limited Vegetables; 1¾ servings Vegetables; ¼ serving Extras.

Per serving: 62 calories, 2 g protein, 3 g fat, 9 g carbohydrate, 244 mg sodium

EASY TOMATO SAUCE
Limited Choice Plan
Makes 2 or 4 servings, about 1 or ½ cup each

2 teaspoons olive oil or vegetable
    oil
½ teaspoon minced fresh garlic
2 cups canned plum tomatoes,
    seeded and crushed
1 tablespoon chopped fresh basil
    or ½ teaspoon dried basil
    leaves

1 tablespoon chopped fresh parsley
    or 1 teaspoon parsley flakes
½ teaspoon salt
Dash freshly ground pepper

In 1-quart saucepan heat oil; add garlic and sauté briefly (*do not brown*). Add tomatoes and bring to a boil. Reduce heat and stir in basil, parsley, salt, and pepper; simmer 10 to 15 minutes.

Each 1-cup serving is equivalent to: 1 serving Fats; 2 servings Vegetables.

Per serving: 95 calories, 3 g protein, 5 g fat, 11 g carbohydrate, 850 mg sodium

Each ½-cup serving is equivalent to: ½ serving Fats; 1 serving Vegetables.

Per serving: 48 calories, 1 g protein, 3 g fat, 6 g carbohydrate, 425 mg sodium

Variation: *Blender Tomato Sauce*—Do not seed or crush tomatoes. Substitute 1 small garlic clove, 6 fresh basil leaves, and 6 parsley sprigs, stems removed, for the minced garlic and chopped herbs. Combine all ingredients in blender container and process until smooth; pour into 1-quart saucepan and bring to a boil. Reduce heat, cover, and simmer for 10 minutes.

RED CLAM SAUCE

Full Choice Plan
Makes 4 Midday or Evening Meal servings, ½ meal each; supplement as required

Serve over cooked linguini or spaghetti. This recipe yields about ¾ cup sauce per serving.

2 teaspoons olive oil
½ cup chopped onion
1 teaspoon minced fresh garlic
3 cups canned plum tomatoes, crushed
1 cup bottled clam juice
2 teaspoons basil leaves
½ teaspoon salt

Dash each oregano leaves and pepper
8 ounces drained canned minced clams
2 tablespoons chopped fresh parsley

In 1½-quart saucepan heat oil; add onion and garlic and sauté about 2 minutes. Add remaining ingredients except clams and parsley and bring to a boil. Reduce heat and simmer, stirring occasionally, for about 15 minutes. Add clams and parsley and cook until thoroughly heated, about 3 minutes longer.

Each serving is equivalent to: ½ serving Fats; ⅛ cup Limited Vegetables; 1½ servings Vegetables; ¼ serving Bonus; 2 ounces Fish.

Per serving: 138 calories, 13 g protein, 5 g fat, 13 g carbohydrate, 814 mg sodium

WHITE CLAM SAUCE

Full Choice Plan
Makes 4 Midday or Evening Meal servings, ½ meal each; supplement as required

Serve over cooked linguini or spaghetti. This recipe yields about ½ cup sauce per serving.

2 teaspoons olive oil
½ teaspoon minced fresh garlic
2 cups bottled clam juice
½ teaspoon each oregano leaves and salt

⅛ teaspoon white pepper
8 ounces drained canned minced clams
2 tablespoons chopped fresh parsley

In 1-quart saucepan heat oil; add garlic and sauté just until golden. Add remaining ingredients except clams and parsley and bring to a boil. Reduce heat and simmer for 5 minutes. Add clams and parsley and cook until thoroughly heated, about 3 minutes longer.

Each serving is equivalent to: ½ serving Fats; ½ serving Bonus; 2 ounces Fish.

Per serving: 102 calories, 12 g protein, 4 g fat, 4 g carbohydrate, 818 mg sodium

"HOLLANDAISE" SAUCE

Limited Choice Plan
Makes 4 servings, about 2 tablespoons each

½ cup Chicken Broth (see page 401)
1 tablespoon cornstarch
2 tablespoons margarine

2 tablespoons mayonnaise
1½ teaspoons lemon juice
Dash each salt, white pepper, and ground red pepper

In small saucepan combine broth and cornstarch and stir to dissolve. Cook over medium heat, stirring constantly, until mixture comes to a boil; continue cooking and stirring until thickened, about 1 minute longer.

Remove from heat and add margarine, a little at a time, stirring after each addition until margarine is melted. Add remaining ingredients and stir to combine.

Each serving is equivalent to: 1 serving Extras; 3 servings Fats.

Per serving: 111 calories, 1 g protein, 11 g fat, 3 g carbohydrate, 143 mg sodium

SWEET MUSTARD SAUCE

Limited Choice Plan
Makes 2 servings

2 tablespoons prepared yellow mustard
2 teaspoons prepared horseradish

2 teaspoons chili sauce
1 teaspoon lemon juice

In small bowl combine all ingredients; cover and chill for about 1 hour before serving.

Each serving is equivalent to: ½ serving Extras.

Per serving: 23 calories, 1 g protein, 1 g fat, 3 g carbohydrate, 232 mg sodium

TARTAR SAUCE

Full Choice Plan
Makes 4 servings, about 1 tablespoon each

Delicious with fish.

¼ cup reduced-calorie mayonnaise
1 teaspoon Dijon-style mustard
⅛ teaspoon each Worcestershire sauce and lemon juice

1 tablespoon pickle relish
1 teaspoon chopped capers
½ teaspoon chopped fresh parsley

In small bowl mix mayonnaise with mustard, Worcestershire sauce, and lemon juice. Stir in pickle relish, capers, and parsley. Serve immediately or cover and refrigerate until ready to use.

Each serving is equivalent to: 1½ servings Fats; ¾ serving Extras.

Per serving: 47 calories, 0.2 g protein, 4 g fat, 3 g carbohydrate, 195 mg sodium

APPLE–YOGURT SAUCE

Full Choice Plan
Makes 1 serving

Serve with baked or broiled chicken.

2 teaspoons reduced-calorie
   margarine
1 small red delicious apple, cored
   and diced

1 teaspoon chopped chives
¼ cup plain unflavored yogurt
Dash ground nutmeg

In small skillet heat margarine, over medium heat, until bubbly; add apple and chives and sauté, stirring occasionally, until apple pieces are soft. Remove from heat* and stir in yogurt and nutmeg. Serve hot.

Each serving is equivalent to: 1 serving Fats; 1 serving Fruits; ½ serving Milk.

Per serving: 122 calories, 2 g protein, 5 g fat, 20 g carbohydrate, 78 mg sodium

* To prevent curdling, be sure to remove skillet from heat before stirring in yogurt.

HOT FRUIT SAUCE

Full Choice Plan
Makes 4 servings

Excellent with ham or chicken.

½ cup diet ginger ale (2 calories
   per 12 fluid ounces)
2 teaspoons arrowroot

1 cup canned crushed pineapple
   (no sugar added), pureed
1 cup canned sliced peaches (no
   sugar added), pureed

In 1-quart saucepan bring ginger ale to a boil and cook until reduced by half. Remove from heat and cool slightly; add arrowroot and stir until smooth. Return to heat, add pureed fruits, and bring to a boil. Reduce heat and simmer for 1 minute; serve hot.

Each serving is equivalent to: ⅙ calorie Specialty Foods; ½ serving Extras; 1 serving Fruits.

Per serving: 61 calories, 1 g protein, 0.1 g fat, 16 g carbohydrate, 10 mg sodium

STRAWBERRY JAM
Full Choice Plan
Makes 8 servings, about ¼ cup each

Use as a spread for toast or pancakes.

1 envelope (four ½-cup servings) strawberry-flavored gelatin
1 cup boiling water

2 cups stawberries, sliced
Grated peel of 2 oranges
Grated peel of 1 lemon

In small heatproof bowl combine gelatin and boiling water, stirring until gelatin is completely dissolved. Stir in strawberries and grated orange and lemon peel; allow to cool, then pour into a glass jar. Cover and refrigerate for at least 1 hour before serving.

Each serving is equivalent to: ½ serving Occasional Substitutes; ¼ serving Fruits.

Per serving: 63 calories, 1 g protein, 0.2 g fat, 15 g carbohydrate, 35 mg sodium

APPLE VINAIGRETTE
Limited Choice Plan
Makes 2 servings, about 3 tablespoons each

⅓ cup apple juice (no sugar added)
2 teaspoons vegetable oil
1 teaspoon each cider vinegar and lemon juice

¼ teaspoon powdered mustard
Dash each salt, pepper, and ground ginger

In small bowl or jar with tight-fitting cover combine all ingredients; stir or cover and shake to mix.

Each serving is equivalent to: ½ serving Fruits; 1 serving Fats.

Per serving: 64 calories, 0.2 g protein, 5 g fat, 5 g carbohydrate, 65 mg sodium

CITRUS VINAIGRETTE
Limited Choice Plan
Makes 1 serving, about 2 tablespoons

Delicious with fruit salad.

1 tablespoon thawed frozen concentrated orange juice (no sugar added)
2 teaspoons rice vinegar

1 teaspoon each basil leaves and chopped chives
1 teaspoon sesame oil
½ teaspoon honey
Dash each salt and pepper

In small bowl or jar with tight-fitting cover combine all ingredients. Stir or cover and shake to mix.

Each serving is equivalent to: ½ serving Fruits; 1 serving Fats; 1 serving Extras.

Per serving: 87 calories, 1 g protein, 5 g fat, 12 g carbohydrate, 131 mg sodium

HERB VINAIGRETTE DRESSING
No Choice Plan
Makes 1 serving, about 2 tablespoons

1 teaspoon each olive and
   vegetable oil
1 teaspoon each red wine vinegar
   and water

1 teaspoon chopped fresh parsley
½ teaspoon Worcestershire sauce
Dash each salt, pepper, and
   artificial sweetener

In small bowl combine all ingredients; beat with whisk or fork until well mixed.
   Each serving is equivalent to: 2 servings Fats.

Per serving: 88 calories, 0.1 g protein, 9 g fat, 1 g carbohydrate, 130 mg sodium

Variations:
   1. Substitute chopped fresh basil for the parsley.
   2. Substitute lemon juice for the vinegar.
   3. *Limited Choice Plan*—Substitute ¼ teaspoon sugar for the artificial sweetener. Add ½ serving Extras to equivalent listing.

Per serving: 91 calories, 0.1 g protein, 9 g fat, 2 g carbohydrate, 130 mg sodium

ANCHOVY DRESSING
Full Choice Plan
Makes 2 or 4 servings, about 2½ or 1¼ tablespoons each

2 tablespoons plus 1½ teaspoons
   red wine vinegar
2 teaspoons drained canned
   mashed anchovies

1 tablespoon plus 1 teaspoon olive
   oil
⅛ teaspoon each basil leaves and
   mashed fresh garlic

In small bowl gradually stir vinegar into anchovies, mixing well to combine. Add oil in a thin stream, beating constantly. Add basil and garlic and stir to combine.
   Each 2½-tablespoon serving is equivalent to: 1 serving Extras; 2 servings Fats.

Per serving: 97 calories, 1 g protein, 10 g fat, 1 g carbohydrate, 53 mg sodium

   Each 1¼-tablespoon serving is equivalent to: ½ serving Extras; 1 serving Fats.

Per serving: 48 calories, 1 g protein, 5 g fat, 0.4 g carbohydrate, 26 mg sodium

CREAMY SALAD DRESSING
Limited Choice Plan
Makes 2 servings

¼ cup evaporated skimmed milk
1 tablespoon lemon juice
½ teaspoon Dijon-style mustard

Dash each salt and pepper
2 teaspoons vegetable oil

In bowl, using a wire whisk or hand beater, combine milk, lemon juice, mustard, salt, and pepper, beating until creamy consistency. Add oil a few drops at a time, beating after each addition, until all oil is used and mixture is well combined.

Each serving is equivalent to: ¼ serving Milk; 1 serving Fats.

Per serving: 70 calories, 2 g protein, 5 g fat, 4 g carbohydrate, 139 mg sodium

HONEY SALAD DRESSING
Limited Choice Plan
Makes 4 servings

1 medium tomato, cut into wedges
2 tablespoons chopped chives
1 tablespoon plus 1 teaspoon
   honey

2 teaspoons rice vinegar
1 teaspoon vegetable oil
¼ teaspoon salt
Dash pepper

In blender container combine all ingredients and process on high speed until mixture is smooth, about 1 minute. Refrigerate, covered, until chilled. Stir well before serving. This dressing will keep for several days in the refrigerator.

Each serving is equivalent to: ½ serving Vegetables; 2 servings Extras; ¼ serving Fats.

Per serving: 41 calories, 0.5 g protein, 1 g fat, 8 g carbohydrate, 137 mg sodium

LEMON–TOMATO DRESSING
Limited Choice Plan
Makes 4 servings, about ¼ cup each

1 cup tomato juice
1 tablespoon cornstarch
2 tablespoons each cider vinegar
   and lemon juice

1 tablespoon chopped fresh parsley
1 garlic clove
Dash each salt and pepper

In small saucepan combine tomato juice and cornstarch and, stirring constantly, bring to a boil. Continue cooking and stirring for 1 minute longer. Cool slightly and transfer to blender container; add remaining ingredients and process until smooth. Refrigerate, covered, until chilled. Shake or stir before serving.

Each serving is equivalent to: ⅓ serving Bonus; ¾ serving Extras. (See page 407 for Full Choice Plan adjustments.)

Per serving: 23 calories, 1 g protein, 0.1 g fat, 6 g carbohydrate, 153 mg sodium

PEANUT BUTTER DRESSING
Full Choice Plan
Makes 2 Midday or Evening Meal servings, ¼ meal each; supplement as required

Serve over salad greens.

1 tablespoon plus 1½ teaspoons peanut butter
1 teaspoon peanut or vegetable oil
Dash ground red pepper
¼ cup water

1 tablespoon rice vinegar or white vinegar
2 teaspoons minced scallion (green onion)
2 teaspoons soy sauce
¼ teaspoon minced fresh garlic

In small saucepan combine peanut butter, oil, and red pepper; heat, stirring constantly, until the consistency of smooth paste. Remove from heat and add remaining ingredients; stir to combine. Serve immediately or cover and refrigerate. Bring to room temperature before serving.

Each serving is equivalent to: 2¼ teaspoons Peanut Butter (¼ serving Protein and ½ serving Fats); ½ serving Fats; 1 teaspoon Limited Vegetables.

Per serving: 97 calories, 4 g protein, 8 g fat, 3 g carbohydrate, 517 mg sodium

PIMIENTO DRESSING
Limited Choice Plan
Makes 4 servings, about 5 tablespoons each

Delicious over a mixed green or tossed salad.

1 cup drained canned pimientos
2 tablespoons rice vinegar

2 teaspoons granulated sugar
¼ teaspoon Dijon-style mustard*

In blender container combine all ingredients and process until smooth.
Each serving is equivalent to: ½ serving Vegetables; 1 serving Extras.

Per serving: 22 calories, 0.4 g protein, 0.3 g fat, 5 g carbohydrate, 21 mg sodium

* For a sharper flavor, increase mustard to ½ teaspoon. Add 4 mg sodium to nutrition figures.

PIQUANT SALAD DRESSING
Limited Choice Plan
Makes 4 servings, about ¼ cup each

This salad dressing is also a delicious marinade for cooked vegetables such as broccoli, cauliflower, and green beans.

1 tablespoon cornstarch
1 cup water
2 tablespoons each lemon juice and rice vinegar
1 tablespoon finely chopped fresh parsley

2 teaspoons chili sauce
1 teaspoon honey
1 teaspoon Worcestershire sauce
1 garlic clove, minced
Dash each artificial sweetener, salt, and pepper

In small saucepan stir cornstarch into water and, stirring constantly, bring to a boil; continue cooking and stirring for 1 minute longer. Transfer to a heatproof bowl and add remaining ingredients; stir well. Cover and chill. Stir again before serving.

Each serving is equivalent to: 1½ servings Extras.

Per serving: 21 calories, 0.2 g protein, trace fat, 5 g carbohydrate, 71 mg sodium

SESAME DRESSING
Limited Choice Plan
Makes 2 or 4 servings, about 2½ or 1¼ tablespoons each

1 tablespoon plus 1 teaspoon vegetable oil
1 teaspoon sesame seed
¼ teaspoon minced fresh garlic

¼ cup rice vinegar
1 teaspoon granulated sugar
¼ teaspoon salt
Dash pepper

In small skillet combine oil and sesame seed and cook over low heat, stirring constantly, until seeds are lightly browned. Stir in garlic and remove from heat.

In small bowl combine rice vinegar, sugar, salt, and pepper; gradually add sesame seed mixture and mix well.

Each 2½-tablespoon serving is equivalent to: 2 servings Fats; 2 servings Extras.

Per serving: 104 calories, 0.4 g protein, 10 g fat, 4 g carbohydrate, 270 mg sodium

Each 1¼-tablespoon serving is equivalent to: 1 serving Fats; 1 serving Extras.

Per serving: 52 calories, 0.2 g protein, 5 g fat, 2 g carbohydrate, 135 mg sodium

YOGURT–MINT DRESSING OR DIP
Limited Choice Plan
Makes 2 servings, about ¼ cup each

½ cup plain unflavored yogurt
2 tablespoons finely chopped fresh mint leaves

1 teaspoon lemon juice
Dash each white pepper, ground red pepper, and salt

In small bowl combine all ingredients and mix well. Cover and refrigerate until ready to serve.

Each serving is equivalent to: ½ serving Milk.

Per serving: 36 calories, 2 g protein, 2 g fat, 3 g carbohydrate, 90 mg sodium

YOGURT–ONION DIP
Limited Choice Plan
Makes 4 servings, about 2 tablespoons each

In a small bowl combine ½ cup plain unflavored yogurt, 1 packet instant onion broth and seasoning mix, and 2 teaspoons chopped chives; cover and chill.

Each serving is equivalent to: ¼ serving Milk; ¼ serving Extras.

Per serving: 20 calories, 1 g protein, 1 g fat, 2 g carbohydrate, 205 mg sodium

Optional

Now you can look at the world through rose-colored wine glasses, for wine and beer are now part of our Food Plan. We've added spirits to the holidays with a ruby-hued Mulled Wine and elegant fruit desserts like Strawberry-Wine Gel and Blueberries in Wine. Even old favorites get a new look, as our Spiced Tea with honey proves.

Guidelines for Using Optional Items
(Full and Limited Choice Plans)

1. The previous food categories make up the total nutrition "package." This category is *optional*. It is included to enhance enjoyment of the Food Plan and to provide variety in recipe development. The caloric values of the items included here have been accounted for in the overall design of the Food Plan. Judicious use of these flavorful items can make the difference between routine eating and a taste adventure.

2. The Optional category is made up of the following groups: Beverages; Condiments; Bonus; Extras; Specialty Foods (Full Choice Plan only); and Occasional Substitutes (Full Choice Plan only).

3. Items from this category may be used for basting; equate items used to the Food Plan.

4. Items from this category may be used in a marinade. If the marinade is discarded, it does not have to be equated to the Food Plan; if consumed, equate to the Food Plan.

5. Chewing gum, regular or artificially sweetened, is a source of calories. Limit intake to no more than 5 pieces daily.

6. *Beverages:*

   A. The following Beverages may be selected in reasonable amounts. It is recommended that at least 6 to 8 cups of water be consumed daily.

club soda	mineral water
coffee	tea
coffee substitutes	water

   B. Beverages may contain only those ingredients that are permitted, but not restricted, on the Food Plan. Therefore, coffee or tea may contain seasonings, flavorings, and/or extracts, but *not* dextrose, sugar, milk, cocoa, starch, vegetable oil, or any other restricted items.

   C. Coffee substitute powders may contain up to 8 calories per teaspoon. Limit the prepared beverage to 2 cups daily.

7. *Condiments:*

   A. All seasonings and condiments may be selected in reasonable amounts. Examples include:

artificial sweeteners	pectin
baking powder	pepper
baking soda	rennin tablets
browning sauce	salt
dehydrated vegetable flakes	seasonings
extracts and flavorings	seaweed
herbs	soy sauce
horseradish	spices
hot sauce (pepper sauce)	teriyaki sauce
lemon juice	vinegar
lime juice (no sugar added)	Worcestershire sauce
mustard	

B. Artificial sweeteners (powders, liquids, or tablets) that contain *up to* 4 calories for the equivalent sweetening power of 2 teaspoons sugar may be used. These products may contain dextrose and/or lactose.

C. Many people consume more sodium (salt) than is needed. Excessive amounts of salt may contribute to elevated blood pressure levels. Therefore, it is suggested that salt consumption be limited. (For those concerned about sodium, our recipes are followed by nutrition information that includes the sodium content per serving.)

8. *Bonus:*

A. On the Full Choice Plan, *up to* 1 Bonus serving may be selected daily. On the Limited Choice Plan, *up to* 1 Bonus serving *or* 3 servings Extras (or a combination thereof) may be selected daily (e.g., ½ serving Bonus and 1½ servings Extras; ¼ serving Bonus and 2¼ servings Extras).

B. The following items may be used as Bonus selections:

Selections	One Serving
Full Choice Plan	
clam juice	1 cup
mixed vegetable juice (commercial or homemade)	1 cup
tomato juice (commercial or homemade)*	1 cup
tomato paste	¼ cup
tomato puree	½ cup
tomato sauce	½ cup

* May be used as a substitute for an asterisked (*) fruit (see Fruits chapter, page 27).

Limited Choice Plan	
mixed vegetable juice	¾ cup
tomato juice	¾ cup

C. Tomato juice and mixed vegetable juice should have *no sugar added.*

D. Choose commercially prepared tomato sauce that is labeled as such (e.g., do *not* select products labeled "spaghetti sauce").

9. *Extras:*

A. On the Full Choice Plan, *up to* 3 servings Extras may be selected daily. On the Limited Choice Plan, *up to* 3 servings Extras *or* 1 Bonus serving (or a combination thereof) may be selected daily (see 8A, page 392).

B. The following items may be used as Extras selections. The items in italics are for the Full Choice Plan only and should *not* be used with the Limited Choice Plan; the item in brackets ([ ]) is for the Limited Choice Plan only and should *not* be used as an Extras selection with the Full Choice Plan. The remaining items may be used with both the Full and Limited Choice Plans.

Selections	One Serving
anchovy, mashed	1 *level teaspoon*
arrowroot	1 level teaspoon
bacon bits, imitation	1 *level teaspoon*
barbecue sauce	2 level teaspoons
beer:	
regular	1 *tablespoon*
light	2 *tablespoons*
bouillon and broth:	
bouillon cube	1
homemade broth, fat free	¾ cup
instant broth and seasoning mix	1 packet
carob powder, unsweetened	1 level teaspoon
cheese, hard (grated or shredded)	1 level teaspoon
cheese, soft	2 *level teaspoons*
chili sauce	2 level teaspoons
cocoa, unsweetened	1 level teaspoon
coconut, shredded (sweetened or unsweetened)	1 level teaspoon
concentrated yeast extract	1 *level teaspoon*
cornstarch	1 level teaspoon
egg white	½
flour	1 level teaspoon
fructose	½ level teaspoon
gelatin, unflavored	½ envelope (about 1½ level teaspoons)
honey	½ level teaspoon
ketchup	2 level teaspoons

Selections	One Serving
matzo meal	1 *level teaspoon*
molasses	½ level teaspoon
miso	1 *level teaspoon*
olives	2
pickle relish	1 *level teaspoon*
potato starch	1 *level teaspoon*
sago	1 *level teaspoon*
seafood cocktail sauce	1 *level teaspoon*
seeds:	
caraway, poppy, sesame, sunflower	½ level teaspoon
[Specialty Foods]	[10 calories]
steak sauce	2 level teaspoons
sugar	½ level teaspoon
syrup	½ level teaspoon
tapioca	1 *level teaspoon*
tomato paste	2 *level teaspoons*
tomato puree	4 *level teaspoons*
tomato sauce	4 *level teaspoons*
wheat germ	1 *level teaspoon*
wine:	
regular	2 *teaspoons*
light	4 *teaspoons*
yeast:	
active dry, brewer's, compressed, torula	1 *level teaspoon*

C. Bouillon cubes and broth and seasoning mixes may contain *up to* 12 calories per serving. Do not use canned broths, consommés, or soups, or dry soup mixes.

D. Homemade broth may be used. Refrigerate until fat congeals on top; remove and discard congealed fat (not necessary for fish or vegetable broth).

E. All table and cooking wines may be used (e.g., Chablis, Burgundy, cooking sherry).

10. *Specialty Foods:*

A. On the Full Choice Plan, up to 20 calories of Specialty Foods may be selected daily. Specialty Foods is *not* a separate group on the Limited Choice Plan; it is included in the Extras group (10 calories equal 1 serving Extras).

B. A Specialty Food is a product that is low-calorie, reduced-calorie, reduced-sugar, low-sugar, low-fat, or dietetic, and includes nutrition labeling.

C. Check labels carefully for calorie count. Do *not* use if label does not indicate calories.

D. Examples of Specialty Foods are:

dietetic mints or candies
low-calorie beverages, carbonated or noncarbonated, or dry mix
low-calorie flavored gelatins
low-calorie ketchup
reduced-calorie fruit-flavored spreads
reduced-calorie salad dressings

11. *Occasional Substitutes* (Full Choice Plan only):
    A. On the Full Choice Plan, 3 Occasional Substitute servings may be selected *weekly* in place of 3 Bonus servings. These servings may be split among days; be sure to omit the proportionate serving of Bonus.
    B. Items from this group may be mixed-and-matched, or they may be split with Bonus selections. If split with a Bonus selection, only the proportion of Occasional Substitutes used counts toward the total of 3 weekly servings.
    C. The following items may be used as Occasional Substitutes selections:

Selections	One Serving
beer	8 fluid ounces
beer, light	12 fluid ounces
gelatin, fruit flavored	½ cup
wine: champagne, red, rosé, or white	4 fluid ounces
wine, light	6 fluid ounces

D. The following list has been designed for the individual who has reached the high end of her/his goal weight (see Goal Weight Charts, pages 15–18) and chooses to continue on the basic Food Plan until a weight lower in the range is reached. You may now expand the list of Occasional Substitutes to include the following foods or 100 calories of any food of your choice. All previous guidelines applicable to Occasional Substitutes apply to this expanded list as well.

Selections	One Serving
Food Plan Categories:	
Fruits	2 servings
Limited Vegetables	2 servings
Milk	1 serving

Selections	*One Serving*
Bread	1 serving
Bread Substitutes	1 serving
Eggs	1
Cheese:	
Soft	½ cup
Semisoft or Hard	1 ounce
Peanut Butter	1 tablespoon
Poultry, Veal, and Game	1 ounce
Meat Group	1 ounce
Fish	1 ounce
Legumes	3 ounces
Fats	3 servings
Additional Items:	
alcoholic beverages:	
dessert wine (cream sherry, port, sauterne, etc.)	2 fluid ounces
brandy, cognac, gin, rum, Scotch, vodka, whiskey, or liqueurs	1 fluid ounce
avocado	¼ medium
bacon, crisp	2 slices
cookies	2 plain or 1 filled
cream, half and half	¼ cup
cream, heavy	2 tablespoons
fruit ice, any flavor	½ cup
nuts, any type	½ ounce
pretzels	1 ounce
sherbet, any flavor	½ cup
sour cream	¼ cup

Pep Up Your Meals with Spices and Herbs

Allspice—A delicate West Indian spice. Flavor resembles a blend of nutmeg, cinnamon, and cloves. Whole, it's a favorite seasoning for pickles, stews, and boiled fish.

Basil—Means "king," and this herb adds the crowning touch to all tomato dishes. Gives zest to eggs, fish, soups, stews, and salads.

Bay Leaf—This dried laurel leaf provides the classic seasoning for stews, soups, pickles, sauces, and fish. Remove the leaf before serving.

Bitters—A liquid blend of herbs and spices, often used in drinks.

Add a few drops to tomato or clam juice. For unusual flavor, try a few drops in scrambled eggs.

Bouquet Garni (Bouquet of Herbs)—A combination of herbs, either tied together or wrapped in cheesecloth and tied into bags. Usually added to soups, stews, and sauces during the last half hour of cooking and removed before serving.

Capers—Pickled buds of the caper bush. They taste like sharp gherkins and are available in both brine and vinegar. Use in sauces and salads.

Cardamom—Native to India. The seeds are delicious in coffee and are used in pickling. Powdered or ground, it adds interesting flavor when sprinkled on melon and other fruits.

Celery Seed—Pungent seed used in stews, coleslaw, potato salad, and salad dressings.

Chervil—Delicate herb of the carrot family. Combines well with other herbs. Delicious fresh or dry, in salads, soups, and egg and cheese dishes.

Chili Powder—The ancient Aztecs are credited for this blend of chili, allspice, red peppers, cumin seed, oregano, garlic powder, and salt. Use sparingly in cocktail sauces, eggs, stews, and meat loaf.

Chives—Have a mild onionlike flavor. Add color and flavor to cottage cheese, eggs, potatoes, vegetable dishes, and soups.

Cinnamon—Bark of the cinnamon tree. Ground and mixed with sugar or artificial sweetener, it's a favorite on French toast, pancakes, and puddings.

Cloves—Nail-shaped dried flower bud. Once available only to the rich, today they can be enjoyed by everyone. Whole, they are used in baking ham, pickling, and drinks. Many desserts call for cloves in ground form.

Coriander—Use this pungent herb sparingly. Gives character to stuffing to be served with poultry, and to pickles. It is one of the many spices found in curry powder.

Cumin—Aromatic seeds used whole or ground in egg and cheese dishes, sauerkraut, meats, rice, pickles, and Mexican foods.

Curry Powder—A blend of spices from India. Used in curries of meat, fish, eggs, and chicken and to perk up leftover stews.

Dill—The tender fresh or dried leaves, as well as the seeds, add a delightful flavor to eggs, cheeses, salads, and potatoes. A favorite in Scandinavian cookery.

Fennel—Has a slight licorice taste. Gives special flavor to apples and steamed fish.

Garlic—This indispensable seasoning is available fresh in clove form, dried in minced and chip forms, and in salt and powder forms.

Ginger—The fresh root is a staple of Oriental cookery. Ground, it is used in soups, stews, and desserts.

Ground Red Pepper—Small hot red pepper, ground and used sparingly to season eggs, meats, and fish.

Italian Seasoning—You can buy this blend of herbs or can make your own by combining basil, oregano, rosemary, ground red pepper, garlic, marjoram, thyme, and sage. Use over fish, meats, poultry, liver, rice, and pasta.

Mace—The lacy covering of the inner shell holding the nutmeg. Delicious in spinach.

Marjoram—Gives nice flavor to peas, green beans, and limas.

Mint—This aromatic herb is delicious with lamb and in cool drinks and hot tea.

Mustard—The whole seed is used in pickling; ground, with a little water added, it's the hot mustard used in Oriental cookery. Prepared mustard is the favorite with frankfurters and is delicious in sauces and salad dressings.

Nutmeg—Traditionally used in desserts. Also adds a special flavor to spinach and brussels sprouts.

Oregano—Wild marjoram, stronger in flavor than its cultivated cousin. Widely used in Mexican and Italian dishes.

Paprika—A member of the pepper family. Available in mild and fiery flavors. Used for color and flavor.

Parsley—Used for flavor and as a garnish. Can be fresh or dried. Fresh is available with either curly or flat leaves. Save the stems to use when preparing broth.

Pepper—Available black and white. Used whole in pickling and soups; ground, in most meat, poultry, fish, egg, and vegetable dishes.

Poultry Seasoning—A mixture of several spices used to season poultry and meats.

Pumpkin Pie Spice—A mixture of cinnamon, ginger, cloves, and nutmeg used to season pumpkin and fruit desserts.

Rosemary—"Rosemary is for remembrance," and its sweet, fresh flavor makes lamb stews, boiled potatoes, turnips, and cauliflower memorable.

Saffron—The world's most expensive spice, so make a little go a long way. For golden color and appetizing flavor, place a pinch in boiling water before adding rice.

Sage—Used in poultry seasoning; this is the perfect complement to poultry, pork, and fish dishes.

Savory—Lightly aromatic; good with green beans, meats, chicken, and scrambled eggs.

Tarragon—Add this anise-flavored herb to vinegar, salad dressings, and sauces for meat, poultry, and seafood.

Thyme—Has a pungent flavor. Use sparingly with clam chowder, onions, eggplant, tomatoes, and celery.

Turmeric—This slightly bitter-tasting herb adds a saffron-like natural coloring to rice, chicken, and seafood.

Vanilla Beans—The source of vanilla extract; used to enhance flavor of custards, puddings, and beverages.

BOUQUET GARNI

Unless otherwise specified, add Bouquet Garni during last 30 minutes of cooking. Remove before serving.

Bouquet Garni #1
Tie together between 2 celery ribs:

4 parsley or chervil sprigs
⅓ bay leaf
2 thyme sprigs

1 leek (white portion only), studded with 2 cloves

Bouquet Garni #2
Wrap the following herbs in a double-thick 4-inch square of cheesecloth and, using undyed or colorfast cotton string, tie into a bag:

½ teaspoon parsley flakes
½ teaspoon celery flakes

¼ teaspoon each thyme and marjoram leaves
Small piece bay leaf

BASIC GELATIN

In saucepan sprinkle **1 envelope unflavored gelatin** * over ½ **cup specified liquid;** let stand a few minutes to soften. Place over low heat and stir until gelatin is dissolved. Remove from heat and add **specified remaining liquid.** Pour into a mold that has been rinsed with cold water.† Cover and chill until firm, about 3 to 4 hours.

To Unmold: Moisten chilled platter with a few drops of cold water. Using a knife or spatula, carefully loosen edges of gelatin from mold. Fill sink or large bowl with warm, *not hot*, water; dip mold into water just to rim for about 10 seconds (be careful not to melt gelatin). Lift mold from water and shake gently to loosen gelatin. Invert platter on top of mold; quickly invert mold and platter together and gently lift off mold.

1 envelope gelatin is equivalent to: 2 servings Extras.

* One envelope gelatin will set about 2 cups liquid.
† Moistening the mold with cold water will make unmolding easier.

TOMATO PRODUCTS

Tomato juice—Available canned or bottled. The juice extracted from ripe tomatoes.

Tomato paste—Available canned. A rich concentration of tomatoes, cooked down until most of the moisture has been removed.

Tomato puree—Available canned. Made from the peeled and seeded pulp of the tomato.

Tomato sauce—Available canned. A combination of tomatoes and seasonings.

Tips for Leftovers: Leftover paste, puree, and sauce are often wasted in the kitchen, yet all can be frozen. Try freezing them in ice cube trays (measure before freezing so that you know how much of the product each cube will yield). Store the cubes in freezer containers or plastic bags. You can then defrost only the amount needed for a recipe.

HOT TOMATO BOUILLON
Full Choice Plan
Makes 6 servings

1 quart plus ½ cup tomato juice
3 cups water

4 packets instant beef broth and
  seasoning mix
Dash hot sauce

Garnish
6 mint sprigs

In 2-quart saucepan combine all ingredients except mint and bring to a boil. Reduce heat and simmer for 5 minutes. Pour into 6 bowls or mugs. Garnish each portion with a mint sprig.

Each serving is equivalent to: ¾ serving Bonus; ⅔ serving Extras.

Per serving: 41 calories, 2 g protein, 0.2 g fat, 9 g carbohydrate, 858 mg sodium

RED-BLOODED MARY MIX
Limited Choice Plan
Makes 1 serving

Only you and the bartender will know that the vodka is missing.

¾ cup tomato juice
1 teaspoon Worcestershire sauce
¼ teaspoon lime juice (no sugar
  added)

Dash each salt, freshly ground
  pepper, and hot sauce
1 lime wedge

In cocktail shaker combine all ingredients except lime wedge; shake. Serve in glass over ice, garnished with lime wedge.

Each serving is equivalent to: 1 serving Bonus. (See page 407 for Full Choice Plan adjustments.)

Per serving: 41 calories, 2 g protein, 0.2 g fat, 9 g carbohydrate, 491 mg sodium

CHICKEN BROTH
Limited Choice Plan
Makes about 2 quarts

It's a good idea to have this in the freezer. Freeze in ¼-cup portions and defrost only what you need for a recipe. A convenient method is to freeze the broth in ice cube trays and then store the cubes in a plastic bag. Using our trays, 2 ice cubes gave us a yield of about ¼ cup.

2 pounds skinned chicken necks
  and backs
3 quarts water
1 large onion
¾ cup each sliced carrots, celery,
  and parsnips

5 parsley stems
3 peppercorns
1 whole clove
⅛ teaspoon thyme leaves

In kettle combine all ingredients and bring to a boil. Reduce heat and remove scum from surface. Partially cover kettle and simmer until liquid is reduced by about a third, about 2½ hours. Strain liquid to remove solids. Refrigerate broth until fat congeals on surface. Remove and discard congealed fat.

¾ cup broth is equivalent to: 1 serving Extras.

Note: Nutrition data are not available for homemade Chicken Broth. Therefore, we are using the nutrition information from commercial broth and seasoning mix. A ¾-cup serving contains 12 calories, 1 g protein, 2 g carbohydrate, sodium data does not apply.

BEEF BROTH
Limited Choice Plan
Makes about 2 quarts

This can be prepared ahead and frozen for future use (see note on Chicken Broth recipe, above).

4 pounds beef and veal bones,
  sawed into pieces
1 cup each sliced celery, carrots,
  and parsnips
1 medium onion, studded with 1
  whole clove

1 gallon water
5 parsley stems
5 peppercorns
¼ teaspoon each thyme and
  rosemary leaves
1 small bay leaf

1. On rack in roasting pan roast bones at 400°F. for 1 hour.
2. While bones are roasting, in separate pan combine celery, carrots, parsnips, and clove-studded onion; roast for 30 minutes.

3. Transfer bones and vegetables to kettle; add remaining ingredients and bring to a boil. Reduce heat and remove scum from surface; partially cover kettle and simmer until liquid is reduced by half, about 3 hours. Strain liquid to remove solids. Refrigerate broth until fat congeals on surface. Remove and discard congealed fat.

¾ cup broth is equivalent to: 1 serving Extras.

Note: Nutrition data are not available for homemade Beef Broth. Therefore, we are using the nutrition information from commercial broth and seasoning mix. A ¾-cup serving contains 12 calories, 1 g protein, 2 g carbohydrate, sodium data does not apply.

FISH BROTH
Limited Choice Plan
Makes about 1 quart

This can be prepared ahead and frozen for future use (see note on Chicken Broth recipe, page 401).

4 pounds fish bones, heads, and
  tails (flounder, fluke, cod, or
  haddock)
2 quarts water
2 cups chopped leeks (white
  portion only)
2 cups chopped celery with leaves
3 parsley stems
1 bay leaf, broken in half
1 peppercorn, cracked

Wash fish parts in cold water. In 4-quart saucepan combine fish parts with remaining ingredients and bring to a rapid boil. Reduce heat and remove scum from surface. Cover and simmer for 45 minutes to 1 hour.

Strain broth through cheesecloth or fine strainer; discard solids. Cool broth, cover and refrigerate, or freeze in measured portions for future use.

¾ cup broth is equivalent to: 1 serving Extras.

Per serving: 12 calories, 2 g protein, 0.1 g fat, 1 g carbohydrate, 14 mg sodium

TURKEY BROTH
Limited Choice Plan
Makes about 3 cups

This broth can be prepared in advance and frozen for use at a later date (see note on Chicken Broth recipe, page 401).

Turkey neck, heart, and gizzard,
  trimmed of all fat
1¼ quarts water
1 teaspoon salt
1 celery rib, cut in half
3 parsley sprigs
1 small bay leaf
¼ teaspoon rosemary leaves
3 peppercorns
1 carrot, scraped and cut into
  pieces
1 medium onion, quartered
1 small parsnip, pared and cut
  into pieces

1. Cut turkey neck into 3 pieces and place in medium saucepan with heart and gizzard. Add water and salt.

2. Make a bouquet garni by tying celery, parsley, bay leaf, rosemary, and peppercorns in a piece of cheesecloth. Add bouquet garni, carrot, onion, and parsnip to saucepan.

3. Bring to a boil and skim scum from surface. Reduce heat and simmer, partially covered, for 2 hours.

4. Strain liquid to remove solids. Refrigerate until fat congeals on surface. Remove and discard congealed fat.

¾ cup broth is equivalent to: 1 serving Extras.

Per serving: 12 calories, 0.4 g protein, 0.1 g fat, 3 g carbohydrate, 576 mg sodium

VEGETABLE BROTH
Limited Choice Plan
Makes about 1 quart

This broth can be prepared in advance and frozen for use at a later date (see note on Chicken Broth recipe, page 401).

1½ cups thickly sliced onions
1 cup each cut-up carrots, celery,
  and parsnips (large chunks)
2 medium tomatoes, cut into
  wedges
6 parsley sprigs
2 bay leaves

2 garlic cloves, crushed
5 peppercorns
½ teaspoon thyme leaves
1 whole clove
1½ quarts water, divided
Dash pepper

1. In metal roasting pan combine all ingredients except water and pepper. Bake at 400°F. for 35 minutes.

2. Transfer vegetable mixture to 3½- or 4-quart saucepan and set aside.

3. Add 1 cup water to roasting pan; place over medium heat and bring to a boil.

4. Using a wooden spoon, scrape browned particles from bottom and sides of pan; transfer mixture to saucepan containing vegetables. Add pepper and remaining water to saucepan; simmer for about 1 hour. Strain liquid, discarding solids.

¾ cup broth is equivalent to: 1 serving Extras.

Note: Nutrition data are not available for homemade Vegetable Broth. Therefore, we are using the nutrition information from commercial broth and seasoning mix. A ¾-cup serving contains 12 calories, 1 g protein, 2 g carbohydrate, sodium data does not apply.

HERBAL TEAS AND SOUP
For each serving:

Herb—In teapot place **1 or 2 tablespoons chopped fresh herbs.** Add **1 cup boiling water.** Cover and let steep for about 5 minutes. Strain and serve. Use as a tea or mix with **1 packet instant broth and seasoning mix** and serve as soup. If broth mix is used, each serving is equivalent to 1 serving Extras.

Per serving: 6 calories, 0.3 g protein, 0.1 g fat, 1 g carbohydrate, 1 mg sodium
With broth mix: 16 calories, 1 g protein, 0.1 g fat, 3 g carbohydrate, 834 mg sodium

Mexican—In saucepan combine **a stick of cinnamon** and **1 cup water** and bring to a boil. Boil for several minutes; remove from heat and add **1 teaspoon tea leaves** or **1 tea bag.** Let steep for about 5 minutes. Strain and serve.

Per serving: 4 calories, 0.2 g protein, 0 g fat, 1 g carbohydrate, 0.2 mg sodium

Mint—In teapot place **⅛ teaspoon mint flakes** or **1 tablespoon chopped fresh mint leaves** and **1 teaspoon tea leaves** or **1 tea bag.** Add **1 cup boiling water** and let steep about 5 minutes. Strain and serve.

Per serving: 3 calories, 0.2 g protein, 0 g fat, 1 g carbohydrate, 0 mg sodium

SPICED ORANGE TEA
Limited Choice Plan
Makes 2 servings, 1 cup each

¼ cup grated orange peel
4 whole cloves, broken into halves
1 cinnamon stick, 2 inches

2 teaspoons tea leaves
2 cups boiling water

In small heatproof bowl or teapot combine first 4 ingredients. Add boiling water, cover, and let stand (steep) for 3 to 5 minutes. Pour through a fine strainer or sieve into teacups.

Per serving: 27 calories, 0.5 g protein, 0.1 g fat, 7 g carbohydrate, 1 mg sodium

SPICED TEA
Limited Choice Plan
Makes 2 servings

2-inch piece lemon peel
2 cardamom seeds
1 whole clove

2 cups water
2 teaspoons Darjeeling tea
1 teaspoon honey

In small saucepan combine lemon peel, cardamom seeds, and clove; add water and bring to a boil. Reduce heat and simmer for 5 minutes. Rinse a small teapot with boiling water. Add tea to pot and pour in spiced water; let stand (steep) for 5 minutes. Strain tea into 2 cups; stir ½ teaspoon honey into each.
Each serving is equivalent to: 1 serving Extras.

Per serving: 14 calories, 0.2 g protein, trace fat, 4 g carbohydrate, 0.3 mg sodium

RICOTTA–OLIVE DIP OR DRESSING
Full Choice Plan
Makes 4 servings

⅓ cup part-skim ricotta cheese
¼ cup plain unflavored yogurt
4 large pimiento-stuffed green
    olives
2 teaspoons chopped chives

1 teaspoon lemon juice
½ teaspoon prepared yellow
    mustard
⅛ teaspoon each garlic powder,
    salt, and red wine vinegar

In blender container or work bowl of food processor combine all ingredients and process just until mixture has a light green color (*do not puree*). Refrigerate, covered, until chilled.

Each serving is equivalent to: 2½ servings Extras; ⅛ serving Milk.

Per serving: 44 calories, 3 g protein, 3 g fat, 2 g carbohydrate, 231 mg sodium

BLUEBERRIES IN WINE
Full Choice Plan
Makes 2 servings

A light, elegant dessert.

2 fluid ounces dry white wine
1 teaspoon each arrowroot and
    granulated sugar
1 cup blueberries

¼ cup plain unflavored yogurt,
    divided
Ground cinnamon

In small saucepan combine wine, arrowroot, and sugar and stir to dissolve; cook over low heat, stirring occasionally, until mixture thickens slightly. Add blueberries and cook until fruit is just heated. Spoon half of fruit mixture into each of 2 dessert dishes; top each portion with 2 tablespoons yogurt and sprinkle with dash cinnamon. Cover and chill.

Each serving is equivalent to: ¼ serving Occasional Substitutes; 1½ servings Extras; 1 serving Fruits; ¼ serving Milk.

Per serving: 100 calories, 2 g protein, 1 g fat, 17 g carbohydrate, 15 mg sodium

STRAWBERRY–WINE GEL
Full Choice Plan
Makes 4 servings

1 cup strawberries, divided
8 fluid ounces dry white wine
1 envelope unflavored gelatin

2 teaspoons granulated sugar
½ cup cold water

1. Reserve 4 whole strawberries for garnish; thinly slice remaining berries and set aside.
2. In small saucepan simmer wine for 3 to 5 minutes.

3. In small heatproof bowl combine gelatin and sugar; add heated wine, stirring until gelatin is completely dissolved. Add water and stir to combine. Cover with plastic wrap and refrigerate until syrupy, 20 to 30 minutes.

4. Chill 4 wine glasses. Rinse an 8 x 8 x 2-inch pan with cold water and shake dry. Arrange sliced berries on bottom of pan. Carefully pour syrupy gelatin mixture over berries and chill until firm, about 30 minutes.

5. To serve, cut firm gel into 1-inch cubes and spoon cubes into chilled glasses; garnish each portion with 1 reserved strawberry.

Each serving is equivalent to: ¼ serving Fruits; ½ serving Occasional Substitutes; 1½ servings Extras.

Per serving: 77 calories, 2 g protein, 0.2 g fat, 8 g carbohydrate, 5 mg sodium

MULLED WINE

Full Choice Plan
Makes 2 servings

8 fluid ounces dry red wine	1-inch piece cinnamon stick
1 lemon slice (¼ inch thick), studded with 1 whole clove	1 teaspoon granulated sugar

In small saucepan combine all ingredients; bring mixture to just below the boiling point. Reduce heat as low as possible and simmer for 10 minutes. Strain wine into 2 cups; serve immediately.

Each serving is equivalent to: 1 serving Occasional Substitutes; 1 serving Extras.

Per serving: 109 calories, 0.2 g protein, trace fat, 8 g carbohydrate, 6 mg sodium

WHITE WINE SPRITZER

Full Choice Plan
Makes 1 serving

Chill a 10-ounce glass. In chilled glass combine **4 fluid ounces chilled white wine** and **½ cup chilled sparkling mineral water;*** serve immediately.

Each serving is equivalent to: 1 serving Occasional Substitutes.

Per serving: 99 calories, 0.1 g protein, 0 g fat, 5 g carbohydrate, 6 mg sodium

* Club soda can be substituted for the mineral water.

Appendix
Full Choice Plan Equivalent Adjustments

When using the following Limited and No Choice Plan recipes in conjunction with the Full Choice Plan, adjust recipe equivalents as indicated below.

Fruits

Cider Cooler	Omit Extras; add 2 calories Specialty Foods
Strawberry–Graham Bananas	Reduce Extras to 1 serving; add 16 calories Specialty Foods
Honey-Glazed Grapefruit Variation	Omit Extras; add 16 calories Specialty Foods
Spiced Peach Pudding	Reduce Extras to ⅔ serving; add 8 calories Specialty Foods

Vegetables

Green and Wax Bean Salad	Increase Vegetables to 2½ servings
Fruited Carrot Salad	Increase Vegetables to 2½ servings
Mandarin–Carrot Loaf with Chive–Yogurt Dressing	Omit Extras; add 8 calories Specialty Foods
Slow-Cooked Carrot Medley	Increase Vegetables to 3½ servings
Braised Celery	Add 1 serving Vegetables
Braised Endive	Add 2½ servings Vegetables
Endive Salad	Increase Vegetables to 3½ servings
Lettuce Stir-Fry	Add 4 servings Vegetables
Romaine and Watercress Salad	Add 3 servings Vegetables
Pickled Radishes	Add 2 servings Vegetables
Mixed Vegetable Kabobs	Increase Vegetables to 3 servings; omit Extras; add 12 calories Specialty Foods
Vegetable Stir-Fry	Increase Vegetables to 2 servings

Milk

Raspberry "Cream"   Omit Extras; add 8 calories
                                   Specialty Foods
Ribbon Mold   Reduce Extras to 1½ servings;
                                   add ⅔ calorie Specialty Foods

Bread and Cereal

Strawberry-Topped Bran Crisps   Reduce Extras to 1 serving; add
                                   16 calories Specialty Foods

Eggs

Open-Face Goldenrod Egg Salad   Increase Vegetables to 1½
  Sandwich   servings
Sugar Cakes Variation   Reduce Extras to 1½ servings;
                                   add 8 calories Specialty Foods

Cheese

Vegetable Cottage Cheese   Increase Vegetables to 2¼
                                   servings
Zucchini–Cheese Salad   Increase Vegetables to 3⅓
                                   servings

Poultry, Veal, and Game

Broiled Chicken—Variation 3   Omit Extras; add 2 calories
                                   Specialty Foods
Chicken Sukiyaki   Increase Vegetables to 1 serving
Tangy Stir-Fried Chicken   Increase Vegetables to 1 serving
Turkey Hash   Increase Vegetables to 1½
                                   servings

Meat Group

Country Beef Steak   Increase Vegetables to 3½
                                   servings; reduce Bonus to ½
                                   serving
Beef Stew   Increase Vegetables to 3 servings
Meatball Stew   Increase Vegetables to 1½
                                   servings

Lamb-Stuffed Yellow Squash	Reduce Bonus to ¾ serving
Pork and Chinese Cabbage in Orange Sauce	Add 1 serving Vegetables; reduce Extras to 1½ servings; add 8 calories Specialty Foods
Spicy Pork and Mushrooms	Reduce Bonus to ⅜ serving
Baked Glazed Ham	Omit Extras; add 10 calories Specialty Foods

Fish

Stir-Fried Fish with Pepper Sauce	Add 1 serving Vegetables
Crab Meat Salad	Increase Vegetables to ½ serving
Shrimp "Cutlets" with Dipping Sauce	Omit Extras; add 16 calories Specialty Foods
Eggplant–Tuna Salad	Increase Vegetables to 2¼ servings
Tuna Salad	Increase Vegetables to 1½ servings

Legumes

Navy Bean Soup	Increase Vegetables to 1 serving; reduce Bonus to ⅜ serving
Bean 'n' Cheese Salad	Increase Vegetables to 2½ servings
Quick Garbanzo Bean Salad	Increase Vegetables to 1½ servings
Kidney Beans Creole	Increase Vegetables to 2 servings; reduce Bonus to ⅜ serving
Stuffed Lettuce Leaves	Increase Vegetables to 1¾ servings

Sauces and Dressings

| Gravy | Increase Vegetables to ½ serving |
| Lemon–Tomato Dressing | Reduce Bonus to ¼ serving |

Optional

| Red-Blooded Mary Mix | Reduce Bonus to ¾ serving |

Dry and Liquid Measure Equivalents

Teaspoons	Tablespoons	Cups	Fluid Ounces
3 teaspoons	1 tablespoon		½ fluid ounce
6 teaspoons	2 tablespoons	⅛ cup	1 fluid ounce
8 teaspoons	2 tablespoons plus 2 teaspoons	⅙ cup	
12 teaspoons	4 tablespoons	¼ cup	2 fluid ounces
15 teaspoons	5 tablespoons	⅓ cup less 1 teaspoon	
16 teaspoons	5 tablespoons plus 1 teaspoon	⅓ cup	
18 teaspoons	6 tablespoons	⅓ cup plus 2 teaspoons	3 fluid ounces
24 teaspoons	8 tablespoons	½ cup	4 fluid ounces
30 teaspoons	10 tablespoons	½ cup plus 2 tablespoons	5 fluid ounces
32 teaspoons	10 tablespoons plus 2 teaspoons	⅔ cup	
36 teaspoons	12 tablespoons	¾ cup	6 fluid ounces
42 teaspoons	14 tablespoons	1 cup less 2 tablespoons	7 fluid ounces
45 teaspoons	15 tablespoons	1 cup less 1 tablespoon	
48 teaspoons	16 tablespoons	1 cup	8 fluid ounces

Note: Measurements of less than ⅛ teaspoon are considered a Dash or a Pinch.

Weight Watchers Metric Conversion Table

TEMPERATURE
To change degrees Fahrenheit to degrees Celsius subtract 32° and multiply by 5/9.

WEIGHT

To Change	To	Multiply by
Ounces	Grams	30.0
Pounds	Kilograms	.48

VOLUME

To Change	To	Multiply by
Teaspoons	Milliliters	5.0
Tablespoons	Milliliters	15.0
Cups	Milliliters	250.0
Cups	Liters	.25
Pints	Liters	.5
Quarts	Liters	1.0
Gallons	Liters	4.0

LENGTH

To Change	To	Multiply by
Inches	Millimeters	25.0
Inches	Centimeters	2.5
Feet	Centimeters	30.0
Yards	Meters	.9

Oven Temperatures

Degrees Fahrenheit	=	Degrees Celsius	Degrees Fahrenheit	=	Degrees Celsius
250		120	400		200
275		140	425		220
300		150	450		230
325		160	475		250
350		180	500		260
375		190	525		270

METRIC SYMBOLS

Symbol	=	Metric Unit	Symbol	=	Metric Unit
g		gram	°C		degrees Celsius
kg		kilogram	mm		millimeter
ml		milliliter	cm		centimeter
l		liter	m		meter

Index